Vladimir Hrubik

# WHEN THEY SAY PEACE SEEK SHELTER

## THE ROAD TO EVADE THE ANTICHRIST

authorHOUSE®

AuthorHouse™
1663 Liberty Drive
Bloomington, IN 47403
www.authorhouse.com
Phone: 1-800-839-8640

First published by AuthorHouse 7/21/2009

ISBN: 978-1-4389-3342-9 (sc)

Library of Congress Control Number: 2009904756

Printed in the United States of America
Bloomington, Indiana

This book is printed on acid-free paper.

Cover design by Elvir Maslovic and Gordon Djordjevic
Photography by Robert Lys
Illustrations by Maria Doric

All Scripture quotations are from the Old and New Testaments
in the King James Version of the Holy Bible.

**Matthew 24:20** *But pray ye that your flight be not in the winter, neither on the Sabbath day:*

**Matthew 24:21** *For then shall be great tribulation, such as was not since the beginning of the world to this time, no, nor ever shall be.*

**Luke 21:35** *For as a snare shall it come on ALL them that dwell on the face of the whole earth.*

**Luke 21:36** *Watch ye therefore, and pray always, that ye may be accounted WORTHY TO ESCAPE all these things that shall come to pass, and to stand before the Son of man.*

**Matthew 24:28** *For wheresoever the carcase is, there will the eagles be gathered together.*

**Luke 21:33** *Heaven and earth shall pass away: but my words shall not pass away.*

# *ACKNOWLEDGEMENTS*

My heart is filled with gratitude towards the God of Israel for His great mercy and love and for the guidance and the revelations He bestowed on me as I was writing this book. It is my fervent desire that this book shall be of benefit to all who seek a deeper understanding of His Word. I am very grateful that the Lord opened the hearts of so many who worked tirelessly and wholeheartedly in helping me to complete this book. Without their help it would not have been possible to accomplish the task which was before me. I am greatly indebted to those who so generously gave of their time and their wisdom, as well as to those from whom I received advice and encouragement in my attempt to complete yet another task from our Lord.

# CONTENTS

# PART THREE
## THE MARRIAGE FEAST OF THE LAMB

# EXAMPLES
## WHICH SHOW THE DEPARTURE FOR ISRAEL

# INTRODUCTION

Many books have been written about the End Times described in the Bible. The authors of these books have made every effort to understand the very essence of the events that will occur here on earth. However, despite these efforts, the events of the End Times have remained a mystery, both for the Christian world and much more so for the non-Christian world which does not study the Bible.

On the other hand, it is known that the Bible is a true Book in which the Almighty God permitted all-important events which occurred on earth to be documented. The Bible is a testimony of this knowledge, which is available to everyone. Examples of events which were prophesied and recorded include the following: The occurrence of the great flood of Noah's time; the judgement of Saul, King of the Jews; God's blessings bestowed upon King David and King Solomon; the judgement of the Jewish people and the time of the Babylonian captivity; the arrival on earth of the world's Saviour, Jesus Christ, and all events relating to Him; the destruction of Jerusalem, and the scattering of the Jewish people all over the world.

Although numerous prophesied events, such as those mentioned above, have already taken place, many are yet to be completed. One of the most important and most sensitive events for humankind is the prophecy concerning the Jewish people, who are today scattered throughout all the countries of the world. God testifies through His Word that the captives of Zion will be returned to their Promised Land, and that He will do better unto them than before.

The prophecies regarding the Jewish people, which we have seen fulfilled, have for hundreds of years made headlines in the world press and other media to the point that humanity has grown tired of listening. These headlines concern terrorism within Israel and the surrounding area; peace processes among Israel, its neighbours, and the Palestinians; and numerous wars. However, the question remains: where is the end to all of this, and how will these events ultimately impact humanity?

At the same time, the readily observable lawlessness among Christians has resulted in humankind's loss of respect for God and His Son, our Lord Jesus Christ. The consequences of this severed relationship between mankind and Christ will be dire in the end and knowing this, many hearts are filled with worry and fear.

Indeed, while studying the Bible, we are faced with the problem of how to interpret this Holy Book in order to gain an accurate understanding. Obviously, an incorrect approach to the study impedes the understanding of God's truth. The answer to this question is not simple, for the message sent by God through prophecy, Jesus' parables, or the Revelation of John, can be understood either literally or spiritually. If approached literally, the Holy Scriptures prompt us to change our lives to be in harmony with the Gospel. If approached spiritually, the same Holy Scriptures become prophetic and cautionary through symbolism. What is necessary for the correct understanding of the message of our Saviour Jesus Christ is 'the comprehension of the heavenly kingdom, which will not come to earth and be seen but will rather be felt in the heart, as declared by Jesus. This kingdom is spiritual, and is ruled by spiritual laws and time. In order to attain it, each person has to be reborn spiritually and become a new type of being. This transformation occurs when the physical body, with its desires and needs, subjugates itself to the Holy Spirit. This means that such a man is served by the body and guided by God's Holy Spirit. Whoever is reborn through baptism and transformed into a new creature, becomes a resident of the kingdom of heaven. In this kingdom of heaven, there is spiritual time and spiritual laws. Without the knowledge of the laws ruling in spiritual time, it is not possible to align all events in the Bible to the correct place in time and space. For this reason, the content of this book is divided into three parts.

In the first part, the reader is given a testimony that the texts in the Bible, regardless of whether they are the parables of Jesus Christ or the Revelation of John, are presented through symbols. An effort has to be made to understand these symbols.

The second part is dedicated to Biblical symbols dealing specifically with spiritual time by which it is titled. Careful study of this chapter is necessary if one wishes to understand the interpretation of the prophecy relating to the last days. The third and final part of this book will be significantly more difficult to comprehend without a proper understanding of symbols relating to spiritual time. We know that in linear time all events go from the past through the present to the future. The language of the New Testament introduces us to the kingdom of heaven where spiritual time rules. A basic characteristic of this kingdom is that time does not flow in a linear manner and that events cannot be determined according to the number of revolutions of the Earth around the Sun. In this kingdom, the notion of present time, i.e., now, is emphasised. A man who possesses the kingdom of heaven in his heart lives in the present, without a past or a future. This concept makes it difficult to understand the Books of the New Testament because we are accustomed to linear time. In linear time, all things have a beginning and an end. Alternatively, in spiritual time, a man only has the present, which lasts for eternity. In the kingdom of heaven, there is no suffering, misfortune, illness, sorrow, misery, old age, or death. Jesus tells us that whosoever believes in Him, and in the One who sent Him, has received eternal life within himself, and has passed from death unto life.

The function of time in this kingdom is that of an event, or a condition. The duration of a condition is not limited by time determinants but rather by focus. Thus, every man who gains the kingdom of heaven through repentance and baptism, and stays focused, i.e. consistent, retains his salvation. Otherwise he will lose it. Therefore, life and death are only conditions of the state man is in. One who is reborn and perseveres in his love toward God and his fellow creatures is alive; in contrast, one who is not reborn and lives according to the body's instincts, is dead. There is no death in the sense of the cessation of existence; therefore, it is written that God shall judge both the dead and the living. The conditions such as *"and because iniquity shall abound, the love of many shall wax cold"* will bring the end of mercy for the gentiles, prophesied in the Bible.

This chapter also clarifies many other symbols which may expand our knowledge of God's will and make the faith, authenticity and depth of providence firm. For these reasons, effort should not be spared when reading this part of the book, even though it is very difficult. If necessary, more difficult parts of the texts should be reread several times, in order for abundant spiritual fruit to be harvested in one's heart. God shall provide a gift of knowledge to every reader because an explanation of the Bible is based on God's unchangeable mind and will thus be much more easily determined.

The third part of the book, titled *the Marriage of the Lamb,* includes an explanation of the End Times through the presentation of a wedding. However, the explanation is in two parts: events happening in the near future and those occurring in the distant future. Events which will occur in the near future are given fuller treatment than events in the more distant future, such as Armageddon, new heaven, and new earth. This is done in order for the reader to gain a general overview of the events to happen until the words *it is done,* from the Revelation of John, are spoken. Presently, it is not necessary to know what will happen in the battle of Armageddon, but it is important to act according to God's will regarding the present and coming events, so that the arrival of these times will not raise fear in our hearts, as God will be with us.

In the course of reading, a rule may be noticed, especially in part three. First, an event from the past is analysed, then an explanation follows of the prophecy relating to both the present and the future. This means that the presentation of the Marriage Dinner of the Lamb is included at the beginning of the third part of the book which occurred in the past, and was recorded in the parable of Jesus Christ described in Matthew 22. In this way, it is clear that the symbolic interpretation is correct, for the events which happened in the past are today a part of history.

The prophecies of the Marriage Supper of the Lamb (Luke 14), describing present and future events, are dealt with later. Since the principle of comparison with the events from the past is used for the supper interpretation, it may be noted that God uses the same or similar symbols in time and space, as shown in the second part, as He does when talking about the End Times through the Marriage Supper of the Lamb. This knowledge comes as a great joy for all people, for it provides a clearer understanding of future events and attention must be paid to what God, through His Word, tells us needs to be done. This is why this book differs from the majority of other writings dealing with the End Times, for it ensures that the symbols relating to the past, the present, and the near future are more easily understood. For example, Ezekiel's prophecy states that dry bones shook. These words do not mean much if they are taken literally. However, if it were known that with his words the prophet, many centuries ago, predicted the suffering of the Jewish people in World War II and the establishment of the state of Israel, these words gain a new significance. In this prophecy of dry bones, the prophet describes in detail the event which must be realized. After the statement that the dry bones are the whole house of Israel, the quake occurs, making the bones adhere to one another. This happened in the period from 1939 to 1948, when the state of Israel was proclaimed. Afterwards, flesh, sinews, and skin are drawn. Skin designates the border of the state: when it is drawn, it shall be a formal body, a state, but without a spirit, or recognition of our Saviour Jesus Christ. Then God orders the prophet to preach with the words: *come from the four winds of breath*, i.e. those in whom the Holy Spirit resides are invited to come to the Marriage Supper of the Lamb in order for the body to formally receive its spirit, or life. In this way, the one who keeps the coming of the Antichrist in the world shall be taken away. When the Holy Spirit (residing in the faithful people of God), departs for Israel, nothing stands in the way for the man of iniquity to shut the door to salvation for the gentiles. When the Holy Spirit manifests itself in Israel, the door of salvation shall be opened to those (Jewish people) who have had a veil over their hearts. Free access to the Marriage Supper of the Lamb shall be ensured to all those who are in Israel at that time. At present, there is a belief that God shall, through His personal intervention, make the Jewish people receive the Spirit and recognize Jesus Christ. These individuals are forgetting that around two thousand years ago God sent John the Baptist and His Son not to immediately convert the people (as if holding a magic wand), but to invite them to new covenant bonds (ask them to repent). With Jesus' second coming to the Jewish people, God does not need to change the doctrine of salvation of His old covenant people, but rather He will do this through His servants. It was written that the eagles (God's sons) would gather where the carcass was, i.e. a body without a spirit. Current events regarding God's old covenant people indicate the time we are in and which prophesied events must be fulfilled. Therefore, it is necessary to pay attention to the events in the Middle East, for they are signs of the times we live in.

The prophecy of the Marriage Supper of the Lamb relating to our present and near future, is a central theme of this book. Through this part of the text, the reader is provided with an explanation of coming events, their impact on the Jewish people, the Christians, humankind in general, and God's expected action plan for His people, giving instruction on how to save them from everything that has to come.

In order for the reader to be convinced of the truth of these explanations, six examples have been chosen from the Old Testament, the New Testament and John's Revelation, to show that the whole Bible presents what Jesus said through the Marriage Supper in Luke 14. The six examples we will consider are: the oath given by God to Abraham and his seed; Ezekiel's prophecies; the Revelation of John; the parable of the Ten Virgins and the words "For when they shall say, Peace and safety...", taken from 1 Thessalonians 5. The parable of the Ten Virgins provides us with additional information on the events, which must happen before *the eagles fly to the carcass*, and what must be done afterwards. In the spiritual midnight, a *cry will occur* i.e., events in the world, which will shake all people, Christians in particular. These sudden events will be a milestone in the life of every man. This will happen when the state of Israel receives the borders desired by this world and when peace is proclaimed. In a short time period of preparation and review, the worthy will receive the call to go to Israel. Others, who are awoken *(because all slumbered and slept),* will become aware of their own unworthiness of God's call because of their ignorance and neglect of the basic principles of the Gospel. From the beginning of the cry until the closing of the door, all those who are ready will be able to enter Israel. Those who, in that period, succeed *to buy oil for their lamps*, will be prevented from entering Israel by a new event occurring throughout the world. Then Israel will represent Noah's Arc of salvation from Antichrist's terror. King Solomon wrote that events are repeated in this world, for he says: *"that which hath been is now; and that which is to be hath already been"*. Likewise, the prophecy of the End Times aligning with the days of Noah and Lot will be fulfilled. When Noah, with his family and all animals, entered the arc, God closed the door and the great flood occurred, destroying everything. In Lot's example, just as he and his family left Sodom, flame mixed with sulphur was poured on Sodom and Gomorrah.

In the sixth and final example, the words *"For when they shall say, Peace and safety..."* are interpreted. Through these words, it is possible to understand, in general terms, what is to happen on Earth. This example is unusual and too complex for many. However, it will certainly be useful for those who feel the urging of the Spirit to research God's will in detail. Therefore, at the end of the sixth example, a comparison of five different prophecies with the prophecy of the Ten Virgins is provided. All the above prophecies speak of the same period. Thus, it is possible to understand that all six prophecies include some of the same steps (events), described in different ways.

Based on this comparison one can develop a diagram of several dozen events in sequence, which have to occur in the near future. This diagram will clearly show that there is **no** biblical support for a pre-tribulation rapture as is commonly being taught in church sermons and in books on the End Times today.

This means that if one is persistent in his efforts to understand the contents of this book, knowledge will be acquired to show that the present spirit, which prophesies in Christianity that Jesus Christ will return as the King of heaven and earth even tonight and take the chosen to heaven (rapture), is obviously not based on God's Word.

God's Word indicates a much more complex message to fallen humankind or sleeping Christianity. Therefore, the last several pages of the text " *For when they shall say, Peace and safety…*" provide a time analysis of our reality through the words of chapters 9 and 11 of the Revelation of St. John. This prophecy, through symbols, in general, summarises the book, the aim of which is to provide a picture of imminent events without the attempt of imposing certain beliefs or of changing anyone's fate. The interpretations analysed in detail are presented, including a large number of quotations, in order for the reader to confirm the interpreted text.

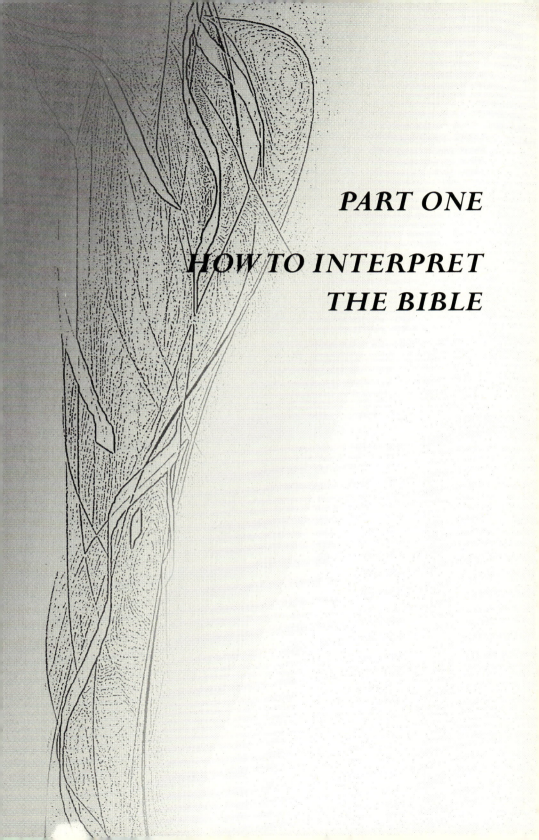

# PART ONE

# HOW TO INTERPRET
# THE BIBLE

*1*

# SYMBOLISM OF THE BIBLE

The manner in which the Bible should be interpreted is still a question
that is asked today, just as it was in the past and as it will be in the
future. There are many arguments concerning the interpretation of the
Bible and, for the time being, those in favour of a literal interpretation
are in the majority. However, most scholars agree that the contents of the
Bible are symbolic. Certainly, it is not wrong if some parts of the Bible are
taken literally. Indeed, it is easier to do so, but what should be done when
a seed is not a seed and tares are not tares? What should be done when
something is not presented logically? Should such ambiguities be ignored
or should one ask oneself whether this was written by chance, whether an
error crept into the translation, or regard this to be of little importance?

Even a literal interpretation of the Bible will prove instructive to a
Christian, because in it he will find eternal spiritual truths and values. On the
other hand, he will be deprived of understanding the depth of God's Word.

Certainly, it may be said that a literal interpretation of the Bible does
not provide a better or a more comprehensive understanding of the Word
of God. Jesus Christ tells simple parables which are easy to understand,
taken from everyday life, to the people and His disciples. The disciples are
clear in their understanding that there is a spiritual message behind these
parables. They speak the following words unto Jesus:

Mt. 13:36   *Then Jesus sent the multitude away, and went into the house:
and his disciples came unto him, saying,* **Declare unto us
the parable of the tares of the field.**[1]

---

1   In the interpretation of the verses, the author felt free to emphasize key words by using
formatting.

If Jesus told the parable of the tares in the field, and if this really explains the tares in a physical sense, then Jesus' disciples need not ask for an explanation. However, they know that Jesus does not tell them the parable "of the tares of the field" without a reason. When a parable is imparted in a spiritual sense, it is necessary to understand its symbols in order to grasp its spiritual dimension.

The Bible is the Book of Life. It does not provide instruction on how a man is to gain eternal life in this body. It is a Book of Knowledge on how to achieve a life of the spirit. Eternal life begins after repentance and after undergoing the Lord's command of baptism. This prolongs life after the death of our earthly body. Therefore, this means that the Bible can only be a spiritual Book. The testimony that this is so is found in the following words:

1 Co.15:50    *Now this I say, brethren, that **flesh and blood cannot inherit the kingdom of God**; neither doth corruption inherit incorruption.*

The complete Bible is provided to humankind only for the human soul, because flesh and blood cannot inherit God's kingdom. If the words written in 1Corinthians 15:50 reach our heart, we will be able to understand the words of our Lord Jesus Christ:

Jn. 18:36    *Jesus answered, **My kingdom is not of this world**: if my kingdom were of this world, then would my servants fight, that I should not be delivered to the Jews: but now is my kingdom not from hence.*

Jn. 18:37    *Pilate therefore said unto him, Art thou a king then? Jesus answered, Thou sayest that I am a king. **To this end was I born, and for this cause came I into the world, that I should bear witness unto the truth.** Every one that is of the truth heareth my voice.*

Our Lord Jesus Christ does not testify to those things which we see with our eyes and which are tangible, but He testifies to the intangible, which we do not see. Jesus declares the truth of the kingdom of heaven, the laws which rule therein, and the path through which mortal man may reach His domain, where justice and eternal life rule. This means that our

Lord Jesus Christ testifies a *spiritual* truth which mortal man should comprehend and believe in.

It is not difficult to understand why God uses our everyday words, the terminology of nature, animals, plants, names of people and events from everyday life such as: a wedding, sowing, harvesting, fishing, shepherds taking care of their flock, etc., when He wants to bring the spiritual world close to us. People act in a similar manner. They use familiar words or the words from Greek or Latin to describe something new, a discovery, to give a name to something that has not existed up to that time.

Since there are many who do not believe that the Bible was written in a symbolical vocabulary, several examples from the Old Testament, the New Testament, and the Revelation of St. John will be stated, in which God explains symbolism to His servants.

Is. 9:14         *Therefore the LORD will cut off from Israel head and tail, branch and rush, in one day.*
Is. 9:15         *The ancient and honourable, he is the head; and **the prophet that teacheth lies, he is the tail.***

In the above example, God, through His Word, shows that the "tail" symbolizes the prophet telling a "lie", and the "head" a respectable man. To verify that this is so, another verse is quoted in which the tail is mentioned:

Re. 12:4        *And his **tail** drew the third part of the stars of heaven, and did cast them to the earth: ...*

When God testifies that the tail symbolizes a prophet telling a lie, it is immediately understood that through false prophecy the stars will be drawn and cast from the sky, as higher spiritual spheres, into the physical sphere, i.e. the earth. When we know what the dragon's tail represents, we immediately understand who is symbolized by the red dragon. Also, based on this, it may be understood whom the dragon confronted and why its goal was to cheat the stars from the sky with its false prophecy. If this line of thinking is followed about the parable of Jesus Christ and the evil winegrowers (Matthew 21:33-41), it will be noticed that the scholars and Pharisees are the dragon's body (the body speaking the Words of God), which deceives God's servants (stars) with its tail to be removed before God's face.

Let us take another example from the Old Testament which includes many symbols. However, attention will be focused only on the three words in bold-face.

Ps. 22:12    *Many bulls have compassed me:* **strong bulls** *of Bashan have beset me round.*

Ps. 22:13    *They gaped upon me with their mouths, as a ravening and a roaring* **lion.**

Ps. 22:14    *I am poured out like water, and all my bones are out of joint: my heart is like wax; it is melted in the midst of my bowels.*

Ps. 22:15    *My strength is dried up like a potsherd; and my tongue cleaveth to my jaws; and thou hast brought me into the dust of death.*

Ps. 22:16    *For* **dogs** *have compassed me: the assembly of the wicked have inclosed me: they pierced my hands and my feet.*

Ps. 22:18    *They part my garments among them, and cast lots upon my vesture.*

There is no doubt that the 22$^{nd}$ Psalm describes the crucifixion of our Lord Jesus Christ. Since this event had already taken place in the past, it is not difficult to understand that the lion symbolizes Satan, that the bulls represent the Jewish clergy, and the dogs were the symbol for the Roman soldiers who crucified Him.

The Revelation of St. John abounds in symbols and it is therefore difficult to single out one example. From the selected fragment, we will discover what waters are and what fine linen is:

Re. 17:1    *And there came one of the seven angels which had the seven vials, and talked with me, saying unto me, Come hither; I will shew unto thee the judgment of* **the great whore that sitteth upon many waters:**

Re. 17:15    *And he saith unto me, The waters which thou sawest, where the whore sitteth,* **are peoples, and multitudes, and nations, and tongues.**

Re. 19:8    *And to her was granted that she should be arrayed in fine linen, clean and white:* **for the fine linen is the righteousness of saints.**

To show that symbolism is also prevalent in the New Testament, an example from the Gospels of Matthew and John will be used:

Mt. 13:24    *Another parable put he forth unto them, saying, The kingdom of heaven is likened unto a man which sowed **good seed** in his field:*

Mt. 13:36    *Then Jesus sent the multitude away, and went into the house: and his disciples came unto him, saying, Declare unto us the parable of the tares of the field.*

Mt. 13:37    *He answered and said unto them, He that soweth the good seed is the Son of man;*

Mt. 13:38    *The field is the world; the good seed are the children of the kingdom; but the tares are the children of the wicked one;*

Mt. 13:39    *The enemy that sowed them is the devil; the harvest is the end of the world; and the reapers are the angels.*

Upon the request of Jesus' disciples, our Lord Jesus Christ gave an explanation, in great detail, of the meaning of symbols from the parable of the man who sowed good seed in his field. This parable is an example of how to interpret His parables, which are prophecies of the New Testament.

From the Gospel of John it is not difficult to guess who the "sheep" are.

Jn. 10:25    *Jesus answered them, I told you, and ye believed not: the works that I do in my Father's name, they bear witness of me.*

Jn. 10:26    *But ye believe not, because **ye are not of my sheep,** as I said unto you.*

Jn. 10:27    ***My sheep hear my voice,** and I know them, and they follow me:*

From the above examples, we can be assured that throughout the Bible, symbols are indeed used for the description of spiritual truths. This example from the Gospel of John clearly proves that everyone must understand the basic symbolism of the parables of our Lord Jesus Christ. A Christian must be clear as to why Jesus Christ calls Himself a shepherd in this example, although He is the Son of God, and why He uses the term "sheep" for His male and female servants. Pay attention to the words from verse 27: ***My sheep hear my voice,** and I know them, and they follow me.* Unless Christians are able to understand the words of Jesus Christ and the symbols He uses, they will question how they should follow their shepherd; and how they should listen to His voice. Education and intellect are not enough for Christians to understand biblical symbols. In addition to the study of the Bible, which contains keys to each symbol, it is necessary to ask the Lord to reveal and clarify His truths.

In the same chapter an astonishing example is found, which should concern us all:

| Jn. 10:1 | *Verily, verily, I say unto you, he that entereth not by the door into the sheepfold, but climbeth up some other way, the same is a thief and a robber,* |
|---|---|
| Jn. 10:2 | *But he that entereth in by the door is the shepherd of the sheep.* |
| Jn. 10:3 | *To him the porter openeth; and the sheep hear his voice: and he calleth his own sheep by name, and leadeth them out.* |
| Jn. 10:6 | *This parable spake Jesus unto them: but **they understood NOT** what things they were which he spake unto them.* |

This example actually provides an answer as to why there are so many interpretations of the Bible, i.e. so many different protestant Christian denominations. An ignorance of God's will and the misunderstanding of God's Word is the main cause of this and an obstacle for many Christians. Therefore, the path of truth and life is disgraced, and sin, disunity, an absence of love, and divisiveness rule in Christianity, and the abomination of desolation is in the holy place.

Jesus' disciples were also unable to understand many of the parables Jesus told to the people, just as we today do not understand them. No one will find justification for his misunderstanding, just as the disciples did not find it. Let us see what our Lord Jesus says to all His servants:

| Mt.13:10 | *And the disciples came, and said unto him, Why speakest thou unto them in parables?* |
|---|---|
| Mt.13:11 | *He answered and said unto them, Because **it is given unto you to know the mysteries of the kingdom of heaven,** but to them it is not given.* |

The Lord testifies that Christians are given knowledge of the secrets of the kingdom of God, i.e. an understanding of the symbolism of Jesus Christ's parables whereby the kingdom of God is described. However, it is a fact that not everyone is given an understanding of these secrets. Therefore, it is not sufficient only to read what a symbol means in order to gain the whole picture, but it is necessary, through prayer and fasting (spiritual and bodily), to be on a quest to understand His truths.

# PART TWO

# SPIRITUAL TIME

# SPIRITUAL TIME IN
# A SPIRITUAL WORLD

One of the most significant symbols in the Bible is "spiritual time". As earthly time passes for this material world, spiritual time also passes for the spiritual world on this earth. Just as this physical world has a material sky, sun, stars, moon, day, year, soil, river, tree, beast, man, etc., the spiritual world also possesses these features.

An understanding of spiritual time which rules the spiritual world, which is used throughout the Bible, illustrates that all spiritual events described in the Bible are set precisely in time and space. Without an understanding of spiritual time, the parables of our Lord Jesus Christ, John's Revelation, prophecies, and laws, according to which several events have to occur, will not be correctly understood.

For example, if there were no words in our language to express the past, present, and future time, how would an activity that occurred in the past or which will occur in the future be explained? This would most certainly be impossible. Also, even though earthly time is used to describe events in the spiritual world, misunderstandings and various interpretations of God's Word occur. There are some that say that a kingdom of a thousand years (the so-called millennium), existed, whereas others say that it exists now, while the majority believes that a kingdom of a thousand years is coming. Misunderstandings and various interpretations have occurred simply due to an incorrect approach. Thus Satan has managed to introduce disunity into Christianity.

The difference between spiritual time and physical time is that the latter moves in a straight line, i.e. events occur chronologically from past to present, to future, while in spiritual time events cause changes which impact the shift of spiritual night into spiritual day.

The notion of spiritual time includes dozens of terms occurring in the Bible. For example: day, night, day of the Lord, terrible day of the Lord, notable day of the Lord, Christ's day, the other day, three days and three nights, 1260 days, 1290 days, 1335 days, 2000 days and nights, for a week, acceptable year of the Lord, kingdom of the millennium, 42 months, 42 days, 40 days, 40 years, three and a half days, time, time and a half time, etc. The term "day" is most frequently found in many of the above forms; therefore, it is necessary to understand what a *spiritual day* is, and also what it includes.

# *SPIRITUAL DAY*

The first mention of a "day" is found immediately on the opening page of the Bible.

Ge. 1:5      *And God called the light **day,** and the darkness he called **night**. And **the evening and the morning were the FIRST DAY.***

From this verse it is evident that the day begins with a period of darkness i.e. night, for it reads: and *the evening and the morning were the first day*, rather than the opposite. There is an embedded belief that Genesis 1 speaks about the creation of the universe and the Earth, and that it refers to an earthly day consisting of 24 hours, or a day lasting for 1000 years according to a verse from the Bible (2$^{nd}$ Peter's), which says that, in front of the Lord, one day is like a thousand years, and a thousand years like one day. However, this occurrence deals with a spiritual day and the creation of a spiritual man, for if we read this chapter carefully, we will see that the sun, moon, and stars were created on the fourth day, and all plants and trees the day before, on the third day. The following question comes to mind: how did the plants grow without the sun? The answer could be that there was light. But where did this light come from if no sun existed? What proof do we have that this day from Genesis 1:5 is actually a spiritual day?

It is not difficult to determine the truth. Let us read the following words spoken by apostle Paul:

2 Co. 3:14      *But their minds were blinded: for until this day remaineth the same vail untaken away in the reading of the old testament; which vail is done away in Christ.*

| 2 Co. 3:16 | *Nevertheless when it shall turn to the Lord, the vail shall be taken away.* |
|---|---|
| 2 Co. 3:17 | *Now the Lord is that Spirit: and where the Spirit of the Lord is, there is liberty.* |

The Word of God clearly states that the Lord reigns in the new covenant time period and the Spirit is where the Lord is, for He is the Holy Spirit. Also, where the Spirit is, there liberty reigns. This means that all things are given to people, in the *spirit* in whom the Holy Spirit resides. Therefore, the Word of God states that a veil shall be taken away from the Jewish nation in the reading of the Old Testament only when they turn to the Lord, when they become the *spirit*, i.e. when they receive Christ's Spirit. However, all those who have Christ's Spirit within them should understand the Old Testament.

Why?

Because the Old Testament was written by the same Spirit as the New Testament, and this Spirit is called God's Spirit. This means that in order to understand the Old Testament, it must be interpreted spiritually.

The "day" in Genesis 1:5 may only be a spiritual day, which includes: a spiritual night (the period of darkness or ignorance of God's will), and day (a period of light when God's will is correctly preached).

Therefore, the Word of God in the New Testament says:

| 1 Th. 5:5 | *Ye are all the children of light, and the children of the day: we are not of the night, nor of darkness.* |
|---|---|

In this verse there is the testimony that Christians are the children of the day. Since they are the children of the day, then the question arises whether the spiritual day includes the same components as an earthly day.

## Components of the Spiritual Day

The spiritual day and earthly day must have the same components. First, let us see what the components of an earthly day are:

1) the sun as an object
2) rays
3) light

The components of a spiritual day (period of light) are:

1) the sun - Jesus Christ, or God, or Israel (in the sense of clergy, scholars, canons, prophets speaking-radiating the Word of God)
2) rays - the Word of God
3) light - eternal life

To confirm that the Word of God actually speaks of the components included in a spiritual day (in the period of light), examples will be stated from the Word of God for each component. First, an example will be provided to illustrate that Jesus is the light of the world, our spiritual sun.

Jn. 8:12      *Then spake Jesus again unto them, saying, **I am the light of the world**: he that followeth me shall not walk in darkness, but shall have the light of life.*

It is written in Psalms that the Word of God is a lamp. A lamp produces light, just as the rays of the sun light this world.

Ps. 119:105   ***Thy word is a lamp** unto my feet, and a light unto my path.*

Several examples will be mentioned for the light as the third component of the spiritual day:

Jn. 1:1      *In the beginning was the Word, and the Word was with God, and the Word was God.*

Jn. 1:4      *In him was life; and **the life was the light of men**.*

17

| | |
|---|---|
| Jn. 1:5 | *And the light shineth in darkness; and the darkness comprehended it not.* |
| 2 Co. 4:4 | *In whom the god of this world hath blinded the minds of them which believe not, lest **the light of the glorious Gospel of Christ,** who is the image of God, should shine unto them.* |
| 2 Co.4:6 | *For God, who commanded the light to shine out of darkness, hath shined in our hearts, to give **the light of the knowledge of the glory of God in the face of Jesus Christ.*** |

Based on the above example from John 1:4, we may conclude that spiritual light in the spiritual world is eternal life for all people. Some may say that it is written in John 1:4 that life was the light for the people rather than eternal life being the light. This is true, but it should be understood that life has eternal value in the spiritual world. In the spiritual world, there is an eternal God, an eternal kingdom, and an eternal law which may not be changed, as well as servants in this kingdom who possess eternal life. There is no night in this kingdom because the day presides. Therefore, when the Word of God speaks of spiritual life, it is actually referring to eternal life.

In the example above, from the second Epistle to the Corinthians, we see that life which is eternal life is described through the comprehension of our Lord Jesus Christ, who is actually our eternal life.

## Definition of Spiritual Day and Spiritual Night

When we come to understand the components which comprise a spiritual day and what they mean, we will then have the necessary knowledge to ascertain whether we are living in day or night. This means that we are able to define the spiritual day. A description of birth, or the beginning of a spiritual day, is found in Matthew's Gospel.

| | |
|---|---|
| Mt. 4:14 | *That it might be fulfilled which was spoken by Esaias the prophet, saying,* |
| Mt. 4:15 | *The land of Zabulon, and the land of Nephthalim, by the way of the sea, beyond Jordan, Galilee of the Gentiles;* |
| Mt. 4:16 | *The people which sat in darkness saw great light; and to them which sat in the region and shadow of death light is sprung up.* |

18

Mt. 4:17        ***From that time Jesus began to preach, and to say,***
                *Repent: for the kingdom of heaven is at hand.*

The Word of God asserts that the beginning of a spiritual day came when Jesus began to teach and speak: *Repent: for the kingdom of heaven is at hand.* This means, when God creates the possibility for the word of salvation to be announced to the people living in darkness and in the shadow of death, it is said that a day has come. This is a general definition of a spiritual day.

Accordingly, spiritual night is spiritual darkness – the ignorance of the truth, a misapprehension due to false teaching or the failure to preach the Word of God. Since a spiritual day is the preaching of the truth of God's Word, it breaks through spiritual darkness like a ray of sun and "enlightens" for mankind the route to salvation. Each spiritual day from Genesis 1 begins with "and there was evening" i.e., with darkness, and ends with the time of light called day. God does not say for the seventh day: "*and the evening and the morning were the seventh day*". He says that He only rested from all His work on the seventh day. (Genesis 2:2).

# THREE SPIRITUAL DAYS AND THREE SPIRITUAL NIGHTS

In the first chapter of Genesis, we are told that there were seven spiritual days. Six days of creation and a seventh day, the day of rest. This means that all earthly events, from the beginning of creation to eternity, are divided into six spiritual days. Three spiritual days relate to the old covenant and three to the new covenant period. The seventh day will be eternity.

This may also be stated in the following manner: from the time when Adam and Eve lost their right to enter into heaven until the time when everything is remedied, i.e. when the salvation of mankind is over and the battle between God and Satan is completed, there will be six nights and six days.

A simplified time line of the old covenant period into three spiritual days and three nights is as follows:

1st spiritual night - From Adam's fall to the end of the flood;

1st spiritual day - From the end of the flood to the Egyptian slavery;

2nd spiritual night- From the Egyptian slavery to the time of departure from Egypt (i.e. until Passover);

2nd spiritual day - From Passover to the Babylonian slavery;

3rd spiritual night - From the Babylonian slavery to the return of the Jews to their land and the temple restoration;

3rd spiritual day - From the restoration of Solomon's temple to the time when the Jewish nation went astray from God.

The events in the new covenant period are also divided into three spiritual days and nights:

1st spiritual night -    Waiting for the arrival of Jesus Christ (His birth) until the beginning of preaching;

1st spiritual day -    From the beginning of Jesus preaching until Judas Iscariot's betrayal;

2nd spiritual night -    From the time of Judas Iscariot's betrayal to the arrival of the Comforter[2]

2nd spiritual day[3] -    From the arrival of the Holy Spirit to the First Zionist Congress.

3rd spiritual night[4]-    From the First Zionist Congress to Israel's entering into new covenant bonds;

3rd spiritual day -    From Israel's entering into the new covenant bonds to the fulfillment of the word "it is done" in John's Revelation.

Let us look at how the new covenant spiritual period, comprised of three spiritual days, is described:

Ho. 5:15    *I will go and return to my place, till they acknowledge their offence, and seek my face: in their affliction they will seek me early.*

Ho. 6:1    *Come, and let us return unto the LORD: for he hath torn, and he will heal us; he hath smitten, and he will bind us up.*

Ho. 6:2    ***After two days** will he revive us: **in the third day** he will raise us up, and we shall live in his sight.*

Ho. 6:3    *Then shall we know, if we follow on to know the LORD: his going forth is prepared as the morning; and he shall come unto us as the rain, as the latter and former rain unto the earth.*

---

[2]    Another name for the Holy Spirit

[3]    The duration of the second spiritual day is the same for Christians and for Jews. The difference is that after the destruction of Jerusalem in 70 AD, the spiritual day turned into night for the Jewish people (Joel 2:1, 2).

[4]    For info on the spiritual night for Christians, see the chapter The Third Spiritual Night.

The offence of the Jewish people, mentioned in verse fifteen which is also the last verse of the 5th chapter of Hosea's prophecy, was the cause of someone's coming back to his place. The Word of God says: *till they acknowledge their offence, and seek my face* (laws). On the basis of the whole text, the conclusion is drawn that this is speaking of our Lord Jesus Christ because no one can come back to his place, i.e. ascend to heaven, unless he has come down from heaven. We know that only our Lord Jesus Christ had done this.

This means that Jesus is saying that He will leave. Where will He go? Obviously to Golgotha to suffer. Then He says: *I will go and return to my place.* The Lord was resurrected after the crucifixion, and ascended to heaven. He came back to His place and sat on the right-hand side of His Father's throne to reign because His place is in heaven. How long will Jesus Christ not know the Jewish people? The Word of God says: *till they acknowledge their offence.*

Pay attention to the last part of the verse: *in their affliction they will seek me early.* Indeed, not even the mercy of being returned to their land after 1900 years of slavery was enough for them to admit their guilt. Therefore, the Word of God predicts hardship for the Jewish nation gathered in Israel. Only hardship will make them admit their guilt and ask for help from God. When the Word says *till they acknowledge their offence*, this means that they are aware of their sin but they intentionally do not want to acknowledge it.

The text further in the Book of the prophet Hosea, states and describes when God will unburden the Jewish people of their unbelief. Hosea 6:2 says: *in the third day he will raise us up.*

This indicates that they will be in trouble in the third spiritual night. And when they recognize their guilt, then the third spiritual day (period of light) will come in order for them to be able to make new covenant bonds.

The third verse states the law according to which this will happen. This is the law of the former and latter rain whose arrival is stated as the arrival of dawn. It is known that the former rain symbolizes the salvation of the gentiles and the latter the salvation of the Jews, which has yet to occur.

Based on the text from the prophet Hosea, it is evident that the new covenant period includes three spiritual days. On the first day, Jesus preaches and goes to suffer, on the second day He returns to His place in heaven, and on the third day He will deliver the Jews from their unbelief. To be assured that the Old Testament period includes three spiritual nights as well as days, the following example will be considered:

Jn. 2:1    *And **the third day** there was a marriage in Cana of Galilee; and the mother of Jesus was there:*

Jn. 2:2    *And both Jesus was called, and his disciples, to the marriage.*

Jn. 2:3    *And when they wanted wine, the mother of Jesus saith unto him, **They have no wine.***

Jn. 2:10   *And saith unto him, Every man at the beginning doth set forth good wine; and when men have well drunk, then that which is worse: but thou hast kept the good wine until now.*

In the first verse, the Word of God testifies that there was a wedding in Cana of Galilee on the third spiritual day, and that Jesus' mother was at that marriage. Jesus Himself was also invited to that wedding. The question is to which ceremony was Jesus invited, to the old or the new covenant wedding, i.e. which third spiritual day is this?

A conclusion may be drawn on the basis of the phrase: *And when they wanted wine,* and the fact that afterwards Jesus ordered new wine representing the new covenant doctrine. This indicates that this is the third old covenant day because the old covenant wine had been poured until Jesus made new wine to be poured during the three new covenant days. This means that Jesus was invited to come to the wedding in the old covenant time period but arrived only when the Jewish nation went astray[5] from God, i.e. He came on the fourth spiritual day (in the period when the night arrived), which is observed from the moment Adam was removed from heaven until the moment of Jesus' birth.

To better understand what the Word of God refers to in this example, it is necessary to point out the symbols occurring therein. The term "marriage" means entering into covenant bonds or a soul's salvation. There are two marriages in the Bible: the old and the new covenant marriage, which indicate the salvation of human souls during these time periods.

The Lord's old covenant marriage was held in Cana of Galilee. The word "Cana" means "cane". It is known that cane is a plant growing in shallow

---

[5]    They ran out of wine.

water. It grows high, and is firm, but it is hollow inside. Also, it is important to note that cane bends as the wind blows.

Cane represents people who are weak and unbalanced, i.e., people guided by the events around them rather than by God's will. The hollowness of the plant indicates that these people are, to an insufficient extent, filled with sap - the will of God. However, because it grows in shallow water, the meaning here is that people ask for salvation from God, but in a shallow, superficial manner.

"Galilee" means a circle, perfection, and an area. Thus, Jesus' mother was in the "area" of cane where the old covenant salvation was taking place. Also, in the Bible, a woman is a symbol of the church or of people. This indicates that during the salvation time period in the Old Testament i.e., on the third spiritual day which was coming to an end, there was a just and pure people from whose genealogy Jesus, the Saviour of the world, was born. On this third spiritual day, Jesus was invited to the old covenant marriage, because the just were awaiting the arrival of their Messiah.

The third spiritual day in the Old Testament also began with a period of darkness. In this third spiritual night, the Babylonian slavery of the Hebrew people occurred. When the Babylonian slavery ended and Solomon's temple was rebuilt, the time period of light occurred, i.e. the third day in the old covenant time period, which lasted several hundred years. It was at the end of this day that the marriage in Cana took place. How do we know that it was nearing its end? Because they had no more wine left.

The Word of God does not say when Jesus and His disciples arrived at the old covenant marriage. It is only stated that there was no wine when they arrived.

Running out of wine means that the time had come when the Jewish people began to sin against God. In other words, spiritual night arrived. The Old Testament lost power in their hearts and could not help them save their souls.

The night when they waited for their Messiah to come may only be the first night from the first spiritual day in the new covenant period. In that night, the Mosaic Law was still preached, though it could no longer help them.

These two examples from the prophet Hosea and John 2 indicate that both the old and the new covenant periods include three spiritual days.

More attention needs to be paid to the spiritual days in the new covenant period. Therefore, all three spiritual days and nights will be individually discussed, followed by a discussion of the Lord's day.

# THE FIRST SPIRITUAL DAY
# OF THE NEW COVENANT PERIOD

## The First Night

The first night or the period of darkness of the first spiritual day is described in the following words:

Lu. 2:7      *And she brought forth her firstborn son, and wrapped him in swaddling clothes, and laid him in a manger; because there was no room for them in the inn.*

Lu. 2:8      *And there were in the same country shepherds abiding in the field, **keeping watch** over their flock **by night.***

In the Gospel according to Luke, it is written that Jesus was born at night. This was the first night of the first spiritual day, or the beginning of the new covenant period. Since the text refers to the Jews who lived in that time, this night testifies that they ignored God's will and were sinful. By reading the Gospel, the conclusion may be drawn that there were two groups of Jews that night. One group is mentioned in verse eight, and reads: *And there were in the same country shepherds abiding in the field, keeping watch over their flock by night.* These shepherds with their sheep were aware of their spiritual condition and joyfully expected the birth of the Messiah because they wanted to be delivered from the burden of their sins.

The second group also expected the birth of the Messiah, but they were afraid when the Wise Men announced to Jerusalem that the King was born. The Wise Men saw the Morning Star, the sign of the Messiah. The Morning Star may be seen at night but it is also seen before dawn for it announces the imminent arrival of the spiritual morning.

Let us list the most important events that occurred in the first night. Jesus was physically born, in other words, God descended from heaven. John the Baptist prepared the way for the Lord. Jesus rejected an alliance with Satan when He was tempted after forty days of fasting and was worthy of taking the Book sealed with seven seals. Jesus was baptized with the Spirit in the Jordan River. The heavens opened and angels served him. Thus, all the preparations for the breaking of the seven seals from the sealed Book are complete.

## The First Day

The following words show that the first spiritual day (or the time period of light) had occurred:

Mt. 4:16    *The people which sat in darkness saw great light; and to them which sat in the region and shadow of death **light is sprung up.***

Mt. 4:17    *From that time Jesus began to preach, and to say, Repent: for the kingdom of heaven is at hand.*

The beginning of Jesus' preaching, which includes the promise that everyone shall receive the gift of eternal life if he follows God's Commandments, meant the time of light for mortal man. Eternal life is the light for the sinful. The time period of light from the first spiritual day lasted around three earthly years, while Jesus preached the Word brought from heaven.

In this three-year time period, the first day, when the Lord preached the words of eternal life, He announced to His disciples that the time shall come when they would desire to see one of the days of the Son of man, the time when the words of eternal life would be preached again. Based on these words, it is concluded that a new period of darkness must occur when the Word will not be preached, i.e. a second spiritual night shall descend.

28

# THE SECOND SPIRITUAL DAY OF THE NEW COVENANT PERIOD

## The Second Night

The following words of Jesus Christ in the Gospel according to Luke announce that the time had come for darkness to occur:

Lu. 22:52    *Then Jesus said unto the chief priests, and captains of the temple, and the elders, which were come to him, Be ye come out, as against a thief, with swords and staves?*

Lu. 22:53    *When I was daily with you in the temple, ye stretched forth no hands against me:* **but this is your hour, and the power of darkness.**

When Jesus was captured, spiritual darkness fell. From that moment, the second spiritual night began in the new covenant period. This means that the preaching of eternal life stopped from this moment on. Jesus, the spiritual Sun, was still among the people but did not emit His life rays i.e., the Word of God. A darkness for sinners began which lasted for 53 earthly days.

Here are some of the most important events from the second spiritual night. A struggle between Satan and Jesus occurred. Satan attempted to kill Jesus but Jesus won because He did not sin. When Jesus was resurrected, thereby achieving victory over death, the old covenant church was abolished. Jesus Christ strengthened the disciples in their faith and taught them about the kingdom of heaven. He ascended to heaven to sit on the right hand side of His Father's throne. Thus, He provided salvation for mankind.

# The Second Day

Jesus' suffering and crucifixion, as well as the coming of a new day were announced in the following verses of the Gospel according to Luke:

| | |
|---|---|
| Lu. 17:22 | *And he said unto the disciples, The days will come, when ye shall desire to see one of the days of the Son of man, and ye shall not see it.* |
| Lu. 17:23 | *And they shall say to you, See here; or, see there: go not after them, nor follow them.* |
| Lu. 17:24 | *For as the lightning, that lighteneth out of the one part under heaven, shineth unto the other part under heaven;* **so shall also the Son of man be in his day.** |
| Lu. 17:25 | *But first must he suffer many things, and be rejected of this generation.* |

Knowing that the second spiritual night was coming in which His crucifixion would occur, the Lord warned His disciples not to doubt in that night and not to follow various voices: *And they shall say to you, See here; or, see there: go not after them, nor follow them.* Why does the Lord say this? There are two reasons.

The first is that when the second spiritual night occurred and when the Lord was resurrected, the disciples tried to look for Him. They went to His grave, but they did not find His body. In that night, the Lord appeared only to the chosen ones who did not expect Him. This is the essence and the rule to be repeated in the future. Servants should not look for God in that night because He never leaves His chosen men without His presence.

The second reason is that after this night, the period of light arrived in this second spiritual day. This means that, regardless of whether the servant looks for his Lord or not, the spiritual day shall come according to God's law. In Luke 17:24, this law is described through the law of lightning and thunder ruling this world. In Hosea 6:3, it says: *his going forth is prepared* **as the morning***; and he shall come unto us as the rain, as the latter and former rain unto the earth.*

At the same time, at the beginning of the second spiritual day, the day of the Son of man begins as follows:

Lu. 17:24    *For as the lightning, that lighteneth out of the one part under heaven, shineth unto the other part under heaven; so shall also the Son of man be in his day.*

It is interesting that apart from these two terms, which have the same beginning in time, the Bible mentions another very important term with the same beginning as the first two, namely the Lord's day. All three spiritual days, which are mutually exclusive, begin with the arrival of the Comforter on earth.

When the apostles receive the Comforter (Holy Spirit), they then begin preaching the Word of life. Thus the second spiritual day is established. The light shone from the preaching and three thousand were baptized in one day. In order to fully understand the laws ruling the spiritual day, attention will be paid to the symbol of lightning which shines from the sky over everything beneath.

The verse from Luke 17:24 needs to be remembered for the realization of mankind's salvation on the second and third days, as well as on the day of the Son of man, explained therein.

According to the laws of physics, an explosion occurs at the clash of two clouds charged with electricity. The resulting sound is called thunder, while the light is called lightning. Let us observe the description of the events in relation to the spiritual world: in the clash of two clouds, which have opposite charges, representing God and Satan, thunder occurs, the voice of the living God. This voice includes eternal life in itself, which is light for man according to John 1:4.

The Word of God says: when lightning shines, everything under the sky in the vicinity also shines. Thus, when it is preached, when the moment that the thunder's echo comes, when the voice of our living God is heard through the preaching of His word, then a man's heart will first hear the offer of eternal life, and only then will man hear what God commands. This means that man sees lightning or light first, i.e. the offer of eternal life, and then hears thunder, the orders of the Word of God. This happens because light travels faster than sound. Depending on how far a man's heart is from God or how far man is from the occurrence of the thunder, the intensity of the sound will have different effects on man. Indeed, the light occurred in this way through the preaching of Jesus in the first day, thus, through the preaching of the Gospel of Jesus the light occurred to the gentiles on the second day. This is how the light shall come to the Jewish people on the third spiritual day.

Another example of the arrival of the second spiritual day will be stated, written in the Gospel to the Hebrews:

He. 4:5     *And in this place again, If they shall enter into my rest.*

He. 4:6     *Seeing therefore it remaineth that some must enter therein, and they to whom it was first preached entered not in because of unbelief:*

He. 4:7     *Again, he limiteth a certain day, saying in David, To day, after so long a time; as it is said, To day if ye will hear his voice, harden not your hearts.*

Salvation was offered first to the Jewish people. Since they refused to make peace with God, through our Lord Jesus Christ the mediator between God and man, the Word of God testifies that God founded a new spiritual day and offered salvation to another people. The seventh verse states that the Word of God was uttered in David's time through Psalm 95: *To day if ye will hear his voice, harden not your hearts.* Reading this seventh verse, it is not quite clear what day and which group of people it is referring to. Is it the time of the old covenant or the new covenant era? However, note the following verse:

He. 4:8     *For if Jesus had given them rest, then would he not afterward have spoken of another day.*

It now becomes clear that it refers to the new covenant time, *if Jesus had given them rest*, He would not have found a new or another spiritual day in which He invited the gentiles:

Ac. 13:46   *Then Paul and Barnabas waxed bold, and said, It was necessary that the Word of God should first have been spoken to you: but seeing ye put it from you, and judge yourselves unworthy of everlasting life, lo, we turn to the Gentiles.*

# THE THIRD SPIRITUAL DAY IN THE NEW COVENANT TIME PERIOD

## The Third Night

When did the second spiritual day end? When did the third night in the new covenant time period occur? Answering these questions presents some difficulty. It is easy to demonstrate that the third night in the New Testament is described in several sections, but it is not easy to determine the moment when darkness began to fall upon all people. This is because each one differs from the other. If the second night is compared with the third, it is seen that darkness suddenly fell in the second night. Jesus was captured and ceased to preach from that moment on. When there is no preaching, the light is not present.

However, the third night gradually arrives. Today, we are waiting for the midnight of the third spiritual night. What does it mean that darkness gradually falls upon the people? It means that the thunder still echoes and the lightning still shines on everything under the sky, but less and less frequently.

To list the most important events of the third spiritual night, it is necessary to note that there are two groups of events which take place in the third night. First, there are those relating to Christians and the others relating to the Jewish people.

For Christians, including the gentiles, the third night is a night of transition. In this night, the preparation for the complete termination of the gentiles' right to establish new covenant bonds shall be established. In order for this to happen, a flood of lawlessness must occur. The Bible must change, so that whoever receives the distorted Word of God loses the right to eternal life. After midnight of the third spiritual night, the Lord's people should be gathered in Israel and, before dawn (the time when the Jewish people should recognize their lawlessness), the punishment of the disobedient servants of God outside Israel shall begin.

In the third night, the Jews should be taken from the Diaspora to their country. And most of God's promises to Abraham, Isaac and Jacob need to be fulfilled. Then the battle of Gog and Israel must occur in order for the door of the third spiritual day to be opened.

Based on the events of the third spiritual night, it can be noted that the beginning of the night comes when God turns His face toward the Jewish people scattered throughout the world. This happened in Basel in 1897, at the Zionist's First Congress, when the decision was made to deal with the creation of the Jewish state. The closing of the door then occurred for the gentiles, while a period of materialism, liberalism, heresy, Biblical corruption, and uniting of whatever may be united, occurred for Christians. Through all these events, the salvation of the gentiles shall be taken away and given to the Jews.

These events from the third spiritual night were announced on the first spiritual day and are described in Matthew 25 through the parable of the Ten Virgins. The whole action of the parable takes place at midnight:

Mt. 25:6       *And **at midnight** there was a cry made, Behold, the Bridegroom cometh; go ye out to meet him.*

In order to get a clear picture of the future from the wording of the parable of the Ten Virgins, it is necessary to read Matthew 24 in its entirety. Here, only those verses will be stated from which the conclusion is drawn that it refers to the midnight of the third spiritual night:

Mt. 24:4       *And Jesus answered and said unto them, Take heed that no man deceive you.*
Mt. 24:5       *For many shall come in my name, saying, I am Christ; and shall deceive many.*
Mt. 24:14      *And this Gospel of the kingdom shall be preached in all the world for a witness unto all nations; **and then shall the end come.***

From verse 14 on, Jesus describes the End Times:

Mt. 24:21     *For then shall be great tribulation, such as was not since the beginning of the world to this time, no, nor ever shall be.*

Mt. 24:24     *For there shall arise false Christs, and false prophets, and shall shew great signs and wonders; insomuch that, if it were possible, they shall deceive the very elect.*

Mt. 24:42     *Watch therefore: for ye know not what hour your Lord doth come.*

After these words, chapter 24 concludes with a warning to future servants:

Mt. 24:50     *The lord of that servant shall come in a day when he looketh not for him, and in an hour that he is not aware of,*

Mt. 24:51     *And shall cut him asunder, and appoint him his portion with the hypocrites: there shall be weeping and gnashing of teeth.*

After everything He had said in Matthew 24, Jesus began to preach the parable of the Ten Virgins by saying:

Mt. 25:1     *Then shall the kingdom of heaven be likened unto ten virgins, . . .*

The above verses indicate that the salvation of the gentiles will be abolished at midnight of the third spiritual night, the time when the false Christs appear, Matthew 24:24.

## The Third Day

We are now in the third spiritual night, nearing midnight, when a voice will be heard: *"Behold, the Bridegroom cometh"*. When the Gospel begins to be preached to the Jewish people, the third spiritual day will dawn. The events which will occur on the third spiritual day are described in Luke 21:

Lu. 21:29     *And he spake to them a parable; Behold the fig tree, and all the trees;*

Lu. 21:30     *When they now shoot forth, ye see and know of your own selves that summer is now nigh at hand.*

Lu. 21:31     *So likewise ye, when ye see these things come to pass, **know ye** **that the kingdom of God is nigh at hand.***

Verse 29 warns us to look at the fig tree i.e., the Jewish people gathering in Israel, as well as at all the trees i.e., the events happening within Christianity. He instructs us to look at the Jewish people for they need to receive salvation. The events happening in Israel and around it are the clock through which God shall show us the coming of their deliverance.

Matthew 24:32 describes in detail the renewal and ripening of fig tree branches:

Mt. 24:32     *Now learn a parable of the fig tree;When his branch is yet tender, and putteth forth leaves, ye know that summer is nigh:*

A branch sprouting symbolizes a generation, i.e. to be covered with leaves is to acknowledge God by one's mouth. A leaf is an individual's soul. This means that when we see the generations multiplying, abundant and prospering, and when the Jews begin to ask God with their mouths, it is known that summer is near. Summer is the season when fruit suddenly ripens and the harvest occurs. This means that the time for making new covenant bonds is near. Indeed, summer means the arrival of the third spiritual day, i.e. their salvation, for verse 31 says: *So likewise ye, when ye see these things come to pass, know ye that the kingdom of God is nigh at hand.* One could think that the kingdom of God relates to Christian followers. However, this is not possible, for those who have fulfilled the order of the Gospel well and live according to the Word of God, are already in the kingdom of God. Thus, if we have received the Holy Spirit and are ruled by Him, then we are in the kingdom of God.

Ro. 14:17     *For the kingdom of God is not meat and drink;but righteousness, and peace, and joy in the Holy Ghost.*

Therefore, any rightful and peaceful heart which possesses the Holy Spirit and enjoys it has the kingdom of God. When this is known, it becomes obvious that the kingdom of God comes only to the Jewish people. A day should dawn only for them when God shall open the door and they will receive the Holy Spirit.

If additional testimony is needed explaining that the arrival of the kingdom of God to the Jewish people is actually the foundation of the third spiritual day, we should continue reading:

Lu. 21:32    *Verily I say unto you, This generation shall not pass away, till all be fulfilled.*

Lu. 21:33    *Heaven and earth shall pass away: but my words shall not pass away.*

Lu. 21:34    *And take heed to yourselves, lest at any time your hearts be overcharged with surfeiting, and drunkenness, and cares of this life, and so **that day** come upon you unawares.*

Lu. 21:35    *For as a snare shall it come on all them that dwell on the face of the whole earth.*

Lu. 21:36    *Watch ye therefore, and pray always, that ye may be accounted worthy to escape all these things that shall come to pass, and to stand before the Son of man.*

In verse 34, Jesus Christ warns us that this day shall come suddenly, and that we have to prepare for it and be worthy. However, if we are not found worthy of it, if the life of Jesus Christ may not be seen in the spirit of our life, the third spiritual day shall come suddenly.

The conclusion is that a Christian cannot fulfill the words from this parable of our Lord unless he understands what comes to that world, for the Word of God commands: *Watch ye therefore, and pray always, that ye may be accounted worthy to escape.*

How will one pray to God to escape the trouble unless he understands this parable of our Lord?

How will he fulfill Jesus' command: *Behold the fig tree, and all the trees,* unless he does so?

How will he see unless he understands what he sees, i.e. doubt whether the Word of God speaks of actual trees or of symbols?

How can he pray for what he does not understand and cannot see? For the Word of God says: *So likewise ye, when ye see these things come to pass…*

Indeed, this is a great problem for Christians today. Darkness envelops people and lawlessness has increased while we wait for the midnight of the third spiritual day to come, which will awaken us all.

The claim that the new covenant period includes three spiritual days will be confirmed by additional examples.

# *THREE SPIRITUAL DAYS*
# *PRESENTED BY EXAMPLES*

In this chapter, I will set events correctly in time and space using spiritual time. Through the explanation provided you will be able to see how knowledge about spiritual time helps us understand the Word of God more properly. Four examples will be presented. The event describing fishing is considered first.

# *JESUS' PARABLE ABOUT FISHING FROM THE GOSPEL OF LUKE*

| | |
|---|---|
| Lu. 5:4 | *Now when he had left speaking, he said unto Simon, Launch out into the deep, and let down your nets for a draught.* |
| Lu. 5:5 | *And Simon answering said unto him, Master, we have toiled* **all the night,** *and have taken nothing: nevertheless at thy word I will let down the net.* |
| Lu. 5:6 | *And when they had this done, they inclosed a great multitude of fishes: and* **their net brake.** |

The question arises: Which spiritual time period is described by the fishing episode in Luke 5:4-6?

The first thing to understand is that this fishing relates to the new covenant time period. Through it, the Lord teaches His disciples that human souls are caught in the sea of the world in the day. He tells them the way they should fish. If they should throw their nets according to God's will, surely, many fish will be caught.

Simon says: *we have toiled all the night.* The question arises on which night did they toil? Does the fishing relate to the first, second, or third night in the new covenant period?

The disciples obviously went fishing in the first night, the time when the Lord had not yet started to preach. In that night, the fishing was unsuccessful. The lost sheep of Israel – the fish – did not want to repent. The catch was a failure.

However, when the Lord began to preach, and the first day dawned (the period of light), Jesus said at that time: *Launch out into the deep, and let down your nets for a draught. And when they had this done, they inclosed a great multitude of fishes: and their net brake.*

The net is a fisherman's tool for catching fish. This means that the disciples possessed the Word of God, with which they catch souls. The

Word of God says that their nets broke due to a multitude of fish. In other words, their preaching had some weaknesses that caused some fish to escape. The disciples' net — the interpretation of the Word of God — was not strong enough, for Jesus did not yet suffer on Golgotha's cross nor had He resurrected. We should remember that many were offended by Jesus:

Jn. 6:66    *From this time many of his disciples turned back and no longer followed him.*

*5.2*

# JESUS' PARABLE ABOUT FISHING FROM THE GOSPEL OF JOHN

The next event which occurred in the new covenant time period speaks about fishing, and is found in the Gospel of John.

| | |
|---|---|
| Jn. 21:3 | *Simon Peter saith unto them, I go a fishing. They say unto him, We also go with thee. They went forth, and entered into a ship immediately; and **that night** they caught nothing.* |
| Jn. 21:4 | *But when **the morning** was now come, Jesus stood on the shore: but the disciples knew not that it was Jesus.* |
| Jn. 21:6 | *And he said unto them, Cast the net on the right side of the ship, and ye shall find. They cast therefore, and now they were not able to draw it for the multitude of fishes.* |
| Jn. 21:11 | *Simon Peter went up, and drew the net to land full of great fishes, an hundred and fifty and three: and for all there were so many, yet was not the net broken.* |

The question arises: in which night did this fishing take place? Obviously, during the time of the second spiritual night, which lasted for 53 earthly days[6], for in verse 14 the Word of God says: *This was now the third time Jesus appeared to his disciples after he was raised from the dead.* They were not successful in catching fish in that second night. Only when the morning dawned in the second spiritual day and when they threw the net on the right, as the Lord told them, did they catch 100 and 50 and 3 big fishes. Nothing in the Bible is insignificant and this number, 153, is important, as we shall see.

---

[6]    If you will add: 3 days of crucifixion up to the resurrection, 40 days after the resurrection up to the ascension of Jesus into heaven, and 10 days up to the descent of the Comforter, you will get 53 days

It is necessary to note that in this example the Word of God does not say that the disciples threw "their" net as in the first example about fishing. The word only refers to "the net". This net for catching 100 and 50 and 3 fishes contains the crucified and resurrected Jesus. This net (teaching), cannot be torn. Fish cannot escape once in it.

1 Jn. 5:18     *We know that* **whosoever is born of God sinneth not;** *but he that is begotten of God keepeth himself, and that wicked one toucheth him not.*

The Lord Jesus Christ testifies that Satan with his might cannot tear any single soul born through the Holy Spirit from His right hand. If Satan had that power, Jesus Christ would not be the king of kings.

The number 153 is not written as a single number, rather it is broken down into three numbers where 100 is a small flock, 50 is the day of the descent of the Holy Spirit (i.e. fish caught through the Holy Spirit), and the number 3 is the Trinity, i.e. the Father, the Son, and the Holy Ghost. These three special numbers as a unit represent a new covenant church made up of the captured fish. The fishing began in the morning of the second day. According to physical experience it is known that water pressure increases when a man goes down to greater depths. This means that deep spiritual water is the place where God's law (water) strongly presses the souls ignoring God's will. Big fish being caught represents grown-up people on the one hand, and their feelings of great sinfulness, on the other.

# JESUS' PARABLE ABOUT THE GOOD SAMARITAN FROM THE GOSPEL OF LUKE

Lu. 10:30    *And Jesus answering said, A certain man went down from Jerusalem to Jericho, and **fell among thieves,** which stripped him of his raiment, and wounded him, and departed, leaving him half dead.*

Lu. 10:31    *And by chance there came down a certain priest that way: and when he saw him, he passed by on the other side.*

Lu. 10:32    *And likewise a Levite, when he was at the place, came and looked on him, and passed by on the other side.*

Lu. 10:33    *But a certain Samaritan, as he journeyed, came where he was: and when he saw him, he had compassion on him,*

Lu. 10:34    ***And went to him, and bound up his wounds, pouring in oil and wine,** and set him on his own beast, and brought him to an inn, and took care of him.*

Lu. 10:35    *And **on the morrow** when he departed, he took out two pence, and gave them to the host, and said unto him, Take care of him; and whatsoever thou spendest more, **when I come again,** I will repay thee.*

In this parable, Jesus is represented as a Good Samaritan. He comes to this world to save the lost, in other words, only the lost sheep of Israel, presented in the parable in the person of the man coming down from Jerusalem to Jericho. He came to save the man who had taken the wrong path. The Word of God says that the road takes him to the town cursed by God. Thus, Jericho symbolizes the town God's blessing does not rest upon.

The parable of the Good Samaritan explains what was happening to this man when Jesus arrived. It is known that Jesus came in the first night in the new covenant period in which the condition of that man is described by the Word of God as follows:

Lu. 10:30      *And Jesus answering said, A certain man went down from Jerusalem to Jericho, and* **fell among thieves,** *which stripped him of his raiment, and wounded him, and departed, leaving him half dead.*

The citizen of Jerusalem, at the time of the arrival of the Good Samaritan, could only have been the one who fulfills the whole law provided by God's servant Moses. Any Israelite who began to treat his God, i.e. His law unfaithfully, went down from Jerusalem, for he began to disrupt the peace he had with God. Almost the whole Jewish nation was more or less faced with this problem.

Ro. 3:10      *As it is written, There is none righteous, no, not one:*

Ro. 3:12      *They are ALL gone out of the way, they are together become unprofitable; there is none that doeth good, no, not one*

In the process of deviating with his heart from God, this man was caught by thieves. In a spiritual sense, this means that the Jewish nation accepted false gods as their god. He was caught, i.e. he was incapable of serving Israel's God.

When they had been caught in Satan's trap, they were not able to follow God's law. Justice, which is the white apparel of each of God's servants, disappeared. They were undressed. And when they were naked, in their shame and great spiritual distress, they sinned against their God. While they were breaching God's law, sin was wounding their souls. They died spiritually, i.e. they became half-dead. The symbol "half-dead" means to be alive bodily and dead spiritually.

This means that Jesus came in this first night of the first spiritual new covenant day, and was described as the Good Samaritan. Jesus testifies that the Jewish clergy and all those responsible for helping a sinful man had failed to do what they were expected to do toward their kinsmen, i.e. to all those feeling spiritually wounded, "undressed", i.e. naked — sinful and helpless while waiting for spiritual healing, for they cannot be delivered from sin without help.

Lu. 10:31      *And by chance there came down a certain priest that way: and* **when he saw him,** *he passed by on the other side.*

Lu. 10:32     *And likewise a Levite, when he was at the place, came and*
              ***looked on him,*** *and passed by on the other side.*
Lu. 10:33     *But a certain Samaritan, as he journeyed, came where he was:*
              *and when he saw him, he had compassion on him,*

Thus, there is no sin in the Samaritan. He possesses the wine and oil. He is always just, always in the light. He does not need the day to see. However, in order for the priest and the Levite to see "that man", the day must dawn, the morning must come, and the Word of our Lord Jesus, the Good Samaritan, must shine on human hearts. The priest and the Levite saw that the Jewish nation, as well as all of mankind, had sinned. However, they did not want to fulfill God's command, thus they took a shorter route – the route of justification in which they did not understand who their kinsmen were. In that day, the Samaritan healed the wounds of the lost sheep of Israel by teaching them repentance; He poured the new covenant wine of God's mercy and love on them. He poured the oil of joy, placed them on His Spirit to take them and brought them into the inn, in His fellowship of the holy.

Lu. 10:35     *And **on the morrow** when he departed, he took out two*
              *pence, and gave them to the host, and said unto him, Take*
              *care of him; and whatsoever thou spendest more, when I come*
              *again, I will repay thee.*

In the second night from the second spiritual day i.e. tomorrow comes after the first spiritual day, it is known that the "Samaritan" was crucified and resurrected. In that night, before leaving, He gave the inn keeper i.e. His disciples (the new covenant priesthood), two pence. A penny symbolizes the Word of God. This means that He gave them the word of the New and the Old Testaments, which is the arch-image of the New Testament, to pay the costs of healing all those waiting for the Samaritan's mercy. Let us remember Jesus' parable about the silver pounds:

Lu. 19:12     *He said therefore, A certain nobleman went into a far country*
              *to receive for himself a kingdom, and to return.*
Lu. 19:13     *And he called **his ten servants,** and delivered them **ten***
              ***pounds,*** *and said unto them, Occupy till I come.*

It is noted that the meaning of the words is almost identical. For the "ten" represents everything. This means that Jesus gave His silver, or the Word of God, to all His servants. He gave the same task to everyone.

Later the "Good Samaritan" went to receive the kingdom. Thus He was able to send the Comforter, whose coming denotes the beginning of the second spiritual day (the period of light) and the new covenant period.

The question may arise: when did the "Good Samaritan" return?

Obviously, He returned in that same second day, for in the parable of the Ten Pounds of Silver it is written that the "Samaritan" returned as a King:

Lu. 19:15    *And it came to pass, that* **when he was returned,** *having received the kingdom, ...*

And that He paid His good servants:

Lu. 19: 17    *And he said unto him, Well, thou good servant: because thou hast been faithful in a very little, have thou authority over ten cities.*

Cities indicate Christian communities among the gentiles. The sense of payment is that the servant (inn keeper), having received the cities, stays in God's mercy to continue with the activity of the Good Samaritan among the gentiles.

In verse 27 he says that the time of the "Samaritan's" arrival, in the sense of the king pronouncing a verdict, was before the destruction of Jerusalem in 70 A.D.

Lu. 19:27    *But those mine enemies, which would not that I should reign over them, bring hither, and slay them before me.*

*5.4*

# *THE OLD COVENANT PASSOVER*

The Passover is one of the most important holidays commanded by God to be celebrated by eternal law. This is the holiday which everyone must celebrate, regardless of whether the person is male or female, Greek or Jew, rich or poor. Every soul has to celebrate the Passover as commanded by the law. Any ignorance to hear or to execute the command results in disastrous effects for the soul. Through the description of the old covenant Passover to mankind, above all regarding the Jews, it is announced what will happen in the future.

To be able to understand the Old Testament wording, it is necessary to remember the words of apostle Paul:

Col. 2:17     *Which are **a shadow of things** to come; but the body is of Christ.*

Apostle Paul says that all Old Testament texts are a shadow of events in the New Testament.

Have we asked ourselves what a shadow is?

For example, when a shadow of a tree with its contours on the ground is observed, it is seen as a two-dimensional picture. Although the tree is three-dimensional and has a certain thickness, through its trunk, a branch or leaf may not be touched, because a shadow is a kind of picture.

What does this mean in a spiritual sense?

This means that in the Old Testament, we read about various events that actually occurred. We see God's law, God's will, His people, commands such as: go and kill all… stone them unto death, etc., but we do not see Christ in all this, a love toward the sinner.

The second thing that may be noted is that if we stand on a tree's shadow, we will notice that it is still three-dimensional, because it enables us to stand in the shadow of that tree and be protected from the direct impact of the sun. What is the point? The point is that every man who stood in a shadow, who fulfilled the Old Testament command, was protected from direct judgment, for the sun symbolizes our God, and the rays are His commands burning anyone who fails to fulfill them.

The third point to be noted is that although the tree's shadow is the picture of that tree on the ground, it is still hard to say, based on the contours of the shadow, which tree is being reflected. Indeed, it is very difficult to see the Old Testament as a shadow of the New Testament. Evidence that this very tree is reflected in the tree's shadow is that they both have the same starting point, which is the root.

What is the starting point of the Old and the New Testaments?

The starting point is the heavenly Trinity. The Son and the Holy Spirit are in God; God and the Holy Spirit are in the Son; and God and the Son are in the Holy Spirit. There are no two different wills of God because there is only one God.

In Colossians 2:17, the Word of God says that the shadow originated from the tree, and this tree is Christ's body. In other words, this tree is the natural olive tree. The root represents Christ, the trunk represents Israel, the branches are generations, while the leaves are God's people, and together this is His church.

This means that all the events described through the Old Testament, which actually occurred, indeed describe the body of Christ and the events in Christ's body in the new covenant time.

Taking all this into consideration, the verses from the Second Book of Moses (Exodus), about the Passover will be reviewed.

Ex. 12:3    *Speak ye unto all the congregation of Israel, saying, In **the tenth day** of this month they shall take to them every man a lamb, according to the house of their fathers, a lamb for an house:*

Ex. 12:6    *And ye shall keep it up until **the fourteenth day** of the same month: and the whole assembly of the congregation of Israel shall kill it **in the evening.***

Ex. 12:7    *And they shall take of the blood, and strike it on the two side posts and on the upper door post of the houses, wherein they shall eat it.*

Ex. 12:8   *And they shall eat the flesh **in that night,** roast with fire, and unleavened bread; and with bitter herbs they shall eat it.*

Ex. 12:10  *And ye shall let nothing of it remain until the morning; and that which remaineth of it **until the morning** ye shall burn with fire.*

Ex. 12:11  *And thus shall ye eat it; with your loins girded, your shoes on your feet, and your staff in your hand; and ye shall eat it in haste: it is the LORD's passover.*

Ex. 12:12  *For I will pass through the land of Egypt **this night,** and will smite all the firstborn in the land of Egypt, both man and beast; and against all the gods of Egypt I will execute judgment: I am the LORD.*

Ex. 12:13  *And the blood shall be to you for a token upon the houses where ye are: and when I see the blood, I will pass over you, and the plague shall not be upon you to destroy you, when I smite the land of Egypt.*

Ex. 12:14  *And this day shall be unto you for a memorial; and ye shall keep it a feast to the LORD throughout your generations; ye shall keep it a feast by an ordinance for ever.*

The Hebrew people celebrated the old covenant law for hundreds of years in the time period of the shadow (Old Testament), although they failed to understand the meaning of the symbols through which this religious holiday is described. The Jews did not understand that the Lamb symbolized our Lord Jesus Christ, and that they would slaughter Him through their lack of faith, i.e. crucify Him on the cross of Golgotha. They could not understand that they lived in the period of the shadow, when the spiritual world, which is to come, is described through physical events that may be seen by the physical eye.

The above verses describe the law of suffering of our Lord Jesus in the future. The Word of God states that the Jews, who are in Egypt, must take the lamb on the tenth day of the first month and keep him until the fourteenth day. This means that the Jewish nation has to keep the chosen lamb during the full four days. And on the fifth day, according to the law, it has to be slaughtered and a sacrifice made.

Mortal man is obliged to know the spiritual time through symbols explaining the path of his salvation, especially that the lamb symbolizes our Lord Jesus Christ. We should remember that Adam and Eve tried to hide their sin, their nakedness, with a fig leaf. A fig symbolizes God's tribe. In other words, Adam and Eve were the first to say to God, when they covered themselves with the fig leaf: God, we are your children, your tribe, forgive us. Conversely, God clothed them in leather. Although He created them, God testifies through them that man's sin cannot be justified by covering oneself with a fig leaf.

Which leather did He clothe them in?

Obviously, in lamb leather, showing that someone in the future will have to give his life in order for their nakedness to be covered and for their sin to be forgiven. Today we know that this sacrifice was made by our Lord Jesus Christ. God showed that only Jesus' sacrifice could cover the nakedness of all his first born children and of the fallen first Adam, as explained in 1 Corinthians 15:22-45, and through this act receive forgiveness for their sin.

For this reason, it was determined that the lamb was to be kept for a full four spiritual days, from the fall of Adam up to the crucifixion of Jesus.

However, at the beginning (in the first spiritual day), mankind went too far in sin. So far that God was forced to bring the great flood to the world. After the flood, people multiplied again so that after releasing the Jewish nation from Egyptian slavery (which symbolizes the slavery of sin and the land of sin), the command for the Passover was given. This command was given at the end of the second old covenant night. The purpose of the command to celebrate the Passover was to remind them after four spiritual days, in the fifth night, that the lamb would be sacrificed, and in that night, God would grant deliverance to all those obeying His will.

It is known that the old covenant period includes three spiritual days. This means that the fourth day is the first day from the new covenant period. And the evening of the fifth day, when the lamb is to be sacrificed, is the second night from the new covenant period.

In the first new covenant night, Jesus was physically born. Then, in the first new covenant day, Jesus preached, while in the second new covenant night, or the fifth night, counting since Adam had been exiled from paradise, our Lord Jesus Christ was crucified on Golgotha's cross.

Ex. 12:6     *And ye shall keep it up until the fourteenth day of the same month: and* **the whole assembly of the congregation of Israel shall kill it in the evening.**

We read in verse six that God's command was that *the whole* assembly from Israel would crucify Jesus on the cross in that night. Indeed, no one was found on that night who was willing to defend Him, even Peter renounced Him three times.

The question arises: since the order was to kill the lamb in the evening of the fifth night, and the Jewish nation did crucify Jesus in that spiritual night, why were they guilty? Where is the explanation to this question given?

Obviously, the explanation lies in the fact that the Jewish nation needed to be taken out of Egypt. Any inhabitant of Egypt as a sinner, may not leave Egypt – sin – by his own strength and become the inhabitant of the Promised Land – land of the just – which in the New Testament is the kingdom of God in our hearts. God testifies that only He may provide an exit to the inhabitants of Egypt. Therefore, He commands the Passover, i.e. the way to achieve this, for all those believing in Him.

In the time of the Pharaohs, two things were important, as they are today. First, to understand that the Jewish nation living in Egypt was in the grip of sin. This means that all Egyptians were in the same state. Spiritual darkness prevailed throughout the Egyptian land. The Jewish nation could not live in justice, for God's law was not in their hearts. Through torture ordered by the Pharaoh, it was shown that they were sinful. The condition to be taken out of slavery in that night was to blindly fulfill God's command. Thus, they had to slaughter the lamb.

In a spiritual sense, for us this means that the Jewish nation shall sin before the coming of the heavenly Lamb, our Lord Jesus Christ. Therefore, all other people who lived on the earth at that time were sinful. This is what the Word of God says:

Ro. 3:10    *As it is written, There is none righteous, no, not one:*
Ro. 3:11    *There is none that understandeth, there is none that seeketh after God.*

The records in the Bible as well as events recorded by history are a testimony that this was actually so. The consequence of the ignorance of God's will was shown through the crucifixion of Jesus Christ, the Son of God. This means that with the arrival of the new covenant period **sinful** man had no choice, the sin had to crucify Jesus. The fact that the Passover or the sacrifice of the lamb was commanded disturbs our hearts and imposes the question: Why is one guilty of what was destined to happen? This question may also be asked: If the sinful Jewish people did not crucify Jesus (although it was impossible for this not to happen), would they still be guilty because they failed to obey God's command?

The answer to both questions would be: yes, they would still be guilty. In the first case, they are guilty for justice did not live within them, and sin did what it had to do. In the second case, they would be guilty again because they failed to fulfill God's command. This means that they remain in spiritual death for they preferred darkness to light. In other words, there is no one to save them from eternal death.

At first sight, this is contradictory, it is simply impossible. But, it is possible, for attention should be paid to the further text of the commanded Passover, in the time of the shadow of things that will come:

| | |
|---|---|
| Ex. 12:7 | ***And they shall take of the blood,*** *and strike it on the two side posts and on the upper door post of the houses, wherein they shall eat it.* |
| Ex. 12:8 | *And **they shall eat the flesh in that night,** roast with fire, and unleavened bread; and with bitter herbs they shall eat it.* |
| Ex. 12:11 | *And thus shall ye eat it; with your loins girded, your shoes on your feet, and your staff in your hand; and ye shall eat it in haste: it is the LORD's Passover.* |

For a Jew or an Egyptian, the conditions for release from Egyptian slavery are as follows:

- To slaughter the lamb on the fifth night.
- With this lamb's blood from the fifth night, to sprinkle both the side posts and the upper door post of the house where they will eat.
- To eat the lamb roasted on the fire.
- To eat raw bread at the same time.
- To eat bitter greens.
- To be belted.
- To wear footwear.
- To carry a staff in the hand.
- To eat quickly.

It is noted that aside from the slaughtering of the sacrificial animal (lamb), God also ordered many other steps to be executed. The first thing the Jewish nation had to do was to apply the lamb's blood to the upper and the side door posts. Then they had to "roast the lamb on the fire", to be ready for eating in the morning.

What does this mean in a spiritual sense?

This means that the Passover is celebrated as a **whole** comprised of several parts. The problem of the Jewish nation was that they slaughtered the Lamb in the new covenant period, and they failed to fulfill the whole second part of the commanded Passover. Therefore, they remained guilty. This means that God let Jesus suffer at the hands of the lawless who, indeed, did not know what they had done, but, at the same time, God also showed them the path of salvation, from this or any other sin.

When they slaughtered the heavenly Lamb, the next step in that night was to apply the Lamb's blood to both side posts. In a spiritual sense, this means that man comprehends that our Lord Jesus Christ is a sacrificial lamb who voluntarily sacrificed Himself for our sins, and put that comprehension on the door of his heart. It is necessary to understand that anyone committing a sin and living in sin crucifies Jesus Christ, i.e. accepts His death. Regardless of the time the man lives in, each sinner caused His death, since every man born of woman lives in sin and should flee from this condition. Therefore, any man in time and space was, and is today, a participant in the crucifixion of Christ.

Both the side posts and the upper door posts on houses where the lamb was to be eaten, had to be sprinkled by blood that same night.

What does "that same night" mean? Why doesn't it say "that night"?

Because it does not refer only to the Jewish people, but to every man in time and space. For sinful man, this fifth night symbolizes the night of the crucifixion of Jesus. This is the time period when man does not understand God's will, and crucifies Christ out of ignorance, i.e. sin. At the same time, this is the night when he realizes his sins. In that same night when man comprehends that he is sinful, he should apply Christ's blood on his side posts.

Let us see how the people living in darkness are described:

Ga. 3:1     *O foolish Galatians, who hath bewitched you, that ye should not obey the truth, before whose eyes Jesus Christ hath been evidently set forth, **crucified among you?***

The words are directed at the Galatians, Christians committing sin, and again crucifying Jesus Christ with their lives. To commit a sin means to crucify Christ. In the present time, this refers to souls who have and have not made a covenant through Jesus with God.

How is this possible?

Following God's will includes listening and obeying the voice of God and refraining from sin. Man himself determines whether Jesus may or may not live in him. Anyone rejecting Jesus with his words or deeds, essentially crucifies Jesus and agrees that He was rightly judged, and thus testifies that he does NOT let Jesus Christ live within him.

Striking the house door with blood where the lamb is eaten represents that the soul understands that it breaches God's will and believes that Jesus is the prophesied Messiah.

The Jewish nation did not want to acknowledge that it was sinful and that it killed the holy and long-awaited Messiah, although God gave testimonies to all those who crucified Him to understand their actions. The Roman captain said:

Mt. 27:54     *Now when the centurion, and they that were with him, watching Jesus, saw the earthquake, and those things that were done, they feared greatly, saying,* **Truly this was the Son of God.**

Let us see how God gave a testimony to the violators of His will that Jesus resurrected and that He was victorious over death and sin:

Mt. 27:51     *And, behold, the veil of the temple was rent in twain from the top to the bottom; and the earth did quake, and the rocks rent;*

Mt. 27:52     *And the graves were opened; and many bodies of the saints which slept arose,*

Mt. 27:53     *And came out of the graves* **after** *his resurrection, and went into the holy city, and appeared unto many.*

Mt. 28:2      *And, behold, there* **was a great earthquake:** *for the angel of the Lord descended from heaven, and came and* **rolled back the stone** *from the door, and* **sat upon it.**

When they did not recognize the resurrected Jesus as their Messiah, they could not *eat the flesh in that night, roast with fire, and unleavened bread; and with bitter herbs.* Roast lamb symbolizes the pains of Jesus who underwent the fire of trouble until all His suffering ended on the cross of Golgotha. To eat the Lamb means to realize the will of Jesus Christ. His will is to be recognized as King by every man with his heart and deeds. Unleavened bread is purity and truth while eating raw bread means that man leads a life of purity, with no sin. Thus, bitter greens mean repenting, and eating them – making a deed of repentance.

1 Co. 5:8    *Therefore let us keep the feast, not with old leaven, neither with the leaven of malice and wickedness; but with the unleavened bread of sincerity and truth.*

Everyone had to gird himself, wear footwear, and carry a staff in his hand.

Ex. 12:11    *And thus shall ye eat it; with your loins girded, your shoes on your feet, and your staff in your hand; and ye shall eat it in haste: it is the LORD's passover.*

What does the verse written in the Epistle to the Ephesians mean?

Ep. 6:14    *Stand therefore, having your loins girt about with truth, and having on the breastplate of righteousness;*

Ep. 6:15    *And your feet shod with the preparation of the Gospel of peace;*

Re. 2:27    *And he shall rule them with a rod of iron; as the vessels of a potter shall they be broken to shivers; ...*

Indeed, the symbolism is incredible. The described event of the Passover seems like a nice story. However, every detail of the story has unusual significance. This significance is vital because it deals with life and death. Through this, man is filled with the fear of God.

Due to their ignorance, many judge rationally what is or is not important in God's will. For example: what is the logic, sense, or importance of the instruction that man in the old covenant time period had to hold a staff in his hand while eating the Passover meal? Does the firstborn's not being killed depend on this? This command seems needless to mortal man, and many say: We do not need the Old Testament (the shadow of things which will come), for it is confusing. But the Lord does not leave room for doubt:

Ex. 12:12    *For I will pass through the land of Egypt **this night**, and will smite all the firstborn in the land of Egypt, both man and beast; and against all the gods of Egypt **I will execute judgment**: I am the LORD.*

If it is understood that the staff symbolizes the Word of God, then we will understand that this Word of God must be kept in a man's hand at all times. To keep in hand the Word of God means to understand, i.e. possess it, and be ready to fulfill it at any moment. Man may not keep the staff temporarily, i.e. to temporarily understand God's will and temporarily obey the Lord and temporarily not do so. While the battle lasted, Moses held his hands upright the whole time, not just temporarily.

When the actual Passover occurred on the fifth night, God said that every firstborn, from man to cattle of all those failing to obey His command, would be killed.

However, no record can be found in the Bible concerning the suffering of the firstborns, of man to cattle, in that fifth night, which lasted for 53 earthly days, when the Lord suffered and was resurrected. It is obvious that the killing of firstborns in Pharaoh's time had a spiritual significance.

This means that in the time of Christ, Egypt represents the hearts (land) that sin. Man needs to flee from such a land. Whoever fails to fulfill what is commanded through the symbols of the old covenant Passover shall be eternally damned. His firstborn, spiritual man, was killed, for when morning came, the Comforter was sent, and all those who failed to fulfill God's command were not saved.

The killing of the firstborns of man to cattle describes two groups of people. Let us remember Cornelius' vision. Creeping things and various impure animals symbolize the gentiles. This means that man is the one who believes in God and is of legal age. Meanwhile, cattle symbolize those fed by man. Eating means the fulfillment of God's will, and feeding with cattle represents the coming of one's household to God.

In that night, all those who fulfilled God's command when the Comforter came, became God's firstborns, or the heirs of heaven.

Ro. 8:29    *For whom he did foreknow, he also did predestinate to be conformed to the image of his Son, that he might be **the firstborn** among many brethren.*

Re. 1:5    *And from Jesus Christ, who is the faithful witness, and **the first begotten of the dead**, and the prince of the kings of the earth. Unto him that loved us, and washed us from our sins in his own blood,*

He. 12:22  *But ye are come unto mount Sion, and unto the city of the living God, the heavenly Jerusalem, and to an innumerable company of angels,*

He. 12:23  *To the general assembly and **church of the firstborn**, which are written in heaven, and to God the Judge of all, and to the spirits of just men made perfect,*

When it is understood that Jesus Christ is God's firstborn and faithful witness, and that we are spiritual firstborns through Christ by virtue of our exit from the world of sin, and that we belong to the assembly and the church of the firstborn, written in heaven, only then will we understand why God says "in the shadow" that the firstborn from every household that fails to celebrate the Passover will be killed.

1 Co. 15:22  *For as in Adam **all** die, even so in Christ shall **all** be made alive.*

1 Co. 15:45  *And so it is written, The **first** man Adam was made a living soul; the **last** Adam was made a quickening spirit.*

# 6

# *THE DAY OF THE LORD*

The next symbol to which attention will be paid is the day of the Lord. It is revealed in several places in the Bible, in verses mentioning the day of the Lord. The following are examples of such verses:

Jl. 2:31    *The sun shall be turned into darkness, and the moon into blood, before **the great and terrible day of the LORD come.***

Mal. 4:5    *Behold, I will send you Elijah the prophet before the coming of **the great and dreadful day of the LORD:***

Ac. 2:20    *The sun shall be turned into darkness, and the moon into blood, before **the great and notable day of the Lord come:***

1Th. 5:2    *For yourselves know perfectly that **the day of the Lord** so cometh as a thief in the night.*

Jl. 3:14    *Multitudes, multitudes in the valley of decision: for **the day of the LORD is near in the valley of decision.***

2 Pe. 3:10    *But **the day of the Lord will come as a thief in the night**; in the which the fervent heat, the earth also and the works that are therein shall be burned up.*

Based on the above verses, several facts may be noted. First, the day of the Lord is referred in the following ways:

-    the day of the Lord
-    the great and dreadful day of the Lord
-    the great and notable day of the Lord
-    the day of the Lord is near in the valley of decision (Jehoshaphat )
-    the day of the Lord coming as a thief in the night

Based on these notions, many draw the conclusion that this speaks of several types of "days of the Lord". Unfortunately, this conclusion is incorrect. There is only one day of the Lord before God. The word "day" itself means the time period when the preaching of the Word of God occurred. We know that several versions of God's will do not exist, before God and in God. This means that several forms of light in God do not exist. The problem exists within man. Man's heart is differently prepared to receive the light, or the Word of God. For this reason, various terms occur for the day of the Lord.

The term "day of the Lord" means the time period in which not only the Word of God is preached, but also the period in which God rules. The Lord's ruling in the day of the Lord is manifested through the ruling of the Holy Spirit or Comforter. The words next to the term "day of the Lord" such as "great", "notable", "dreadful", "in the valley of decision", "as a thief in the night", describe the group of people the message is directed toward. This means that based on these words we may understand who the term is referring to.

The fact that a difference in time occurs may also be noted from the above verses, for one verse says that the day of the Lord has already been, while another announces that it is yet to come. For example, the words from the verse of Malachi 4:5, that Elijah the prophet would be sent before the coming of the great and dreadful day of the Lord, were fulfilled 2000 years ago.

To be able to know whether Elijah the prophet has already been, we have to know whom he represents. This is written in the Gospel of Matthew:

Mt. 11:10    *For this is he, of whom it is written, Behold, I send my messenger before thy face, which shall prepare thy way before thee.*
Mt. 11:11    *Verily I say unto you, Among them that are born of women there hath not risen a greater than John the Baptist: notwithstanding he that is least in the kingdom of heaven is greater than he.*
Mt. 11:14    *And if ye will receive it, **this is Elias, which was for to come.***
Mt. 11:15    *He that hath ears to hear, let him hear.*

It is written to us that John the Baptist is Elijah who was prophesied to come to prepare the path of our Lord Jesus Christ. Also, based on these few words, it may be concluded that the day of the Lord could not come until John the Baptist had lived, for the Word of God says: *I will send you Elijah the prophet **before the coming** of the great and dreadful day of the Lord.*

The following is an example from which we can see that the day of the Lord shall come in the future:

| | |
|---|---|
| 2 Pe. 3:9 | *The Lord is not slack concerning his promise, as some men count slackness; but is longsuffering to us-ward, not willing that any should perish, but that all should come to repentance.* |
| 2 Pe. 3:10 | *But the day of the Lord **will come** as a thief in the night; in the which the heavens shall pass away with a great noise, and the elements shall melt with fervent heat, the earth also and the works that are therein shall be burned up.* |

The above examples clearly indicate that the Word of God announces the coming of the day of the Lord in various times. Man may think that the case is the same as with Elijah. The first time, Elijah came to earth born of a woman as a prophet, and the second time, hundreds of years later, he came to prepare the path of the Lord, and was born of Elizabeth and became John the Baptist.

The day of the Lord does not occur in this manner. The day of the Lord is the day of mercy for mankind, the day in which human souls are saved through the sacrifice of the Lord Jesus Christ. Since Jesus Christ suffered once for the sins of mankind, God gave a time period to man in which he could achieve salvation. This day is called the day of the Lord.

| | |
|---|---|
| Ac. 2:14 | *But Peter, standing up with the eleven, lifted up his voice, and said unto them, Ye men of Judea, and all ye that dwell at Jerusalem, be this known unto you, and hearken to my words:* |
| Ac. 2:15 | *For these are not drunken, as ye suppose, seeing it is but the third hour of the day.* |
| Ac. 2:16 | *But **this is that which was spoken by the prophet Joel**;* |

The Comforter descended to God's servants awaiting fulfillment of the Father's promise, causing them to begin preaching the Lord's words in many tongues. This caused many to believe that these servants were overcome with drunkenness. However, apostle Peter explains that they were not drunk, but that this was the fulfillment of the words spoken by the prophet

Joel. This means that the words written in Joel 2 describe the event found in Acts 2, which includes the coming of the Comforter and the consequences for human hearts. Perhaps some may wonder: how long shall the Comforter influence human hearts?

Obviously, as long as He shall be present in this material world. It is known to us that the Comforter has been assigned the task of fulfilling **the entire** will of God. This includes the waging of a war against the spirit of darkness until the final victory, which will occur in the battle of Armageddon.

The event of the descending of the Comforter to Christ's servants is found further in Acts 2:

| | |
|---|---|
| Ac. 2:17 | *And it shall come to pass in the last days, saith God, I will pour out of my Spirit upon all flesh: and your sons and your daughters shall prophecy, and your young men shall see visions, and your old men shall dream dreams:* |
| Ac. 2:18 | ***And on my servants and on my handmaidens I will pour out in those days of my Spirit;*** *and they shall prophecy:* |
| Ac. 2:19 | *And I will shew wonders in heaven above, and signs in the earth beneath; blood, and fire, and vapour of smoke:* |
| Ac. 2:20 | *The sun shall be turned into darkness, and the moon into blood, before the great and **notable** day of the Lord come:* |
| Ac. 2:21 | *And it shall come to pass, that whosoever shall call on the name of the Lord shall be saved.* |

Through the descent of the Comforter, the day of the Lord is founded. However, before His arrival the things described in verse 20 must occur. A verse almost identical to this one is found in the Book of the Prophet Joel:

| | |
|---|---|
| Jl. 2:31 | *The sun shall be turned into darkness, and the moon into blood, before the great and **terrible** day of the LORD come.* |

The only difference is that one verse speaks of the notable day of the Lord, and the other of the terrible day of the Lord. Both verses do, however, speak of the same time period. What does God want to convey to us through these words? It is obvious that for any servant fulfilling His will, this will be a notable day of the Lord because he will receive the gift of the Holy Spirit. For all those opposing God's will, the notable day shall turn into the terrible day of the Lord because they will not be blessed with the Holy

Spirit by God. This is terrible because eternal damnation shall prevail for the opponents of God's will.

In addition to the fact that this day shall be beneficial for one group and terrible for the other, we should understand that: *The sun shall be turned into darkness, and the moon into blood.* According to the Word of God, this will happen *before* the arrival of the Comforter, i.e. the day of the Lord announced by the following events:

Ac. 2:19      *And I will shew wonders in heaven above, and signs in the earth beneath; blood, and fire, and vapour of smoke:*

Ac. 2:20      *The sun shall be turned into darkness, and the moon into blood, **before** the great and notable day of the Lord come:*

Heaven and earth are symbols here, for, if observed in a physical sense, no one has seen blood in heaven up to this day. In heaven, the human eye sees the sun, moon, stars, comets, meteors, rather than blood. However, in a spiritual sense, the spiritual eye may see blood, flames, and the fumes of smoke. These effects are miracles and great signs for the spiritual world. All these symbols may have a positive or a negative spiritual connotation. This means that the possibilities are numerous. According to the message sent by God, the reader should understand that the message is given both in a positive and a negative sense.

At the time of the preaching of Jesus Christ, the Jewish people could see, both the old and the new covenant heaven simultaneously. This means there are two suns and two moons. One heaven was worn-out, and scrolled like an old scroll, and another began to shine with all its might.

In the old covenant heaven, the sun that sent forth the Word of God (rays of light), was old covenant Israel, i.e. the old covenant clergy, and the moon was the old covenant church. God, like the sun, can never lose His brightness. Unfortunately, people who received the power to perform God's work, not God himself, made the sun go dark with their transgressions.

In the new covenant heaven, Jesus Christ is our sun. The new covenant Israel, with the new covenant clergy emitting light (the Word of God) is identified with Christ; the moon is the new covenant church, i.e. His body.

The words in verse twenty state that the sun shall turn into darkness. Obviously, God or Jesus Christ cannot become dark. In the spiritual world, God and Jesus Christ shall eternally emit their heavenly light. However, the clergy, who are like the sun and its rays, the old covenant Israel, the old covenant sun incapable of recognizing Jesus, turned into darkness. They defamed Jesus and His clergy with their activities to such an extent that Jesus, with His clergy as the new covenant sun, became dark for the Jewish nation, although He is not darkness before God. These events were, and still are today, miracles and great signs of the history of the Jewish people .

In general, the meaning of other notions from Acts 2:19 is as follows:

> Blood – God's law
>
> Flame – the tongue speaking words

Smoke – creation of the spirit from the words spoken by the tongue

Let us consider these symbols for a moment.

The soul is in the blood. When man sins the soul becomes sinful, as does the blood. From this fact it may be immediately concluded that in a spiritual sense there are several types of blood.

He. 9:12    *Neither by the blood of goats and calves, but by his own blood he entered in once into the holy place, having obtained eternal redemption for us.*

He. 9:13    *For if the blood of bulls and of goats, and the ashes of an heifer sprinkling the unclean, sanctifieth to the purifying of the flesh:*

Spilt blood, in a positive sense, represents the sacrifice of life for the redemption of sin. However, the Acts of the Apostles say that the moon turned into blood. The Word of God does not say that the moon spilled blood nor does it explain whether blood has a positive or a negative meaning. On the basis of the first part of the verse, this is presented in a negative sense because the sun turned into darkness, the conclusion is drawn that blood must have a negative connotation.

Ac. 2:20    *The sun shall **be turned** into darkness, and **the moon into blood**, before the great and notable day of the Lord come:*

Blood in a negative sense is the law, which may no longer provide spiritual life to man. Let us read the words written in Revelation:

Re. 16:3          *And the second angel poured out his vial upon the sea; and it became as the blood of a dead man: and every living soul died in the sea.*

In the verse above there is a description of events which should occur in the future, and, based on this, we can better understand what the term the "moon turned to blood" means.

In Revelation 16:3 we find a description of the punishment God determined for those who have received the beast's mark and who respect its image. An angel poured a vial on the sea, i.e. on all the gentiles, which caused the sea (the world) to turn into *"the blood of a dead man"*. Every living soul died. This means that all the people who lived in the sea and who had blood in themselves in which the "living soul" resided, died from the poured vial, because the water turned into the blood of a dead man.

This should be further clarified. Pouring out of a vial means that the general law shall be enacted (because the Antichrist system rules), which will determine a particular belief, i.e. sacrificing, through which any living soul (Christian) shall spiritually die. This refers only to those living among the gentiles.

Now, let us apply this explanation to Acts 2:19. The Word of God says that before the Comforter, i.e. the day of the Lord comes, the old covenant church shall turn into blood (law). This means the blood (a law) which shall not be able to give spiritual life to people. This was what actually happened. The Mosaic Law was abolished, and God replaced it with His righteousness, a faith in redemption through Jesus. Failing to recognize Jesus, the old covenant Israel became the darkness and the old covenant moon could not bear living children to God. The old covenant moon is giving birth even today, but these spiritual children are not spiritually alive for God. All of this began occurring *before* the great and notable day of the Lord had come.

Now, let us see what fire and smoke represent:

Ja. 3:6          *And **the tongue is a fire**, a world of iniquity: so is the tongue among our members, that it defileth the whole body, and setteth on fire the course of nature; and it is set on fire of hell.*

It was written that the tongue is fire, and this fire produces words — smoke (spirit). When words are evil, the smoke is black – the spirit is evil. In

Acts 2:20, we read that the sun became black, i.e. the intensity and volume of the evil spirit were so high that the sky became black. All those who were looking at the sun in heaven could not see it.

This means that at the beginning of Jesus' preaching the Old Testament church and its preaching were abolished. In other words, it turned into "blood which cannot give life". Listening to Jesus, the Jewish priesthood could not believe that through the deeds of the law, which they preach, justification before God could no longer be acquired. Through this, the fire occurred, i.e. the human tongue which raised its voice against Jesus' teaching. Also, through these words, the evil spirit was created which denied Him as the Messiah.

Another important question is worthy of our attention. Why is it written that the day of the Lord shall come several times?

Because there are two folds in this world. The first fold is the Jewish nation. The second fold of sheep are the gentiles.

Jn. 10:16     *And other sheep I have, which are not of this fold: them also I must bring, and they shall hear my voice; and there shall be one fold, and one shepherd.*

According to the Word of God, the end of mercy for the gentiles shall come, and salvation will be granted to the Jewish nation. This means that the veil covering the eyes of the Jewish nation shall be removed and they will believe in Jesus Christ. In other words: the day of salvation shall come to them again, i.e. the present terrible day of the Lord shall turn into a great and notable one, while the present notable day of the Lord shall turn into a terrible day for the gentiles. They will be under the Antichrist system and will lose their right to be included into covenant bonds. This fact means that all statements indicating the arrival of the day of the Lord in the future relate to the Jewish nation in Israel, who will receive the Holy Spirit through baptism. Three sections from the Bible will be mentioned.

Ro.11:25     *For I would not, brethren, that ye should be ignorant of this mystery, lest ye should be wise in your own conceits; that blindness in part is happened to Israel, until the fulness of the Gentiles be come in.*

1 Th. 5:2     *For yourselves know perfectly that the day of the Lord so cometh as a thief in the night.*

68

1 Th. 5:3     *For when they shall say, Peace and safety; then sudden destruction cometh upon them, as travail upon a woman with child; and they shall not escape.*

In the previously mentioned verses, it is said that the day of the Lord may not come to the Jewish nation until certain events have occurred. One of the crucial events is the declaration of peace in the Middle East. The second is the fulfillment of the number of saved gentiles. Once the number of saved gentiles is fulfilled the Holy Spirit will depart.

When this happens, the day of the Lord is near in the valley of decision:

Jl. 3:14     *Multitudes, multitudes in the valley of decision: for **the day of the LORD is near in the valley of decision.***

After the Holy Spirit leaves the gentiles, the battle in the valley of decision shall occur (Jehoshaphat valley). Gog and Magog[7] shall come upon Israel. These events are a condition for the dawning of the spiritual morning for the Jewish nation, i.e. gaining the right to make covenant bonds.

Finally, let us state the words which are disturbing to many people:

2 Pe. 3:10     *But **the day of the Lord will come as a thief in the night**; in the which the heavens shall pass away with a great noise, and the elements shall melt with fervent heat, the earth also and the works that are therein shall be burned up.*

The majority of Christians who read the verse from Peter's second Epistle believe that the Lord is speaking of the destruction of the universe, i.e. the end of the world. However, if one knows that the Lord's day means the acquisition of the right of salvation for souls, then the words "*in the which the heavens shall pass away with a great noise, and the elements shall melt with fervent heat, the earth also and the works that are therein shall be burned up*" cannot mean the physical destruction of the universe. Obviously, the Word of God speaks about the spiritual heaven which shall be destroyed and the spiritual earth which shall burn.

---

[7]     Gog and Magog are two of the world's spirits waging war against God's deeds. Gog symbolizes materialism and Magog symbolizes idolatry.

The symbol "heaven" describes what Christianity in gentile countries shall experience when the day of the Lord comes to the Jewish nation. The symbol "earth" describes the hearts of Christians (for they live in a materialistic way) in that time.

# 7

# THE LAST DAY

Another spiritual day mentioned in the Bible whose meaning is almost identical to the day of the Lord is the last day:

Jn. 6:40     *And this is the will of him that sent me, that **every one** which **seeth the Son**, and believeth on him, may have everlasting life: and I will raise him up **at the last day.***

In the above verse, the Word of God says that the resurrection shall occur on the last day. On that day, anyone who sees and believes in the Son shall gain eternal life. Seeing and believing are conditions for receiving everlasting life. This means that anyone who turns to God and wants to release himself from the chains of sin and eternal death must see the Son and believe in Him. This is a completely illogical statement for man who interprets these words as seeing through physical eyes. If something is seen, how can it be believed in?

However, if these words are observed with spiritual eyes, then, it is understood that the Son is in the Spirit. Since the Son is seen in the Spirit, then we have to believe in Him. It is interesting to note that the Jewish nation, at the time of Jesus' preaching, looked at Jesus with physical eyes and did not see the Son in Him. Because the Jewish nation did not see the Son, they could not believe in Him. This means that in the new covenant time period, anyone who wants to acquire everlasting life must always observe with spiritual eyes messages from God coming through God's Son, the prophets, God's servants, or the Word of God.

Everlasting life is obtained through the resurrection which is baptism.[8] However, why is it written that the resurrection will come on the last day? What is the last day?

Since baptism is on the last day, this is the day salvation is offered to fallen man. After this, a new spiritual day for salvation shall not be found. Also, this is the day of the Lord for the Lord is in it. Therefore, man has to see the *Son* with spiritual eyes to be able to repent, undergo the Lord's command, resurrect to God, and obtain everlasting life.

However, some believe that this relates to the last earthly day at the end of the world, that the resurrection will come in the last twenty-four hours. Others believe that this relates to the last day of the creation of the world i.e. the seventh day (everlasting Saturday), in which God rested from work. Therefore, many think that the resurrection will be in heaven in the everlasting Saturday, and there are also those who believe the opposite.

It should not be forgotten that God is the God of the living rather than of the dead. These words clearly testify that the resurrection, i.e. revival (spiritual), shall occur on earth. One does not go to heaven dead in order for his soul to be revived. Let us see what Jesus said to Martha:

Jn. 11:23    *Jesus saith unto her, Thy brother shall rise again.*
Jn. 11:24    *Martha saith unto him, I know that he shall rise again in the resurrection **at the last day.***

From Martha's words, it is seen that mortal man knew that the resurrection would occur on the last day. However, Jesus replies to her that man, even if he dies physically, shall live after death:

Jn. 11:25    *Jesus said unto her, **I am the resurrection, and the life**: he that believeth in me, **though he were dead, yet shall he LIVE:***

This means that man does not need to wait for revival after a physical death. Why? Because once the soul resurrects to God to live, it shall no

---

[8] ·    Explained in the chapter "The Kingdom of the Millennium".

longer die (unless it deviates from the Lord and His commands). God is the God of the living rather than of the dead:

| | |
|---|---|
| 1 Jn. 5:10 | *He that believeth on the Son of God hath the witness in himself: he that believeth not God hath made him a liar; because he believeth not the record that God gave of his Son.* |
| 1 Jn. 5:11 | *And this is the record, that God hath given to us eternal life, and this life is in his Son.* |
| 1 Jn. 5:12 | ***He that hath the Son hath life;*** *and he that hath not the Son of God hath not life.* |
| 1 Jn. 5.13 | *These things have I written unto you that believe on the name of the Son of God; that ye may know that ye have eternal life, and that ye may believe on the name of the Son of God.* |

Just as a seed has to die in order for a plant to be revived, we also have to die through baptism in order for our soul to be resurrected, hidden in God:

| | |
|---|---|
| Col. 3:1 | *If ye then be **risen with Christ,** seek those things which are above, where Christ sitteth on the right hand of God.* |
| Col. 3:2 | *Set your affection on things above, not on things on the earth.* |
| Col. 3:3 | ***For ye are dead,*** *and your **life is hid with Christ in God.*** |
| Col. 3:4 | *When Christ, who is our life, **shall appear,** then **shall ye also appear with him in glory.*** |

This means that our resurrected soul, living with Christ, does not need to resurrect a second time. It needs only to appear in glory. Based on this, it is seen that this last day on earth is the time period in which God offers mortal man the right to pass from spiritual death to life through baptism, which will only happen in the notable day of the Lord.

# 8

# *EVERLASTING SABBATH*

God gave the Jewish nation the Sabbath to celebrate as the seventh day, or the day of rest. The eternal law mentions the seventh day as the day when God rested from the creation of the world. This day of rest applied to all, which means it applied to slaves as well as cattle. One was not allowed to work on this day, because it was required to be celebrated, i.e. dedicated to God. Failure to observe the Sabbath was a sin severely punished. During this time, the Pharisees made such an extreme celebration of the Sabbath that not even good deeds such as healing could be performed on this day. This was the situation Jesus found when He was among them. To show them the true sense of the day, He performed good deeds and healed on the Sabbath. They felt that He did not respect the Sabbath.

Through Jesus Christ's arrival and preaching about man's reconciliation with God, making peace or rest with God, a new spiritual meaning was given to the Sabbath. Peace with God is obtained only through repentance and baptism with water and the Holy Spirit. Through baptism (resurrection), i.e. rebirth, man enters rest with God here on earth – the everlasting Sabbath[9].

He.4:10        *For he that is entered into his rest, he also hath*
                      *ceased from his own works, as God did from his.*
He.4:11        *Let us labour therefore to enter into that rest, lest any man*
                      *fall after the same example of unbelief.*

In Hebrews 3, it is written that this creation of rest was first announced to the Jews. However, they refused the Lord's invitation due to their sin and unbelief:

---

[9]    The everlasting Sabbath is described in detail in part three: The Marriage Feast of the Lamb.

He. 3:17 *But with whom was he grieved forty years? was it not with them that had sinned, whose carcases fell in the wilderness?*

He. 3:18 *And to whom sware he that they should not enter into his rest, but to them that believed not?*

He. 3:19 **So we see that they could NOT enter in because of unbelief.**

Thus, entering into rest was given to those believing in Him:

He. 4:3 *For we which have believed do enter into rest, as he said, As I have sworn in my wrath, if they shall enter into my rest: although the works were finished from the foundation of the world.*

He. 4:4 *For he spake in a certain place of the seventh day on this wise, And God did rest the seventh day from all his works.*

He. 4:5 *And in this place again, If they shall enter into my rest.*

The message given to people is that one should enter the seventh day, the day of rest. Peace with God is found only on the seventh day, the everlasting Sabbath. Entering into rest is a commandment to every soul. Whoever rejects this entrance into peace with God, i.e. rest, shall be destroyed. Whoever sins intentionally, and does not observe God's order, is pronounced a terrible judgment by God: *"they shall not enter into my rest"*. Therefore, the door to the everlasting Sabbath (Saturday) is on earth.

He. 4:6 *Seeing therefore it remaineth that some must enter therein, and they to whom it was first preached entered not in because of unbelief:*

He. 4:7 **Again, he limiteth a certain day,** *saying in David,* **TO DAY**, *after so long a time; as it is said, To day if ye will hear his voice, harden not your hearts.*

He. 4:8 **For if Jesus had given them rest, then would he not afterward have spoken of another day.**

Man may only enter into that rest in the day called "today", which is, at the same time, the last day:

Jn. 6:44 *No man can come to me, except the Father which hath sent me draw him: and I will raise him up at* **the last day.**

76

This means that the day "today" is the "last spiritual day" granted by God to mankind to be at peace with God.

Perhaps you may wonder why it is necessary for God to use several terms, such as: the day of the Lord, the last day, today, which, essentially, mean one and the same. In order for the events and messages to be correctly defined, we must be aware of the difference between them.

| | |
|---|---|
| The last day | By this term, mankind is warned that it will not receive another chance for salvation (resurrection). |
| Day of the Lord | Is the time given for the repentance of a fold, either Jewish or gentile. Also, the beginning of salvation of some fold is announced through the day of the Lord. |
| Day today | By this term God says that from the moment man hears the words of life, it is for him the last day (chance). This is the day of the Lord. |

# 9

# *THE KINGDOM*
# *OF THE MILLENNIUM*

I n Christianity, a belief exists about an earthly kingdom of one thousand years, in which our Lord Jesus Christ, when He comes a second time, will sit on an earthly throne in Jerusalem and reign a thousand earthly years.

Most Christians have accepted this explanation. At the same time, this explanation has made it impossible to properly understand Christ's messages, which are given through the parables of Jesus Christ, the Epistles, John's Revelation and the Old Testament, because it does not rest on the foundation of God's word. The kingdom of one thousand years is one symbol of spiritual time appearing in the Bible. This symbol allows us to better understand future events.

Proof that the theory of Christ's earthly kingdom of one thousand years is untenable is found in God's Word.

## Discussion of the Kingdom of One Thousand Years

God gave Jesus Christ all power on heaven and earth:

Mt.28:18   *And Jesus came and spake unto them, saying,* **All power is given unto me in heaven and in earth.**

The question is this: Do we believe that these words of Jesus Christ are true?

If we were to ask individuals the meaning of this Scripture, we would probably receive a variety of answers. Some would say that Jesus Christ does not reign on this earth, where evil and lawlessness are rampant. Most would say that Satan rules the earth rather than Jesus Christ. Also, they would present scriptural evidence implying that our Lord will establish His kingdom on earth in the future and will reign for a thousand years with His followers, i.e. with the Jewish people. It is obvious: we do not all understand the words of God in the same way.

Our Lord testifies above that He is given all power in heaven and on earth. He rules this earth by His own will. Nevertheless, He allows wars, iniquity, poverty, lawlessness, starvation, pestilence etc. All these issues happen not because Satan is in power but because mortal man was given a free will to choose between darkness and light, between justice and injustice, between eternal life and eternal death. Jesus Christ lets every man choose whom he will serve. Hence, much evil exists. Satan has no power to work his free will because there is a limit set upon darkness. Satan is the king of sin but Christ is the king of this earth. Therefore, Satan is bound as a result of his limited power. It is written:

Ro. 13:1   *Let every soul be subject unto the higher powers. For* **there is NO power but of God:** *the powers that be are ordained of God.*

Ro. 13:2   *Whosoever therefore resisteth the power, resisteth* **the ordinance** *of God: and they that resist shall receive to themselves damnation.*

God allowed feudal, capitalist, communist, Islamic, pagan, etc. powers to be established over nations, and in the end God will allow the Antichrist to rule on earth. He ordains powers over nations and removes them at will. In light of God's Word thus far mentioned, why do some of us doubt that Christ reigns on this earth? Perhaps there are those who would like Him to rule in a different way. Let us question the following words:

Ep. 1:20   *Which he wrought in Christ, when he raised him from the dead, and set him at his own right hand in the heavenly places,*

Ep. 1:21   *Far* **above all** *principality, and power, and might, and dominion, and* **every** *name that is named,* **not only in this world,** *but also in that which is to come:*

Ep. 1:22   **And hath put all things** *under his feet, and gave him to be* **the head over all things** *to the church,*

Ep. 1:23   *Which is his body, the fulness of him that filleth all in all.*

After reading the preceding words of our Lord, can anyone preach that "some other kingdom will come on earth", where people will live for a thousand years under a new economy, new laws, new ministers etc.?

These words testify that Jesus Christ has come to rule over all principalities and powers in this world and the world which is to come. It is not possible to preach another doctrine.

Let us now read what Satan said to Jesus Christ:

Lu. 4:5     *And the devil, taking him up into an high mountain, shewed unto him all the kingdoms of the world in a moment of time.*
Lu. 4:6     *And the devil said unto him, **All this** power will I give thee, and the glory of them: for that is **delivered** unto me; and to whomsoever I will I give it.*

What an incredible lie. Satan is the father of lies and here he demonstrates his nature.

In whom do we believe, in God or in Satan? He that holds the power has the kingdom. If we believe the devil rules this earth then he is loose and executing his will, and God has no power over the kingdoms on earth. Conversely, if we believe God, let us read His words:

Mt. 12:28     *But if I cast out devils by the Spirit of God, then the kingdom of God is come unto you.*
Mt. 12:29     *Or else how can one enter into a strong man's house, and spoil his goods, except he first bind the strong man? and **then** he will spoil his house.*

This to us is known through faith, and we believe that God could, and this very day can destroy all evil on earth in a twinkling of an eye. Also, we do believe that God could destroy sinful mortal man who submitted to Satan and listened to his voice at the time of Jesus' crucifixion. In addition, we do believe that Jesus had the power to call ten thousand angels to defend His life at the time of His crucifixion. We firmly believe that He won the victory over Satan on the cross and conquered death through His resurrection. We are convinced the sacrifice of Jesus Christ enabled those who were spiritually dead and slaves to sin to come alive to God by fulfilling His ordinances.

By this we also know that Satan does not have the power to keep a man in the bonds of sin (prison — bottomless pit) if he prayerfully strives for eternal life. In addition, we know that Satan does not have the power to return righteous man back into sin if he loves God and keeps His commandments. Nor to keep a sinner in the shackles of sin if he asks the Lord for help and truly desires to glorify God's name. Nevertheless, we are not able to understand that the power of Satan is limited, saying: how can this now be Christ's kingdom when our eyes see such evil?

When we pose such questions, it means that we do not believe the words of Jesus. Or that we do not believe that He came on this sinful earth, in the house where Satan lives (among people, among the hearts of man, submitted to sin, i.e. Satan), to conquer the master of that house and to bind him so that He will be able to spoil his house. If the Lord does not spoil Satan's house, how is it possible that we believe that we are delivered from Satan's slavery, from spiritual prison and that we are saved?

Is. 61:1    *The Spirit of the Lord GOD is upon me; because the LORD hath anointed me to preach good tidings unto the meek; he hath sent me to bind up the brokenhearted, to proclaim liberty to the captives, and **the opening of the prison** to them that are bound;*

The evidence of these examples is insufficient proof for many. They agree that Christ's spiritual kingdom does exist today. They present evidence that Christ's earthly kingdom is yet to come.

However, His words are powerful:

Jn. 18:36    *Jesus answered, My kingdom is not of this world: **if my kingdom were** of this world, then would my servants fight, that I should not be delivered to the Jews: but now is my kingdom not from hence.*

Undoubtedly, Jesus Christ testifies that His kingdom is spiritual. It is in this world but not of this world.

Proof that Jesus Christ will establish an earthly kingdom[10] cannot be found anywhere in the Word of God. As the Scripture says, if His kingdom were of this world, then His servants would fight for their master not to

---

[10]    Earthly kingdom which will last a thousand earthly years.

be delivered to the Jews. Nevertheless, nowhere in God's word can any evidence be found that His servants defended Him. Therefore, Christ's earthly kingdom cannot exist as long as the day of the Lord lasts. The coming of Christ's earthly kingdom would be in direct opposition to the New Testament and would falsify Christ's doctrine.

Obviously, a problem has arisen because we do not differentiate between the words "to have power over someone" and "to create a kingdom for someone" (for the human soul).

Jesus gained victory over Satan through His resurrection. His followers and the earth were given to Him for governance. The authority of Christ is carried out over Satan and his followers, i.e. his house, in such a way that He places the world's governments according to His will. Through this He deals directly with all events, and makes it impossible for Satan to become organized. For those followers of Satan who realize their mistake through the Word of God, the Lord makes it possible to be delivered from the slavery of sin and allows them to enter into His spiritual kingdom of a thousand years.

In order to be persuaded that the servants of Jesus Christ are not allowed to defend their Lord in the earthly kingdom as Jesus testified in John 18:36 let us cite events from the battle which advocates of an earthly kingdom claimed was Armageddon. This is the battle when Satan came and compassed "the camp of the saints". This is also the town were Jesus Christ should be. Furthermore, this is a description of the end of the kingdom of a thousand years.

Re. 20:8    *And shall go out to deceive the nations which are in the four quarters of the earth, Gog, and Magog, to gather them together to battle: the number of whom is as the sand of the sea.*

Re. 20:9    *And they went up on the breadth of the earth, and compassed the camp of the saints about, and the beloved city: and fire came down from God out of heaven, and devoured them.*

A description of this battle, which will occur at the end of the kingdom of a thousand years, provides a testimony that Christ's servants will not defend the king of the holy city. Help came down from heaven in the form of fire and devoured the enemies. Therefore, the final battle of Armageddon will take place in Christ's spiritual kingdom.

Our Lord Jesus Christ testifies the truth in the next example, when He alone speaks of the purpose of His coming:

Jn. 18:37    *Pilate therefore said unto him, Art thou a king then? Jesus answered, Thou sayest that I am a king.* **To this end was I born,** *and for this cause came I into the world,* **that I should bear witness unto the truth.** *Every one that is of the truth heareth my voice.*

Christ's words are powerful: *To this end I was born, and for this cause came I into the world, that I should bear witness unto the truth.*

These words, however, caused Pilate to pose the following question:

Jn. 18:38    *Pilate saith unto him, What is* **truth?**

It's a wonder Pilate posed such a question since he heard all of the wonders Jesus performed during the time of His preaching. In addition, his wife dreamed a dream warning Pilate not to bring about the wrong judgment. Unfortunately, this was not sufficient evidence to erase his doubt and to allow him to understand the truth of Jesus. We are not much better than Pilate when we cannot believe in the following truths:

- His kingdom is not of this world
- His kingdom will not come to be seen
- His kingdom is not eating and drinking

There is no need to prove the truthfulness of the things we can touch and see. This is why our Lord Jesus Christ says: *everyone that is of the truth heareth my* **voice.** This means we must believe and have complete trust in the Lord, in His truth, and in His testimony, which gives life to the world (John 6:33-35).

Jesus Christ came from heaven to earth to bear witness of spiritual things which cannot be seen with the eye nor touched by the hand. He came to witness the spiritual kingdom.

Lu. 17:20    *And when he was demanded of the Pharisees, when the kingdom of God should come, he answered them and said, The kingdom of God cometh not with observation:*

Pharisees, scribes and Jews were waiting for the earthly kingdom of God to come. They were expecting Christ to conquer their enemies so that they could rule over mankind with their Messiah.

Can we, as spiritual beings, wait for the kingdom of this world to come, as did those Jews? Just as the Jews were waiting for the Messiah to free them from the Romans, we are waiting the Messiah to free us from evil, disease and sin. Are we expecting to live a blessed life of 1000 years in this earthly body?

When Jesus entered Jerusalem on a donkey, the multitude thought their expectations were being fulfilled. He was received like the king of kings. However, to their surprise, instead of going into the king's palace to sit on the throne, our Lord went into the temple of God to expel sinfulness. The multitude was disappointed. Their hope vanished as they realized they were to remain slaves of the Romans. Their hearts changed and they began to chant: crucify him, crucify him.

Lu. 19:45    *And he went into the temple, and began **to cast out** them that sold therein, and them that bought;*
Lu. 19:46    *Saying unto them, It is written, My house is the house of prayer: but ye have made it a den of thieves.*

Will we turn against the Lord, just as the Jewish nation did in the past, when we perceive our own mistakes concerning the coming of Christ's earthly kingdom? When we realize, in our disappointment, that the door to the Wedding Supper of the Lamb is closed, will we receive the Antichrist as our king?

Based on the aforementioned information, we can understand that the Lord Jesus Christ testifies of heavenly matters, which cannot be seen by the physical eye. Testimonies exist of our invisible God, the invisible heavenly kingdom, invisible heavenly law of love which will reign in that invisible heavenly kingdom, and the path which leads sinners into that heavenly kingdom. This is why Jesus Christ was born. Also, Jesus entered this world to testify about heavenly (spiritual) truths, many of which still cannot be received.

Can anyone show, through the Gospels, Letters, John's Revelation, and the prophets, that our Lord will establish a visible kingdom upon His second coming, a kingdom with perfect peace where the lion will graze grass, where there will be neither sorrow nor earthly sickness, and where man will not be required to bear his cross?

There are no such words in the Gospel. Instead it is written:

Mt.10:34     *Think not that I am come to send peace on earth:* **I came not to send peace, but a sword.**

Mt.10:35     *For I am come to set a man at variance against his father, and the daughter against her mother, and the daughter in law against her mother in law.*

Mt.10:36     *And a man's foes shall be they of his own household.*

Mt.10:37     *He that loveth father or mother more than me is not worthy of me: and he that loveth son or daughter more than me is not worthy of me.*

Mt.10:38     **And he that taketh not his cross,** *and followeth after me, is not worthy of me.*

This is the Gospel which our Lord Jesus Christ brought to this earth. There is no other Gospel.

Our Lord explains further:

Lu. 17:21     *Neither shall they say, Lo here! or, lo there! for, behold,* **the kingdom of God is within you.**

This is the kingdom that our Lord has brought to this earth. There is no other kingdom, for it is written: *Neither shall they say, lo here! or, lo there!* We cannot say lo, here is the kingdom of this world, when such a kingdom does not exist.

Is there anyone who can show through the Epistles that our Lord will establish a kingdom of this world upon His second coming?

There are no such words in the Epistles, but instead we read the following:

2 Co. 5:15     *And that he died for all, that they which live should not henceforth live unto themselves, but unto him which died for them, and rose again.*

2 Co. 5:16     *Wherefore henceforth* **know we no man after the flesh:** *yea, though we have known Christ after the flesh, yet* **now henceforth know we him no more.**

From the time when our Lord Jesus Christ ascended to heaven, no one else will be sent to this earth in the flesh. No prophet, nor angel, not even God himself will come to this earth in the flesh, before the salvation of mankind is attained. In support of this let us read the following words:

Th. 4:17     *Then we which are alive and remain shall be **caught up** together with them in the clouds, to meet the Lord in the air: and so shall we **ever be** with the Lord.*

Th. 4:18     *Wherefore **comfort** one another with these words.*

From these words can we conclude that our Lord will establish His kingdom in this world upon His second coming, and that He will rule from Jerusalem for a thousand years? Definitely not!

Can anyone prove from John's Revelation that our Lord will establish His kingdom in this world upon His second coming?

Surely, there are no such words found in John's Revelation. Some people do, however, quote John's Revelation to support their claim of an earthly kingdom. We read:

Re. 20:5     *But the rest of the dead lived not again until the thousand years were finished. **This is the first resurrection.***

Re. 20:6     *Blessed and holy is he that hath part in the first resurrection: on such the second death hath no power, but they shall be priests of God and of Christ, and shall reign with him a thousand years.*

The Word of God says that the first resurrection is in the kingdom of the millennium. The first resurrection is the resurrection which initially happens to man. Sinful man is alive (in the body) but is spiritually dead. This spiritually dead man has to be revived or resurrected.

Lu. 15:24     *For this my son **was dead, and is alive again**; he was lost, and is found. And they began to be merry.*

Col. 3:1     ***If ye then be risen with Christ,** seek those things which are above, where Christ sitteth on the right hand of God.*

The first resurrection is baptism. Only through the fulfillment of the New Testament Commandment of being born again, can the spiritually dead be revived to a life in God. It is not possible to take part in the first resurrection without the ordinance of baptism.

Jn. 3:3    *Jesus answered and said unto him, Verily, verily, I say unto thee, Except a man be born again, he **cannot** see the kingdom of God.*

If we understand the meaning of the first resurrection, we cannot doubt the meaning of the kingdom of the millennium. However, if we do not trust Christ's words then the question becomes: which testimony can help us to understand God's truth?

Let us remind ourselves for a moment of what is written in the Word of God:

Mt. 10:38    *And he that taketh not **his cross**, and followeth after me, is not worthy of me.*

Mt. 3:11    *I indeed baptize you with water unto repentance. but he that cometh after me is mightier than I, whose shoes I am not worthy to bear: he shall baptize you **with the Holy Ghost, and with fire:***

There is an opinion that bliss will prevail in the kingdom of this world where there will no longer exist any tears, sin, pain or evil. Conversely, the first resurrection, i.e. baptism, will prevail. How will God's law, which says that man must take his cross, be fulfilled if there is no suffering, tears, pain and so on? Also, how will our Lord baptize us with fire?

Indeed, the doctrine of the kingdom of this world is in contrast to the very fundamental doctrine of the Gospels which is unchangeable.

Is there anyone who can prove through the prophesies of the Old Testament that our Lord will establish a kingdom of this world upon His second coming?

Verily, there are no words in the prophesies of the Old Testament, but many use the Old Testament to prove their claims. Let us look at one of the most cited passages:

Is. 11:1    *And there shall come forth a rod out of the stem of Jesse, and a Branch shall grow out of his roots:*

| | |
|---|---|
| Is.11:2 | *And the spirit of the LORD shall rest upon him, the spirit of wisdom and understanding, the spirit of counsel and might, the spirit of knowledge and of the fear of the LORD;* |
| Is.11:3 | *And shall make him of quick understanding in the fear of the LORD: and he shall not judge after the sight of his eyes, neither reprove after the hearing of his ears:* |
| Is.11:4 | *But with righteousness shall he judge the poor, and reprove with equity for the meek of the earth: and he shall smite the earth:* **with the rod of his mouth,** *and* **with the breath of his lips** *shall he slay the wicked.* |
| Is.11:5 | *And righteousness shall be the girdle of his loins, and faithfulness the girdle of his reins.* |

| | |
|---|---|
| Rod of his mouth | - the Word of God – as law |
| Breath of his lips | - the Word of God – as the Spirit of God who condemns sinfulness (burning) |
| Earth | - human hearts (in the general sense – as in the parable of the sower). In the specific sense: good ground represents faithful people. |

Let us not forget that the Word of God says that our Lord shall reprove the meek of the earth. The meek are God's faithful ones. This reference speaks of the reproof given to those faithful people. How can there be reproof in the kingdom of this world if its followers claim there are no tears, pain, sin, etc. in it? The conclusion is that this chapter is not about the kingdom of this world. Rather it is about Christ's kingdom which we can see today, and which is in fact the spiritual kingdom of the millennium.

The advent of Jesus Christ's coming to this earth, which occurred almost 2000 years ago, is described in the first five verses of Isaiah's prophecy. We can all agree on this. We can also agree that our Lord did not smite the earth on which we walk *with the rod of his mouth* but rather he smote the earthliness of our hearts. Lastly, we can also agree that he slays the wicked with his word, i.e. with the *breath of his mouth*, for it is written:

| | |
|---|---|
| Jn. 12:48 | *He that rejecteth me, and receiveth not my words, hath one that judgeth him:* **the word that I have spoken, the same shall judge him in the last day.** |

However, the advocates of Christ's earthly kingdom claim that there is a time gap of 2000 years between the fifth and the sixth verse because the *"lion shall eat straw like the ox"* and other similar things, have not yet occurred. Let us read some additional verses:

Is. 11:6    *The wolf also shall dwell with the lamb, and the leopard shall lie down with the kid; and the calf and the young lion and the fatling together; and a little child shall lead them.*

Is. 11:7    *And the cow and the bear shall feed; their young ones shall lie down together: and* **the lion shall eat straw like the ox.**

Is. 11:8    *And the sucking child shall play on the hole of the asp, and the weaned child shall put his hand on the cockatrice' den.*

Is. 11:9    *They shall not hurt nor destroy in* **all my holy mountain**: *for the earth shall be full of the knowledge of the LORD, as the waters cover the sea.*

Is. 11:10   *And* **in that day** *there shall be a root of Jesse, which shall stand for an ensign of the people; to it shall the Gentiles SEEK: and* **his rest shall be glorious.**

We can observe two important things from the text of verses 6 to 10. First, in that time people will seek after the root of Jesse, i.e. salvation by Jesus Christ. Furthermore, it shall stand for an ensign of the people. In other words, Christianity will develop *and his rest shall indeed be glorious*. Secondly, *"the lion shall eat straw like the ox"*. In order to know when this shall occur, we must first know what the holy mountain is. Is it a spiritual or tangible mountain? Where is this mountain? Is it in America, Israel, Europe, China or elsewhere? Also, we must know if Mount Zion is a holy mountain, and how many *"holy mountains"* our Lord possesses?

When we answer these questions, the next question concerning the meaning of the mountain of our Lord will become quite clear, regardless of whether we are talking about a lion as a wild beast or something else.

Let us see what our Lord says:

Je. 50:5    *They shall ask the way to Zion with their faces thitherward, saying, Come, and* **let us join ourselves to the LORD in a perpetual covenant that shall not be forgotten.**

Je. 50:6    *My people hath been lost sheep: their shepherds have caused them to go astray, they have* **turned them away on the mountains**: *they have gone from mountain to hill,* **they have forgotten their restingplace.**

Je. 50:7     *All that found them have devoured them: and their adversaries said, We offend not, because they have sinned against the LORD, the habitation of justice, even the LORD, the hope of their fathers.*

These words were directed to the Jews in the flesh, people blinded by God and unable to be saved. The Jewish nation to this day does not believe in our Lord, Jesus Christ. They roam different (spiritual) mountains. They wander from one spirit to another instead of returning to the Lord's Zion, to their God, their place of rest. Other nations devour and torment them because they have sinned against our Lord. God has denied them His protection because of their sin of crucifying Jesus Christ and casting away the salvation He had offered. God has allowed other nations to devour them, throughout history and to the present day.

Ro. 11:30     *For as ye in times past have not believed God, yet have now obtained mercy through their unbelief:*
Ro. 11:31     *Even so have **these also now** not believed, that through your mercy **they also may** obtain mercy.*

Indeed, the mountain of the Lord is a spiritual mountain. It represents the spiritual people of God. The holy mountain of the Lord is higher than every other mountain. It is the purest, holiest and highest on this earth, the only mountain acknowledged by the Lord, the most beautiful woman. It is holy because it is everlasting.

The holy mountain is the resting place of our Lord.

Is. 2:3     *And **many people shall go** and say, Come ye, and let us go **up to the mountain of the LORD,** to the house of the God of Jacob; and he will teach us of his ways, and we will walk in his paths: for out of Zion shall go forth the law, and the word of the LORD from Jerusalem.*

The Word of God is clear: the holy mountain of the Lord is a spiritual mountain. Only those who were spiritually born, who passed through the ordinance of baptism, are on this spiritual mountain. Also, there are no wild beasts on it. Wolves, lions, snakes, foxes and other beasts which have not spared God's flock in the past and have mingled among God's people are not residents of the Lord's holy mountain. Tares and different beasts are not holy. Nothing unclean and evil can enter the kingdom of God. If a believer sins, God takes peace from such a person and automatically that person is expelled from the kingdom of God. Only those who are holy are on the Lord's holy mountain because God Himself resides on it.

For a better understanding of the symbolism that our Lord uses let us read the following verses:

Is. 35:8     *And an highway shall be there, and a way, and it shall be called* **The way of holiness; the unclean shall not pass over it;** *but it shall be for those: the wayfaring men, though* **fools, shall not err therein.**

Is. 35:9     *No lion shall be there, nor any ravenous beast shall go up thereon, it shall not be found there; but the redeemed shall walk there:*

Is. 35:10    *And* **the ransomed** *of the LORD shall return, and come to Zion with songs and everlasting joy upon their heads: they shall obtain joy and gladness, and sorrow and sighing shall flee away.*

It is evident that no beasts can dwell in the kingdom of God, on the holy mountain of our Lord. Every man who is like a beast has to repent and be born again. This is the time when our Lord takes a wolf and a lion on his pastures. The lion grazes the grass of the Lord's pastures together with a lamb, a calf and a kid. They lie together in God's pen on the Lord's mountain in peace.

The eleventh chapter of Isaiah's prophecy clearly describes Christ's kingdom which He brought from heaven as spiritual; this the kingdom that many call "*the kingdom of the millennium*" because this term was used in Revelation. That heavenly kingdom has been on earth since the Holy Comforter was sent by Jesus Christ.

We can find a testimony that this is so in Isaiah 11. When the kingdom of the millennium comes to its end, the Lord will **then** do the following:

Is. 11:11    *And it shall come to pass in that day, that the Lord shall set his hand* **again** *the second time to recover the remnant of his people, which shall be left, from Assyria, and from Egypt, and from Pathros, and from Cush, and from Elam, and from Shinar, and from Hamath, and from the islands of the sea.*

Is. 11:12    *And he shall set up an ensign for the nations, and shall assemble **the outcasts** of Israel, and **gather together the dispersed** of Judah from the four corners of the earth.*

It is evident that the Lord shall assemble the Jewish people together again at the end of the kingdom of the millennium. Today we are witnessing these events. It was written that *the Lord shall set his hand again to recover the remnant of his people* – He shall assemble the outcasts of Israel and the dispersed of Judah from the four corners of the earth, as we are now witnessing.

So, according to Isaiah 11, the kingdom of the millennium lasts from the time that the Holy Comforter was sent by Jesus Christ to this earth and up to this day. Today, we are living at the end of the kingdom of the millennium given to the gentiles. Presently, Satan is being loosed and Christianity is sinking into spiritual darkness; the spiritual midnight is coming.

It is further written in this chapter how the Jewish people will fight against their neighbours, the Arabs:

Is. 11:13    *The envy also of Ephraim shall depart, and the adversaries of Judah shall be cut off: Ephraim shall not envy Judah, and Judah shall not vex Ephraim.*

Is. 11:14    *But they **shall fly upon the shoulders** of the Philistines toward the west; they **shall spoil them** of the east together: they shall lay their hand upon Edom and Moab; and the children of Ammon **shall obey them.***

When the kingdom of the millennium comes to its end, Judah will fight (*shall fly upon*) neighbouring nations, spoil them, and the children of Ammon, i.e. Jordanians, shall obey him. In the last fifty years, Israel fought its neighbouring countries five times, each time repossessing new land. However, these wars are apart from the battle of Armageddon although they are occurring at the end of the kingdom of the millennium. This is proof that the kingdom of the millennium is a spiritual kingdom whose completion we are witnessing.

The advocates of the kingdom of the millennium on earth testify that Jesus Christ will bind Satan and establish His kingdom on earth upon His second coming. In this kingdom of this world Jesus will reign with the Jewish people on this planet for the following thousand years. His throne shall be in Jerusalem and He will spend a thousand years here on earth. At the end of His reign Satan will be set loose and then the final battle of Armageddon will begin. After this comes the end of the world.

Conversely, it is written:

Re. 16:14    *For they are the spirits of devils, working miracles, which go forth unto the kings of the earth and of the whole world, to gather them to the battle of that great day of God Almighty.*

Re. 16:15    **Behold, I come as a thief.** *Blessed is he that watcheth, and keepeth his garments, lest he walk naked, and they see his shame.*

Re. 16:16    *And he gathered them together into a place called in the Hebrew tongue Armageddon.*

Analyze these words!

If people think that Christ's kingdom of this world will exist, that our Lord will sit on His throne in Jerusalem and that the battle of Armageddon will take place at the end of the kingdom of the millennium, how can the words *"Behold, I come as a thief"* be fulfilled? If Jesus is going to sit in Jerusalem then His coming is not sudden nor is it secret. His presence is proclaimed and public.

Our Lord, Jesus Christ, will come as a thief in the night, suddenly, in the near future and not after a thousand years. Scoffers will come prior to the fulfillment of His words, walking after their own lusts, and there will be those who say: *Where is the promise of His coming?*

2 Pe. 3:3    *Knowing this first, that there shall come in the last days* **scoffers,** *walking after their own lusts,*

2 Pe. 3:4    *And saying,* **Where is the promise of his coming?** *for since the fathers fell asleep, all things continue as they were from the beginning of the creation.*

God is longsuffering because lawlessness is immense. This is in contradiction to the words of advocates who say that sheer bliss rather than lawlessness reigns in this kingdom. Therefore, there is no room to speak about the creation of an earthly kingdom

2 Pe. 3:9    *The Lord is not slack concerning his promise, as some men count slackness; but **is longsuffering to us-ward**, not willing that any should perish, but that **all** should come to repentance.*

2 Pe. 3:10    *But the day of the Lord will come as a thief in the night; in the which the heavens shall pass away with a great noise, and the elements shall melt with fervent heat, the earth also and the works that are therein shall be burned up.*

Jesus Christ cannot sit in Jerusalem and reign in the flesh over the whole world, unlike the words of advocates for Christ's kingdom in this world, because it is written: *for they are the spirits of devils, working miracles, which go forth unto the kings of the earth and of the whole world.* How can kings other than our Lord Jesus Christ exist in this world? In such a kingdom of this world, kings as well as Jesus Christ are not a possibility. It is obvious that this interpretation is incorrect and an earthly kingdom does not exist.

Therefore, the following is written in the Word of God:

Lu. 22:29    *And I **appoint unto you** a kingdom, as my Father hath appointed unto me;*

Lu. 22:30    *That ye may eat and drink at my table in **my kingdom**, and sit on thrones judging the twelve tribes of Israel.*

Lu. 22:31    *And the Lord said, Simon, Simon, behold, Satan hath desired to have you, that he may sift you as wheat:*

Lu. 22:32    *But I have prayed for thee, that thy faith fail not: and when thou art converted, **strengthen** thy brethren.*

He. 11:6    *But without faith it is impossible to please him: for he that cometh to God must believe that he is, and that he is a rewarder of them that diligently seek him.*

Our Lord, Jesus Christ, clearly says that He has given His kingdom to His faithful people. In one of these verses He also says to Simon: *But I have prayed for thee, that thy faith fail not.* One must have faith in order to partake of the heavenly kingdom. In addition, our Lord commanded Peter, when he was converted from his unbelief and violation, to strengthen his brethren in the faith of Christ's kingdom contained in the hearts of believers. That commandment is still in power because Christ's Gospel is unchangeable.

If a believer wants to see the face of God and find himself on the right side of God's heavenly throne, he must fulfill the required conditions. Our

Lord provides a testimony of two of these conditions in the Epistle to the Hebrews: without faith it is impossible to please God.

Only through faith can a man draw nigh unto God and be placed on the right side of His throne. According to the Word of God there is no difference between people because all of humankind is under sin. Therefore, everyone must be born again in order to see the kingdom of God. Every man born of woman, without exception, must repent and be baptized by water, fire and the Holy Ghost.

In order for this condition, which was set by God Himself, to be fulfilled, none from heaven since Christ shall be sent to earth to deliver a message to mankind. Even God Himself shall not come to establish a kingdom of this world.

This condition cannot be fulfilled with a mortal's understanding of the kingdom of the millennium. Advocates say that Jesus Christ will be in Jerusalem. None can seek our God and Saviour by faith, when it is known that He sits on His throne in Jerusalem.

In John's Revelation it is written that in the kingdom of a thousand years, only those who do not worship the beast in his image or receive the mark upon their foreheads or hands, will live (be revived) through the first resurrection. The remaining dead will not live again until the thousand years have passed.

This means that a question arises. What will happen after the kingdom of a thousand is finished on earth? Who are those dead who will additionally (later on) resurrect?

Verily, a correct interpretation of spiritual time will go a long way in helping us to understand God's truth.

2 Pe. 3:8     *But, beloved, be not ignorant of this one thing, that one day is with the Lord as a thousand years, and a thousand years as one day.*

If 2 Peter 3:8: is interpreted in the sense of spiritual time, confusion about the future arrival of the kingdom of one thousand years will not arise. Upon reading this verse, many believe that God created the universe and the earth in six days, which means six thousand years. It has been scientifically proven that rocks and the remains of dinosaurs are millions of years old. Obviously, these present interpretations of the Bible, as well as scientific facts, prove that this cannot be so. Believers also claim that Christ will restore fallen mankind in six days, which means in six thousand years. After this Christ will create a kingdom of a thousand years, lasting one thousand earthly years. Together this adds up to seven thousand years. Obviously, today this explanation does not provide a satisfactory answer. Four thousand years elapsed from the time years began being numbered before A.D., add two thousand years since the birth of Christ, and it will add up to six thousand years. Today we are already in the seventh day, actually six thousand and eight. According to the theory of the earthly kingdom, Jesus Christ was already supposed to have come to this earth in order to sit for eight years on His earthly throne in Jerusalem. Afterwards, the church of Christ already should have ascended from this earth. Accordingly, the salvation of mankind should eventually be accomplished. Our eyes, however, see something else. Let us see what this looks like from the standpoint of spiritual time.

An interpretation from the standpoint of spiritual time is based on 2 Peter 3:8. Verily, a thousand years is as one day and one day is as a thousand years in a spiritual sense.

Mortal man comprehends what he sees; he recognizes one earthly day as twelve hours of darkness and twelve hours of light. Man likes to apply his understanding of earthly time to the Bible in a literal sense. This means, when we read that one day is a thousand years before God, our human mind is steered in the direction that a thousand years should be divided into five hundred years of darkness and five hundred years of light. If we think back to the time of the Babylonian captivity of the Jewish nation, we can see that the captivity of one spiritual night lasted seventy earthly years and not five hundred. The Babylonian captivity of the Jewish nation represents the third night from the third spiritual day in the old covenant time period. Also, the preaching of Jesus did not last five hundred earthly years, rather it lasted three years. These three years represent the first spiritual day (as light) in the new covenant time period. Consider the salvation of the gentiles in the second spiritual day (as light) which lasted around one thousand eight hundred and sixty years rather than five hundred years.

Spiritual events described in the Bible confirm that a spiritual day does not depend on the spin of the Earth around the Sun or other objects in the universe. It depends on the law which reigns in heaven. Obviously, this law is eternity. In eternity everything is subject to God's will. Everything God does is part of eternity. This means, the seventh day is eternity. The first six days are also a part of eternity. In addition to these seven days, every chronological term used to describe earthly occurrences, is connected with eternity and events in eternity. Also, every adverb which stands beside a term describing a certain time period actually describes specific happenings from eternity, through which God tries to send us a message.

Here is our big problem. We do not pay enough attention to numbers and their significance, nor do we pay attention to words which follow terms explaining certain time periods. Verily, we should know why Jesus preached for only three years. For example, why did He not preach for eleven years? What is the spiritual meaning of these three years?

Why was the Jewish nation in Babylonian captivity for seventy years or seven times ten years? Why was the Holy Comforter sent on the fiftieth day? In addition, why did Jesus not eat and drink for exactly forty days and forty nights? Could other numbers have been used instead?

Surely, no other numbers could have been used because through these numbers God sent us additional messages, which we have been poorly interpreting. Confusion has been growing as a result of our misunderstanding. Also, questions concerning the kingdom of a thousand years have been developing.

The Word of God says that one day before God is like a thousand years.

| | |
|---|---|
| 2 Pe.3: 8 | *But, beloved, be not ignorant of this one thing, that one day is with the Lord as a thousand years, and a thousand years as one day.* |
| 2 Pe.3:9 | *The Lord is not slack concerning his promise, as some men count slackness; but is longsuffering to us-ward, not willing that any should perish, but that all should come to repentance.* |
| 2 Pe.3:10 | **But the day of the Lord will come** *as a thief in the night; in the which the heavens shall pass away with a great noise, and the elements shall melt with fervent heat, the earth also and the works that are therein shall be burned up.* |

From the moment of baptism, a man becomes a living servant of God and reigns over sin. If we carefully read these verses again, we will note that the day lasting one thousand years is actually the Lord's day. Only in the Lord's day is life delivered through baptism. This is the first resurrection.

Through baptism, a soul passes from death into spiritual life. This spiritual life has eternal value.

Before God, the Lord's day, in which the transition from death to life occurs, and which occurred on earth, is equal to a thousand years. This means, a thousand years has eternal value on earth. This is why the number one thousand symbolizes eternity.

On earth there is only one Lord's day (already lasting almost two thousand years) as well as one kingdom of a thousand years. This means, the Lord's day and the kingdom of one thousand years take place in the same time period. This is why the Word of God warns us that we should know that before God the Lord's day is described as a thousand years, and is also a part of eternity with God.

Souls which pass from death to eternal life, through the sacrament of baptism, need to live somewhere. The Word of God says that they will live in the kingdom of a thousand years. After baptism, man becomes a living servant of God, who from that moment on reigns with Christ over sin, in His spiritual eternal kingdom on earth called the kingdom of a thousand years.

Re. 20:4     *... and they lived and reigned with Christ a thousand years.*

Righteousness, peace and joy in the Holy Ghost reign in this kingdom according to the law of love towards God and one's neighbours.

Every creation unfolds in six steps. The length of these steps is not bound by the spinning of the Earth around the Sun. These steps are bound by God's will which governs according to the rules of spiritual days. At the creation of the universe and this earth, some days actually lasted for millions of years. This is why rocks are millions of years old and the bones of dinosaurs are hundreds of thousands of years old.

The length of spiritual days varies from the time when Adam and Eve were banished from paradise on this earth, to the time when God rebuilds destruction. Some days lasted three years and some two thousand years, as needed, for God's ordered will to be fulfilled. God banished Adam and Eve from paradise, because they sinned, but He will eventually restore fallen mankind for six spiritual days and nights. This is the law. The seventh day is eternity, for creation will have been completed. The seventh day does not coincide with wars, death, earthly bodies, or with darkness. This is why it is not logical for Armageddon, or the ultimate war between God and Satan, to occur at the end of this day. If we would accept the teachings about the kingdom of a thousand years (which is possible to count as a thousand years) then these thousand years would be that seventh day.

It is necessary to understand one more characteristic of the kingdom of one thousand years, which will have a big influence on our understanding of the End Times. This is the same characteristic of the Lord's day.

Before God, only one Lord's day exists, the day in which people can be saved. However, since the Lord has two folds, we will find verses in the Bible which speak of the Lord's day in the past, present and future tense, depending to which fold salvation is made available.

**We also find this rule in the kingdom of one thousand years.** This means, that at the time the notable day of the Lord comes to its fold, the kingdom of a thousand years begins.

It is important to note that the notable day of the Lord and the kingdom of a thousand years, in the time of the coming of the Comforter, up to the destruction of Jerusalem, (we will call this the first period), contains the following components for the Jewish people: the image of the beast, the mark of the beast, the unloosing of Satan, the judgment, the opening of the Books and the final judgment.

We also find these components in the time of the notable day of the Lord and the kingdom of a thousand for the gentiles (the second period). The notable day of the Lord and the kingdom of a thousand years for the gentiles are stretched from the time of the destruction of Jerusalem up to midnight of the third new covenant night.

However, some differences will be present in the third period, when the Jewish nation again receives the right to enter into new covenant bonds, i.e. when the notable day of the Lord comes to them as a thief in the night and they receive the kingdom of a thousand years to reign with Christ in the Spirit over sin. This third period will not contain all of the components which appear in the first two periods because a transitional period no longer exists. Secondly, at the end of this third time period the final battle between God and Satan (Armageddon) will occur.

# The Kingdom of a Thousand Years
# Through the 20<sup>th</sup> Chapter of John's Revelation

When the Comforter was sent to this earth, salvation was announced to the lost sheep of Israel from the Jewish fold. The notable day of the Lord for the Jewish nation began from this moment. The Jewish people were given the right to enter into new covenant bonds. From the time of the coming of the Comforter to the destruction of Jerusalem, the kingdom of a thousand years began for everyone who believed and was baptized in the name of Jesus Christ and became a Christian. This is the kingdom in which Christ reigns over sin. We can find a description of this kingdom in Revelation 20:1-5 which must be examined for the sake of present events.

In the first two verses we find a description of the battle between the Son of God and Satan. This battle contains everything which God had to do to Satan to enable the establishment of a millennial kingdom in souls who believe in the Lord Jesus Christ, who will be able to resurrect through the ordinance of baptism, and who will reign over sin in the kingdom of a thousand years.

Re. 20:2     *And he laid hold on the dragon, that old serpent, which is the Devil, and Satan, and bound him a thousand years,*

Re. 20:3     *And cast him into the bottomless pit, and shut him up, and set a seal upon him, that he should deceive the nations no more, till the thousand years should be fulfilled: and after that he must be loosed a **little** season.*

In order for the final battle to begin Jesus had to seize Satan. Jesus won this battle. The battle which Jesus won allowed Him to bind Satan. Obviously, the next step was to cast him into prison. The door of this prison (the bottomless pit) was closed and sealed so that no one could change it until God orders differently.

This is what Jesus did two thousand years ago. It is represented through the following steps:

Seize -     Judas' betrayal made it possible for Jesus to seize Satan. Thus the final battle began.

| | |
|---|---|
| Battle - | Jesus then allowed Himself to be judged and crucified on Golgotha's cross. |
| Victory - | Jesus is victorious in the battle, for He fulfilled His Father's will, and released the Spirit. |
| Bound - | Jesus Christ resurrected. Through this event, Satan was bound (his power), because death was conquered and could no longer reign over mortal man as long as man fulfilled the will of God. |
| Cast - | After the resurrection Jesus Christ declared Himself to His disciples and gave them the Spirit. Thus Jesus separated light from darkness, showing who is worthy of the glory. Satan was thus forced into darkness. |
| Shut him up - | The Lord became the King of kings when He ascended into heaven to sit on the right hand side of His father's throne. Satan's fate was settled. The door of his prison was shut. |
| Set a seal - | By sending the Comforter, the door of the bottomless pit was sealed so that Satan cannot change anything. |

From the following verses we can see which souls will be able to believe in Jesus Christ and be baptized. These verses describe the kingdom of a thousand years, which is given to the Jewish nation and which will last from the time of the coming of the Comforter up to the destruction of Jerusalem.

| | |
|---|---|
| Re. 20:4 | *And I saw thrones, and they sat upon them, and judgment was given unto them: and I saw the souls of them that were beheaded for the witness of Jesus, and for the Word of God, and which had not worshipped the beast, neither his image, neither had received his mark upon their foreheads, or in their hands; and they lived and reigned with Christ a thousand years.* |
| Re. 20:5 | *But the rest of the dead lived not again until the thousand years were finished.* |

At the beginning of the fourth verse the following words are written: *And I saw thrones, and they sat upon them, and judgment was given unto them.*

The throne represents power. John saw the throne and those who sat on it. We can find an explanation of these words in the following words spoken by our Lord Jesus Christ.

Mt. 19:28    *And Jesus said unto them, Verily I say unto you, That ye which have followed me, in the regeneration when the Son of man shall sit in the throne of his glory,* **ye also shall sit upon twelve thrones,** *judging the twelve tribes of Israel*

On the day of Pentecost when the Comforter descended upon the apostles, they received power, i.e. they sat on the thrones and began to judge.

What does judgement represent?

Judgment represents the granting of permission for baptism. This means that sinners (those who are condemned to eternal death), who testify of a repentant soul and who bear the fruits of repentance, will appear in court before the church of God (as a jury) and the priesthood (as judges), who in the name of God, and through the Word of God (His law), will judge (decide) them and consider their request to pass from eternal damnation to eternal life (conditionally).

The Word of God testifies that only those sinners who were *beheaded for the witness of Jesus and for the Word of God* were positively absolved, i.e. able to be baptized and receive the gift of eternal life (Holy Spirit). To be beheaded for the witness of Jesus, and for the Word of God, represents those Jews from the Jewish nation who believed Jesus and were not ashamed to testify for His name. As a consequence of their testimony they were often beheaded. The old covenant priesthood excommunicated them and cast them out of the synagogues.

The next group of worthy people were those who had not worshipped the beast nor his image, nor did they receive his mark upon their foreheads or hands. This part of the verse is very difficult to comprehend for those who understand the kingdom of God in an incorrect sense.

In Revelation 20:4,5 the Word of God testifies that Satan had his seal and his image at the time of the apostles' preaching and up to the destruction of Jerusalem, even though he was bound. Christians mostly believe that Satan must be loosed in order for man to possess the image and the seal. Some also believe that this will occur in the near future. Most do not comprehend that Satan, during the time of the apostles, already possessed the image. The apostles fought it wholeheartedly. That image was for the Jewish people. Satan has another image for us, the gentiles. Certainly, the image of the beast is present among us today. The beast is capturing great numbers and stamping many. We as Christians do not preach about the beast for we do not understand what the beast represents.

In a general sense, the image represents a picture of holy things. This picture cannot provide eternal life because it is two- dimensional. A picture provides only an image of something. Conversely, the body is three dimensional and provides eternal life. In the past, our Lord Jesus Christ brought the Word of God from heaven. This Word was transformed into **flesh.**

Jn. 1:14     *And the Word was made **flesh,** and dwelt among us, (and we beheld his glory, the glory as of the only begotten of the Father,) full of grace and truth.*

The Word of God is flesh because Jesus Christ is in it, our eternal life. The old covenant Word of God as a shadow of goods which will come gives a description of this Holy Flesh. Through the coming of Jesus Christ, the old covenant was replaced because it lost power in the hearts of Jewish people. The new covenant word became flesh (three dimensional) providing eternal life. The old covenant, on the other hand, was transformed into a picture, something which cannot give life (two dimensional).

Ga. 5:4     *Christ is become of no effect unto you, whosoever of you are justified by the law; ye are fallen from grace.*

When the Lord began preaching, the priesthood of the old covenant church was against Him. A spiritual war began. The priesthood was transformed into a beast. The weapon which was warring against Jesus and His followers was the image. Through this image, seals on the foreheads and right hands were given. Only those who worshiped the image received this seal. This means, the old covenant was transformed into an image when it was replaced with the new covenant Word. Those who accepted the old covenant worshiped the image. This means that those who were circumcised and kept certain ceremonial practices, accepted this seal on their foreheads.

Also, those who exercised the deeds of the law accepted the seal on their right hands.

Therefore, every Jew who did not accept the old covenant in his heart had the opportunity to turn to Jesus, be revived and reign with Jesus for a thousand years. A thousand years symbolizes an eternal kingdom on this earth. The fourth verse refers to the Jewish nation up to the destruction of Jerusalem. The following words stand written in the fifth verse:

Re. 20:5    *But **the rest of the dead** lived not again until the thousand years were finished. This is the first resurrection.*

The term *the rest of the dead* refers to the gentiles. They could not be revived until the thousand years for the Jewish nation were fulfilled. The period of a thousand years then begins for them. In essence, this period has already lasted nineteen hundred years. Now let us see how these thousand years are described for the gentiles at the time of the first resurrection.

Re. 20:6    ***Blessed and holy is he*** *that hath part in the first resurrection: on such the second death hath no power, but they shall be priests of God and of Christ, and shall reign with him a thousand years.*

Through the words *"Blessed and holy is **he** that hath part in the first resurrection"* the Word of God is saying that not every gentile in the Lord Jesus Christ will believe, i.e. only those who take part in the first resurrection will be blessed.

The same events are occurring in the second time period of a thousand years, which is given to the gentiles.

Re. 20:7    *And when the thousand years are expired, Satan shall be loosed out of his prison,*

The third verse from Revelation 20 says that Satan will be loosed from his prison for a little season at the end of the thousand years given to the Jewish nation. Conversely, at the end of the thousand years, given to the gentiles, it is written that Satan will be released from his prison with a certain purpose:

Re. 20:8      *And shall go out to deceive the nations which are in the four quarters of the earth, Gog, and Magog, to gather them together to battle: the number of whom is as the sand of the sea.*

Take note that God allowed Satan to be loosed at the end of both periods of a thousand years. There are several reasons why God gave Satan the opportunity to deceive man at the end of the time period of a thousand years. The first reason is that judgment has to come, judgment in the sense of the abolishment of the right of the first resurrection (baptism). In other words, this means the following: when the right to enter into covenant bonds is abolished for one group of people (fold), the way is opened for another group to enter into these covenant bonds. The time period of Satan's loosening serves as a transitional period for another group or nation to receive the possibility of salvation. The transitional time period actually shows that those who have the right to enter into covenant bonds are no longer worthy of mercy. It says:

Ac. 28:26      *Saying, Go unto this people, and say, Hearing ye shall hear, and shall not understand; and seeing ye shall see, and not perceive:*

Ac. 28:27      *For the heart of this people is waxed gross, and their ears are dull of hearing, and their eyes have they closed; lest they should see with their eyes, and hear with their ears, and understand with their heart, and should be converted, and I should heal them.*

Ac. 28:28      *Be it known therefore unto you, that the salvation of God is sent unto the Gentiles, and that they will hear it.*

Judgment, which was passed on the Jewish nation at the end of the first time period of a thousand years, is described in Daniel 7:

Da. 7:21      *I beheld, and the same horn made war with the saints, and prevailed against them;*

Da. 7:22      *Until the Ancient of days came, and judgment was given to the saints of the most High; and the time came that the saints possessed the kingdom.*

It is written in the 21st verse that the beast warred against the saints. These *saints* are followers of Jesus Christ for they have the gift of the Holy

Spirit. Afterwards, it is cited that these saints were losing the war. In the Book of Acts it is written that at the end of the time given for the salvation of the Jewish nation, Jews who have embraced Christianity will begin to return to the deeds of the law in large numbers. These saints started losing the war, although this did not last for a long time. The beast prevailed until the final moments of judgment (for the first time period) arrived. The Book was opened on this judgment and every one received according to their deeds. Finally, the time for the execution of the judgement arrived, i.e. the destruction and punishment of Jerusalem and the Jewish nation. We can find a description of these events in the following words:

Da. 7:11    *I beheld then because of the voice of the great words which the horn spake: I beheld even till the beast was slain, and his body destroyed, and given to the burning flame.*

First, the beast was slain. The beast's soul represents the temple in Jerusalem. When the Mosaic Law was in power, it required every Jew to come into the temple and bring a sacrifice once a year. This law was commanded by God. The Roman Empire, however, eventually abolished this practice entirely. Through destruction of the temple the beast was destroyed. A Jewish person who was not slain was taken into captivity and exiled. When they came into captivity, a burning flame (trouble) burned everything against God's will. This flame will continue burning until the Jewish people return to God. Nothing will remain of the beast in the end. The earthly Temple in Jerusalem will never be able to be rebuilt because thereby the life of the beast would be restored.

It is hard for many to believe that the Jewish nation had already been judged. Many Christians believe that the Book will be opened at the end in heaven and that judgment will be passed there. However, the Word of God states that judgement will take place on earth, in a spiritual sense. If we understand that the destruction of Jerusalem has resulted from the pronounced judgement declared upon the opening of the Books nineteen hundred and fifty earthly years earlier, we will understand that the words which are written in Revelation 20:12 describe the judgment of the gentiles (at the end of the second time period).

Re. 20:12    *And I saw the dead, small and great, stand before God; and the books were opened: and another book was opened, which is the book of life: and the dead were judged out of those things which were written in the books, according to their works.*

Re. 20:15    *And whosoever was not found written in the book of life **was cast into the lake of fire.***

To be cast into the lake of fire represents all those names not found in the Book of Life to be under the Antichrist's reign. Where will the names written in the Book of Life be?

Re.15:1    *And I saw another sign in heaven, great and marvellous, seven angels having the seven last plagues; for in them is filled up the wrath of God.*

Re.15:2    *And I saw as it were a sea of glass mingled with fire: and them that had gotten the victory over the beast, and over his image, and over his mark, and over the number of his name, stand on the sea of glass, having the harps of God.*

Those who are victorious over the beast, his image, his mark, and the number of his name are obviously those who were preserved in the glorious faith of Christ. The first verse describes the time period when these events will occur. They will take place before the seven last plagues of God's wrath are poured out in the time of the Antichrist's reign. This means, before the seventh trumpet sounds or before the Antichrist is revealed, Christians from the gentiles will battle against the image of the beast. At this time Gog and Magog will encompass the camp of the saints.

Those individuals whose names are written in the Book of Life will be present in this camp. This camp will be found in Israel. Judgement will come after the battle and after the Books are opened. It will now be possible for the Antichrist to appear.

When the Jewish nation receives the right to enter into covenant bonds (the third time period), they will reign with Christ a thousand years. During this time, the image of the beast and the seals will not be present inside Israel, the holy camp. The image, the seals and Antichrist himself will reign outside of Israel.

*10*

# THE SON OF MAN

The Son of man is one of the symbols which appears in a spiritual time frame and is also important for the understanding of God's word. Many different verses are written in the Bible about the Son of man. Upon reading these words, a question arises: who does the Son of man represents? God's word says that the Son of man symbolizes our Lord Jesus Christ.

Mt. 20:18    *Behold, we go up to Jerusalem; and **the Son of man** shall be betrayed unto the chief priests and unto the scribes, and they shall condemn him to death,*
Mt. 20:19    *And shall deliver him to the Gentiles to mock, and to scourge, and to crucify him: and the third day he shall rise again.*

Jesus Christ, being the Son of God, is called the Son of man in this example. Why is Jesus described through this symbol and what is the essence of this message? Satan, the enemy of the Lord, is trying to confuse mortal man so that he cannot be saved.

1Jn. 4:3    *And every spirit that confesseth not that Jesus Christ is come in the flesh is not of God: and this is that spirit of antichrist, whereof ye have heard that it should come; and even now already is it in the world.*

Mortal man can only be saved if he admits and believes that the Son of man came in the flesh, was born of an earthly woman, felt human emotions such as: pain, tiredness, hunger, joy, sadness, and suffered a cruel death as a righteous man for our sins, resurrected and ascended to heaven to sit on the right hand side of God's throne, reigning together with the Father. This is why mortal man must clearly be told that the Lord is the Son of man who opened His arms on the cross granting salvation. This is the reason why the

Word of God in the 18$^{th}$ and 19$^{th}$ verses testifies that "the Son of man came from heaven to be crucified and arise on the third day".

Jesus is described in two ways in the 18$^{th}$ and 19$^{th}$ verses under the term "the Son of man". Firstly, He is described as Jesus the crucified, who is like man in the flesh, except free of sin, and secondly, as the resurrected Jesus, or the Son of man, who went through the closed door. This Jesus also told Thomas to *"put your finger in my wounds"*, ate earthly food, and shed blood on the cross. Furthermore, after His resurrection, Jesus taught the disciples for forty days and forty nights about God's kingdom. Finally, He ascended to heaven because He fulfilled His Father's will and became Jesus Christ (the high priest and the Saviour of the world).

The symbol "the Son of man" is used in a spiritual sense:

Mt. 16:27    *For the Son of man shall come in the glory of his Father with his angels; and then he shall reward every man according to his works.*

Mt. 16:28    *Verily I say unto you, There be some standing here, which shall not taste of death, **till they see the Son of man coming in his kingdom.***

The kingdom of the Son of man is actually God's kingdom. It began through the Comforter who came two thousand years ago. He descended upon Christ's disciples, and after this, they began preaching the Word of God. In this way the Son of man (the Word of God) started to walk in His kingdom through Christ's disciples. In other words, Jesus Christ in the Spirit, like the Word of God, began to reign in the hearts of His servants – His angels.

## The Essence of the Symbol Son of Man

In a spiritual sense the Son of man has two meanings: one for righteous people, and another for sinners.

For a sinner who has a desire to escape spiritual death, the essence of the message carried out through the symbol Son of man is that Jesus sacrificed himself for sinners, stretched out His arms, and took the cross to give life to all sinners (obviously today this is in the Spirit). Therefore, when a sinner turns to the resurrected Jesus, the Son of man will strengthen him in faith concerning the kingdom of God (again, obviously in the Spirit). The conclusion is thus: when we read the phrase "Son of man" in the Bible the message for the sinner (unrepentant or not baptized) brings a blessing.

What kind of message did the Son of man carry for Christians, i.e. the righteous (those who made a covenant of faithfulness)?

Lu. 21:36    *Watch ye therefore, and pray always, that ye may be accounted worthy to escape all these things that shall come to pass, and* **to stand before the Son of man.**

It is not enough for the righteous man to be righteous only in order to escape and stand before the Son of man. The Word of God says that Christians must prove themselves, i.e. be worthy. This is why this verse speaks against the teaching, which says that the church will be raptured before tribulation. Obviously, God has a different plan.

Righteous man cannot escape by his own will and depart to heaven: to him a special place will be given where he will hide from tribulation and where he will stand before the Son of man.

The word to "stand" before the Son of man represents a readiness of the worthy people to fulfill the will of the Son of man. Conversely, some may say that the meaning is rather that Jesus will come down from heaven unto earth and righteous men will gather around Him. Obviously, this will not happen. Secondly, this is not possible because it is in complete contradiction to the essence of God's word. The Son of man is present on earth through His word, in the Spirit. Let us remember the words which Jesus Christ spoke before His ascension from this earth:

Mt.28:19    *Go ye therefore, and teach all nations, baptizing them in the name of the Father, and of the Son, and of the Holy Ghost:*
Mt.28:20    *Teaching them to observe all things whatsoever I have commanded you: and,* **lo, I am with you ALWAYS, even unto the end of the world. Amen.**

For righteous man who became worthy, this means that the Son of man brings a message of mercy and Godly testimony that He fulfilled the will of God's word.

Spiritual eyes can see the Son of man in the clouds. The clouds are a spiritual term, which denotes righteous men. Just as clouds contain water, which gives life, righteous people will also have the Spirit of God within them, providing them with eternal life.

## Whom Do the Clouds Symbolize?

There are clouds with and without water. Clouds without water symbolise unrighteous people.

Jude 12    *These are spots in your feasts of charity, when they feast with you, feeding themselves without fear: **clouds they are without water,** carried about of winds; trees whose fruit withereth, without fruit, twice dead, plucked up by the roots;*

Why do clouds without water symbolize ungodly servants?

In a spiritual sense, one meaning of water is the Spirit. Just as the ungodly servants are without the Lord's spirit, or empty, a cloud without water is also empty. A cloud without water cannot bring a blessing to an earthly (unrepentant) heart because the cloud does not possess the Spirit. The description of the ungodly, clouds without water is very hard:

2 Pe. 2:15    ***Which have forsaken the right way,*** *and are gone astray, following the way of Balaam the son of Bosor, who loved the wages of unrighteousness;*

2 Pe. 2:16    *But was rebuked for his iniquity: the dumb ass speaking with man's voice forbad the madness of the prophet.*

2 Pe. 2:17    *These are **wells without water, CLOUDS** that are carried with **a tempest**; to whom the mist of darkness is reserved for ever.*

2 Pe. 2:13    *And shall receive the reward of unrighteousness, as they that count it pleasure to riot in the day time. Spots they are and blemishes, sporting themselves with their own deceivings while **they feast with you;***

2 Pe. 2:14    *Having eyes full of adultery, and that cannot cease from sin; beguiling unstable souls: an heart they have exercised with covetous practices; cursed children:*

Water-bearing clouds symbolize righteous people because righteous people do not live their lives according to the laws of the earth, or of this world. Righteous people struggle to live a new life, a heavenly life. They are led by the Spirit through this earthly life, just as these earthly clouds are

112

led by the wind. Although we cannot see the wind, it has the great power to carry and move clouds. Similarly, we cannot see the Spirit but again the Spirit has the great strength to move, carry, and revive.

## Whom Does One Cloud Symbolize?

When "clouds" symbolize righteous people, we then ask ourselves whom does one cloud, which has the power to take the resurrected Lord into heaven, symbolize?

Ac. 1:9    *And when he had spoken these things, while they beheld, he was taken up; **and a cloud received him** out of their sight.*

Let us look at other examples from God's Word:

Ex. 19:9    *And the LORD said unto Moses, Lo, I come unto thee in **a thick cloud**, that the people may hear when I speak with thee, and believe thee forever. And Moses told the words of the people unto the LORD.*

Ex. 19:16    *And it came to pass on the third day in the morning, that there were thunders and lightnings, and **a thick cloud** upon the mount, and the voice of the trumpet exceeding loud; so that all the people that was in the camp trembled.*

Ex. 34:4    *And he hewed two tables of stone like unto the first; and Moses rose up early in the morning, and went up unto mount Sinai, as the LORD had commanded him, and took in his hand the two tables of stone.*

Ex. 34:5    *And **the LORD descended in the cloud,** and stood with him there, and proclaimed the name of the LORD.*

The next example is harder to understand if one does not know the meaning of the term "glory of the Lord".

Ex. 40:34    *Then **a cloud covered the tent of the congregation**, and the glory of the LORD filled the tabernacle.*

Ex. 40:35    *And Moses was not able to enter into the tent of the congregation, because **the cloud** abode thereon, and the glory of the LORD filled the tabernacle.*

Therefore, until the Lord was present in the cloud and covered the tent of the congregation, filling the tabernacle with His presence, no one was able to enter the tabernacle, including Moses. We can find similar examples in John's Revelation:

Re. 15:8    *And the temple was filled with* **smoke** *from the glory of God, and from his power; and* **NO man was able to enter into the temple,** *till the seven plagues of the seven angels were fulfilled.*

Although there are many more examples in the Gospel, let us conclude by quoting one:

Mt. 17:5    *While he yet spake, behold,* **a bright cloud** *overshadowed them: and behold a voice out of the cloud, which said, This is my beloved Son, in whom I am well pleased; hear ye him.*

We note that a difference exists in the description of "clouds" and "one cloud". Clouds are described with adjectives like "watery" and "without water". A cloud is described as being "thick" in the Old Testament, or "bright" in the Gospel. Every account of a cloud in which God appears speaks of a voice coming from it. We see that God's word testifies that "thickness" is not in darkness but rather in light which is life eternal for people, John 1:1-5.

Obviously, a cloud which has the power to carry our resurrected Lord into heaven, from Acts 1:9, is our Lord God alone. God came down from heaven in the form of a cloud for His Son, who fulfilled His holy will. When the Lord ascended into heaven, His Father was already waiting for Him in a cloud. Also, when the Lord was united with His Father in the cloud, His Father-Cloud took Him and brought Him into heaven and put Him on the right hand side of His throne so that He may reign with Him over heaven and earth.

However, if it is not known unto us what a cloud or clouds symbolize, then the words *"shall so come in like manner as ye have seen him go into heaven"* will leave a strong impression on us. Therefore, when we are reading similar words in Revelation 1:7 *"behold, he cometh with clouds; and EVERY eye shall see him"*, we come to the conclusion that the Word is speaking about the second coming of the Lord.

114

# Why Is "to See the Son of Man on the Clouds" Not Christ's Second Coming?

Most believers conclude that all of these verses in God's Word, which speak of the Son of man's appearance in the clouds, describe the second coming of our Lord Jesus Christ. They base their faith on the words of the apostle in Acts 1:1, that the Lord's coming will be the same as His departure. However, in essence there remains a large difference, which will lead readers of the Word of God in a completely different direction because these verses do not describe the second coming of the Lord.

The confusion arises because we do not take note of important details such as the Lord ascended into heaven by **one** cloud and all other verses say that people will see the Lord in the **clouds**, actually in the righteous ones.

Here are a few examples:

Mt. 26:64   *Jesus saith unto him, Thou hast said: nevertheless I say unto you, Hereafter shall ye see the Son of man sitting on the right hand of power, and coming in **the clouds** of heaven.*

Da. 7:13   *I saw in the night visions, and, behold, one like the Son of man came with **the clouds** of heaven, and came to the Ancient of days, and they brought him near before him.*

Lu. 21:27   *And then shall they see the Son of man coming in **a cloud**[11] with power and great glory.*

Mt. 24:30   *And then shall appear the sign of the Son of man in heaven: and then shall all the tribes of the earth mourn, and they shall see the Son of man coming in **the clouds** of heaven with power and great glory.*

Mk. 13:26   *And then shall they see the Son of man coming in **the clouds** with great power and glory.*

Re. 1:7   *Behold, he cometh with **clouds;** and every eye shall see him, and they also which pierced him: and all kindreds of the earth shall wail because of him. Even so, Amen.*

---

[11]   It is necessary to note that Matthew 26:64, Luke 21:27 and Mark 13:26 speak about the same event. In this example one cloud in a spiritual sense represents God's people as one body. The Jewish people should recognize the Son of man in that body (the Word of God – Jesus Christ).

If the clouds represent the righteous ones, the above verses should be a sufficient testimony that the Word of God describes something other than the second coming of Jesus Christ.

## What Does It Mean that People Will Be Able to See the Son of Man Sitting on the Right Hand Side of God's Throne?

In the Gospel according to St. Matthew, the Lord Jesus Christ testified to the high priest, to whom the truth of God should have been known, that from the moment of the delivered judgement the Son of man will be seen in the clouds:

Mt. 26:64     *Jesus saith unto him, Thou hast said: nevertheless I say unto you, Hereafter **shall ye see** the Son of man **sitting** on the right hand of power, and **coming** in **the clouds** of heaven.*

In addition, the Lord testifies that we also will see Him sitting on the right hand side of God. Do we see Him sitting on the right side of God's throne? Obviously, we see Him because it is only possible to see the Lord with spiritual eyes of faith, sitting on the right hand side of God's throne and coming in the clouds of heaven. In order for spiritual eyes of faith to be opened and receive sight, we must believe everything that the Word of God prophesied. When we believe, only then will the occurrences which are happening on this earth be a testimony of the fulfillment of God's truth through the reigning of our Lord Jesus Christ. The following verses describe how spiritual eyes are able to see Jesus Christ sitting and reigning on the right hand side of His father's throne:

Lu. 19:12     *He said therefore, A certain nobleman went into a far country to receive for himself a kingdom, and to return.*

Lu. 19:13     *And he called his ten servants, and delivered them ten pounds, and said unto them, Occupy till I come.*

Lu. 19:14     *But his citizens hated him, and sent a message after him, saying, We will not have this man to reign over us.*

Lu. 19:15     *And it came to pass, that when he was returned, **having received the kingdom**, then he commanded ...*

Lu. 19:27     *But those mine enemies, which would not that I should reign over them, bring hither, and slay them before me.*

Those who believe the Word of God have a testimony that these words of God were fulfilled. The Jewish nation felt that they were righteous and therefore, they hated our Lord Jesus Christ who brought them the message that they must repent. That is why they killed Him. Forty days after the Lord's resurrection He ascended into heaven, returning to His Father to receive the kingdom, and to return, as explained in Luke 19:13. Verily, the Lord returned in the spirit like a king sitting on the right hand side of His Father's throne. He asked for an account from His servants. He pronounced and executed His judgment. He slew evil Jews with the sword of the Roman Empire. Jerusalem was destroyed and burned. He dispersed the remaining Jews around the whole world, just as the Word of God testified would happen if they did not submit to the mighty hand of God.

The fulfillment of the judgment upon the Jewish nation is a testimony for the Christian people that our Lord Jesus Christ, the Son of man, who was crucified for our sins, is sitting and reigning on the right hand side of our Father's throne.

When the Lord Jesus Christ came as King in the spirit to seek an account from the Jewish nation (Luke 19:12-27), the words that He came "like the Son of man", to save, cannot be found in the Word of God for that time period. Instead He is described as a king (Luke 19:15). Only in the Book of Daniel is it written, for that time period (70 A.D.), that He came **like** the Son of man fulfilling the judgment like the king of heaven.

Da. 7:13      *I saw in the night visions, and, behold, one **LIKE the Son of man** came with the **clouds** of heaven, and came to the Ancient of days, and they brought him near before him.*

As the above example shows, we can see how the Lord is reigning and fulfilling the judgment, in other words, sitting on the right hand side of the power that is His Father's throne.

## What Does "that People Will Be Able to See the Son of Man Walking Upon Heavenly Clouds" Mean?

This means that every sinner who is coming to Christ must first see the Son of God and believe in Him in order to pass through baptismal ordinances and inherit eternal life. The Son can only be seen as the Son of man who was

117

crucified for the sins of humankind and who is walking on the clouds. Jesus Christ testifies that people will be able to see Him coming in the clouds of heaven after His crucifixion:

Mt.26:64     *Jesus saith unto him, Thou hast said: nevertheless I say unto you, Hereafter shall ye **see** the Son of man sitting on the right hand of power, and **coming** in **the clouds** of heaven.*

Since clouds symbolize the righteous ones, to see the Son of man walking on the clouds means to see crucified Jesus in the life of the righteous ones. Jesus Christ must be seen in the lives of Christians because He lives in them. The Word of God speaks:

Ga.5:24     *And they that are Christ's have crucified the flesh with the affections and lusts.*
Ga.5:25     *If we live in the Spirit, let us also walk in the Spirit.*

Therefore, every sinner who is **not able** (blessed) to see Jesus the crucified in Christians (clouds of heaven) and believe the Word, will not have the opportunity to pass through God's baptismal ordinances. This can be explained in a different manner: how is it possible for an individual to seek salvation if he cannot see the Lord Jesus living among the Christians in a congregation? Jesus Christ clearly states to the high priest that humankind will see Him after His crucifixion only in His new covenant people. Verily, those words were and continue to be fulfilled to this day.

## Why Is It Possible to See the Son of Man Only on the Heavenly Clouds?

One of the reasons why the Son of man can only be seen on the clouds is because our Lord Jesus Christ reigns in heaven and on earth. It is possible to reign on earth from heaven, but it is not possible to reign in heaven from earth. This is why the reign of our Lord Jesus Christ over earth must only be in the heavenly way – spiritual way – through the Holy Spirit. If Jesus reigns in the spirit, the earthly kingdom of the millennium can never exist, because the earth is not, and neither can it be, the center of everything.

The Son of man can be seen walking on the clouds because His message is directed toward sinners who should see Jesus Christ in Christians and repent. The lives of the clouds (Christians) will show that the crucified Son of man does truly live within them. Do they sincerely have the Holy Spirit within them or are they empty and without water.

From the expounded material we can conclude that the different verses which mention "*they shall see the Son of man coming in the clouds*", are a message of blessing announcing an opportunity to either fold, gentile or Jewish, of entering into new covenant bonds and reigning with Jesus in clouds over sin.

For this reason we must be careful when reading verses which contain the phrase "to see the Son of man in the clouds". They describe different time periods in the Lord's day which occurred in the last two thousand years, and those which are yet to come.

| | |
|---|---|
| Mt. 16:27 | *For the Son of man shall come in the glory of his Father with his angels; and then he shall reward every man according to his works.* |
| Mt. 16:28 | *Verily I say unto you, There be some standing here, which shall not taste of death, till they see the Son of man coming in his kingdom.* |

When the Great Comforter came, the crucified Son of man with His angels or clouds was seen *coming in* His kingdom. It is clearly written that these words were fulfilled some two thousand years ago. The words written in the next verses, however, have not even begun to be fulfilled:

| | |
|---|---|
| Mt. 24:14 | *And this Gospel of the kingdom shall be preached in all the world for a witness unto all nations; and then shall the end come.* |
| Mt. 24:30 | *And then shall appear the sign of the Son of man in heaven: and then shall all the tribes of the earth mourn, and they shall see the Son of man coming in the clouds of heaven with power and great glory.* |

It is clear that there exists a great time difference between the verses "*till they see the Son of man coming in his kingdom*" and "*they shall see the Son of man coming in the clouds of heaven with power and great glory*".

There is also a difference in the terms. The first verse says that the Son of man will be seen with His angels, and the second that He will be seen in the clouds, actually angels. What is the meaning of these differences?

The meaning is to reveal the turning points.

## The Turning Points in the New Covenant Period Described by Verses Containing the Term "They Shall See the Son of Man in Clouds"

There are five turning points in the new covenant period:

| | |
|---|---|
| First | The beginning of the salvation of humankind |
| Second | The removal of salvation from the Jewish nation. |
| Third | The transfer of salvation to the gentiles. |
| Fourth | The removal of salvation from the gentiles. |
| Fifth | The beginning of the new salvation for the Jewish nation gathered in Israel. |

For these turning points we should expect to find in God's word, that the coming of our Lord Jesus Christ be in the spirit described through the symbol the Son of man.

Likewise, in these various time periods the spiritual coming of our Lord Jesus Christ is described through the words Lord, lord, Bridegroom, king and servant, depending on which group the message was sent, either to those who made a new covenant or to those who did not make a new covenant of mercy.

## First Turning Point: The Beginning of the Salvation of Humankind

The first turning point takes place at the coming of the Holy Comforter who declares free entry into new covenant bonds for the Jewish people (and for all humankind). In order for the Jewish people to enter into new covenant bonds they first needed to see and then to believe. This means that they had to see some of Christ's disciples full of the Holy Spirit, and their deeds made through the Holy Spirit in order to believe or to see the Holy Comforter in the form of flames above the apostles' heads.

Verily, we read in Acts that the Holy Spirit descended from heaven as fire and sat upon each of Christ's disciples. After this event, God's servants began to preach the word of salvation. People in that time who sought salvation for their souls, and who were gathered in Jerusalem from different parts of the world, could see the Son of man in the heavenly clouds. In that very first day of preaching three thousand souls saw the Son of man in the clouds and were baptized.

In Revelation, we can only come across one verse which speaks of the appearance of the Son of man. That verse is found at the beginning of Revelation and describes who will have the right to make a covenant with God through our mediator the "crucified Son of Man":

Re. 1:7        *Behold, he cometh with clouds; and **EVERY eye** shall see him, and they also which pierced him: and all kindreds of the earth shall wail because of him. Even so, Amen.*

Every sinful eye that sees Him in the righteous ones – the clouds – and believes in Him, will have the right to be saved, i.e. to wail because of Him. Verily, every sinner's eye and the eyes of those who killed Him cried. But when they recognize that they trespassed the will of God they will keep crying after Him until the words written in Revelation 16:17 *"it is done"* have been fulfilled. This verse in general announces the salvation of humankind and this is why it is found at the beginning of Revelation.

In addition to the verses quoted from John's Revelation, the announcement of salvation, using the words the "Son of man" can be found in the Gospel. However, the description in the Gospel is in the sense of the coming of the kingdom of God to earth by means of thunder and lightning. We know that these phenomena do not come from a clear sky but from the clouds. In essence, a more complex description of the Son of man in the clouds can be found in the Gospel according to St. Luke, without the word clouds being used.

Lu. 17:20      *And when he was demanded of the Pharisees, when the kingdom of God should come, he answered them and said, The kingdom of God cometh not with observation:*

Lu. 17:21     *Neither shall they say, Lo here! or, lo there! for, behold, the*
              *kingdom of God is within you.*

Jesus Christ answers the Pharisees' question directly. He testifies that His kingdom is in the spirit. It will not be possible to say *Lo here* or *Lo there* because that kingdom of God is invisible, it is within one's heart.

Ro. 14:17     *For the kingdom of God is not meat and drink; but righteousness,*
              *and peace, and joy in the Holy Ghost.*

The components of the kingdom are peace and the presence of the Holy Spirit. Therefore, only through the fulfillment of God's righteousness, that is God's requirements, is it possible to achieve complete peace. It is God's will that every man repents, brings forth the fruits of repentance, and is baptized so that he may be sealed with the Holy Spirit. This could only be achieved by a soul when the Great Comforter was sent to earth. This means that from that moment God's kingdom began. However, the Lord continued His teaching and said:

Lu. 17:22     *And he said unto the disciples, The days will come, when ye*
              *shall desire to see* **one of the days of the Son of man,**
              *and ye shall not see it.*
Lu. 17:23     *And they shall say to you, See here; or, see there: go not after*
              *them, nor follow them.*
Lu. 17:24     *For as the lightning, that lighteneth out of the one part under*
              *heaven, shineth unto the other part under heaven;* **so shall**
              **also the Son of man be in his day.**
Lu. 17:25     **But first must he suffer many things, and be**
              **rejected of this generation.**

The Lord testifies that before the day of the Son of man comes, of which is God's kingdom and the Son of man will be seen in the clouds, spiritual night will descend. Verily, this proves the words written in Luke 17:25. Only in that spiritual night, when Jesus Christ is physically absent, will the disciples desire to see "one day"[12] of the Son of man and that is exactly what happened. Jesus was killed and in that spiritual night when the Word of God

---

[12]   One day is in quotation marks because there are more spiritual days.

was not preached publicly, the disciples desired to see one day of the Son of man or the day when the words of salvation and the words of the crucified Son of man are preached. Therefore, the spiritual time when the word of salvation is preached to a fold is described through the term the "day of the Son of man" (or days). Conversely, when salvation refers to all of humankind the term "Son of man in his day" is used. The following verse describes this in an amazing way:

Lu. 17:24    *For as the lightning, that lighteneth out of the one part under heaven, shineth unto the other part under heaven; so shall also the Son of man be in **his day.***

According to examples quoted above, the Lord explains the way in which salvation on this earth will be executed in the time when the Son of man appears, described by the term "the day of the Son of man". This means that the day of the Son of man for the Jewish nation began when the Great Comforter came to this earth and ended when Jerusalem was destroyed in 70 A.D. The day of the Son of man for the gentiles also started in that time and should now soon end.

## Second Turning Point: The Removal of Salvation From the Jewish Nation

Two thousand years ago, the Jewish nation was not an ordinary nation. According to the Mosaic Law, every Jew was circumcised. God and His law were not unknown to them. The testimony of the Messiah was before their eyes. They were God's nation. The Word of God testifies that "He came unto His own and His own received Him not". The salvation of Jesus Christ was first offered unto them. When they rejected salvation judgment was executed, which was ready long ago, for God knew in His providence that this would happen. Jesus Christ came to execute this judgment. He came not as the Son of man with outstretched arms and pierced hands to save them, but like a king to execute judgment. We know what happened and how Jerusalem was cruelly destroyed. The temple was razed to its foundation. This is why there is no written word concerning the coming of the Son of man in the clouds of heaven, because the blessed times for the Jewish nation were over.

However, the question arises whether the coming of the Son of man is written for His faithful people, for the Christians of that time who were also in trouble during the destruction of Jerusalem. Let us see what is written:

Lu. 21:20    *And when ye shall see Jerusalem compassed with armies, then* **know** *that the desolation thereof is nigh.*

Lu. 21:24    *And they shall fall by the edge of the sword, and shall be led away captive into all nations: and Jerusalem shall be trodden down of the Gentiles, until the times of the Gentiles be fulfilled.*

The message through the Son of man was also not withheld from Christians, since the time of anguish for the Jewish people was also a time of pain for Christians. The description was not given in symbols to Christians so that there could be no room for doubt concerning what would happen when the Roman army came to besiege Jerusalem. At that time, the Roman Empire was the leading military power in the world. This means that whoever believed in the Word of God knew what he should do. Since a direct announcement was given concerning the events, no other warnings were provided. Whoever did not heed the message of God's Word had to endure the consequences of his actions.

## Third Turning Point: The Transfer of Salvation to the Gentiles

The transfer of the right of salvation to the gentiles occurred after the destruction of Jerusalem. An announcement was expected for this period (because a time of blessing was near), so that gentiles will see the Son of man on the clouds, believe in Him and be resurrected in newness of life to God. After the destruction of Jerusalem Christians from the Jewish nation were dispersed throughout the world. However, before Jerusalem was destroyed the following event took place:

Da. 7:21    *I beheld, and the same horn made war with the saints, and* **prevailed against them;**

Da. 7:22    *Until the Ancient of days came, and judgment was given to the saints of the most High; and the time came that the saints possessed the kingdom.*

124

Just as God ordained that the anointment be removed from King Saul for trespassing against His will, and that David be anointed King of Israel, the same thing happened in the new covenant time period when the preaching of salvation began. King Saul could not accept God's decision and as a result spent forty years trying to kill King David, just as the old covenant church did. Jesus Christ abolished the old covenant church, God gave a testimony, and the Jewish nation could not accept it. For forty years, the old covenant church tried to destroy the new covenant church, i.e. "*made war with the saints*" just as it is written in Daniel 7:21, until the judgment was pronounced that the beast should be slain, his body destroyed, and given to the burning flame. The spirit which denied that Jesus Christ was the Messiah, represents the beast in the spirit. The Jewish clergy and the Jewish people accepted that spirit and in this way became the body of the beast. Through the destruction of the temple the priesthood was not able to keep the service, and the beast was slain. Through the dispersion of the Jewish people throughout the whole world, its body was destroyed. In addition, the sword that was put out throughout history, that tribulation, and burning flame, burned the spirit, which rejected the Lord as Messiah. The following verses refer to the time after the destruction of Jerusalem:

Da. 7:13   *I saw in the night visions, and, behold, one **like** the Son of man came with the clouds of heaven, and came to the Ancient of days, and they brought him near before him.*

Da. 7:14   *And there was given him **dominion, and glory, and a kingdom**, that ALL people, nations, and languages, should serve him: his dominion is an everlasting dominion, which shall not pass away, and his kingdom that which shall not be destroyed.*

Let us take note that the Word of God does not speak that the Son of Man was going on the clouds in glory. Because He could not. In the midst of the Jewish nation He was losing the battle with the beast. Rather than Christians growing in number, masses of converted Jews began returning to the old covenant.

This means that the Jewish nation did not glorify His name and this is why the apostle speaks in Acts: *but seeing ye put it from you, and judge yourselves unworthy of everlasting life, lo, we turn to the Gentiles*. Verily, when Christians from the Jewish nation turned to the gentiles after the destruction of Jerusalem, the name of the Lord Jesus Christ was glorified. This is why it is written: *And there was given him **dominion, and GLORY, and a kingdom**, that ALL people, nations, and languages, should serve him.*

Many of us will ask: is there a difference between the terms "**like** the Son of man with clouds" and "the Son of man on the clouds". There certainly is. "The Son of man on the clouds" offers salvation. However, when it is written "like the Son of man" it means that He is reigning and governing eternally over those who willingly submit to Him. Therefore, the term "like the Son of man" describes Jesus Christ in the Spirit like a King.

This is why it is written that "like the Son of man" was "*brought near before the Ancient of days*" *which* means that "the Son of man" stood before God. These words describe a readiness to go in a new action. That action is to go with His clouds unto the gentiles *to spoil house of the strong one* (Satan).

## Fourth Turning Point:
## The Removal of Salvation From the Gentiles

When will the time of mercy expire for the gentiles? When will Christians who find mercy by the will of God be taken to the Wedding Feast of the Lamb? How will salvation be taken away from the gentiles? There are more assumptions. Most believe that a rapture of the church will occur. However, the words written in Matthew 24:37-51 and Luke 17:26-37 point in a completely different direction. This event is described in both Gospels with similar words, and begins thus:

Lu. 17:26      *And as it was in the days of Noe, so shall it be also **in the days** of the Son of man.*

Mt. 24:37      *But as the days of Noah were, so **shall also** the coming of the Son of man be.*

For many these two verses speak identically.

In principle, they speak in the same manner: However, a difference still exists between them. In the verse from Luke, the Word of God describes in general terms the kind of situation which existed and still exists in Christianity through the entire past until today. Yet, the words from Matthew 24:37

describe the state of Christianity right before the time comes for Christians to depart for Israel and remind us that there will be no difference.

What does Noah's time represent in a spiritual sense?

Noah's time represents the time when the Gospel is preached to the gentiles. Just as Noah preached a warning to his generation that they should live life well, pleasing God, in order to avoid a cataclysm, the same happens in the days which God ordered for the salvation of the gentiles. In the time of Christianity, Christ's priesthood (as Noah) warns everyone about God's intention, simultaneously preparing their own house (God's people) for a cataclysm, i.e. the coming of the Antichrist (spiritual flood).

The term "days of the Son of man" also represents the period of time which is given to the gentiles for their salvation. The reason is that the word "days" encompasses the time of light from the second spiritual day and the period of darkness (third night) from the third spiritual day.

However, the words written in the Gospel according to St. Matthew describe our time and state that there will be no difference. Before the arrival of the Son of man the nature of people and of Christians will not be changed, just as it had not changed in Noah's time.

Mt. 24:38    *For as in the days that were **before** the flood they were eating and drinking, marrying and giving in marriage, until the day that Noe entered into the ark,*

Mt. 24:39    *And knew not until the flood came, and took them all away;* ***so shall also the coming of the Son of man be.***

Noah's preaching was completed at the same time as the ark was finished. The fulfillment of God's judgment which God prophesied for that generation, followed, and the great flood began.

Our case will be the same. When the number of saved gentiles is fulfilled the righteous who are worthy will enter the ark (Israel). A great spiritual flood will come after this (the Antichrist system). From that moment on, the gentiles will not be able to see the Son of man in the clouds, for the clouds will be hidden in the "ark".

We may conclude that the Word of God does not speak about the rapture of the church or taking her into heaven, rather the Word of God speaks that the church will be led into "Noah's ark". This action takes place on earth just as in Noah's time.

Many people believe that verse 38 refers to those people not baptized in the name of Christ. However, this is not so. These words refer to Christians because they developed a negligent relationship toward God's will. This is why the words from verse 39 (*so shall also the coming of the Son of man be*) sound somehow strange. In the first moment, it is not clear to whom these words are directed, i.e. to whom the Son of man will come. In essence, the Son of man is coming to save someone from something. The Son of man always sacrifices Himself for the sake of another.

Until now, we have established that the Son of man comes on the heavenly clouds to save sinful people. However, in verse 39 it is written that the Son of man will come **alone,** without the clouds. If the Son of man does not come to sinful people, to whom will He come? Is it possible for the Son of man to come to the clouds (righteous ones) when He is already in the clouds (righteous ones)?

It is indeed possible. We need to be reminded that the Word of God testifies that the Holy Spirit will announce God's truth to his servants at the appropriate time. This means that the Holy Spirit has a desire to announce God's truth to God's servants in their time of need through the Word of God in the form of the Son of man.

From all the points mentioned, we see that the word of the Holy Spirit wanting to save man will come to us. In the parable of the Ten Virgins it is quoted that the Bridegroom will come alone and will take the ready ones (from the wise virgins) to the feast. The following verses also speak of the separation in which one group of believers in that night will be taken to the body.

| | |
|---|---|
| Mt. 24:40 | *Then shall two be in the field; the one shall be taken, and the other left.* |
| Mt. 24:41 | *Two women shall be grinding at the mill; the one shall be taken, and the other left.* |
| Mt. 24:42 | *Watch therefore: for ye know not what hour your* **Lord** *doth come.* |

These three verses are identical to the parable of the Ten Virgins. The Son of man, the Lord in the Spirit, comes to His own, unto the wise and foolish in Christ's faith. He comes to those who prepare themselves for the coming of the spiritual flood and to those who are concerned only with earthly cares. The latter will not be aware of the call, i.e. of the coming of the Son of man in the form of the Bridegroom who has the desire to save the Jewish people. They will also not go to the wedding (unto salvation of the Jewish people which will be in Israel). Why will they not notice the coming of the Bridegroom? Because if an individual is not concerned with the truth of the Word of God then the Word of God will not have any effect upon that particular individual's heart. Who will see Jesus in that night, when He comes in Spirit through His word to His servants? Only those who have oil enabling them to trim their lamps will see Him. In other words, only those who have faith in the coming of the Bridegroom to the Jewish people will be able to fulfill his faith and come with the Word of God – the Bridegroom – to the wedding feast of the Jewish people.

The several cited examples prove that God does not use the term *to see the Son of man in the clouds,* for the time when the right to enter into new covenant bonds is abolished for the gentiles, rather He uses the term **when the Son of man is REVEALED,** for God is no longer referring to unrepentant people:

Lu. 17:29    *But the same day that Lot went out of Sodom it rained fire and brimstone from heaven, and destroyed them all.*
Lu. 17:30    *Even thus shall it be in the day* **when the Son of man is REVEALED.**

To whom will the Son of man be revealed? Obviously, He will be revealed to those who listen to Him and await Him. The Son of man will be revealed to those who are called when the time approaches, i.e. to those who earlier heard the words "come, everything is ready" through preaching, reading, conversation etc. Those who are found worthy and have found mercy, will urgently obey the voice of the Word, Spirit, Son of man, and Bridegroom and will flee to Israel. This is why the Son of Man sends a message to believers through the words of the Gospel, to be on guard, for He will come to them as a Lord who reckons with His servants.

In order to receive judgment it is necessary to stand before the Son of man.

Lu. 21:34    *And take heed to yourselves, lest at any time your hearts be overcharged with surfeiting, and drunkenness, and cares of this life, and so that day come upon you unawares.*

129

Lu. 21:36     *Watch ye therefore, and pray always, that ye may be accounted worthy to escape all these things that shall come to pass, and* **to STAND before the Son of man.**

In order for man to be considered worthy to stand before the Son, he must fulfill everything quoted throughout this text. Thoughts such as: "I think I am a good enough Christian" or "I am not sure if it is essential to go to Israel, nor am I interested in finding out at this moment, but I know that God is love and will deliver me from trouble when the time comes", are no longer helpful. We must take heed that our hearts are not overcharged with surfeiting and drunkenness. In other words, we should not be overly involved with this world, nor should we live according to the spirit of the flesh. In addition, our walk in life cannot be watered with unfriendliness, selfishness, or pride and our hearts cannot be overcharged with the cares of this world so that we will not be separated from the Lord and His commandments.

When we fulfill the issue discussed above, we must then be on guard, examining the Word of God and praying, to prepare ourselves for our departure to Israel.

Only then will we have the hope of finding mercy before the Lord and be considered worthy to escape all these things that shall come to pass. When man escapes and enters Noah's ark he will stand before the Son of man who is sitting upon the throne of glory, to receive His condemnation or His blessing.

Mt. 25:31     *When the Son of man shall come in his glory, and all the holy angels with him, then shall he sit upon the throne of his glory:*

The words which say that the Son of man will come in His glory speak to us and mean that salvation for the gentiles is complete because the name of Jesus Christ was glorified. Jesus Christ will come to the Jewish nation with this glorified name and with His angels to help them because the time for the transfer of salvation will have come.

What does it mean when we read that the Son of man in Israel will sit on the throne of His glory?

The word of the Gospel represents the Son of man. The throne symbolizes the place from which one governs. The Lord's altar is the place from which the Word of God reigns. The word glory describes someone who has won a battle and who will come in glory only if he is the victor. To *sit* represents that someone consolidated his power. Therefore, *to sit upon the throne of his glory* represents the Word of God which consolidated its power on the Lord's altar in Israel.

Does this mean that up to this moment the Word of God did not sit upon the throne of its glory? Just like that:

Mt. 24:14    *And this Gospel of the kingdom shall be preached in all the world for a witness unto all nations; and then shall the end come.*

Mt. 24:15    *When ye therefore shall see the abomination of desolation, spoken of by Daniel the prophet, stand* **in the holy place,** *(whoso readeth, let him understand:)*

The purest water, i.e. God's doctrine, must come from the altar, the holy place, because it is holy. That which comes from man is not allowed to be preached from the altar. However, this is not so in Christianity today. The Son of man does not sit on the throne of His glory nor does the Law of God reign. There is no denomination which did not add or take away from the holy Word of God. Also, the simplest of God's commandments are not honoured. This is why the Ten Virgins (Matthew 25) fell asleep. They sleep for the spiritual world. Those who sleep do not know what is happening around them. In addition, in the spiritual world those who are spiritually asleep do not know what the Word of God speaks. Therefore, because they do not understand the Word of God, it cannot be fulfilled.

When Christians gather in Israel, the word of the Gospel will again be God to His servants in Christ. The word of the Gospel will then take over the power in God's congregations and will also sit on the throne of his glory. The first thing which will occur within Israel will be the judgment amongst Christians, for there will be some goats among God's people.

Mt. 25:32    *And before him shall be gathered all nations: and he shall separate them one from another, as a shepherd divideth his sheep from the goats:*

# Fifth Turning Point:
## The Beginning of New Salvation for the Jewish Nation Gathered in Israel

The separation of the sheep from the goats is a condition which must be fulfilled in order for the Jewish nation to see the Son of man on the heavenly clouds. This is described in the next verse:

Mt. 24:30   *And THEN shall **appear the SIGN of the Son of man in heaven**: and then shall all the tribes of the earth mourn, and they **shall see the Son of man coming in the clouds of heaven** with power and great glory.*

Until a sign of the Son of man in heaven appears, the Jewish nation will not be able to see the Son of man on the clouds. In addition, until the servants of God, filled with the Holy Spirit from different Christian denominations, understand that they are the body of Christ, and that they must have peace and holiness amongst them, the sign of the Son of man in spiritual heaven will not appear.

What does the sign of the Son of man in heaven represent?

It represents a united, cleansed, whitened son, a new covenant Israel, i.e. Ephraim's son. Only then will the Jewish nation be able to see the crucified Jesus in God's nation and believe in Him. It is written:

Jn. 17:21   *That they all may be one; as thou, Father, art in me, and I in thee, that they also may be one in us: that the world may believe that thou hast sent me.*

Jn. 17:22   *And the glory which thou gavest me I have given them; that they may be one, even as we are one:*

When this happens the way will be opened for all the tribes of the earth to mourn, and they will see the Son of man coming in the clouds of heaven with power and great glory. This will mark the beginning of the Supper of the Wedding Feast of the Lamb.

# PART THREE

# THE MARRIAGE FEAST
# OF THE LAMB

# 11

# THE MARRIAGE FEAST
# OF THE LAMB

There are two parables about the marriage feast in the New Testament. Jesus narrates both. The first one, describing the Dinner of the Wedding Feast, is found in Matthew 22, and the second, dealing with the Marriage Supper of the Lamb, is contained in Luke 14.

Both parables are communicated in similar words. This similarity may confuse the reader at first sight, for it seems that the same event is in question. However, when spiritual time is taken into consideration, it becomes evident that the Supper of the Marriage Feast from Luke 14, which is generally interpreted as a call to repentance for the gentiles, will happen in the future.

However, let us start from the beginning, from the parable or prophecy about the kingdom of heaven told by Jesus in the Gospel according to St. Matthew. The parable begins with the following words:

Mt. 22:2    *The kingdom of heaven is like unto a certain king, which made **a marriage** for his son,*

The king who made a marriage for his son, Jesus Christ, is the Lord God. A wedding in the heavenly kingdom is similar in meaning to the wedding of a man and a woman on this earth. At a wedding ceremony, two individuals make a covenant of faithfulness and love unto death. In a spiritual sense, a repentant person enters into covenant bonds with Jesus Christ, the Bridegroom, and makes a covenant of faithfulness and love unto death.

We all know that God is a spirit. The kingdom that He has given to His Son and our Lord, Jesus Christ, is a spiritual kingdom. Righteousness, peace and joy in the Holy Ghost (Romans 14:17), reign in this spiritual kingdom. To attain righteousness, peace and joy in the Holy Ghost, a sinner is called unto the Wedding of His Son, in other words, he is called to enter into covenant bonds with Jesus Christ.

Ask yourself this question: Why did Jesus come on this earth?

It is easy to answer this question. Jesus came to save sinful humankind. It proceeds then, that the marriage represents the salvation of every single soul as well as all of humankind. The process of salvation began when the Spirit Comforter was sent to earth.

Why is the kingdom of heaven compared to a wedding?

Because light and eternal life reign in it. One can enter the heavenly kingdom only through marriage, for a marriage is part of the kingdom of heaven. Not just anyone can come to the wedding feast. Only those invited are permitted to attend. When someone receives an invitation, it should be accepted. To decline an invitation proffered by God is a grave offence. When a person decides to accept the invitation, he has to prepare himself for the wedding. He needs to buy a wedding garment and dress in it. The gifts which will be presented must be bought. In addition, he should go to the wedding and pass through the door of the wedding. He has to sit at the wedding table, eat, drink and rejoice. In general terms, these steps must be taken in the process of going to the wedding. However, since marriage is a spiritual event, these steps need to be interpreted in a spiritual sense.

When a man receives an invitation to a wedding feast, he must first repent in order to enter the kingdom of God.

Mt. 4:17    *From that time Jesus began to preach, and to say, Repent: for the kingdom of heaven is at hand.*

Without faith and repentance, it is not possible to be dressed in the wedding garment, which is righteousness. Without repentance, it is not possible to bring forth good fruit of repentance toward God. Without everything mentioned, a man cannot bring his heart as a gift to God. However, when a man attains all this, then the time has come to enter the Lamb's Wedding in the kingdom of God through the ordinance of baptism.

Jn. 10:9    *I am the door: by me if any man enter in, he shall be saved, and shall go in and out, and find pasture.*

The door to the Lamb's marriage is our Lord Jesus Christ Himself as word of His Spirit. By going through the ordinance of the Gospel, man is spiritually reborn and is sealed with the Holy Ghost.

Why is it necessary to be reborn?

It is necessary for man to be *reborn* because in his previous life, he was dead to the will of God and to the spiritual world of light. A man spiritually dead cannot please God, cannot live according to God's law. However, through baptism by water man is reborn for the spiritual world. This is why the second half of the verse from John 10:9 reads: *and shall go in and out, and find pasture*. These words mean that through baptism one enters into the spiritual world and into spiritual life. Once spiritually reborn, he will go out into the light of the spiritual day. Thus, when he is out in the light of spiritual day, he will find pasture; actually he will eat, drink and rejoice at God's table in the kingdom of God. In other words, a marriage is the place where a covenant with God is made and performed through the mediator our Lord Jesus Christ.

Marriage, which God prepared for His Son, our Lord Jesus Christ, has two parts: a Dinner and Supper. The call for the Marriage Dinner of the Lamb is described in Matthew 22.

Mt.22:4     *Again, he sent forth other servants, saying, tell them which are bidden, Behold, I have prepared my **dinner**: my oxen and my fatlings are killed, and all things are ready: come unto the marriage.*

The call for the Supper is described in Luke 14, and John's Revelation 19.

Lu. 14:16    *Then said he unto him, A certain man made a **great supper,** and bade many:*

Re. 19:9     *And he saith unto me, Write, Blessed are they which are called unto the **marriage supper** of the Lamb. And he saith unto me, These are the true sayings of God.*

These two parts of the wedding are inseparable and represent a unity described through the symbol of marriage. Everything written in the Books of the New Testament including John's Revelation is related to the events concerning the marriage.

137

The question is, why is it so important to note that only one marriage exists, consisting of two connected parts, rather than two marriages?

Because it designates that there is only one ordinance of baptism carried out in the same manner. Furthermore, it illustrates that there is only one new covenant church, which means that before God there is only one nation redeemed through Jesus Christ, and so on.

Why does marriage consist of two parts? Because Jesus Christ has two folds:

Jn. 10:16      *And other sheep I have, which are not of this fold: them also I must bring, and they shall hear my voice; and there shall be one fold, and one shepherd.*

Each part of the marriage is dedicated to one fold. The Marriage Dinner of the Lamb refers to the salvation of the gentiles and the Marriage Supper of the Lamb to the salvation of the Jews. In the verse quoted above, the Word of God testifies three facts:

First testimony -      That Jesus Christ has sheep in two folds, for it is written: *And other sheep I have, which are not of this fold.*

Second testimony -      That Jesus Christ will go to another fold to find His sheep. The Word of God reads; *them also I must bring.* It is not possible to bring the sheep from another fold if the Lord does not go among the gentiles to seek them out. The testimony that He will find them, that the gentiles will believe in Christ, is found in the words: *they shall hear my voice.* This second testimony has already been fulfilled.

Third testimony -      The two folds will be united, for it is written: *and there shall be one fold, and one shepherd.* The unification of two folds is not possible if Christians, firstly, do not go to Israel and secondly, if the Jewish people do not believe in Christ. Only if these two things come to pass will Jesus Christ become a shepherd to all. This testimony has not yet been fulfilled.

The first two testimonies are found in Mathew 22. The Marriage Dinner of the Lamb or the salvation of the gentiles is described through this parable and its symbols. However, their salvation was announced earlier in the Old Testament.

# THE MARRIAGE DINNER
# OF THE LAMB

In a general sense, Proverbs describes what God prepared so that the salvation of humankind could begin:

Pr. 9:1   *Wisdom hath builded her house, she hath hewn out her seven pillars:*
Pr. 9:2   *She hath killed her beasts; she hath mingled her wine; she hath also furnished her table.*
Pr. 9:3   **She hath sent forth her MAIDENS:** *she crieth upon the highest places of the city,*
Pr. 9:4   *Whoso is simple, let him turn in hither: as for him that wanteth understanding, she saith to him,*
Pr. 9:5   *Come, eat of **my bread,** and drink of the wine which **I** have mingled.*
Pr. 9:6   *Forsake the foolish, and live; and go in the way of understanding.*

This means that the Lord should have:

1.  Built her house (in the heart of people)
2.  Hewn her seven pillars (i.e. strengthened His house through His servants)
3.  Killed her beasts (sacrificed prophets and His servants for the sake of our salvation)
4.  Mingled her wine (Jesus Christ spilt His blood and resurrected)
5.  Furnished her table (ascended into heaven, to sit on the right hand side of the Father's throne, i.e. to become a king and to send the Comforter)
6.  Sent forth her maidens (started calling unto the marriage)

God built Himself a house to reside in when He created a pious heart. If we do what the Lord commands, then we have God within us. If we retreat from His commandments, then we become without God. The process of building people's hearts began through Abraham, actually through the faith of Abraham. The faithful heart, or house in which God resides, is strengthened with seven hewn pillars. Every large building has its own pillars. The quality and size of the pillars determine how solid the building is. The house and its pillars are a unit, an entity. A house which is built on rock cannot be harmed by winds. Jesus is the rock, the perfect rock for a building. Our forefathers, Abraham, Isaac, Jacob, the prophets, and other holy servants of God, are also a part of the hewn pillars on which the building of an Israelite's heart is built. Through the hearts of Abraham, Isaac and Jacob, the father of Israel, the house was filled with beasts, and the beast in the herd was killed, i.e. sacrificed for God's will and for our salvation. Every prophet sent to the Jewish nation for the sake of our salvation was sacrificed (killed).

Then the wine was mingled – Jesus Christ brought the new covenant Word, gave His life for us, spilt His blood, and was resurrected, after which the table was set in the kingdom of God at the Wedding Feast of the Lamb (entering into a covenant). To make entering into the covenant possible, the Lord first sent the Comforter who descended on the apostles and Christ's disciples, after which they began to preach and invite guests to the wedding.

Ac. 2:14    *But Peter, standing up with the eleven, **lifted up his voice**, and said unto them, Ye men of Judaea, and all ye that dwell at Jerusalem, be this known unto you, and **hearken to my words:***

Ac. 2:21    *And it shall come to pass, that whosoever shall call on the name of the Lord **shall be saved.***

Now let us see how all this is described in the Gospel according to St. Matthew.

Jesus came to the Jewish people to invite them to enter into new covenant bonds:

Mt. 15:24    *But he answered and said, **I am not sent** BUT UNTO **the lost sheep of the house of Israel.***

142

These words clearly say that verily Jesus was sent only unto the lost sheep of Israel. Why was He sent only to them and not to some other nation? Why were they so special? Because the Jews were monotheist who believed in a single God and had God's law to govern them, at the time when all other nations where ether polytheist or pagan. However, over time the Jews began drifting away from the law. The law did not have the power to keep them away from sin. This is why Jesus Christ was first sent to them to deliver them from sin. There was no point for Jesus to go to other nations which did not believe in God, nor lived according to God's commandments. God had announced this to the Jewish nation through many prophets, hundreds of years earlier, before Jesus was sent to earth. When the time came, Jesus lifted His voice and called on the Jewish nation to repent and to make a new covenant with God, in order to be delivered from their sinfulness.

Mt. 22:3    *And sent forth his servants **to call them that were bidden** to the wedding: and they would not come.*

This means that in the time of Jesus' preaching, which had lasted for three years up to His crucifixion, Jesus sent His disciples (servants) to call them that were bidden (lost sheep of Israel) to repent and to make a new covenant with God, i.e. to come to the wedding. However, the answer of the Jewish nation to His invitation was: *and they would not come.* They refused to recognize Jesus as the Son of God and to accept Him as their Saviour and redeemer of their souls from eternal death. This is why they killed Him on Golgotha's cross.

Lu. 23:23    *And they were instant with loud voices, requiring that he might be crucified. And the voices of them and of the chief priests **prevailed.***

After this invitation, which the Jews did not accept, God sent a second call:

Mt. 22:4    ***Again,** he sent forth other servants, saying, Tell them which are bidden, Behold, I have prepared my dinner: my oxen and my fatlings are killed, and all things are ready: come unto the **marriage.***

After Christ's crucifixion, our Lord once again sent His servants to the house of Israel. The Word of God refers to these servants as *other servants* for they were now filled with the Holy Ghost. Jesus gave spiritual power to these *other servants*. He poured the Holy Ghost on Christ's disciples who became His apostles. The Jewish people were called a second time, but now by other servants, to come to the Lamb's Wedding.

Ac. 2:38    *Then Peter said unto them, Repent, and be baptized every one of you in the name of Jesus Christ for the remission of sins, and ye shall receive the gift of the Holy Ghost.*

The Word of God directly says what the servants of Christ who received the gift of the Holy Spirit, should speak to the Jewish nation in His name. It is written: *Tell them, which are bidden, Behold, I have prepared **my dinner**: my oxen and my fatlings are killed, and **all** things are ready: come unto the marriage.*

It is written in the Word of God that the apostles, with all of Christ's servants, should preach that dinner is prepared for the Jewish nation. With the words "dinner is ready", God dispels the Jewish nation's doubts. They should not wait for anything else to come from heaven. This is why the sentence ends with the words: *and **all** things are ready: come unto the marriage.*

In other words, God made all the necessary preparations so that the salvation of humankind could begin: dinner was prepared, *the oxen and fatlings are killed.* All things are ready and He invites guests to the wedding. We do the same when we invite guests to our home for dinner. We prepare the food and the place where we will receive guests. It proceeds that the preparation for the feast can be divided into two parts: one that refers to food preparation and the other which entails work on arranging the location where the feast will take place. Both activities happen simultaneously. When we have finished both parts, we can say that everything is ready. God does the same.

Who are His *oxen and fatlings, which are killed?* These are all servants from Adam who were sacrificed for the salvation of humankind. All prophets and God's chosen ones up to John the Baptist were tortured and killed. Even John himself was beheaded in prison and in the end, our Lord, Jesus Christ, died on Golgotha. He as the Word, as the bread of life, spilt His blood for the children of God. Indeed, all food is prepared for God's future children who will be born into the kingdom of God.

The Second part in the preparation for the marriage is described through: *all things are ready*. What has God achieved by sacrificing His servants? God's nation was created. The law was given to man so that he knows what is good and what is evil. Through the sacrifice of His servants, God showed His judgment and the way for men to find mercy in front of Him. Those who listen will be convinced of the incredible mercy God shows to His servants and that God is more powerful than Satan. According to the Word of God this is only a small part of all the things that God has accomplished by sacrificing His servants.

With Jesus Christ's arrival, the final preparations for the dinner had begun. Jesus Christ refused an alliance with Satan when He was tempted in the wilderness. He was thus made worthy to take the Book sealed with the seven seals and break the seals. The seven seals represent the seven crucial events through which the Old Testament was abolished and the New Testament put into power. This enabled the Dinner of the Marriage Feast of the Lamb to begin. Through these seven crucial events, or deeds, which only Jesus could accomplish, a complete new covenant doctrine was established. The word of salvation, peace and the keys of the kingdom were handed over to His servants. The new covenant church was established (as His wife), new covenant wine — His blood — was spilt for our sins, His body - our daily bread - was broken for us that we may start to eat. Death was conquered by Jesus' resurrection (the seventh seal was broken). Satan was bound so that the marriage could begin. The Old Testament church with its ordinances was abolished. The new covenant was sealed and made unchangeable by the spilling of Christ's blood, the veil was rent in half and the way into the Holy of Holies was opened. Thus, the prayers of sinners which were sent in the name of Jesus Christ, were to appear before the throne of God. In the end, the Holy Comforter was poured on the apostles and other disciples. Indeed, all things were ready.

Nothing else will be done for sinful humankind. No additional message will come from heaven, no prophet will be sent from heaven for sinful mortal man; the Gospel of Jesus Christ is the only thing that is left for humankind. Here is what the resurrected Jesus says:

Mt. 28:17    *And when they saw him, they worshipped him: but some doubted.*

| Mt. 28:18 | *And Jesus came and spake unto them, saying, All power is given unto me in heaven and in earth.* |
| Mt. 28:19 | *Go ye therefore, and teach all nations, baptizing them in the name of the Father, and of the Son, and of the Holy Ghost:* |
| Mt. 28:20 | *Teaching them **to observe all** things whatsoever I have commanded you: and, lo, I am with you always, even unto the end of the world. Amen.* |

The resurrected Jesus sends a message to all Christians that their obligation is to teach people who oppose God everything that He commanded and that this will not change unto the end of this world. In addition, Jesus said that He will be with His servants in the Spirit in all days unto the end. Therefore, these words do not permit any preaching which is not based on the foundation of His Gospel.

In order to help His servants perform this task, Jesus Christ left an additional explanation of the Gospel through His parables, the Epistles, and John's Revelation. John's Revelation and the Epistles cannot oppose the Gospel, for they are an integral part of the Gospel. This is why the beginning of John's Revelation starts with the words: *to shew unto his servants things which must shortly come to pass.*

| Re. 1:1 | *The Revelation of Jesus Christ, which God gave unto him, to shew unto his servants things which must shortly come to pass; and he sent and signified it by his angel unto his servant John:* |

The Word which God gave to humankind is unchangeable; therefore, the words which speak of the Marriage Dinner are also unchangeable.

| Mt. 22:4 | *AGAIN, he sent forth other servants, saying, Tell them which are bidden, Behold, I have prepared my **dinner**: my oxen and my fatlings are killed, and ALL things are ready: come unto the marriage.* |

The last words from the previous verse: *come unto the marriage* represent the second call to the Jewish people which they did not heed; instead they made excuses:

| Mt. 22:5 | But they made light of it, and went their ways, one to **his** farm, another to **his** merchandise: |
|---|---|
| Mt. 22:6 | And **the remnant** took his servants, and entreated them spitefully, and slew them. |

There were two groups of Jews who opposed Christ's invitation to repentance and reconciliation with the living God through Jesus Christ.

The first group did not pay heed to the call for it is written that one went to his farm and the other to his merchandise. In a physical sense to go to a farm designates to till the soil because it brings forth food and drink. In a spiritual sense, a farm or land represents the Jewish nation or people's hearts, and to eat and drink from the farm's fruits designates the fulfillment of one's will (in this case one's own will).

To what kind of **his** *farm* and **his** *merchandise* did the old covenant Jewish people go?

Clearly, they went to a spiritual farm and spiritual merchandise. To the old covenant Jewish people, the spiritual farm and spiritual merchandise were the Old Testament Law. The words "to purchase" and "to sell" have a spiritual meaning. Purchasing denotes listening and learning the words of the Old Testament, while selling denotes preaching the doctrine.

Let us now see how apostle Paul describes the refusal of the Jewish nation to enter into new covenant bonds:

| Ac. 28:24 | And some believed the things which were spoken, and some believed not. |
|---|---|
| Ac. 28:25 | And when they agreed not among themselves, they departed, after that Paul had spoken one word, Well spake the Holy Ghost by Esaias the prophet unto our fathers, |
| Ac. 28:26 | Saying, Go unto this people, and say, Hearing ye shall hear, and shall not understand; and seeing ye shall see, and not perceive: |
| Ac. 28:27 | For the heart of this people is waxed gross, and their ears are dull of hearing, and their eyes have they closed; lest they should see with their eyes, and hear with their ears, and understand with their heart, and **should be converted, and I should heal them.** |

However, the other group of Jews decided to fight against the Christian faith. It is written *the remnant took his servants, and entreated them spitefully, and slew them.* It is known that all the apostles were slain except for John, who died from natural causes. Stephen's execution was written about, as was Saul's journey to Damascus to capture Christians, to reprimand, to torture, and to kill them.

Mt. 22:7      *But when the king heard thereof, he was wroth: and he sent forth his armies, and destroyed those murderers, and burned up their city.*

It is written that when Almighty God heard what had happened, He was angry. Judgment was pronounced. The salvation of the Jewish people was revoked and transferred to the gentiles.

Ac. 28:28      ***Be it known*** *therefore unto you, that the salvation of God is sent unto the Gentiles, and that they will hear it.*

The army was sent to destroy the murderers and burn their city. According to historical evidence, the Roman army destroyed Jerusalem and set it on fire. The temple of God was pulled down. A million Jews were killed by sword, famine and pestilence and another million were taken into captivity. Above all, their persecution has lasted to this day. Indeed, a terrible judgment was pronounced and executed fully.

Mt. 22:8      *Then saith he to his servants, The wedding is ready, but they which were bidden were not worthy.*
Mt. 22:9      *Go ye therefore into the highways, and* **as many as** *ye shall find, bid to the marriage.*

Indeed, the Jewish people were not worthy. Christ's servants went into gentile countries and everyone both good and bad, at the crossroads of their lives, was bidden to come to the Marriage Dinner of the Lamb. Today we are standing witness to the grace and glory of God's love, for many have accepted His invitation, repented, brought forth fruits of repentance, been baptized in the name of the Father, the Son and the Holy Spirit, received the gift of the Holy Ghost and sat at the table at the Marriage Dinner of the Lamb, drinking and celebrating. The dinner is, however, coming to its end. The entering of gentiles into covenant bonds is ending because the following is now approaching:

| Ro. 11:25 | *For I would not, brethren, that ye should be ignorant of this mystery, lest ye should be wise in your own conceits; that blindness in part is happened to Israel, **until** the fulness of the Gentiles be come in.* |
| Ro.11:27 | *For this is **my covenant** unto them, when I shall take away their sins.* |

When the Marriage Dinner is over – when the number of gentiles is complete – the Lord will call the Jewish people to the Marriage Supper of the Lamb, in other words, to enter the new covenant bonds. The Jewish people will be grafted to the good olive tree to which the gentiles have already been grafted.

| Ro.11:23 | *And they also, **if they abide not still in unbelief, shall be grafted in**: for God is able to graft them in again.* |

Being the new covenant people, we believe that the gentiles' right to enter into new covenant bonds will be revoked when the necessary number of saved gentiles is attained. We cannot deny the existence of the Marriage Dinner of the Lamb at which the gentiles have been feasting for nineteen hundred years, and likewise of the Marriage Supper of the Lamb because it is written so. Nevertheless, it seems that it has not been revealed who is being referred to by these words.

Apostle Paul, who was sent among the gentiles, said; *"For I would not, brethren, that ye should be ignorant of this mystery"*. The question is: do we feel that we were told a great mystery? Let us ask ourselves, how do we value these words in our heart? Why would the apostle reveal this great mystery by the will of God if it were not important for us to know it? Have we noticed that in Romans 11, apostle Paul turns the attention of the children of God to the fact that a sentence will be pronounced, so that the Jewish people can be grafted to the good olive tree?

Perhaps some would ask why it is necessary to be judged before salvation has been transferred. Can they be grafted to the good olive tree, to which we are grafted, without judgment being pronounced on us? Obviously, they cannot, for when this is done, the Jews will become members of different Christian denominations. Let us be frank: if it were possible for the Jewish people to believe in Christ, among gentiles, which Christian denomination or whose teaching would we recommend? For Jesus Christ clearly says:

Mt. 25:5          *While the Bridegroom tarried, they all slumbered and slept.*

This relates to the virgins — denominations, congregations, individuals — which prepare those who desire to make a covenant with the Bridegroom. Among those slumbering — sinning — and sleeping — who are not aware they are living in sin — virgins, which teaching would you recommend to the Jewish people so that they could be grafted successfully to the good olive tree and stay on it? Maybe we would point our finger at this or that denomination, but then it would not be necessary to establish the Marriage Supper of the Lamb. Could God, in this case, call them to the Marriage Dinner of the Lamb a second time?

They cannot be called to the Dinner a second time, for this is against God's law and God's will. If this were possible, the Jewish nation would have, for the past two thousand years of their exile, believed in the Messiah here among the gentiles, and been baptized because the Word of God spread throughout the whole world. In addition, every Christian country has Jews. Recently, a few major wars have taken place so that the Jewish people could return to their land and believe:

World War I —        The Ottoman Empire had to withdraw from Palestine, after which it came under the patronage of Britain. By the terms of the Balfour Declaration, Jews were given the right to buy land in Palestine, but they moved there only in small numbers.

World War II —       The Jewish people paid for Israel, their country, with the lives of six million Jews.

After WW II —        There were five wars fought with Arab countries so that Israel could come into possession of lands belonging to it.

Is there no other way for the Jewish people to return to their land and believe in Christ?

No, there is no other way, for every jot from the Word of God has to be fulfilled.

150

| De. 30:15 | ***See, I have set before thee this day life and good, and death and evil;*** |
|---|---|
| De. 30:16 | *In that **I command thee** this day to love the LORD thy God, to walk in his ways, and to keep his commandments and his statutes and his judgments, that thou mayest live and multiply: and the LORD thy God shall bless thee in the land whither thou goest to possess it.* |
| De. 30:17 | *But **if thine heart turn away**, so that thou wilt not hear, but shalt be drawn away, and worship other gods, and serve them;* |
| De. 30:19 | ***I call heaven and earth to record this day** against you, that I have set before you life and death, blessing and cursing: therefore choose life, that both thou and thy seed may live:* |
| De. 30:1 | *And it shall come to pass, **when all these things are come upon thee**,* |
| De. 30:2 | ***And shalt return** unto the LORD thy God, and shalt obey his voice according to all that I command thee this day, thou and thy children, with all thine heart, and with all thy soul;* |
| De. 30:3 | *That **then** the LORD thy God **will turn** thy captivity, and have compassion upon thee, and **will return and gather thee** from all the nations, whither the LORD thy God hath scattered thee.* |
| De. 30:4 | ***If** any of thine be driven out unto the outmost parts of heaven, from thence will the LORD thy God gather thee, and from thence will he fetch thee:* |
| De. 30:5 | *And the LORD thy God **will bring thee into the land** which thy fathers possessed, and thou shalt possess it; and he will do thee good, and multiply thee above thy fathers.* |
| De. 30:6 | *And the LORD thy God **will circumcise thine heart, and the heart** of thy seed, to love the LORD thy God with all thine heart, and with all thy soul, that thou mayest live.* |

This is the covenant which Almighty God gave to the sons of Israel through His servant Moses, and from which we can see the future sequence of events. The Jewish people have to be brought back to their land, which was promised to their forefathers Abraham, Isaac and Jacob. Their hearts will then be circumcised, i.e. turned to Him. It is not possible to change the will of God. Therefore, there is no other way but for the Lord God to bring them to their land. The judgment of Christians must then be carried out; the children of God have to be taken to Israel because salvation has to be removed from the gentiles. The Jewish people must be grafted to the good olive tree. Before this takes place, however, the Antichrist has to come and the door to the Marriage Supper of the Lamb must be closed. This is the part of the law according to which events must occur. All prophesies of our Lord, Jesus Christ, have to be fulfilled. Can anyone doubt the fulfillment of the prophesies of the Talents, the Ten Virgins, the Unjust Judge, the Eagles, the Two in One Bed, the Borrowing of Three Loaves of Bread, not to mention John's Revelation?

# THE MARRIAGE SUPPER
# OF THE LAMB

The following is written in John's Revelation:

Re. 19:7    *Let us be glad and rejoice, and give honour to him: for the marriage of the Lamb is come, and his wife hath made herself ready.*

Re. 19:8    *And to her was granted that she should be arrayed in fine linen, clean and white: for the fine linen is the righteousness of saints.*

Re. 19:9    *And he saith unto me, Write,* **Blessed are they which are called unto the marriage supper of the Lamb.** *And he saith unto me, These are the true sayings of God.*

Verily, before us are the unbelievable words of God, for which God alone testifies are true. When we read these words today, many of us have difficulty believing them because present Christianity believes differently. Their faith is based on rapture before tribulation and an earthly kingdom of the millennium. The invitation to the Marriage Supper of the Lamb simply does not fit in with this belief. Our disbelief made our Lord testify that these words are truthful and that the Lamb's wife will be invited to the Marriage Supper of the Lamb. In addition, the belief that God's faithful people represent the Lamb's wife does not fit into present-day Christianity. There are several reasons for this.

The first reason stems from the belief that the Marriage Supper and, therefore, the Marriage itself, take place in heaven. Even before the Marriage Supper the Word of God addresses God's people as a wife. Obviously, the belief that the Marriage Supper takes place in heaven is wrong, especially if we understand that marriage represents an individual's salvation; in heaven there is no correction of one's life path, no baptism, and no salvation.

The second reason results from the belief that the church is the bride. According to this belief, marriage must take place in heaven. However, it is written in the letter to the Corinthians that the Lord is the head and the new covenant church is His body. Only a husband and wife can be one body, not a bride and Bridegroom. This means that friends of God, or the penitents who prepare themselves to be baptized – to make a covenant of mercy – represent the bride.

The third reason derives from the belief of many that we do not have any connection with the Jewish people. Those who believe this cannot see how the salvation of the Jewish people depends on Christians – wife of the Lamb – or what God's reason is for leading us into Israel. Quite simply, they do not see the purpose of a departure for Israel, nor of believing in the words of God: *blessed are they, which are called unto the marriage supper of the Lamb.*

In the Gospel according to St. Luke, we have a description of the Marriage Supper of the Lamb from a different perspective.

| | |
|---|---|
| Lu. 14:1 | *And it came to pass, as he went into the house of one of the chief Pharisees to eat bread on the sabbath day, that they watched him.* |
| Lu. 14:2 | *And, behold, there was a certain man before him which had the dropsy.* |
| Lu. 14:3 | *And Jesus answering spake unto the lawyers and Pharisees, saying, Is it lawful to heal on the sabbath day?* |
| Lu. 14:4 | *And they held their peace. And he took him, and healed him, and let him go;* |

The chief of the Pharisees calls Jesus to eat bread in his house. However, lawmakers and Pharisees who kept an eye on Jesus were also gathered in his house. Knowing why they were gathered and had brought a man with a serious illness before Him, Jesus posed the question: *is it lawful to heal on the Sabbath day?*

The lawmakers and Pharisees did not answer this question. Jesus then healed the man despite the fact that it was the Sabbath day.

What spiritual message did Jesus send us through this event?

We know that the Old Testament is a shadow of things to come through the New Testament. This is why the Old Testament, or Jewish Sabbath – if we can put it this way — has a spiritual meaning. God gave the Jewish nation a law by which they were obligated to celebrate the Sabbath eternally. The intention of this law for the Sabbath day was to make a man do God's will rather than his own.

Is. 58:13    *If thou turn away thy foot from the sabbath, from doing thy pleasure on my holy day; and call the sabbath a delight, the holy of the LORD, honourable; and shalt honour him, not doing thine own ways, nor finding thine own pleasure, nor speaking thine own words:*

Is. 58:14    *Then shalt thou delight thyself in the LORD; and I will cause thee to ride upon the high places of the earth, and feed thee with the heritage of Jacob thy father: for the mouth of the LORD hath spoken it.*

The door of the eternal Sabbath is here on earth. This means that the old covenant Sabbath, which lasted twenty four earthly hours, is a shadow of the New Testament eternal Sabbath, which begins from the moment a person is baptized or from the moment of one's entering into peace with God through our mediator Jesus Christ. Such a person stays in this eternal Sabbath as long as he keeps peace, which he gained, or as long as he fulfills God's will rather than his own.

The Jewish nation should have been at peace with God through the fulfillment of the Sabbath law. On such a Sabbath day, Jesus came into "the house" of one of the chief Pharisees to eat bread.

In a spiritual sense, to eat denotes the fulfillment of God's will, while the Pharisee's house denotes a spiritual house. A house is a place where we eat, or a place where righteous man fulfills God's will. Israel of that time was the place where righteous people fulfilled God's will, i.e. ate.

It so happened that at the place of the fulfillment of God's will, at the place of eating, a man with a serious illness suddenly stood before Jesus. Evidently, this sick man was of Jewish origin. In a spiritual sense, he represents the sinful Jewish nation, or the lost sheep of Israel. Jesus knew that the lawmakers and the Pharisees, who should have understood the law of God and taught people the law, in essence did not understand it. Jesus' testimony of this is in the fact that they did not help the sick man on the Sabbath. This is why Jesus asked: *is it lawful to heal on the Sabbath day?*

This means that only the righteous can be in the earthly Sabbath because it is a shadow of the eternal Sabbath to come. Therefore, Jesus asks whether a righteous man who lives in that "spiritual Sabbath" is allowed to heal the sick. Those who understand the will of God should know that it is exactly what God commands the righteous people to do, to dedicate their lives to healing sinful humankind. The healing of sinful ones is food for the righteous who live in the Lord's Saturday.

This is why righteous Jesus came to earth, to heal the sinful. He is in the eternal Saturday. There is no Monday, Thursday, Saturday, or Sunday for Jesus and for all righteous men, days when it is forbidden to preach, heal, baptize or deliver sinful men from the deep pit of sin.

This is why Jesus asked them:

Lu. 14:5    ...*Which of you shall have an ass or an ox fallen into a pit, and will not straightway pull him out on the sabbath day?*

Without the intention to offend anyone, the spiritual meaning of a donkey and an ox must be explained in order to understand the spiritual meaning of Jesus' question. In a spiritual sense, a donkey represents people, in this case the Jewish nation, and an ox symbolizes a priest or priesthood. In fact, Jesus asked them: if you are righteous, if you are in the Sabbath, in peace with God, which of you would not help a brother or priest if you had been a witness to his surrender to sin or to his mistaken understanding of the Sabbath, a time when righteous man will execute justice?

From the Word of God we can see that the earthly Sabbath has a spiritual meaning for Jesus. This is why it seemed to the Jews that Jesus did not respect their Sabbath. They did not comprehend the meaning of the earthly Saturday, which was given to them for a celebration. By healing a sick man on the Sabbath and by using the example of a donkey and an ox falling into a pit, Jesus tried to point out the spiritual meaning of the earthly Sabbath, which is a shadow of the eternal Sabbath.

In the verses that follow, Jesus begins to explain to the Jewish priesthood and to all people the meaning of the eternal Sabbath, or the New Testament Sabbath, through the arrival of the Marriage Dinner and Supper at which sick people are healed in the New Testament time:

| Lu. 14:7 | *And he put forth a parable **to those which were bidden,** when he marked how they chose out the chief rooms; saying unto them.* |
|---|---|
| Lu. 14:8 | *When thou art bidden of any man to a wedding, sit not down in the highest room; lest a more honourable man than thou be bidden of him;* |
| Lu. 14:9 | *And he that bade thee and him come and say to thee, Give this man place; and thou begin with shame to take the lowest room.* |

Since marriage represents the deliverance from sin, the one extending invitations to the wedding can only be the Lord God. Only He has the power to deliver us from sin, to invite guests to the Marriage of His Son. In addition, God determines the position that one will take in His kingdom. Therefore, through this example God warns the entire Jewish nation and its priesthood – all the "guests" in the Pharisee's house – not to expect to be priests of Jesus Christ – to sit down in the highest room – when He invites them into new covenant bonds. It is up to God to decide who will sit in the highest room, who will be His apostle, His priest, and His servant.

With these words, Jesus shows what will happen in the time of the New Testament Sabbath. He then addressed the Jewish priesthood directly, telling them which group of people they should concentrate their preaching in the New Testament time on.

| Lu. 14:12 | *Then said he also **to him that bade him**, When thou MAKEST **a dinner** or **a supper**, call not thy friends, nor thy brethren, neither thy kinsmen, nor thy rich neighbours; lest they also bid thee again, and a recompence be made thee.* |
|---|---|

The message to the Jewish priesthood is that they should not invite *"their friends, nor their brethren, neither their kinsmen, nor their rich neighbours; lest they also bid thee again, and a recompense be made thee"* to a dinner or supper.

"Thy" friends, brethren, kinsmen, and rich neighbours are all those who know the will of God, who believe in Jesus and are connected with the priesthood which invites guests to dinner and supper. Therefore, a friend is the one who knows the will of his Lord, a brother is a brother in faith who also knows the will of God, and kinsmen are those who have a blood kinship – here a spiritual kinship – and who know the will of God. A rich neighbour is one who spiritually lives beside you and is familiar with everything because he is your neighbour. There is no need to invite those who believe in Jesus to the Dinner or Supper, for they know of it and have already fulfilled the will of God.

| | |
|---|---|
| Lu. 14:13 | *But when thou makest a feast, call the poor, the maimed, the lame, the blind:* |
| Lu. 14:14 | *And thou shalt be blessed; for they cannot recompense thee: for thou shalt be recompensed at the resurrection of the just.* |

Is should be noted that "feast" is a term which means either dinner or supper. Thus the given commandment is valid for both. Jesus says that it is necessary to call the poor, the maimed, the lame, and the blind from the Jewish nation, or all those who do not recognize Jesus as the Saviour of their souls, the Messiah of Israel, to this first feast which is being prepared — Marriage Dinner of the Lamb — and will begin with the arrival of the Holy Comforter.

In the time of preparation of the feast for the Marriage Supper of the Lamb, which is at hand, Christ's priesthood has to once again call the poor, the maimed, the lame, and the blind; all those Christians who do not believe in the departure to the Marriage Supper of the Lamb. However, once they believe, they cannot return to those who have declared God's truth, because they already believe. It does not matter which group of servants declares God's truth, those who announced Dinner or those who today are announcing the arrival of the Marriage Supper of the Lamb.

This is why it is written that wages will return to those who call the poor, the maimed, the lame, and the blind at the time of the resurrection of the righteous, in the time of the Holy Comforter's reign.

| | |
|---|---|
| Lu. 14:15 | *And when one of them that sat at meat with him heard these things, he said unto him, Blessed is he that **shall eat bread in the kingdom of God**.* |

We should note that, in a spiritual sense, when someone is sitting, it represents a person who is firm in his belief, or intention. Thus, when a Jew who follows the Mosaic Law, is sitting at the meat in the Pharisee's house, he is expressing his resolve to fulfill God's will according to the Mosaic Law, and working zealously toward this.

158

All those who sat at meat in the Pharisee's house listened to the new covenant teaching of Jesus. Among these were some who understood Jesus' words, for they said: *Blessed is he that shall eat bread in the kingdom of God.*

What does it mean to eat bread in the kingdom of God?

In order to answer this question it is necessary to know what the kingdom of God represents, where it is, when it will come and whether there is a difference between the terms "to eat bread in the kingdom of God" versus "to eat bread in the Pharisee's house"?

The kingdom of God begins only through the coming of the Comforter, namely, the reign of the Comforter creates the kingdom of God. This is the reason why there is a difference between eating bread in the Pharisee's house according to the Mosaic Law – deeds according the law – and eating bread in the house of the Holy Spirit, according to Christ's Law: "*love thy God with all thy soul and thy neighbour as thyself*".

When some among those present realized the essence of Jesus' coming to this earth and His doctrine about the Marriage Dinner and Supper, they said: *Blessed is he that shall eat bread in the kingdom of God*, in other words, blessed is he who spares no effort for God's namesake. After this, Jesus began to prophesy the things that will happen at the Great Supper. It proceeds that this prophecy is directed at those eating bread in the kingdom of God presently and in the future. In other words, those who have already made a covenant of mercy with God through our mediator, our Lord Jesus Christ.

## The Call for Supper

Presently the Dinner is coming to an end, more than nineteen hundred years since it began, and the invitation from God to the Great Supper of the Lamb's Marriage is before us.

Lu. 14:16      *Then said he unto him, A certain man* **made a great Supper***, and bade many:*

Considering this 16th verse it can be concluded that firstly, God has finished all preparations so that the Supper can begin for it is written: *made a great supper;* secondly, during the period of preparation it was announced that Supper will soon start and guests were invited; thirdly, many guests were invited. This means that the call to the Great Supper is not hidden from Christianity.

We should note that preparations for the Marriage Supper of the Lamb are now almost complete. However, presently the call has not yet been forwarded. The invitations to both Dinner and Supper are quoted below for the sake of an easier understanding of the similarities and the differences between them:

The call for Dinner:

Mt. 22:4    *Again, he sent forth other servants, saying, Tell them which are bidden, Behold, I have prepared my DINNER: my oxen and my fatlings are killed, and* **ALL things are ready: come** *unto the marriage.*

The call for Supper:

Lu. 14:17    *And sent his servant* **at SUPPER time** *to say to them that were bidden,* **Come;** *for* **ALL things are now ready.**

We may note that the manner of the invitation for Supper is the same as for the Marriage Dinner.

Firstly, everything has to be ready. The servant is then sent to tell the guests that preparations are complete and those invited should come. What makes them different is the fact that in order for the Marriage Dinner to start a description of the final preparations is given while a description is not provided for the Marriage Supper. It is contained in other prophecies of Jesus Christ.

The next important difference is in the number of servants sent to call the guests. One servant is sent to call the guests to Supper while many servants were sent to invite guests to Dinner.

In order for the servant sent to invite guests to the wedding, or for the words from Luke 14:17 to be fulfilled, all preparations for the Marriage Supper of the Lamb have to be finished. The preparations that God made and is still making presently for the Wedding Supper of the Lamb have to be divided into two parts: those relating to the Jewish nation and those relating to Christians.

## Preparations to Be Accomplished
## Relating to the Jewish Nation so That the Words *All Things Are Now Ready* Can Be Pronounced

Knowing when the words *all things are now ready* will be heard we must be clear about the purpose of the Supper, what it represents, for whom it is made and where it will take place. We also need to know who the guests are, what kind of food will be prepared for the Supper etc. Only then will we understand after which event the words: *verily, all things are now ready* will be heard. It is not possible to answer these questions without finding places in the Bible from which it is evident what will happen to the Jewish nation in the future.

God will return the Jewish people into their land in response to the words of their prayer:

Ps. 106:47    *Save us, O LORD our God, and gather us from among the heathen, to give thanks unto thy holy name, and to triumph in thy praise.*

The afflictions and the prayers of the Jewish nation were the reason God said the following:

Ps. 106:44    *Nevertheless he regarded their affliction, when he heard their cry:*

Ps. 106:45    *And* **he remembered for them his covenant,** *and repented according to the multitude of his mercies.*

Ps. 106:46    *He made them also to be pitied of all those that carried them captives.*

Eze. 36:21    *But I had pity for mine holy name, which the house of Israel had profaned among the heathen, whither they went.*

Eze. 36:22    *Therefore say unto the house of Israel, thus saith the Lord GOD; I do not this for your sakes, O house of Israel, but for mine holy name's sake, which ye have profaned among the heathen, whither ye went.*

Eze. 36:23    *And I will sanctify my great name, which was profaned among the heathen, which ye have profaned in the midst of them; and the heathen shall know that I am the LORD, saith the Lord GOD, when I shall be sanctified in you before their eyes.*

Eze. 36:24    *For I will take you from among the heathen, and gather you out of all countries, and will bring you into your own land.*

*God remembered for them his covenant when he heard their cry* and their prayer. They received mercy not for their righteousness but for His *holy name's sake.* In other words, Supper of the Marriage Feast of the Lamb is being prepared because it is God's will that they be saved through it.

Before the sound of *"all things are now ready"* is heard, the following has to occur:

Eze. 37:7      *So I prophesied as I was commanded: and as I prophesied, there was **a noise,** and behold **a shaking,** and the bones **came together,** bone to his bone.*

Eze. 37:8      *And when I beheld, lo, the sinews and the flesh **came up** upon them, and **the skin covered them above**: but there was no breath in them.*

From the events listed below, only the first one is contained in Ezekiel 37:4. All the others are from the seventh and eighth verses. These seven steps represent the chronological order of events, so that the words *all things are now ready* can be heard. They also create a picture of what is presently unfolding right before our eyes.

1) As I prophesied
2) There was a noise
3) Behold a shaking
4) The bones came together to his bone
5) The sinews and the flesh came up upon them
6) The skin covered them above
7) But there was no breath in them (in the body)

**1) As I prophesied (tell them).** The first step represents the beginning of preparations for the Marriage Supper of the Lamb, which took place when God began to organize the Jewish nation – to unite their hearts – so that the Jewish state could be established. In this way, the location where the Supper will take place has been created. This happened at the Zionist Congress held in Basel in 1897, when a decision was made to start working on the formation of a Jewish state and, subsequently, on the return of Jews dispersed throughout the world to Palestine.

**2) There was a noise (voice).** Palestine was under the rule of the Muslim Ottoman Empire which did not permit the immigration of Jews into Palestine. However, after the First World War Palestine came under the administration of Christian Great Brittan, which brought forth the Balfour Declaration in 1917, according to which Jews were given the right to emigrate to Palestine where they were allowed to buy land. This started the voice that Jews began creating their state and emigrating into it.

Normally, we would expect to find words on immigration and the purchase of land in Palestine of that time by the Jewish nation further in the process of preparations for the Marriage Supper of the Lamb. We instead find the strange words *behold a shaking*.

**3) Behold a shaking.** The meaning of these words corresponds with the words from Psalm 106:46. *He made them also to be pitied of all those that carried them captive.*

Shaking refers to the events surrounding the Second World War, which began in 1938. It caused the genocide of the Jews by which all hearts of the Jewish people became upset and people began to pity them. Surely, many asked themselves the question: Why did God allow such an unimaginable cataclysm to come upon the whole world, especially upon Christians and Jews?

We should look for the cause in the following facts: due to their own interests Christian Europe and America were not ready to give to the Jewish people their own state. They interfered politically. On the other hand, the Jewish nation was not ready to hear the voice upon receiving the Balfour Declaration, nor were they ready to enter into Palestine. They were buying land cheaply from the Palestinian and Arab population, but they were not ready to leave for Palestine because life there was very hard. The life they led in Europe and America was more to their liking. This was a big insult toward God.

Therefore, God sent His first warning. A great economic depression came upon the world. Poverty spread over "Egypt". The message to the Jewish nation was clear; enter into Palestine. However, they did not hear it. Thus the cataclysm came.

Observe how God, through the symbol of shaking, clearly describes the shakeup of the human heart. The heart symbolizes the earth, if we recall Jesus' parable about the sower who sows good seed.

**4) The bones came together bone to bone.** After the Second World War and the huge destruction of the Jewish people, the Jews tried to enter Palestine. This process lasted from 1945 to 1948. The skeleton was formed when every bone came to his bone.

Only when the hearts of the Jewish people understood that God would protect them from the enemy only in their own state, did God allow the creation of the state of Israel on May 18, 1948. The proclamation of the state of Israel represents the creation of the skeleton from dry bones. Dry bones symbolize the house of Israel. They are dry because they do not possess the Holy Spirit who is Jesus Christ.

**5) The sinews and the flesh came upon them.** The official gathering of the Jewish nation into their country started in 1948. Christians have been able to follow this process unfolding, by the will of God, for the past 59 years.

**6) The skin covers them above.** The skin is the border of a body. To put the skin over the body represents recognition by the neighbouring countries of Israel's right to exist as a state in the Middle East. In addition, to put the skin on means the drawing of an international border between Israel and its neighbouring states. For many years, its neighbours did not recognize the state of Israel. This means a border was not drawn. The first state to do this was Egypt in 1978. Jordan followed by officially drawing a border in 1994. Syria, Lebanon and Palestine however still have not done so.

**7) But there was no breath in them.** Through these words, God explains that the Jewish nation gathered in Israel should be observed as a body. When we understand that God describes Israel through the word *body* only then will we be able to raise such questions as: When was this body conceived? When is it going to be delivered? Is this body a son or a daughter? When will it be revived for the spiritual world? Who is the mother of this body? Are there other records in the Bible concerning the body which does not possess the spirit of Christ?

After the body was dressed in skin, the prophet saw the body without its spirit – the Spirit of Christ. Recognition by its neighbours in the Middle East of Israel's right to exist and the drawing of borders, made it possible for the prophet to see the body. Only when the prophet sees it, will we be able to see it as well.

It should be noted that the body, which the prophet saw has not yet been delivered. Once the skin covers the body it will be ready for deliverance. From this moment on, the fulfillment of the next event referring to the Jewish nation will begin:

1 Th. 5:3     *For when they shall say, Peace and safety; then sudden destruction cometh upon them, as travail upon a woman with child; and they shall not escape.*

Namely, once the covering of the body by skin proceeds, peace will be announced. Israel, Palestine and other hostile neighbouring countries will sign an agreement. It should be mentioned that this will happen at spiritual midnight of the third spiritual day, described in the parable of the Ten Virgins (Matthew 25). The preparations for the Marriage Supper of the Lamb will end once the skin covers the body. Then the message – *all things are now ready* – will be heard.

## Preparations to Be Accomplished Relating to Christians so That the Words *All Things Are Now Ready* Can Be Pronounced

In order to understand what has to occur in Christianity so that the words *all things are now ready* are spoken, we must read the words of Jesus:

Mt. 13:24     *Another parable put he forth unto them, saying, The kingdom of heaven is likened unto a man which sowed good seed in **his** field:*

Mt. 13:25     *But while men slept, his enemy came and sowed tares among the wheat, and went his way.*

Mt. 13:26     *But when the blade was sprung up, and brought forth fruit, then appeared the tares also.*

Mt. 13:27     *So the servants of the householder came and said unto him, Sir, didst not thou sow good seed in thy field? from whence then hath it tares?*

Mt. 13:28     *He said unto them, An enemy hath done this. The servants said unto him, Wilt thou then that we go and gather them up?*

Mt. 13:29     *But he said, Nay; lest while ye gather up the tares, ye root up also the wheat with them.*

165

Mt. 13:30      *Let both grow together until the harvest: and in the time of harvest I will say to the reapers,* **Gather ye together** *first the tares, and* **bind them** *in bundles to burn them: but gather the wheat into my barn.*

This parable or prophecy of our Lord Jesus Christ describes the events which will occur on this earth before the harvest time and the harvest. The Word of God asserts that some who did not repent fully, or the wholly unrepentant, entered into new covenant bonds. Furthermore, we read that such a state should be left until the time of the harvest when our Lord will separate the tares from the wheat through His reapers.

The key question is when does harvest time commence? When harvesting begins, the tares are first gathered. In the second phase of harvesting the binding of the tares into bundles is performed. In the third phase, wheat is carried into the barn. Lastly, the tares will be cast into the furnace of fire in phase four and *wheat shall shine forth as the sun in the kingdom of their Father.*

All of these phases refer to Christians in gentiles. This is to say that the parable from Matthew 13 deals with events that will take place at the end of the Marriage Dinner, in the End Times that began from the moment God started to build the Jewish nation. We should note that the End Times begin simultaneously both for the Jewish nation and for Christians.

The essence of the End Times coming for Christians is the revoking of salvation and the pronouncement of judgment upon them. For the Jewish people, the arrival of the End Times has a different meaning. Their time of captivity among the gentiles will end and the events of the End Times will bring them the right to once again enter into new covenant bonds and receive the gift of eternal life.

The rise of the Jewish nation began at the First Zionist Congress, held in 1897, when a decision was made to start working on the creation of the state of Israel. Likewise, the gathering of the tares also has its origin about that time.

What is the meaning of gathering?

To gather represents clustering around a nucleus. Let us now see who the Word of God says the tares are, who will gather them and who will bind them into bundles:

| Mt. 13:36 | *Then Jesus sent the multitude away, and went into the house: and his disciples came unto him, saying, Declare unto us the parable of the tares of the field.* |
| Mt. 13:37 | *He answered and said unto them, He that soweth the good seed is the Son of man;* |
| Mt. 13:38 | *The field is the world; the good seed are the children of the kingdom; but the tares are the children of the wicked one;* |
| Mt. 13:39 | *The enemy that sowed them is the devil;* **the harvest is the end of the world;** *and the reapers are the angels.* |
| Mt. 13:40 | *As therefore the tares are gathered and burned in the fire;* **so shall it be** *in the end of this world.* |
| Mt. 13:41 | *The Son of man shall send forth his angels, and* **they shall gather** *out of his kingdom all things that offend, and them which do iniquity;* |
| Mt. 13:42 | *And shall cast them into a furnace of fire: there shall be wailing and gnashing of teeth.* |
| Mt. 13:43 | *Then shall the righteous* **shine forth as the sun** *in the kingdom of their Father.* **Who hath ears to hear, let him hear.** |

The Lord Jesus Christ says that the tares are all Christians who bring offence to His kingdom and do iniquity. He says that harvesting will be performed by His angels for it is written in the 39th verse: *the reapers are the angels.* The angels are His priests who reap and preach the Word.

We need to understand that the purpose of gathering and binding the tares into bundles is to separate those who are an offence to Christianity and do iniquity from those who live in righteousness before God.

The question is: are reapers – angels – who gather and bind the tares the same as those that carry wheat into the barn?

The answer is that there are two kinds of reapers, or angels. The Word of God asserts this in the 38th, 39th and 40th verses.

A reaper is a servant of God, whether he is good or bad. A good reaper is responsible for wheat while an evil reaper is responsible for tares.

Perhaps there will be some who will not agree that Jesus Christ has two kinds of reapers. However, it is necessary to understand that all activities in the kingdom of God are carried out only through the Word. This means that only by words are tares gathered and bound in bundles in order to be burned in the furnace of fire. Wheat is also gathered into the barn by the Word. There is no other way. Consequently, a servant of

God cannot simultaneously be a fountain of the Holy Spirit and a false spirit. Evil reapers gather tares and bind them in bundles with false spirits, or unclean preaching, while good reapers carry wheat into the barn with proper explanations of the Word of God.

Presently, through materialism, liberalism and ecumenism evil reapers gather and bind tares into bundles. These spirits reign in Christianity because evil angels must fulfill their task. Therefore, false spirits are preached in our time. Bibles containing new concepts greatly propagate false preaching. Just as a bundle of tares is bound with a rope consisting of many braided threads, so are tares, in a spiritual sense, bound with many unclean spirits.

Why?

Because when the time comes for good angels – the reapers – to preach the Word so that wheat can be brought into the barn, the tares will not be able to receive the Word for they will be bound with many false spirits – different beliefs. Christians who do not have true faith, or the knowledge of the mysteries of the kingdom of God, will not be able to do anything.

The following question arises: why is it necessary to separate the tares from the wheat? Could God not do the opposite, and put the wheat into the barn first? If God were to act in this way, there would be no need to gather and bind the tares. However, this is not possible, for it opposes God's law. Eventually, if the tares were not bound with other beliefs, and while the wheat is carried into the barn, the tares could say we are wheat as well and want to go to the Marriage Supper of the Lamb, because the barn is the place of the Lamb's Wedding.

According to the law of God every trespass will be punished, every deed will receive wages on earth and even more so in heaven. Those who are baptized in the name of Christ have submitted to the law of Christ because they made a covenant of faithfulness with God:

Ec. 5:4     *When thou vowest a vow unto God, defer not to pay it; for he hath no pleasure in fools:* **pay that which thou hast vowed.**

However, if they do not fulfill their covenant and they do not listen to the spoken Word of God, they are fools and *the sword will devour everyone* who is counted in His nation.

Is. 1:19    *If ye be willing and obedient, ye shall eat the good of the land:*

Is. 1:20    *But if ye refuse and rebel, ye shall be devoured with the sword: for the mouth of the LORD hath spoken it.*

The will of God is clear from the above-cited words. The disobedience of God's servants in the kingdom of God is not permitted. This is why God will separate the wheat from the tares when the time comes for judgment to be carried out. Another reason for the separation of wheat from tares is God's intention to cast the tares into a furnace of fire.

What is a furnace of fire in a spiritual sense?

A furnace of fire is a place where a Christian's spiritual house is tested, to determine the material from which it is built. This place is the Antichrist system where the spiritual house of those Christians not finding mercy to be carried into the barn will be tried by fire (troubles). The "barn" represents Israel where the Marriage Supper of the Lamb will be held.

It is necessary to know that God will never punish His servants unless He gives them a testimony of their sins and calls them to return from their sinfulness. This is why God binds the tares first for He is giving a testimony to trespassers of His will in the areas of their trespasses.

For example, in the time of the preaching of our Lord Jesus Christ, God showed the Jewish nation their iniquity by allowing them to crucify His Son. He then gave them a chance to return from their iniquity by offering them the right to enter into new covenant bonds. When they rejected him, judgment followed. The Romans sent their army, destroyed Jerusalem, put down the temple, killed many people and took the rest into captivity. In addition, a veil was put over their hearts so that they could not believe in Jesus Christ unto the present day.

Something similar to this will happen to us Christians. First, through the gathering and binding of Christians with false spirits, God uncovers His servants with false beliefs, showing to all their hearts and faith.

Then, at the spiritual midnight, when the **cry** is made – when troubles start – and all are awakened, the tares and the wheat, or as the Word of God says, the wise and the foolish, God will show His servants their sins. This testimony will be given to them through the realization that they were sleeping, that they did not have enough oil in their lamps nor were their lamps trimmed. God will offer His servants deliverance from their transgressions by showing them their sinfulness – through the words written in the parable of the Ten Virgins. He will offer them deliverance from the bonds of false spirits by His call into the barn for the departure to Israel. Judgment will befall those who refuse to go through the Antichrist system.

Therefore, it is written:

2 Co. 13:5     *Examine yourselves, whether ye be in the faith; prove your own selves. Know ye not your own selves, how that Jesus Christ is in you, except ye be reprobates?*

Based on the expounded material it follows that the words *all things are now ready* indicate that peace in the Middle East has been proclaimed between Israel and its enemies. Borders will be set and Israel's right to exist will be recognized. On the other hand, at the same time all Christians who prove themselves not worthy of eternal life will be bound into bundles, which means they will accept the teachings of many different creeds not based on the Word of God.

It only remains to be seen who the guests at the Marriage Supper and who the servant is whom God sent to call them unto the Supper when everything is ready.

Lu. 14:17     *And **sent his servant** at supper time to say to them that were bidden, Come; for all things are now ready.*

The guests are those Christians to whom the Marriage Supper of the Lamb was announced and who were told to be prepared for it. Who is the servant? Obviously, it is Jesus Christ. There are several places in the Bible where Jesus is named as the servant:

Is. 53:11     *He shall see of the travail of his soul, and shall be satisfied: by his knowledge shall my righteous **servant** justify many; for he shall bear their iniquities.*

Is. 53:12     *Therefore will I divide him a portion with the great, and he shall divide the spoil with the strong; because he hath poured out his soul unto death: and he was numbered with the transgressors; and he bare the sin of many, and made intercession for the transgressors.*

170

Is. 42:1          *Behold my servant, whom I uphold; mine elect, in whom my*
                  *soul delighteth; I have put my spirit upon him: he shall bring*
                  *forth judgment to the Gentiles.*

In John's Revelation the word *angel* is used for Jesus Christ who extends the invitation to the Great Supper:

Re. 19:17         *And I saw **an angel** standing in the sun; and he cried with*
                  *a loud voice, saying to all the fowls that fly in the midst of*
                  *heaven, Come and gather yourselves together unto the supper*
                  *of the great God;*

We can conclude that Jesus Christ is the only one with the power to stand in the sun, or to be in unity with the sun from the fact that the sun symbolizes the Lord God. He is the covenant Angel – the messenger – sent to call guests to the Great Supper of God.

How is He sent?

Through the Word. It is written that *he cried with a loud voice* while standing in the sun. The **voice** of the Angel reaches the fowls, all fowls that fly between heaven and earth, which is to say all those that live spiritually and not earthily. We all know that the voice of the angel, His Word, will reach all hearts that listen.

From the presented words, it follows that it is important to realize the power of the Word. We are created by the Word and we will be justified or condemned by the Word. Without the Word nothing can be accomplished. The new covenant Word is God, for it is His will. Jesus Christ is the Word. At the same time, the Word is the prophet-servant, for it tells us what will happen in the future. Today, as in ancient times, Christ's Word announces the judgment to all nations. Christ's Word invites guests to the Marriage Supper of the Lamb. In the midnight voice of the angel, Christ in the spirit will call and say: it is time, come.

Who will be able to hear? Rather, how can we hear the voice of the angel? What sort of heart and ears must we have?

The foolish virgins awoke, but in the darkness they could not see with their eyes the invisible Bridegroom, Jesus Christ in the spirit, whose bride, the Jewish nation, should repent and be baptized at the Marriage Supper of the Lamb.

Why could the foolish virgins not see the Bridegroom?

Because the following two requirements needed to be fulfilled: to possess oil – faith, knowledge of the Holy Word of God – and to light their lamps – fulfill the will of God.

Verily, it is not possible to be written; and He sent His servants to call them to the Supper of the Lamb.

Why?

Because the virgins who prepared the bride slumbered and slept. If they had not slumbered and slept, they would have reminded others to get ready for the Supper of the Lamb. The Word of Christ concerning the Supper of the Lamb cannot be proclaimed through preachers who slumber and sleep.

## Excuses of the guests and their gathering

After the long preparations for the Marriage Supper of the Lamb are finished, the words *it is all ready* will be heard. God will then send His servant to call all guests unto the Marriage Supper of the Lamb. When the guests hear the call, through the words of Jesus Christ in the Spirit, to come unto the Marriage Supper of the Lamb, because everything is ready, they will begin making excuses:

Lu. 14:18    *And they **all with one consent began to make excuse**. The first said unto him, I have bought a piece of ground, and I must needs go and see it: I pray thee have me excused.*

Lu. 14:19    *And another said, I have bought five yoke of oxen, and I go to prove them: I pray thee have me excused.*

Lu. 14:20    *And another said, I have married a wife, and therefore I cannot come.*

Simply unbelievable! All the invited guests made excuses claiming they were unable to come to the Supper and prayed to be excused from the Marriage Supper of the Lord. This means that the Lord Jesus Christ, who is presently praying for us, also informs His Father about happenings among His people. It is not possible to hide the thoughts of our heart from our Lord. God and our Lord Jesus Christ knows when our heart resists hearing the will of God.

Let us compare these three verses to events in the time when Jesus preached to the Jewish nation for three years. We can notice amazing similarities during this time.

A similarity exists in the fact that Jesus came to His people and all of them renounced Him. We read in Acts 1:15 that only 120 souls remained in the end that did not waver in their faith. The Word of God says: *To His own came and they received Him not.* Just imagine that, from a few million Jews only 120 of them in one accord, at one place prayed and waited upon Jesus' promise.

Now let us face the truth: what has been written about the Supper? It has been written that from all of Christianity, which numbers over a billion Christians, all will begin making excuses when the call to go to the Marriage Supper of the Lamb – to Israel – comes. How interesting! It does not suit anyone to obey the call, the voice of the Word of God, the angel who is Jesus Christ in the Spirit.

Let us consider the excuses given by the invited guests. The excuses given by God's servants at the Marriage Dinner and Marriage Supper will be compared.

Three groups of Jews did not care about the invitation for the Dinner because:

1) One went to his farm (Matthew 22:5)
2) The other to his merchandise (Matthew 22:5)
3) And the remaining took His servants, treated them spitefully and slew them (Matthew 22:5)

At the invitation for the Supper, Christians will excuse themselves in the following manner:

1) I have bought a piece of ground. (Which means that it is now his land)
2) I have bought five yoke of oxen. (They are now his oxen)
3) I have married a wife

In both cases, the way of making excuses is the same. The three examples, which represent three types of people, show what happened when God

173

called the Jewish nation into covenant bonds through the arrival of the Holy Comforter. We know this for certain, for it is part of history. It becomes clear, according to historical fact, why God emphasizes that every one of them returned into "his". What does *his* represent? One thing is certain: if a man will say *mine*, then it is not God's. The Old Testament was God's and is God's today. However, when it was abolished, every Jew who returned to that old law was returning to "his", which is now against the will of God.

We can see from reading the prophesied words about the Marriage Dinner (Matthew 22) which has already happened, that God through *returning on his* (one's own) describes the Jewish nation which rejected the call of Jesus Christ which came through His servants.

The words referring to the first group, which returned to their farm, explain how the will of the Jewish people reacted when they received a direct invitation to enter into new covenant bonds.

The words referring to the second group which returned to their merchandise, show how the will of the Jewish priesthood reacted when they were called into new covenant bonds.

The words referring to the third group say that a certain number of Jewish people and the priesthood will be so sure in their belief that they will begin killing Christians.

We can come to the conclusion that Christians will act similarly when they hear the call to the Marriage Supper (Luke 14:18), from the manner in which the Jews behaved when they received the call to the Marriage Dinner.

Lu. 14:18    *And they all with one consent began to make excuse. The first said unto him, I have bought a piece of ground, and I must needs go and see it: I pray thee have me excused.*

A piece of ground is a source of food for man. He works it and lives from it. For a spiritual man, a Christian, a piece of ground symbolizes the place where he fulfills the will of God. There is a big difference between what the Jewish people did in the past and what Christians will do in the future when they are called unto the Marriage Supper. In the past, a Jew simply did not accept a "new doctrine" and returned unto his old field, into the Old Testament doctrine. However, a Christian does something more, actually something worse. A Christian buys new ground. He is not pleased with the piece of ground he already has, ground with which Jesus Christ as the king of heaven and earth blessed him.

A Jew in the past did not care for the call. However, a Christian now excuses himself and justifies his actions.

Let us be reminded of the words written in the Gospel according to St. Matthew:

Mt. 13:41    *..and **they shall gather** out of his kingdom all things that offend, and them which do iniquity;*

These words say that a Christian's *new ground,* or the place where he fulfills God's will, is an offense and an iniquity, that he accepted – bought – materialism and liberalism as a way of life in faith, a piece of ground that feeds his soul. This is why it is written *I must needs go and see it.* Visually, a man receives a picture of what he has bought and then rejoices in it and finds pleasure. This is to say that Christians will excuse themselves by asserting that they accepted materialistic Christianity as a way of life in the faith of Christ and that they rejoice in it. They are completely satisfied with the spiritual life they have, and have no need for a call to Supper or for anything additional.

The second group of invited guests excused themselves in this way:

Lu. 14:19    *And another said, I have bought five yoke of oxen, and I go to prove them: I pray thee have me excused.*

This group of Christians found an excuse for turning down the call to come to the Supper in buying five yoke of oxen. The five yoke of oxen is five times two oxen, which is ten oxen altogether. These oxen will help them in their work. An ox, in a spiritual sense, symbolizes a priest. The number ten represents all, i.e. all priesthood. They work together for they are equally yoked; however, since they are divided it shows that among them there are those who are wise and those who are foolish.

When one of the guests says, *I go to prove them* it means that he must ask them for advice. However, since he knows their belief, the answer *I go to prove them* is only an excuse. Because he just bought five yoke of oxen, he had his oxen already given from the Lord. Therefore, he buys new oxen only because he is not pleased with the old ones.

This can be said in the following manner: I cannot accept the invitation to come to the Supper because my priesthood, whom I believe – I bought them, so they are mine – teaches me differently.

In essence, the verse from Luke 14:19 is the same as in Matthew concerning the invitation for the Marriage Dinner. In Matthew, a priest went to his merchandise, i.e. preaching of the Mosaic Law, yet at Supper a Christian went seeking new oxen because he was not pleased with those he had. After finding them, he bought them. A guest knows exactly what the "new" priests – the five yoke of oxen – will teach him. Naturally, they will teach people the things that please them. This includes avoiding preaching about going to the Marriage Supper.

The third excuse says what he believes:

Lu. 14:20     *And another said, I have married a wife, and therefore I cannot come.*

I have married a wife. This means, I became one body with this woman, or one body with people who do not believe in the departure for the Marriage Supper. In other words, I do not believe and I cannot come.

Comparing this excuse with the third example of the Marriage Dinner where it is written the *remnant took his servants and entreated them spitefully, and slew them* (Matthew 22:5) we will see that essentially, in a spiritual sense, no difference exists between them. For when you believe differently from what has been written in the Bible, the Word of God is thrown away or killed in one's heart as if it had never existed. Thus, the "servant" is killed.

When guests refused to come unto the Marriage Supper of the Lamb, the servant – the Word of God, Jesus Christ in the Spirit – revealed this to His Father. However, something similar happened when the servants invited guests to the Marriage Dinner. In that time, the Pharisees, scribes, lawyers, noblemen, and people who blindly obeyed the priesthood, did not recognize Jesus Christ as their Messiah. Those who were counted as "healthy" departed from God.

Now, the most competent in Christianity, those denominations that are counted as having a sound foundation in the Word of God, reject the invitation to come to the Marriage Supper of the Lamb.

176

Lu. 14:21    *So that servant came, and shewed his lord these things. Then the master of the house being angry said to his servant, Go out quickly into the streets and lanes of* **the city,** *and bring in hither the poor, and the maimed, and the halt, and the blind.*

Having heard this, the master of the house — God, sent the second invitation for the Marriage Supper through His servant. This time, God turned His focus on a special category of Christians. In a general sense, this category is composed of the poor, the maimed, the halt and the blind. All of them are citizens of a city which is evidently God's city. It is written:

He. 12:22    *But ye are come unto mount Sion, and unto* **the city** *of the living God, the heavenly Jerusalem, and to an innumerable company of angels,*
He. 12:23    *To the general assembly and church of the firstborn, which are written in heaven, and to God the Judge of all, and to the spirits of just men made perfect,*
He. 12:24    *And to Jesus the mediator of the new covenant, and to the blood of sprinkling, that speaketh better things than that of Abel.*

That city is spiritual Jerusalem, mount Zion, God's people. God gives instructions to the "servant: *go out quickly into the streets and lanes*".

What do the streets and lanes in that city represent?

Streets and lanes are for traveling. To reach a certain place one must use the streets of a spiritual city. A spiritual man living in a spiritual city has no choice but to walk the streets and lanes of the city in order to do his spiritual work. First, the spiritual man must make a decision in his heart of what to do. When a faithful man decides to do a deed he then chooses which street of the spiritual city to take to reach his destination. Only one way, which is Jesus Christ, takes a man into the spiritual city. Moreover, even this "*one way*"forks into many streets and lanes. This means that the servant has to go among the hearts of those who travel these streets. Only those who want to do the deeds that please God and our Saviour, Jesus Christ, wish to sacrifice themselves for His Holy Name, to walk the streets of peace, justice, love, meekness and endurance, are called by the servant to come to the Supper of the Lamb, regardless of whether they are spiritually poor, maimed, blind and lame.

177

It is very important to note that God requires of the servant to go **quickly** into the streets and lanes of the city. These words are in accordance with the prophecy of the Ten Virgins, for there is no time for doubt.

| | |
|---|---|
| Mt. 25:9 | *But the wise answered, saying, Not so; lest there be not enough for us and you: but go ye rather to them that sell, and buy for yourselves.* |
| Mt. 25:10 | *And while they went to buy, the Bridegroom came; and they that were ready went in with him to the marriage: and the door was shut.* |

While the foolish virgins were buying oil, the wise virgins entered the Marriage Supper and the door was shut. This means that there was not enough time for the wise virgins to give oil to the foolish ones.

It remains to be seen who the poor, the maimed, the halt and the blind are.

The poor are the first among four categories of Christians to be brought unto the Marriage Supper by the servant. Surely, the Word speaks about the spiritually poor, or those who for different reasons did not have an opportunity to receive ample spiritual knowledge. This probably applies to those who are poor in the spirit through no fault of their own.

The second group are the maimed, those who were born spiritually through the process of baptism. In their case, something was not completely right during the process of repentance and in bringing the fruit of repentance before baptism. They are now living in the spiritual world as the spiritually maimed.

The third group are the halt. This group consists of those who were delivered for the spiritual world through baptism as spiritually healthy souls. They sinned in their spiritual life, and by God's mercy were healed. Some consequences however remain, so they are walking as the lame through their spiritual life.

The fourth group, those who are spiritually blind, are in the worst position. Simply put, they have no spiritual knowledge and cannot see. They are forced to let others lead them, because they are unable to live spiritually independent lives in the blessed faith of our Lord Jesus Christ.

When Jesus in the Spirit gathered the spiritually poor, the maimed, the crippled and the blind from Christianity, He revealed to His Father that there was still some room left in His house.

Lu. 14:22    *And the servant said, Lord, it is done as thou hast commanded, and yet there is room.*

Lu. 14:23    *And the lord said unto the servant, Go out into the highways and hedges, and* **compel** *them to come in, that my house may be filled.*

Then Jesus in the Spirit — the Word of God — received a new commandment: *Go out into the highways and hedges, and* **compel** *them to come in, that my house may be filled.*

The house where the righteous dwell with the unrighteous is Israel. This is the place where the Marriage Supper will be held. When the servant said to His Lord "there is still some room left", a severe commandment was pronounced: *compel them.* This commandment applies to Christians who are still *out into the highways and hedges.*

We should remember that the Jewish nation rejected an entrance into Palestine despite the great world depression that God used to force them. This "gentle" warning did not bring any fruit. Then came the words *shake dry bones,* shake the Jewish nation. This small word "shake" actually describes the killing of six million Jews in World War II. A cataclysm that shook the hearts of the Jewish nation, dispersed throughout the whole world.

Formerly it was said, that the servant turned to gather the poor, the maimed, the crippled and the blind when Christians refused to respond. How do you think the servant is going to gather them? Will He do this by his free will or by force, through faith or through the fear of God?

Verily, the servant gathered them by the fear of God, which awakened the sleepy virgins who went out to wait for the Bridegroom (Matthew 25). This fear was caused by a cry in the middle of the night, namely, by dangerous occurrences in the world from which the foolish and the wise virgins awoke.

However, *compel them* is a much stronger term than *cry.* Usually we say that for a small nail we need a small hammer yet a bigger nail requires a bigger hammer. Obviously, for those on the highways and hedges, special measures are needed to convince them that going to the Marriage Supper of the Lamb is necessary.

What does it mean to go out into the highways?

Before God, there is only one way in accordance with His will - the doctrine of our Lord Jesus Christ. Jesus Himself said: *I am the way*.

However, a misunderstanding of the Word of God has allowed many to build for themselves an auxiliary way alongside God's path, which they respect as the greatest commandment of God. They fear God, work in His vineyard and respect Him but partly preach their own doctrine. Clearly, their way – teaching – is the supporting rock of the whole denomination. These believers do not have enough oil nor enough knowledge of the divine things to do the complete will of God. Of course, God and Jesus Christ are not pleased with this. God, however, still has His people who perform His will even in such fellowships. The Word of God refers to these when it reads; **compel** *them to come in, that my house may be filled.*

What does it mean to be in the hedges?

In a general sense, a fence defends someone's property from the unwanted. Christians should be fenced with God's protection, with the keeping of His commandments.

Yet there are those who have put up their own fences rather than God's walls around themselves. Many denominations live in faith enclosed by human commandments which do not please God. Humans make different laws and ordinances only to be different from other Christians and from the rest of the world. In this way, they are protected from the changes that are coming. By enclosing themselves with the rules that God did not command, they live encapsulated lives, separated from the children of God and transgressing the will of God, especially the commandment about unity and love. Also, because they differ from others, many of them fall into the trap of considering themselves better than they really are. God however, also has many among the hedges of His people who are saved from such sins.

Is. 65:5    *Which say, Stand by thyself, come not near to me; for I am holier than thou. These are a smoke in my nose, a fire that burneth all the day.*

God ordered that His servant compel some members of these groups to come to the Marriage Supper, *that his house may be filled.* To be convinced that the word "compel" really describes the great tribulation we will read the following verses:

Mt. 24:19    *And woe unto them that are with child, and to them that give suck in those days!*

Mt. 24:20    *But pray ye that your flight be not in **the winter**, neither on **the sabbath** day:*

Mt. 24:21    *For then shall be **great tribulation**, such as was not since the beginning of the world to this time, no, nor ever shall be.*

The Great tribulation begins in spiritual midnight which contains a spiritual winter and a spiritual Sabbath. We should note the order of events:

- first comes the **midnight** as an event.
- Then comes the **flight** or going away of the spiritually halt, the blind, the lame and the poor to the Marriage Supper of the Lamb. It is written: *pray ye*. Note that this is a flight before the arrival of the Sabbath and of winter. The cry at midnight is forcing this group to flee.
- After this comes the **flight in winter**. Through tribulation, the servant gathers those among the hedges and highways who are "*not with child*" – have no sin – and those who give no "*suck*" – who do not live in sin.
- The next phase is the **flight on the Sabbath**. When the servant finished gathering among the hedges and highways, his job was finished, for he did not get another order from God to go and gather the faithful for the Lamb's Supper. However, if that is so, the question is who is fleeing on the Sabbath? We read on:

Mt. 25:11    *Afterward came also the other virgins, saying, Lord, Lord, **open to us**.*

The foolish virgins will be fleeing to the wedding on the Sabbath. It will be too late for no one can go to the wedding on the Sabbath.

Why will the foolish virgins flee or try to enter the wedding on the Sabbath?

The Sabbath symbolizes the period when man should rest from his work. In a spiritual sense, the Word of God sent a message to all, that preparations for the Marriage Supper, which relates to the gentiles, are finished. Guests from the gentiles are gathered. In other words, the salvation of the gentiles has ended, the reign of the Antichrist has begun, and Satan is loose and sifting wheat as he pleases. The hour of temptation which shall come upon all the world has begun.

It is interesting to note that not even the tribulation of the **winter** will move the foolish virgins who have not enough oil to find refuge at the Lamb's Wedding i.e. in Israel. Instead, the foolish virgins are buying oil. Winter symbolizes the Third World War, the time when *love of many shall wax cold* and everything will be cold among the nations. In such times, it will be very difficult to travel or to flee.

Lu. 14:24      *For I say unto you, That none of those men which were bidden shall taste of* **my** *supper.*

To turn down God's invitation to the Marriage Supper of the Lamb is a great offence against God. To despise His call is a great sin. This sin is so great that God will erase the names of those who reject his call from the Book of Life. Therefore, the following words were written to us:

Mt. 25:12      *But he answered and said, Verily I say unto you, I know you not.*

The Word of God, following a description of the Marriage Supper and in addition to Luke 14, warns all Christians with surprising severity:

Lu. 14:25      *And there went great multitudes with him: and he turned, and said unto them,*
Lu. 14:27      *And whosoever doth not bear his cross, and come after me, cannot be my disciple.*

Verily, it is a great sin not to respond to the call to the Marriage Supper.

Lu. 14:28      *For which of you, intending to build a tower, sitteth not down first, and counteth the cost, whether he have sufficient to finish it?*

Lu. 14:29    *Lest haply, after he hath laid the foundation, and is not able to finish it, all that behold it begin to mock him,*

Lu. 14:33    *So likewise, whosoever he be of you that forsaketh not all that he hath, he cannot be my disciple.*

Lu. 14:34    *Salt is good: but if the salt have lost his savour, wherewith shall it be seasoned?*

Lu. 14:35    *It is neither fit for the land, nor yet for the dunghill; but men cast it OUT.* **He that hath ears to hear, let him hear.**

Today's generation of Christians does not have a choice, just as Christians in the past did not have a choice: Noah — before the great flood, Lot — before the destruction of Sodom and the Jews in the time of preaching of the Lord Jesus. The will of God must be done.

There are other places in the Bible from which we can see that Christians will go to the Marriage Supper of the Lamb.

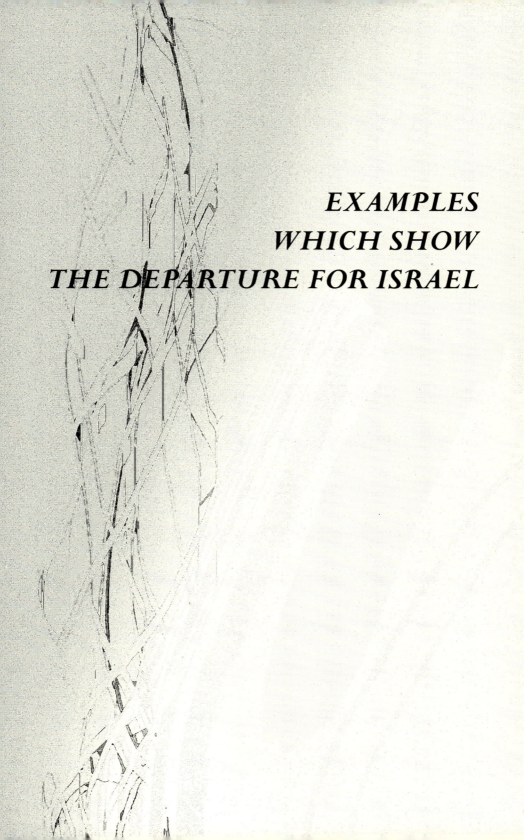

*EXAMPLES*
*WHICH SHOW*
*THE DEPARTURE FOR ISRAEL*

Examples are chosen in such a way as to include the Old Testament, the Gospels, the Epistles and Revelation of John.

*12*

# THE BOOK OF THE PROPHET EZEKIEL, CHAPTER 36

If we carefully analyze the entire 36<sup>th</sup> chapter from the Book of Ezekiel, we will come to astonishing revelations. In this chapter God reveals how He is going to deliver the Jewish nation from bondage among the gentiles. Also, here we can find a general description of the main events presently occurring in the Middle East.

Since our goal is to show those verses in the Bible which refer to the migration of Christians to the Marriage Supper of the Lamb, we will concentrate on verses which apply to present day.

In the beginning of this chapter God is talking to the people, i.e. to the mountains of Israel. These verses read as follows:

Eze. 36:1     *Also, thou son of man, prophecy unto the mountains of Israel, and say, Ye mountains of Israel, hear the word of the LORD:*

Eze. 36:2     *Thus saith the Lord GOD; Because the enemy hath said against you, Aha, even the ancient high places are ours in possession:*

Eze. 36:3     *Therefore prophecy and say, Thus saith the Lord GOD; Because they have made you desolate, and swallowed you up on every side, that ye might be a possession unto the residue of the heathen, and ye are taken up in the lips of talkers, and are an infamy of the people:*

A mountain in a spiritual sense represents a group of people who share the same belief. This belief is raised above other beliefs. This refers to the Jewish belief that the promises of God which they received possess eternal value. These promises are what the Scripture refers to as "the ancient high places", elevated for all eternity. God promised the first Jew, who was

Abraham, that if he walked in the footsteps of God, both he and his seed would become the children of God. God also promised that his seed would multiply like the stars in the sky. Finally, the Lord promised Abraham land and many other blessings. Nevertheless, the enemy captured the ancient high places for its own.

Eze. 36:2    *...Aha, even* **the ancient high places are ours in possession:**

Ezekiel 36:2 says that the enemy appropriated all the promises of God which actually belonged to the Jewish people believing in God for themselves. Besides, by appropriating eternal promises, the enemy desolated and devoured the Jewish people so that they would become the possession of the people of this world.

Eze. 36:3    *Therefore prophecy and say, Thus saith the Lord GOD;* **Because they have made you desolate, and swallowed you up on every side,** *that ye might be a possession unto the residue of the heathen, and ye are taken up in the lips of talkers, and are an infamy of the people:*

To become the possession of other people means to become as other people or blend into another nation. Furthermore, this means that the enemy wanted the Jewish people to forget that they are Jews, to abandon their faith in God as well as their customs, and become like all other people.

Therefore, as soon as the enemy of the Jewish people had the chance, they sold them to the sons of Greece and other nations so that they could take their land.

Nevertheless, God did not allow the Jewish people to become the possession of this world. They only became the talk and infamy of the people of this world.

The Jews, even while in captivity, possessed the faith in their hearts to marry only among themselves. They did not mingle with the gentiles. The Jews therefore preserved their national and religious identity, while at the same time keeping with the traditions and the belief that they would find God's grace once again and that God would return them to their land.

As Christians, we know that their hope and belief will one day turn into complete joy. The announcement of this is written in the following verses.

Eze. 36:4  *Therefore, ye mountains of Israel, hear the word of the Lord of God; Thus saith the Lord God to the mountains, and to the hills, to the rivers, and to the valleys, to the desolate wastes, and to the cities that are forsaken, which became a prey and derision to the residue of the heathen that round about;*

Eze. 36:5  *Therefore thus saith the Lord GOD; Surely **in the fire of my jealousy have I spoken against the residue of the heathen**, and against all have appointed my land into their possession with the joy of all their heart, with despiteful minds, to cast it out for a prey.*

In Ezekiel 34:4 a message is sent to the Jewish people[13] that God will end derision and suffering inflicted by other nations. His words: *in the fire of my jealousy have I spoken against the residue of the heathen, and against all have appointed my land into their possession with the joy of all their heart, with despiteful minds, to cast it out for a prey,* surely will not give restful sleep to the enemy.

It is a historical fact that Roman soldiers desolated Jerusalem and took the Jews into captivity. The land was left desolate. When the enemy saw this, they became greedy, took the Jewish land and said "now it is ours". It is important to note that God named the Jewish enemy. First He named them "the other people" and then Edom which is today Saudi Arabia. In the Book of the prophet Joel we can find who these "other people" are.

Jl. 3:1  *For, behold, in those days, and in that time, when I shall bring again the captivity of Judah and Jerusalem,*

Jl. 3:2  *I will also gather **all nations**, and will bring them down into the valley of Jehoshaphat, and will plead with them there for my people and for my heritage Israel, whom they have scattered among the nations, and parted my land.*

Jl. 3:3  *And they have cast lots for my people; and have given a boy for an harlot, and sold a girl for wine, that they might drink.*

Jl. 3:4  *Yea, and what have ye to do with me, O **Tyre**, and **Zidon**, and **all the coasts of Palestine**? will ye render me a recompence? and if ye recompense me, swiftly and speedily will I return your recompence upon your own head;*

---

[13] God uses the following symbols to describe the unrepentant hearts of the Jewish people: mountains, hills, rivers, valleys, desolate wastes, and forsaken cities.

Jl. 3:5    *Because ye have taken my silver and my gold, and have carried into your temples my goodly pleasant things:*

Jl. 3:6    *The children also of Judah and the children of Jerusalem have ye sold unto the Grecians, that ye might remove them far from their border.*

From this text we can acknowledge that all nations are guilty of treating the Jewish people in this way while they were in captivity among the gentiles. God especially accuses Lebanon (Tire and Sidon) and all the coasts of Palestine, otherwise known as the Palestinians. Perhaps you will ask why?

They are guilty because they committed great sins. The first sin they committed involved taking God's land with joy in their hearts and spiteful minds. The land where Tire and Sidon lie belongs to the Jewish people, according to the order of God. The West Bank, which great powers of this world want to pronounce as the Palestinian State, belongs to the Jewish tribe of Judah. Jesus Christ comes from the tribe of Judah.

All land and all that is in it is the property of our God of Israel. Nevertheless, it is important to note that in the past God designated a part of the land for His people, who believe in Him and obey His commandments. God did not designate the wide land of Siberia for His people, nor Canada with four hundred thousands lakes and countless rivers and forests, but a small piece of land in the Middle East, which is for the most part a desert.

Humanity cannot blame the Creator for giving His people the best, biggest, and most fertile mineral land on this planet. Nevertheless, the enemy should have known that God's land cannot be taken because it was given as an inheritance only to His people. When God decided to remove the Jewish people from His land because of their sin, the land remained desolate. When the enemy saw this they were not allowed to enter because God designated this land only for His people.

In the sight of God this is a great sin, especially from Christian nations who do not understand that the land God designated for His servants cannot be divided according to human laws and human understanding of problems.

Also, they took God's silver and gold, goodly and pleasant things, and carried them into their temples. Silver symbolizes the Word of God and gold the servants of God. To further explain these symbols an example

190

will be illustrated. Islam teaches that Abraham sacrificed Ishmael, his son from the slave Hagar, whom Sarai[14] gave to her husband Abram[15] for an heir. Nevertheless, we know that it was Isaac, Sarah's son, who was born according to God's promise and was sacrificed to God. Therefore, the Word of God was twisted to look like the inheritance and all blessings belonged to the descendants of Ishmael. In other words, the descendants of Ishmael were made to look like God's people.

A temple was built at the place where Abraham sacrificed his son, according to the will of God. The Romans destroyed this temple when they captured Jerusalem. Later, the enemy of the Jewish people (who captured the land) built a mosque in its place.

Today, this mosque is considered to be one of the holiest places for the Islamic people, and Palestinians insist that Jerusalem is their city, given to them by God. But God of Israel said: Jerusalem is my city. This is why today the enemy of the Jewish people wants to divide this city between the Jews and the Palestinians.

Indeed, while the Jewish people (mountains of Israel) were in captivity and without His blessings, believing that one day they will find grace before the God of Israel, their enemy perpetrated its deeds. By taking their land, their ancient high places, holy places, and destroying them (because they were without protection), the heart of the enemy became sublime. They thought the God who created heaven, earth, man, and all things seen and unseen, accepted them as His people.

Nevertheless, God returned the slaves of Zion back to their land as He promised. This was a shock for those who captured God's land. Let us read a message from God to the enemies of the mountains of Israel.

Eze. 36:6    *Prophecy therefore concerning the land of Israel, and say unto the mountains, and to the hills, to the rivers, and to the valleys, Thus saith the Lord GOD; Behold, I have spoken in my jealousy and in my fury, because ye have borne the shame of the heathen:*

---

[14]    Sarai became Sarah when God made a covenant with Abram, Genesis 17:15.
[15]    Abram became Abraham when God made a covenant with him, Genesis 17:5.

Eze. 36:7    *Therefore thus saith the Lord GOD;* **I have lifted up mine hand,** *Surely the heathen that are about you, they shall bear their shame.*

In the sixth verse, God reveals that He will end the shame that the Jews endured from their enemies because of their belief that God will return them to their land. This belief materialized when God allowed Israel to be proclaimed a country after 1900 years of captivity.

In the seventh verse it says that the enemy will not be able to destroy the Jewish people gathered in Israel anymore ("*I have lifted up mine hand*") and that the nations surrounding Israel will be without protection. Indeed, in the last fifty years, the Arabic countries have lost five major wars against Israel.

The following verse indicates that the Marriage Supper of the Lamb will occur in the future.

Eze. 36:8    *But ye, O mountains of Israel, ye shall shoot forth your branches,* **and yield your fruit to my people of Israel; for they are at hand to come.**

When Israel was established, God lifted His hand against the enemies of the Jewish people. The mountains of Israel started shooting their branches which represents the coming of the new generations. According to Jewish law a new generation comes every 20 years, which means that soon a fourth generation will appear (counting from 1948).

The next event which God reveals is that the mountains of Israel will yield their fruit to God's people of Israel which will soon come.

In other words, this means that the multiplying and gathering of Jewish people in Israel is the fruit of their belief in God's promises. The Jewish people gathered in Israel will be given to God's people, or Christians, as a gift, because they will soon come. Christians became God's people or new covenant Israel, when they acknowledged Jesus Christ.

These words are the law. All the events at the end of time will happen according to this law. God tells us that He will first gather the slaves of Zion (Jewish people according to the flesh) and then He will bring them to new covenant Israel (Christians).

In addition to the prophet Ezekiel, the Gospels also talk about building the country of Israel using the symbol of a branch.

| Mt. 24:32 | *Now learn a parable of the fig tree; When his branch is yet tender, and putteth forth leaves, ye know that summer is nigh:* |
| Mt. 24:33 | *So likewise ye, when ye shall see all these things, know that it is near, even at the doors.* |
| Mt. 24:34 | *Verily I say unto you, This generation shall not pass, till all these things be fulfilled.* |
| Mt. 24:35 | *Heaven and earth shall pass away, but my words shall not pass away.* |

To understand the events in the world, we need to observe the fig tree which symbolizes the Jewish nation. Jesus withered the fig tree by His word because it did not bear fruit (Matthew 21:19). The fig tree withered away when the Romans destroyed Jerusalem and enslaved the Jewish people. The fig tree withered away because the Holy Spirit was not among them.

Today in Israel the same fig tree branches are becoming tender and this generation shall not pass till all these things are fulfilled. According to the Word of God one generation is seventy to eighty years. This means that all prophecy concerning the Jewish people should be fulfilled when we add eighty years to the year when Israel was established or when the branches started to become tender. If we add seventy or eighty to the year 1948 we get the year 2018 or 2028. During this time the Jewish people will make a covenant with God through Jesus Christ and Armageddon will happen. Of course, no one knows the exact date.

Some may ask the question: why is it necessary for Christians to go to Israel? The answer is found in the next verse:

| Eze. 36:9 | *For, behold, I am for you, and I will turn unto you, and ye shall be tilled and sown:* |

God reveals that He will pay special attention to the Jewish people in Israel because He will be among them. This means that He will take special care of them. He will rule within their hearts.

The third thing that God reveals is that the mountains of Israel will be tilled and sown. We know that soil (the hearts of men) needs to be prepared for seeding before sowing. In other words, God will let trouble fall upon them so that they can repent and admit their sin, or to prepare their hearts for the execution of His will.

Only then will the time come for sowing. In other words, the time for the preaching of the Gospel of Jesus Christ by Christians will come.

The next two verses summarize everything God will do to the Jewish people before the time comes to bring Christians to Israel.

Eze. 36:10    *And I will multiply men upon you, all the house of Israel, even all of it: and the cities shall be inhabited, and the wastes shall be builded:*

Eze. 36:11    *And I will multiply upon you man and beast; and they shall increase and bring fruit: and I will settle you after your old estates, and will do better unto you than at your beginnings: and ye shall know that I am the LORD.*

He will settle them like they were before and do better by them than previously. Only then will they know that the God of Israel is their God.

In the end, He will bring His people to Israel.

Eze. 36:12    *Yea, **I will cause men to walk upon you, even MY people Israel;** and they shall possess thee, and thou shalt be their inheritance, and thou shalt NO more henceforth bereave them of men.*

When reading this 12th verse, no Christian should hesitate when considering whether it is necessary to go to Israel or not. We see that God gave a direct message to all Christians so that His servants do not hesitate. He openly tells us:

1) That He will cause men to walk upon them, even His people Israel (Christians).

2) They (Christians) will possess the mountains of Israel or the house of Israel.

3) The mountains of Israel will be their (Christians) inheritance.

4) From now on the mountains of Israel (Jewish people) will not be deprived of man or body of Christ, His people of Israel.

In all other places in the Bible, this was described through symbols. Therefore, Christians should pay special attention to Ezekiel 36, so that they will not be confused with different interpretations of God's Word.

When God gave a testimony that He will bring His people Israel to the Jewish people, He immediately explained why He was going to do this. They have to inherit the mountains of Israel. The question is, how can man inherit another man? Or how can Christians inherit the Jewish people according to flesh.

Through the process of inheritance, certain things become possessions of the successor. In a spiritual sense, the Jews are to become a possession of Christians or a part of Christians.

This means that the Christians will inherit the Jews in a spiritual sense and that the Jews will become spiritual brothers of the Christians. This will happen when the Jews acknowledge that they killed their Messiah Jesus Christ, repent, and fulfill the ordinances of Christ's Gospels.

God's will is unchangeable. The mountains of Israel will be the inheritance of His people Israel. To avoid any doubt God says: *thou shalt NO more henceforth bereave them of men.*

This is an unbelievable testimony to the truthfulness of God's Word. We all know what Jesus told the Jewish people 1950 years ago.

Mt. 23:37    *O Jerusalem, Jerusalem, thou that killest the prophets, and stonest them **which are SENT unto thee,** how often would I have gathered thy children together, even as a hen gathereth her chickens under her wings, and ye would not!*

All those sent to the Jewish people up to the destruction of Jerusalem and after His crucifixion were killed or stoned. Let us remember the prophets, John the Baptist, Jesus, Stephen, and the apostles. When the Lord now sends His people Israel (Christians) to the Jewish people they will not be exterminated. Rather, Christians will walk upon them as the Word says.

Verily, the first twelve verses from the Book of Ezekiel 36 openly speak about bringing His new covenant Israel to the Jewish people so they can become one nation. Christians cannot go back to the Mosaic Law because the Jewish people who believe in the Mosaic Law must repent and accept Christ's Law.

# 13

# ONE FOLD AND ONE SHEPHERD

God does not hide His will or laws from man, if man allows the Words of God to reach his heart. This is why Jesus openly speaks of the task which was entrusted to Him by His Father: to unite the sheep from the two folds. God announced His intention from the very beginning: through Abraham in the Old Testament and in the New Testament through Jesus Christ. This announcement will be more obvious if we are clear on the meaning of "woman" and clear on the usage of the male and female principles in the Bible. Only then will we be able to understand from which tribe of Jacob Christians have originated.

## Jesus' Announcement of the Unification of the Two Folds

The unification of the two folds is announced through the following words of our Lord Jesus Christ:

Jn. 10:3     *To him the porter openeth; and the sheep hear his voice: and he calleth his own sheep by name, and leadeth them out.*

Jn. 10:4     *And when he putteth forth his own sheep, he goeth before them, and the sheep follow him: for they know his voice.*

Jn. 10:16    *And other sheep I have, which are not of this fold: them also I must bring, and they shall hear my voice;* **and there shall be one fold, and one shepherd.**

One fold and one shepherd is the law of heaven. In heaven two folds cannot exist. Two represents divisiveness and disunity. There is no disunity in heaven. Light cannot be mixed with darkness. Righteousness and unrighteousness cannot coexist. Jesus testifies that on this earth He has sheep in two folds, the Jewish and Gentile. The task He was given by His father was to make one fold, which will love the Triune God of Israel.

The owner of these two folds is Jesus' Father, our heavenly God. He is the porter who allows Jesus to enter both folds and lead the sheep out into the good pasture.

Jesus says that He will lead (only) His sheep from the Jewish nation as well as from the gentile fold into the New Testament pasture. In other words, all Jews from the Jewish fold and gentiles from the gentile fold will not believe in Him.

Verily, when Jesus came to the Jewish nation, they did not accept Him as their king. This is why they crucified Him on Golgotha's cross. After the crucifixion the Comforter was sent, Jesus in the Spirit, through His apostles and His followers, who went out again into the Jewish fold to lead His sheep into the pasture.

To lead sheep out into the pasture represents the acceptance of Jesus Christ's teachings and the passage through the ordinance of baptism. When a Jew is led out into the pasture it means that he is being led away from the Mosaic Law. Likewise, when someone is led from the gentile fold, he is led away from unbelief and idolatry. When Jesus has led His sheep away from these two folds, He will never return them. We can find a testimony that Jesus made His own fold in His Words: *I am the door*. The door to what? Obviously, the door to the fold where the kingdom of God rules.

When Jesus sent the Comforter from heaven, the apostles invited the Jewish nation a second time to remove themselves from the Mosaic Law. By refusing to leave, they showed themselves to be unworthy of eternal life. At that time Jesus Christ was not able to accomplish the task He was given because of the unbelief of the Jewish people. Also, through this the gentiles received the opportunity for salvation:

Ro. 11:11      *I say then, Have they stumbled that they should fall? God forbid: but rather through their fall salvation is come unto the Gentiles, for to provoke them to jealousy.*

In the same chapter we read:

Ro. 11:30      *For as ye in times past have not believed God, yet have now obtained mercy through their unbelief:*

| Ro. 11:31 | *Even so have these also now not believed, that through your mercy they also may obtain mercy.* |
| Ro. 11:32 | *For God hath concluded them all in unbelief, that he might have mercy upon all.* |

The point of their unbelief was that the gentiles could be saved. However, the Word of God proclaims that the salvation of the gentiles will soon come to an end so that the Jewish nation can be redeemed. In the 31st verse it is written that *they also may obtain mercy.*

Several more verses deal with their obtaining God's mercy:

| Ro. 11:25 | *For I would not, brethren, that ye should be ignorant of this mystery, lest ye should be wise in your own conceits; that blindness in part is happened to Israel, until the fulness of the Gentiles be come in.* |
| Ro. 11:26 | *And so all Israel shall be saved: as it is written, There shall come out of Sion the Deliverer, and shall turn away ungodliness from Jacob:* |
| Ro. 11:27 | *For this is my covenant unto them, when I shall take away their sins.* |

Every verse quoted contains a fact of great importance. The first verse says that the Jews will be spiritually blind until a certain number of gentiles are saved. In the next verse we are told that they will be saved when the Deliverer comes from Zion (Christianity). This verse says two things: first, that the Jewish nation will gather in their land. This is not openly written but is a condition for the second event, which is to bring the Deliverer from Zion to the Jewish nation.

Here the Word of God directly states that God will bring His servants from Christianity, where the Holy Spirit resides, to help Jacob – the Jewish nation – turn away from ungodliness.

In the 27th verse it is written that God gave a covenant to the Jews, that He will force them to repent. Actually, He will bring such troubles upon them that they will repent. They will have no choice but to believe Jesus Christ and thus achieve salvation.

According to Romans 11, we can see that the Jewish nation's belief in Christ will unfold in four steps:

1) The salvation of a certain number of gentiles
2) The return of the Jews to their land at the end of the period given for the salvation of the gentiles
3) The departure of Christians to Israel
4) The arrival of a major tribulation upon Israel which will cause them to be humbled and to recognize their sin. Their sins will be forcefully taken away from them so they may be saved.

It may seem that the words from Romans 11 do not speak of uniting the sheep from the two folds only because we have not quoted all the verses from chapter 11. Let us read these words:

Ro. 11:17     *And if some of the branches be broken off, and thou, being a wild olive tree, wert grafted in among them, and with them partakest of the root and fatness of the olive tree;*

The same words which have already been written in many places in the Bible are repeated here again, that through the unbelief of the Jewish nation, the gentiles – the wild olive tree – will receive the right to be God's nation, to be grafted onto the olive tree through baptism. In this way they become partakers of the root and fatness of the olive tree. They become part of the natural olive tree and God's nation. The root symbolizes Jesus Christ – the Messiah – and the fatness of the olive tree represents the Holy Ghost who originates from the root.

Ro. 11:22     *Behold therefore the goodness and severity of God: on them which fell, severity; but toward thee, goodness,* **if thou continue in his goodness: otherwise thou also shalt be cut off.**

These words announce the end of salvation for the gentiles. The gentile people could have remained God's people if they had stayed in God's goodness. What does it mean to stay in God's goodness? It means to stay in the beliefs and deeds which brought them into the bonds of the new covenant by which they became part of the natural olive tree.

Christians can be spared being cut off from God's nation only if they believe, and do what Jesus said and did:

Ro. 11:23     *And they also, if they abide not still in unbelief, shall be grafted in: for God is able to graft them in again.*

This verse states that God will gather the sheep from the two folds and unite them into one fold. Let us note: Jesus' doctrine is clear: the Jews will be grafted onto the natural olive tree. This means that they will be grafted onto Christians who are today a part of the natural olive tree.

In addition to the grafting of the Jewish nation onto Christians, God also announces the judgment upon Christians, which will be held on this earth. All those who do not accept His doctrine in its fullness will be cut off from God's people. Most Christians will experience what the Jewish nation had in the past when they did not accept Jesus' teaching.

Now let us ponder for a moment: What do we Christians believe in? This is important because our beliefs will determine whether we shall be cut off from the natural olive tree.

Today, we preach and believe that we have finished our task on this earth. Jesus Christ will come for a second time to take us into heaven. He can come at any moment. Rapture is at hand. Jesus will come to take us before tribulation or amidst tribulation and other, similar combinations of beliefs.

At the same time most Christians have assumed the belief that we are not Jews in the flesh but in spirit only, though we admit that Jesus was a Jew according to the flesh. We also believe Jesus Christ's words: *I am the head and you are my body.* We firmly believe that Abraham, Isaac, and Jacob are our forefathers and again most Christians say that we do not have anything to do with the Jews in Israel. Our hearts do not recognize them as our earthly brothers. We Christians do not feel that we are Jews according to the flesh, through the faith of Abraham, and that Israel is our land on this Earth. We do not contemplate their salvation, for we believe that God will take care of that. Seldom do we pray for them, and more often not at all.

The Second World War in which one of the worst crimes in the history of mankind was committed, is a testimony that our hearts are far from God's will.

Who committed this crime?

Obviously, those people whose hatred of the Jews was unbounded. It is a sad fact that this occurred in Christian Europe. During this dire time of genocide, the Christian priesthood remained silent.

Let us not ignore what is happening even today. Who is pleading for the land which God ordered for the Jewish nation to be divided between Israel and its enemy? It is mostly the Christian countries: America, Europe, Russia and the United Nation.

Can any good come from such a belief?

Verily, Jesus Christ does not regard our unbelief, rather He says:

Jn. 10:16    *And other sheep I have, which are not of this fold: them also I must bring, and they shall hear my voice;* **and there shall be one fold, and one shepherd.**

Our Lord Jesus Christ knows that He has a small flock in Christianity who will hear His invitation to come to Israel. His task, for which He came to this earth, was to give His life for the sins of the whole world. He will accomplish this when there is one fold and one shepherd.

One fold and one shepherd is the law of the Bible. The entire Bible speaks about unity. Unity is the highest stage of love. There are many examples in the Bible of unification between Christians and the Jewish nation according to the flesh. One of these, which is rarely mentioned, is the example of Abraham.

## Announcement of One Fold and One Shepherd Through Abraham

Because one fold and one shepherd is the law, the Word of God has been speaking about this from the beginning of the faith which was proclaimed by Abraham. The salvation which God gave to humankind has a foundation not only in the faith of Abraham but also in our forefathers Isaac and Jacob. This means that through Abraham, Isaac and Jacob God will make one fold from the Jews and the gentiles, with Jesus Christ as high priest:

He. 11:17    *By faith Abraham, when he was tried, offered up Isaac: and he that had received the promises offered up his only begotten son,*

He. 11:18    *Of whom it was said, That in Isaac shall thy seed be called:*

He. 11:19    **Accounting that God was able to raise him up, even from the dead;** *from whence also he received him in a figure.*

God took Abraham to be the father not only of the Jewish people but also of us who belong to the gentiles, because he believed that God could raise the dead:

Ro. 4:17    *(As it is written, **I have made thee a father of many nations,**) before him whom he believed, even God, who quickeneth the dead, and calleth those things which be not as though they were.*

This is important to note because here the Word of God testifies that from the beginning it was God's intention to have one fold.

Since Abraham is the father of us and the Jewish nation, it means that all the promises which God made to Abraham have been passed to both nations. God explains this through His servant, the apostle Paul, in the following verses.

Ro. 4:11    *And he received the sign of circumcision, a seal of the righteousness of the faith which he had yet being uncircumcised: that he might be the father of all them that believe, though they be not circumcised; that righteousness might be imputed unto them also:*

Ro. 4:12    *And the father of circumcision to them who are not of the circumcision only, **but who also walk in the steps of that faith of our father Abraham, which he had being yet uncircumcised.***

Ro. 4:13    *For the promise, that he should be the heir of the world, was not to Abraham, **OR to his seed,** through the law, but through the righteousness of faith.*

The Word of God states that **all** who **WALK** in the steps of our father Abraham's faith when he was uncircumcised are to receive the promise. In other words, if we execute the faith of Abraham, God will fulfill the promise He made to Abraham and unto his seed as well.

In the next verse we will find an even clearer explanation:

Ga. 3:16    *Now to Abraham and his seed were the promises made. He saith not, And to seeds, as of many; but as of one, **And to thy seed, WHICH IS CHRIST.***

Let us remember these words:

## THE SEED OF ABRAHAM IS CHRIST

If one believes that he is not of the seed of Abraham then he is also not Christ's. Pay attention to what the Word says: only those who have the faith of Abraham can be called Christians. This cannot be any different. Furthermore, these promises belong only to that single seed.

This verse from the Epistle to the Galatians testifies of one fold and one shepherd. There is no other possibility. The Jewish nation must be grafted onto Christians — on Christ — in order to be one seed.

The same is said in the Epistle to the Galatians:

Ga. 3:23      *But before faith came, we were kept under the law, shut up unto the faith which should afterwards be revealed.*

Ga. 3:24      *Wherefore the law was our schoolmaster to bring us unto Christ, that we might be justified by faith.*

Ga. 3:25      *But after that faith is come, we are no longer under a schoolmaster.*

Ga. 3:26      *For ye are all the children of God by faith in Christ Jesus.*

Ga. 3:27      *For as many of you as have been baptized into Christ have put on Christ.*

Ga. 3:28      *There is neither Jew nor Greek, there is neither bond nor free, there is neither male nor female: for ye are all one in Christ Jesus.*

Ga. 3:29      **And if ye be Christ's, then are ye Abraham's SEED, and heirs according to the promise.**

However, we can find words which concern us in the Epistle to the Romans:

Ro. 9:6      *Not as though the Word of God hath taken none effect. For they are not ALL Israel, which are of Israel:*

Ro. 9:7      *Neither, because they are the seed of Abraham, are they ALL children: but, In Isaac shall thy seed be called.*

Ro. 9:8      *That is, They which are the children of the flesh, these are not the children of God: but the children of the promise are counted for the seed.*

Ga. 4:28      **Now we, brethren, as Isaac was, are the children of promise.**

As in the past, all descendants of Israel were not "Israelites". Likewise today, all the people of the New Testament are not "Israelites of the New Testament". Therefore, all those who are "the Seed of Abraham" – all who believe that Jesus was crucified and resurrected – do not necessarily belong to Christ. Only those who offer themselves as a sacrifice to God, as Isaac was sacrificed, are accepted as God's children.

It is inevitable that among us there are wise and foolish individuals, those who glorify God and others who put Him to shame. We understand that two different groups of people exist. However, we do not know to which group we belong. Let us read a rather complex dialogue between Christ and the Pharisees, which is found in the Gospel according to St. John.

Jn. 8:33   *They answered him, We be Abraham's seed, and were never in bondage to any man: how sayest thou, Ye shall be made free?*

Pay attention once again to the words, "the seed of Abraham". The Jews knew that they were "the seed of Abraham" and truly his descendants according to the flesh. Since they were descendants of Abraham they believed that all promises and all blessings belonged to them. Truly, it is so and it must be so. In this passage the Pharisees chastise the Lord: *"we are the seed of Abraham, we were never slaves unto anyone, and therefore, how can you say that we are going to be freed"?* The Pharisees were astonished and puzzled by Christ's words that they needed to be freed from "something" since they believed that the only thing they needed to do was to receive the promised blessings. However, since they harboured such opinions in their hearts they could not understand Christ's mission, nor accept their need for repentance.

Now let us see how Christ responded to the Pharisees.

Jn. 8:34   *Jesus answered them, Verily, verily, I say unto you, Whosoever committeth sin is the servant of sin.*

Jn. 8:35   *And the servant abideth not in the house for ever: but the Son abideth ever.*

Jn. 8:36   *If the Son therefore shall make you free, ye shall be free indeed.*

Jn. 8:37   ***I know that ye are Abraham's seed;** but ye seek to kill me, **because my word hath no place in you.***

As in the past, the Jews do claim Abraham to be their father, and we, too, claim that our father is Abraham and that we are Christ's servants. Furthermore, as in the past, the words of Jesus have no place in the hearts of the Jewish nation. Likewise today, the words of Jesus Christ regarding one fold and one shepherd have no place in the hearts of present-day Christians. In the same manner as the Jews sought to kill Jesus in the past, the voice of Him who spoke against their heart, we spiritually kill — throw off, deny, do not believe — the Word of God (two prophets Revelation 11:3,7,8) in our hearts, because we will not listen to the testimony of God's will.

In order to have the perfect faith of Abraham, we as his seed and as Christians need to understand what exactly God promised to that only seed, which is Christ. If we do not know what God promised unto us through Abraham, then how can we have "the faith of Abraham"? For Abraham believed what God promised to him and to his seed, which is Christ:

Ge. 17:4    *As for me, behold, my covenant is with thee, and thou shalt be a father of many nations.*

Did God fulfill His promise to Abraham? Of course He did. After 2000 years the Word of God is still preached and Abraham has become the father of many nations.

Ge. 17:5    *Neither shall thy name any more be called Abram, **but thy name shall be Abraham;** for a father of many nations have I made thee.*

Today we know that God has fulfilled even this.

Ge. 17:6    *And I will make thee exceeding fruitful, and I will make nations of thee, and kings shall come out of thee.*

Verily, the words of this covenant are completely fulfilled as are the words of the next covenant which states that the God of Abraham is our God.

Ge. 17:7     *And I will establish my covenant between ME and THEE and THY SEED after thee in their generations **for an everlasting covenant**, to be a God unto thee, and to thy seed after thee.*

However, the words of the next covenant have not yet been fulfilled:

Ge. 17:8     *And I will give unto thee, and to THY SEED after thee, the land wherein thou art a stranger, **ALL the land of Canaan, for an everlasting possession;** and I will be their God.*

Christians have not yet received all the land of Canaan for an everlasting possession. In fact, these words create a big problem. Presently, we have chosen what is suitable to us from the covenant God made with Abraham and his seed. We have become choosy like the Jewish nation in the past. The Lord clearly indicated to the Pharisees that they had difficulty believing because they could not hear the will of God due to their own reasoning. To those of us with a materialistic attitude, the spiritual world is unrealistic. When Christians gradually turn materialistic in their hearts and minds, such Christians find themselves driven and guided by their own reasoning rather than by the Word of God.

The fulfillment of God's promise to Abraham, in which He promised to multiply his seed, began with Jesus Christ two thousand years later. This seems completely illogical. According to human reasoning, if God promises something to us we expect the fulfillment to occur according to our own timing and logic. However, four thousand years after Abraham received the promise from God the time has come for us to receive Israel as our country. This goes against our logic.

However, we cannot change the following words of God:

Ga. 3:29     *And **if ye be Christ's, then are ye Abraham's SEED**, and heirs according to the promise.*

Ga. 3:16     *Now to Abraham and his seed were the promises made. He saith not, And to seeds, as of many; but as of one, And **to thy seed, WHICH IS CHRIST**.*

Ge. 17:8     *And I will give unto thee, and to thy seed after thee, the land wherein thou art a stranger, **ALL THE LAND of Canaan, for an everlasting possession;** and I will be their GOD.*

Through the uttered covenant, the promises and the first born blessing given to Abraham, Isaac, Jacob and to us (the seed of Abraham), God has ordered all the important events which will occur on this earth up to the words "*it is done*" (Revelation 16.17). Events mentioned in the covenant cannot be changed, regardless of whether we are able to understand them or not. In the following words we can find a testimony that God ordered future happenings through Abraham:

Ge. 49:1    *And Jacob called unto his sons, and said, Gather yourselves together, that I may tell you that which shall befall you in the last days.*

It is written that the *Old Testament is a shadow of things to come.* Our forefather Jacob, in this shadow of things, gathered his sons to reveal to them what will happen up to the words "it is done". Through the Spirit of God Jacob revealed the distant future to his sons, as well as to us.

Herein, then, lies the problem. Christianity went astray because it did not pay enough attention to the promises God made to our forefathers Abraham, Isaac, and Jacob. This is why we do not understand the events of the End Times, present and future happenings which must occur. We failed to take into account that we are one body with our forefathers. It is not preached that Christians are also Jews in the flesh and that the land where Israel is now situated is given to us as our country. This is why Christianity cannot understand that we are ordered to return into our land in the near future.

Surely, our spiritual land is heaven, where God abides. No one denies this truth. However, when Christians finish their task among the gentiles the moment will have come for their return to their land.

Because we do not pay attention to the fact that we are also Jews in the body and that before God it is greater to be a Jew by the faith of Abraham than it is to be a Jew through Abraham by the law, the question regarding which of Jacob's tribes we belong to seldom enters our mind.

It is not easy to answer this question because our forefather had two wives. His first wife, Leah, was given to him according to custom and his second wife, Rachel, was received from love through mercy. When we discover from which wife we originate, we will then be clear as to which of

Jacob's tribes we Christians belong to. However, it is necessary to establish what a "woman", in a general sense, symbolizes in the Bible.

## The Meaning of "Woman" in the Bible

The answer is found in the Epistle to the Ephesians:

| | |
|---|---|
| Ep. 5:22 | *Wives, submit yourselves unto your own husbands, as unto the Lord.* |
| Ep. 5:23 | *For the husband is the head of the wife, even as Christ is the head of the church: and he is the saviour of the body.* |
| Ep. 5:29 | *For no man ever yet hated his own flesh; but nourisheth and cherisheth it, even as the Lord the church:* |
| Ep. 5:30 | *For we are members of his body, of his flesh, and of his bones.* |
| Ep. 5:31 | *For this cause shall a man leave his father and mother, and shall be joined unto his wife, and they two shall be one flesh.* |
| Ep. 5:32 | **This is a great mystery: but I speak concerning Christ and the church.** |

In a general sense in the Bible, a woman represents a nation or a church. If the apostle did not emphasize the relationship of these words to Christ and to the church, we would easily think that these words were addressed to husbands and wives. However, so that we are sure that this is so, the apostle says the following words in the 33$^{rd}$ verse, that the law of one body also refers to husbands and wives in the flesh. It is evident from this that the same laws rule both the material and the spiritual world. We can understand the spiritual world by observing the material world. The law of unity is the essence of all things visible and invisible. The two, which are not in unity, or which are not one, represent negativity which opposes God.

From the following verses it is possible to see who Abraham, Isaac and Jacob's wives represent in a general sense.

| | |
|---|---|
| Ga. 4:22 | *For it is written, that Abraham had two sons, the one by a bondmaid, the other by a freewoman.* |
| Ga. 4:23 | *But he who was of the bondwoman was born after the flesh; but he of the freewoman was by promise.* |
| Ga. 4:24 | **Which things are an allegory:** *for these are the two covenants; the one from the mount Sinai, which gendereth to bondage, which is Agar.* |

| Ga. 4:25 | *For this Agar is mount Sinai in Arabia, and answereth to Jerusalem which now is, and is in bondage with her children.* |
| Ga. 4:26 | *But Jerusalem which is above is free,* **which is the mother of us all.** |
| Ga. 4:27 | *For it is written, Rejoice, thou barren that bearest not; break forth and cry, thou that travailest not: for the desolate hath many more children than she which hath an husband.* |
| Ga. 4:28 | *Now we, brethren, as Isaac was,* **are the children of promise.** |
| Ga. 4:29 | *But as then he that was born after the flesh persecuted him that was born after the Spirit, even so it is now.* |

Incredibly, the apostle says that Sarah, Abraham's wife, represents the upper, free Jerusalem and that we are the children of that free Jerusalem; through Rebecca, Isaac's wife, we represent the children of promise, again of the same upper Jerusalem (verse 28). It follows that Abraham, Isaac and Jacob's wives, namely Sarah, Rebecca, Leah, and Rachel symbolize upper Jerusalem. Since we are members of that free, upper (heavenly) Jerusalem, the covenant of freedom or the law of mercy through promise which was given to Abraham reigns over us.

The creation of upper Jerusalem through the wives of our forefathers is partially described in the Book of the prophet Ezekiel:

| Eze. 16:2 | *Son of man, cause Jerusalem to know her abominations,* |
| Eze. 16:3 | *And say, Thus saith the Lord GOD unto Jerusalem; Thy birth and thy nativity is of the land of Canaan; thy father was an Amorite, and thy mother an Hittite.* |
| Eze. 16:4 | *And as for thy nativity, in the day thou wast born thy navel was not cut, neither wast thou washed in water to supple thee; thou wast not salted at all, nor swaddled at all.* |
| Eze. 16:5 | *...; but thou wast cast out in the open field, to the lothing of thy person, in the day that thou wast born.* |
| Eze. 16:7 | **I have caused thee to multiply as the bud of the field,** *and thou hast increased and waxen great, and thou art come to excellent ornaments: thy breasts are fashioned, and thine hair is grown, whereas thou wast naked and bare.* |

| Eze. 16:8 | *Now when I passed by thee, and looked upon thee, behold, thy time was the time of love; and I spread my skirt over thee, and covered thy nakedness: yea, I sware unto thee, and entered into a covenant with thee, saith the Lord GOD, and thou becamest mine.* |
|---|---|
| Eze. 16:9 | *Then washed I thee with water; ...* |
| Eze. 16:10 | *I clothed thee also with broidered work, ...* |
| Eze. 16:11 | *I decked thee also with ornaments, ...* |
| Eze. 16:14 | *And thy renown went forth among the heathen for thy beauty: for it was perfect through my comeliness, which I had put upon thee, saith the Lord GOD.* |
| Eze. 16:15 | *But thou didst trust in thine own beauty, and playedst the harlot because of thy renown, and pouredst out thy fornications on every one that passed by; his it was...* |

Verily, the description is unbelievable and fascinating. Every word has its own special meaning and trying to interpret them all would lead us off topic. However, it is necessary to give a brief explanation.

The tribe of the Amorites symbolizes Satan because the Amorites were committing terrible sins. The Hittites, however, symbolize idolatry. Jerusalem was created through these two negatives. The Word of God says that Jerusalem is a "woman" who was created from earth, respectively from human hearts. A heart brings forth fruit when the seed – the spirit – in the form of the word, enters into it. Therefore, the earth symbolizes people who believe in God.

In the beginning human hearts contained the spirit of idolatry and a spirit that opposed God. Jerusalem was born through these two sprits. Jerusalem symbolizes a city (people-nation) longing to be at peace with God. God's people, or citizens of Jerusalem, will appear when faith (as seed), which seeks obedience to God, enters into union with the woman (as the earth) – the human heart which falls in love with God. There is no other way to bring forth children of the faith.

If this is hard to comprehend then ponder the marriage between a young man and a young woman. When a young woman gets married she changes her last name and is ready to bring forth children to her husband.

What does the changing of one's last name represent?

It represents a woman becoming a part of her husband. She is submitting to him. The children that she delivers will take her husband's last name because they are his children.

It is written that every spirit (of man) which sins is enslaved in a mortal body. In addition, every spirit (of man) who wishes to be delivered from sinfulness, death, become righteous and be dressed in an eternal incorruptible body must enter into a union with the righteous heavenly spirit. The human heart (spirit of a sinful man) must "marry" and become one body with the heavenly spirit, must submit to faith (Abraham), be sacrificed (Isaac), and must desire to receive the first born blessings (Jacob) of God and to overcome the spiritual battle (to become Israel). It is not enough to simply enter into the union. In every marriage a husband expects a wife to give birth. If a woman does not give birth all is in vain. Without an heir the family name dies out. Let us say this in a different manner.

Through the union of Abraham and Sarah, or, through the union of faith and the human heart, God's nation was **conceived** (began), because the seed of faith fell on good ground. Through Jacob, his two wives and two handmaids given as wives, twelve sons were delivered; a nation of upper Jerusalem was **born**.

Since on the day of its birth the umbilical cord of upper Jerusalem was not cut, this means that upper Jerusalem continued to be fed with idolatry from its mother. Let us be reminded of an incident when Rachel stole idols from her father's house.

After this, it was not washed clean in water. In other words, they did not go through the process of repentance – remember the hatred Jacob's sons showed toward their brother Joseph. They were then not salted with salt (with God's righteousness), nor were they swaddled at all, in other words, they were not given the law. Swaddling clothes symbolize the law because they are white and clean. The color white denotes righteousness and the assignment of the swaddle is to remove human impurity. This is what God's law does to man. And they were *cast out in the open field*. Upper Jerusalem, as eleven sons – Joseph had already been sold into Egypt – was cast out in the field when they were brought into captivity in Egypt. Through four hundred years of slavery, the Jewish nation multiplied and grew up spiritually. To grow up spiritually means to come to the knowledge of God. Their spiritual

212

maturity happened through the ten wonders which God did through His servant Moses.

Through the characters in the Bible some spirits, or nations, are described. For the sake of this statement an example of the wives of our forefathers Abraham, Isaac, and Jacob was used. However, the use of the male and female principle in the Bible is much more complex. At the same time it gives a deeper understanding of the Word of God.

## Male and Female Principle in the Bible

Upper Jerusalem as a nation was delivered through Jacob's sons. Hereafter, the Word of God refers to it in masculine terms. However, when it was in captivity in Egypt it was described as a maid — a woman who made abominations. This means that in certain cases one nation is described through the masculine or the feminine gender. Why is this so? Or, why does the human heart contain both the male principle (Abraham, Isaac, Israel, Bridegroom, Son etc.), as well as the female principle, described as upper Jerusalem?

Because in a material world the female principle receives the seed, gives birth and multiplies according to the husband's will and is subordinated to the husband's authority. The woman together with her husband is one body, although she is still not a male. The same holds true in the spiritual world. A woman, a virgin, a widow, a bride etc. always represents a nation or a church which must submit to the will of the Word of God.

The male principle (God, Word, thought, spirit, etc.) creates and shapes. A house can never make itself because it is designed by the spirit. Also, all things are recorded in the seed. The male principle is used when a certain spirit is described which reigns in the spiritual world and to whom human hearts (as a woman) should submit.

For example: Jesus Christ as a male principle is the Son and human hearts should submit to that Spirit. When a heart submits itself to the Son, it enters into a union with Him. It is then possible to bring forth fruit.

Let us be reminded of the words which are written for the Jewish nation as they were being led from Egypt. This was the time when the Jewish nation submitted to the mighty hand of God. Because they submitted, Moses was able to lead them from Egypt. Conversely, when the Jewish nation, as upper

Jerusalem, submitted to the will of God, the Word of God does not refer to the Jewish people as upper Jerusalem (or as a woman). The Word describes them as His son Israel, the spirit which will dominate:

Ex. 4:22    *And thou shalt say unto Pharaoh, Thus saith the LORD, Israel is **my son**, even my firstborn:*

Let us consider another example, the parable of the Ten Virgins which symbolizes all of Christianity, wise and foolish, who were sent to await the Bridegroom. This Christianity is described through the feminine gender. The entire message is centered on virgins as the female principle awaiting the Bridegroom (male principle). This means that the virgins should be subordinated to the Spirit of the Bridegroom. A virgin who is not ready is not able to see the Bridegroom. This happens because the hearts of the virgins are not ready to accept the seed (commandment) from the Bridegroom and enter the wedding with this Spirit.

It may sound strange, but everything is based on the male and female principle relation. The question is only what does the male as the seed and the female as the earth represent, irrespective of whether it is grass, a tree, bird, fish, animal, man, building or spiritual world.

Sometimes we may find a message directed toward the masculine gender, when God sends a message to the Spirit of creation. Let us consider an example from Revelation 14. In the first verse it is written:

Re. 14:1    *And I looked, and, lo, a **Lamb** stood on the mount Sion, and with him an hundred forty and four thousand, ...*

Re. 14:4    *These are they which were not defiled with women; for they **are virgins**. ...*

The Lamb is of a masculine gender and those who are with Him are of the same gender, because they were not defiled with women. This means that the Lamb is the Spirit who creates. The only Lamb able to create is Jesus Christ in the Spirit. A description is provided through a lamb, because the role of the lamb is to be sacrificed, to take sins upon itself. Those who follow the Lamb are Christians who submitted to this Spirit and who are ready to follow the Lamb wherever it goes and to be sacrificed with it.

214

Virgins who enter the wedding are actually the one hundred and forty four thousand (this is a symbol and is thus not countable) who follow the Lamb. The Bridegroom and the Lamb are one person, i.e. Jesus Christ in the Spirit. More precisely, the Bridegroom is the Spirit of Jesus Christ who desires to enter into a union with someone. In the parable of the Ten Virgins the Word of God cites that the Bridegroom, Jesus Christ in the Spirit (Word), desires to make a covenant with the Jewish nation gathered in Israel where the Great Supper will be held. Conversely, in John's Revelation, the Word of God, as the Lamb, wants to be sacrificed, take on the sins of others and go somewhere. This somewhere can be Israel, for it remains that only here the Lamb can be sacrificed for the sins of the Jewish nation, the seed of Abraham according to law. It means that the virgins or those who were not defiled with women will follow the Bridegroom or the Lamb (in essence there is no difference), and go to fulfill the task. A man by himself cannot do anything. The Spirit (the Son) must lead him. If a man does not believe, how can he be led by the Spirit? Faith comes only through preaching, listening to the Word of God, meditation, etc.

## To Which of Jacob's Tribe Do Christians Belong?

Historically observed, the fact is that Abraham and his wife Sarah delivered Isaac, whom Abraham offered as a sacrifice upon God's request. Isaac with Rebbekah delivered twins, Esau and Jacob. Through many events, Jacob took the firstborn blessing from his brother Esau, which was earlier prophesied by God. Being deprived of the firstborn blessing, Esau's heart was filled with hate. This was the reason why Jacob sheltered himself at Laban's place, where he fell in love with his younger daughter Rachel and asked her to be his wife. Laban promised to give Jacob his daughter. However, due to different circumstances Jacob was deceived by Laban and instead married Rachel's older sister Leah first. According to custom, a week after his marriage to Leah, Jacob was permitted to marry Rachel, whom he had originally loved, in exchange for an additional seven years of service to Laban.

Now let us examine the spiritual side of these events; spiritual man was conceived through faith (through Abraham). The spiritual man, who believes in the God of Israel and who decides to sacrifice himself (because "Jacob" was

215

born within him) and receive a testimony from God through His sacrifice, must enter into a union with upper Jerusalem (that carnal man may submit to the spiritual) in order to continue growing in the honourable faith of God. Faith and sacrifice in a union with upper Jerusalem delivered two bodies, the twins; one who did not care for the firstborn blessing although it belonged to him (Esau), and the other who cared for the firstborn blessing though it did not belong to him (Jacob).

God gave a testimony that the body who loves the firstborn blessing (Jacob) will prevail. When it prevails, faith, sacrifice and love toward the firstborn blessing will enter in the form of one body into a union with two wives, or with the two upper Jerusalem.

Let us note: Jacob and his two wives are one inseparable body. Only this body can create God's nation – the twelve sons, again as one inseparable body.

Jacob received his first wife, Leah, through common law (law of custom). Although Jacob disliked this union, through it he had to learn certain rules of life. In a spiritual sense this union represents that one must first comprehend the law of God's will - faith, sacrifice through a fear of God and love towards the firstborn blessing (Jacob). Jacob did not comprehend this law until his ten sons were born.

Reuben was Jacob's first son to receive the firstborn blessing. However, Reuben lost this blessing by having sinned. Had he not lost the firstborn blessing, the salvation of humankind would have come through the law for the law was the firstborn from the twelve tribes, i.e. from God's nation.

Since the law could not remain as the firstborn, God allowed Leah and Reuben together to sell the firstborn blessing to Rachel, the wife whom Jacob loved.

Rachel symbolizes upper Jerusalem who delivers through love. This means that Christianity comes from Rachel. However, Leah and Rachel are sisters. They are one bone and one blood. Jesus Christ said: *I did not come to destroy the law, or the prophets, but to fulfill.* Jesus cannot destroy the law for He comes through the Law. This means that Jesus is from Leah, from Judah's tribe.

Judah is the fourth son of Leah. Since Reuben, Simeon and Levi sinned, the firstborn blessing which belongs only to Leah's children was passed to Judah. This is the reason why the Jewish nation which lived according to the

216

Mosaic Law is referred to as Judah, the firstborn from the law. Conversely, Jesus is the firstborn from the dead who was revealed through the law. Therefore, Jesus must be from Judah's tribe, for this tribe is the firstborn according to the common law.

When Jesus came to this earth through the law, as a Lion of the tribe of Judah, the root of David, Leah's children who relied on the law, killed Jesus. They killed Him because He had removed the priority (primogeniture) of common law. Instead of that law, the new law of mercy and love as a newborn was placed, which comes through Rachel's firstborn son Joseph. A testimony that the priority of common law will be removed is described in the blessing given to Leah's son Judah:

Ge. 49:1     *And Jacob called unto his sons, and said,* **Gather yourselves together, that I may tell you that which shall befall you in the last days.**

Ge. 49:9     *Judah is a lion's whelp: from the prey, my son, thou art gone up: he stooped down, he couched as a lion, and as an old lion; who shall rouse him up?*

God announced that Judah would fall asleep as an old lion (confident) and that no one other than Himself would be able nor would dare wake him. To sleep symbolizes to be in sin. Through this symbol God is announcing that Judah, i.e. all Jews according to the law, will fall into sin and in their sin they will be confident as an old lion. In other words, those who live according to the Mosaic Law will fall into such sin from which no one other than God will be able to deliver them (to wake them up, to prove them) because they are blinded by confidence. The type of sin in question is explained in the next verse:

Ge. 49:10    *The sceptre shall not depart from Judah, nor a lawgiver from between his feet, until Shiloh come; and unto him shall the gathering of the people be.*

The Word says that Judah stooped down and crouched as an old lion, because the sceptre departed from him when the appointed time came. This means that the priority of the Mosaic Law represented by the sceptre was taken away. In addition, God Himself departed from his feet. Why? Because, they killed Jesus, their Messiah.

God departed from Judah but God continues to be with Jesus. We have a testimony of this through the words that *unto him shall the gathering of the people be* as well as in the words of the 11ᵗʰ and 12ᵗʰ verses:

Ge. 49:11    *Binding his foal unto the vine, and his ass's colt unto the choice vine; he washed his garments in wine, and his clothes in the blood of grapes:*

Ge. 49:12    *His eyes shall be red with wine, and his teeth white with milk.*

Here is what has been written in Matthew:

Mt. 21:7    *And brought the ass, and the colt, and put on them their clothes, and they set him thereon.*

The ass whereon no man sat except Jesus symbolizes the Jewish people who believe in Him. Jesus will bind this part of the Jewish nation on the vine.

What does the vine represent?

Jn. 15:5    *I am the vine, ye are the branches: He that abideth in me, and I in him, the same bringeth forth much fruit: for without me ye can do nothing.*

The vine represents Jesus Christ who will bind those from the Jewish nation who believe in Him. How will He bind them? He will bind them through His doctrine and ordinance of baptism, i.e. the Holy Spirit.

The Word of God also says in Genesis 49:11 that the ass's colt will be bound unto the choice vine. In John 15:5 the Word of God tells us that Christians are this choice vine. The colt which is of masculine gender will sow the seed in the future when it grows up. The ass's colt was born when Jesus preached His doctrine which means that the colt symbolizes the future priesthood of Christ. This is why the colt follows his Lord Jesus and mother – the Jewish people who believe in Him.

Now let us read the words that describe the binding of the colt to the choice vine or how Jesus bound His disciples with the following commandment:

Mt. 28:18    *And Jesus came and spake unto them, saying, All power is given unto me in heaven and in earth.*

Mt. 28:19    *Go ye therefore, and teach all nations, baptizing them in the name of the Father, and of the Son, and of the Holy Ghost:*

If we compare the words from Genesis 49:11 with Jesus' words from the Gospel where He asked His disciples to bring Him an ass and a colt, we may notice that the disciples first had to unloose the ass (Matthew 21:2) and then bring it to their Lord. In other words, they had to set free the Jewish people from the Mosaic Law in order to be able to bring it closer to the Lord.

In Genesis 49:11 it is also written that: *he washed his garments in wine, and his clothes in the blood of grapes:*

Wine symbolizes Jesus' blood, i.e. the Spirit (law) of the new covenant which intoxicates human souls and leads them to perform good deeds through the love of God. A garment in a general sense symbolizes the decorative element by which we cover our body. Jesus' garment represents God's righteousness and *to wash* symbolically represents justification. On the basis of the provided explanation *to wash garment in wine* denotes to be justified in the sacrifice laid down for all mankind by which Jesus covers His body, God's nation.

In the Book of the prophet Isaiah we read that the garment of vengeance is the zeal in the fulfillment of God's will:

Is. 59:17    *For he put on righteousness as a breastplate, and an helmet of salvation upon his head; and he put on the garments of vengeance for clothing, and was clad with zeal as a cloak.*

The juice of grapes represents Jesus' deeds. When the Lord clad His body with clothing and washed His cloak in the juice of grapes it means that His "body" received additional protection (justification) through His zeal.

It is certain that every word from the cited blessing given to Jacob's sons has a deep spiritual meaning that was fulfilled in the past and is being fulfilled in our time exactly as written in Genesis 49:1: *Gather yourselves together, that I may tell you that which shall befall you in the last days.*

Since Jacob had twelve sons we can come to the conclusion that the number twelve will be divided, because the Jews as a nation, and the children of Leah, did not recognize Jesus Christ as the firstborn from the dead. Conversely, Rachel's children did. Is this correct? Certainly not. It is necessary to understand that in the end there can only be one shepherd before God. This means that the twelve will be transformed into ONE nation. The blessing of Moses spoken through the will of God for Leah's sons shows us that in the end there will only be one fold and one shepherd.

De. 33:7    *And this is the blessing of Judah: and he said,* **Hear, LORD, the voice of Judah, and bring him unto his people:** *let his hands be sufficient for him; and be thou an help to him from his enemies.*

We know that these words of blessing must be fulfilled. There is no possibility that they will not be fulfilled. The first item to note in this blessing is the plea that God grant a prayerful voice of Judah; to all Jews from Abraham according to the law and not according to faith. Then it is written: *bring him unto his people.*

On the one hand these words testify that Judah is rejected by God, and on the other that Judah should be returned unto God's people. To return unto God's nation is possible only through an acknowledgment that they killed Jesus and by going through the ordinance of baptism. Today, Christianity is the natural olive tree and only onto this tree can God's new covenant nation be grafted.

Therefore, only Judah's people, those from Abraham according to the law, can be grafted onto Abraham's seed by their faith in Christ. There is no other way. We must constantly be aware that the number twelve is indivisible in our hearts because it represents God's nation as a whole. The olive tree cannot be divided, namely Jesus and His body cannot be divided. Israel (Jacob) and his body which is made up of two upper Jerusalems (Leah and Rachel) cannot be torn apart (split into two camps). There is only one church of the firstborn. Before God there is only one shepherd and one fold, and only one heavenly kingdom with one law.

The future unity of Leah and Rachel's sons is announced through the buying of the firstborn blessing. Future Christianity is described through the sale of the firstborn blessing and through Rachel as upper Jerusalem, who delivers through love.

Ge. 30:14    *And Reuben went in the days of wheat harvest, and found mandrakes in the field, and brought them unto his mother Leah. Then Rachel said to Leah, Give me, I pray thee, of thy son's mandrakes.*

Ge. 30:15    *And she said unto her, Is it a small matter that thou hast taken my husband? And wouldest thou take away my son's mandrakes also? And Rachel said, Therefore he shall lie with thee to night for thy son's mandrakes.*

Ge. 30:16    *And Jacob came out of the field in the evening, and **Leah** went out to meet him, and **said, Thou must come in unto me;** for surely **I have HIRED thee with my son's mandrakes.** And he lay with her that night.*

In order to be able to understand the meaning of selling the mandrake one must know that the mandrake symbolizes fertility, obtains riches, and reveals the future. Since Rachel bought the mandrakes, this indicates that her children will be blessed with these blessings. The sense of these blessings is primarily spiritual. Thus, through this act Rachel (the law of mercy and love) obtained a blessing of spiritual riches and fertility for her children, while at the same time revealing their spiritual future. She comes by this lawfully, for it was bought from Leah.

If we read the blessing which was poured out upon Joseph, Rachel's firstborn son, it becomes clear what Rachel procured through her purchase of the mandrakes:

First she purchased fertility:

Ge. 49:22    ***Joseph is** a fruitful bough, even **a fruitful bough by a well;** whose branches run over the wall:*

A bough symbolizes a generation, therefore, through this symbol the Word tells us that Joseph represents the generation that will bring forth spiritual fruit to Israel. This bough is placed beside a well – Jesus Christ with His new covenant doctrine – from which it draws strength and life; its bountiful blessings. The branches of this fruitful bough run over the wall. The wall represents protection. In a spiritual world protection comes only from God. The Word of God says that Christianity will multiply from the blessings it will draw from the well. Christianity will multiply to such an extent that it will run over the wall, i.e. over the point of God's protection.

Actually, this is an announcement that deviation from the faith will occur from spiritual welfare which Christianity will draw from the spiritual well.

Secondly, riches were purchased:

Ge. 49:23　*The archers have sorely grieved him, and shot at him, and hated him:*

Ge. 49:24　*But his bow abode in strength, and the arms of his hands were made strong by the hands of the mighty God of Jacob; (from thence **is the SHEPHERD, the stone of Israel:**)*

Ge. 49:25　*Even by the God of thy father, who shall help thee; and by the Almighty, **who shall bless thee** with blessings of heaven above, blessings of the deep that lieth under, blessings of the breasts, and of the womb:*

Ge. 49:26　*The blessings of thy father have prevailed above the blessings of my progenitors unto the utmost bound of the everlasting hills: they shall be on the head of Joseph, and on the crown of the head of him that was separate from his brethren.*

In the above verses we find a description of unimaginable riches that will be poured upon Joseph's bough and branches. One of the most valuable blessings given is that Jesus Christ has chosen the apostles and established a Christian priesthood from Joseph's bough, i.e. became the shepherd, the stone of (new covenant) Israel.

Thirdly, a testimony that the firstborn blessing will be upon Joseph's bough and branches is given:

Ge. 37:3　*Now Israel loved Joseph more than all his children, because he was the son of his old age: and he made him a coat of many colours.*

Ge. 37:4　*And when his brethren saw that their father loved him more than all his brethren, they hated him, and could not speak peaceably unto him.*

Ge. 37:5　*And Joseph dreamed a dream, and he told it his brethren: and they hated him yet the more.*

Ge. 37:6　*And he said unto them, Hear, I pray you, this dream which I have dreamed:*

Ge. 37:7　*For, behold, we were binding sheaves in the field, and, lo, **my sheaf arose, and also stood upright; and, behold, your sheaves stood round about, and made obeisance to my sheaf.***

| | |
|---|---|
| Ge. 37:8 | *And his brethren said to him,* **Shalt thou indeed reign over us? or shalt thou indeed have dominion over us?** *And they hated him yet the more for his dreams, and for his words.* |
| Ge. 37:9 | *And he dreamed yet another dream, and told it his brethren, and said, Behold, I have dreamed a dream more; and, behold,* **the sun and the moon and the eleven stars made obeisance to me.** |
| Ge. 37:10 | *And he told it to his father, and to his brethren: and his father rebuked him, and said unto him, What is this dream that thou hast dreamed?* **Shall I and thy mother and thy brethren indeed come to bow down ourselves to thee to the earth?** |
| Ge. 37:11 | *And his brethren envied him;* **but his father OBSERVED the saying.** |

Joseph's father (Israel) received a great testimony that the firstborn blessing would be transferred to Joseph. He kept these words in his heart. He knew that Rachel's firstborn would receive the firstborn blessing. Even Joseph's brothers themselves interpreted the dream and said; *shall thou indeed reign over us?* They knew that it was a message from God. Therefore, it is written that *they hated him yet the more for his dreams.* Father Israel also understood that this was a message from God. This is why it is written; *but his father observed the saying.*

These two dreams clearly revealed that Rachel's children would possess the firstborn blessing and through it reign over Leah's children. The Mosaic Law cannot be above Christ's Law of mercy and love.

If we were asked how many sons Israel (Jacob) had, many who read the Old Testament would say twelve. However, it would be more accurate to say fourteen, because Israel took two of Joseph's sons, Manasseh and Ephraim, who were born in the land of Egypt, as his own:

| | |
|---|---|
| Ge. 48:1 | *And it came to pass after these things, that one told Joseph, Behold, thy father is sick: and he took with him his two sons, Manasseh and Ephraim.* |
| Ge. 48:2 | *And one told Jacob, and said, Behold, thy son Joseph cometh unto thee: and Israel strengthened himself, and sat upon the bed.* |
| Ge. 48:3 | *And Jacob said unto Joseph, God Almighty appeared unto me at Luz in the land of Canaan, and blessed me,* |

| Ge. 48:4 | *And said unto me, Behold, I will make thee fruitful, and multiply thee, and I will make of thee a multitude of people; and will give this land **to thy seed** after thee **for an everlasting possession.*** |
|---|---|
| Ge. 48:5 | *And now **thy two sons, Ephraim and Manasseh,** which were born unto thee in the land of Egypt BEFORE I came unto thee into Egypt, **are mine;** as Reuben and Simeon, they shall be mine.* |
| Ge. 48:8 | *And Israel beheld Joseph's sons, and said, Who are these?* |
| Ge. 48:9 | *And Joseph said unto his father, They are my sons, whom God hath given me in this place. And he said, Bring them, I pray thee, unto me, and I will bless them.* |
| Ge. 48:17 | *And when Joseph saw that his father laid his right hand upon the head of Ephraim, it displeased him: and he held up his father's hand, to remove it from Ephraim's head unto Manasseh's head.* |
| Ge. 48:18 | *And Joseph said unto his father, Not so, my father: for this is the firstborn; put thy right hand upon his head.* |
| Ge. 48:19 | *And his father refused, and said, I know it, my son, I know it: he also shall become a people, and he also shall be great: but **truly his younger brother shall be greater than he, and his seed shall become a multitude of nations.*** |

The quoted text provides us with a testimony that only Ephraim, of the tribes of Israel, received the firstborn blessing from his father Israel, rather than from Jacob. All prophesies to occur on this earth have been completed with Ephraim. And most importantly, all previous promises of God belong to him as the last on whom the firstborn blessing was bestowed.

Who does Ephraim represent?

We should note some facts: when Joseph was sold to Egypt, the Pharaoh gave him for a wife the daughter of Potipher, the priest. Through this Joseph became one body with Asenath (Genesis 41:45) who was of gentile origin. Let us also be reminded of the blessing given to Joseph: *from thence is the shepherd* (Genesis 49:24). This means that God ordered Joseph to be the shepherd – a priest to Israel. This is why he could only marry a priest's daughter. In addition, this is a sign that the God of Israel will choose priests descending from Joseph's sons for Himself in the time of Christianity.

Through God's providence, Joseph spent his life in Egypt pleasing God. Even though he was married to Asenath, he did not accept Egypt's gods. His wife also accepted the God of Israel as her God. This means that

Joseph's wife is upper Jerusalem from the gentiles. Asenath delivered several children, although it was determined by God that her first two sons would be taken away from her and become tribes of Israel through His will. This is a key event to which little attention is paid.

In the quoted verses (Genesis 48:1-19) we have a testimony that Jacob really had fourteen sons after he took his grandsons, Manasseh and Ephraim. Fourteen tribes did not exist. We know that Dan's tribe was erased from the inheritance, because his name is not mentioned in John's Revelation. Thus, thirteen tribes remain. Since the old covenant is a shadow of things to come, the number thirteen must likewise appear in the new covenant.

Verily, Jesus had twelve apostles. When Judas Iscariot betrayed Jesus, he was erased from the apostleship. Matthew was chosen to be the new apostle. After this, Jesus Christ called Paul into service. Therefore, the number thirteen appears again.

Why were there thirteen tribes of Israel and thirteen apostles of Jesus Christ?

This question is very important, especially because we know that the number thirteen contradicts the rule which states that a nation is described through the number twelve. There must be a reason for this. First we can note that the thirteen apostles represent the priesthood of the nation which, surprisingly at the moment, consists of thirteen tribes. According to spiritual law this is not possible. Secondly, twelve tribes have twelve apostles, so Ephraim's tribe, the 13$^{th}$ tribe, was created (born) among the gentiles through Joseph as a Jew and his gentile wife Asenath. This means, that Ephraim's tribe symbolizes the gentiles. Thus, their priesthood has to be of gentile origin. Apostle Paul, ordered by God to be an apostle to the gentiles, is of such origin. Although his father was a Jew his mother was of gentile origin. It is written in Acts 22:25: *is it lawful for you to scourge a man that is a Roman.*

The existence of two folds is the reason for the appearance of the number thirteen. One flock of the saved, described by the number twelve, is from the Jewish fold and the second flock, represented by the number one, is from the gentile fold. Let us be reminded of God's words that only Ephraim received the firstborn blessing from his father Israel. This means that no one can take this blessing from him.

Based on this, we can conclude that the number twelve will be grafted on the number one and will become one with it.

Eze. 36:12    *Yea, I will cause men to walk upon you, even MY people Israel; and **they shall possess thee, and thou shalt be their inheritance,** and thou shalt no more henceforth bereave them of men.*

Since the number twelve always represents a nation this means that the nation will be described through the twelve tribes and the priesthood through the twelve apostles. But the seed of Abraham through faith which is Christ, Ephraim's tribe, will possess the firstborn right.

In John's Revelation we can find a testimony that two nations will be united into one fold in the near future:

Re. 7:4    *And I heard the number of them which were sealed: and there were sealed an hundred and forty and four thousand of **all the tribes of the children of Israel.***

Re. 7:5    *Of the tribe of Juda were sealed twelve thousand. Of the tribe of Reuben were sealed twelve thousand. Of the tribe of Gad were sealed twelve thousand.*

Re. 7:8    *Of the tribe of Zebulon were sealed twelve thousand. Of the tribe of Joseph were sealed twelve thousand. Of the tribe of Benjamin were sealed twelve thousand.*

John's Revelation refers only to the new covenant time period, to those sealed with the Holy Spirit. Based on this fact, it follows that in the seventh chapter the Word of God describes those sealed with the Holy Spirit from the Jewish nation. The names of all twelve tribes of Israel are listed in Revelation 7:5-8. Twelve thousand will be saved from each tribe. All of Jacob's sons are named except for Dan and Ephraim. Dan's tribe has been removed from the inheritance (*he is a snake and he judges his brothers*), while Ephraim, who received the biggest firstborn blessing, is not among the twelve.

However, in the 9th verse we have a description of those saved from the gentiles, those from Ephraim's tribe.

Re. 7:9     *After this I beheld, and, lo, **a great multitude, which no man could number,** of all nations, and kindreds, and people, and tongues, stood before the throne, and before the Lamb, clothed with white robes, and palms in their hands;*

Verily, the multitude that stood before the Lamb's throne were those sealed from Ephraim's seed. This is the thirteenth tribe. Let us be reminded of the blessing father Israel gave to Ephraim: *truly his younger brother shall be greater than he, and his seed shall become a multitude of nations,* the great multitude of nations from Revelation 7:9.

A question arises: why does chapter seven of John's Revelation separately cite those sealed from the twelve tribes and those from Ephraim's tribe as if they were two different nations?

It is because Jesus' words about one fold and one shepherd had not yet been fulfilled. A testimony of this is found in the fact that the Jewish people have a veil over their eyes, and are scattered across this globe. When the words about one fold and one shepherd come to be true, the Jewish people will no longer be out of Israel because there will only be a "lake of fire" and a "camp of the saints" on this earth.

The first verses of John's Revelation, chapter seven, announce that in the beginning Christians will be described as two folds because a portion of the Jewish people have yet to believe:

Re. 7:1     *And after these things I saw four angels standing on the four corners of the earth, holding the four winds of the earth, that the wind should not blow on the earth, nor on the sea, nor on any tree.*

Re. 7:2     *And I saw another angel ascending from the east, having the seal of the living God: and he cried with a loud voice to the four angels, to whom it was given to hurt the earth and the sea,*

Re. 7:3     *Saying, Hurt not the earth, neither the sea, nor the trees, till we have sealed the servants of our God in their foreheads.*

God ordered four angels to *hurt not the earth, neither the sea, nor the trees till He seals His servants.* Through this order God made it possible for three groups of people to believe in Jesus Christ: those who believe in the God of Israel (the earth), those who do not believe in Him (the sea) and the people who bring forth fruit to God, those who live according to His commandments (the trees).

Angels were told the words "hurt not" at the time when the four winds of earth did not blow on the earth, neither the sea, nor on any tree. When the sealing of servants among the gentiles is over or when the number of those saved from the gentiles is fulfilled, the four angels will be set free. When this happens no one can be sealed by God's seal (which God recognizes) except those who are in the camp of saints (Revelation 20:9).

The four angels will be let loose at the sounding of the sixth trumpet.

Re. 9:13     *And the sixth angel sounded, and I heard a voice from the four horns of the golden altar which is before God,*

Re. 9:14     *Saying to the sixth angel which had the trumpet, **Loose the four angels** which are bound in the great river Euphrates*

Re. 9:15     *And the four angels were loosed, which were prepared for an hour, and a day, and a month, and a year, for **to slay the third part of men.***

The voice of the sixth angel who will sound the trumpet is calling the sheep of Christ among the gentiles to come to Israel, so that the words of Jesus concerning one fold and one shepherd may be fulfilled. Through their departure, more and more angels will be set free because one third of the world must be slain and the Antichrist must establish his power. In other words, no gentile will be saved because for him the day of mercy is over.

Therefore, until the sound of the sixth trumpet is heard, the words of Jesus speaking of one fold cannot be fulfilled. This is why the seventh chapter of Revelation describes these 144,000 from the twelve tribes of Israel and the great multitude (Ephraim) as two folds.

If we read Revelation 21, which refers to our time, we will be provided with further proof that there exists one fold and one shepherd.

*14*

# THE NEW HEAVEN
# AND
# THE NEW EARTH

The verity of Jesus' words about one shepherd and one fold honouring Him as high priest can be found in Revelation 21. This chapter is dedicated to the new heaven, the new earth and the New Jerusalem, referred to by many as the Golden Jerusalem. There exist today divergent beliefs about the new heaven and the new earth, one centered on the question of where the "Golden Jerusalem" should descend. It has become customary thinking for many to believe that the New Jerusalem will be a real town built of earthly gold in heaven and will then be sent down to Earth. In essence, most believe that the present universe will be destroyed and a new one created, the new heaven and the new Earth[16]. In order for us to show the truthfulness of Jesus' word concerning one fold, it is necessary to understand what the new heaven and earth represent in a spiritual sense. Only through an explanation of the New Jerusalem will we be able to show the unity of these two folds.

## A Heaven and an Earth

Heaven and earth are mentioned in the Bible in many places. As with everything else in the Bible, both heaven and earth can be interpreted in a literal or a spiritual sense. In general, the earth in a spiritual sense represents the heart of man who believes God. Words used to describe earth, such as good, thorny, wilderness, sea sand, new earth etc., help us understand the state of an individual's heart or the heart of an entire nation. For example,

---

[16]    Many believe that God will create a new planet.

if the earth is described as a wilderness, the "wilderness" represents the servants of God who have not submitted to His will and who do not have the Spirit of God within them. They are arid (empty) like the wilderness which lacks water. In the same manner, when the earth is good, water will fall on her good seed, and bear fruit:

Mk. 4:20     *And these are they which are sown on good ground; such as hear the word, and receive it, and bring forth fruit, some thirtyfold, some sixty, and some an hundred.*

In a general spiritual sense, heaven represents the nation whose task it is to light the path of individuals walking in darkness (sin) in a spiritual night, by the stars and the moon. The Bible speaks of heaven in different terms, such as: heavens, third heaven, present heaven, new heaven etc. This means that God is portraying a different group of His people who in the history of mankind had the task of illuminating, i.e. preaching to people living contrary to God's will. If we know which heaven depicts which group, we will then be able to discern which historical time period is being illustrated.

Certainly, heaven and earth can sometimes be understood in a literal sense. However, we should note that the message is primarily sent in a spiritual sense. The moment we accept the reality of these terms in a spiritual sense, we will accept the existence of a spiritual heaven and earth on this globe.

The first chapter of Genesis begins with the creation of the first heaven and earth in the first spiritual day. This day lasted from Adam's fall up to the end of the great flood, when people went astray from God:

Ge. 1:1     *In the beginning God created the heaven and the earth.*
Ge. 1:2     *And the earth was without form, and void; and darkness was upon the face of the deep. And the Spirit of God moved upon the face of the waters.*
Ge. 1:3     *And God said, Let there be light: and there was light.*
Ge. 1:4     *And God saw the light, that it was good: and God **divided** the light from the darkness.*
Ge. 1:5     *And God called the light Day, and the darkness he called Night. And the evening and the morning were the first day.*

Although God created heaven and earth at the very beginning, their creation is not highlighted. The focus is on the creation of light in the midst of existing darkness. Why? Because Adam and Eve had already sinned. Their hearts knew God. This means, their hearts are the earth, although the earth is void and without form (in darkness). The earth is without form because they did not honour God's will. It is void because they did not have the Spirit of God in them.

The 3rd verse speaks of the creation of light, i.e. God created light through Abel (generation – line of light) and divided light from darkness through the flood. In this manner a sinful man was drowned and a righteous man was delivered. This means that heaven and earth, or the world which existed from Adam to the flood, had perished:

2 Pe. 3:5   *For this they willingly are ignorant of, that by the Word of God the heavens were of old, and the earth standing out of the water and in the water:*

2 Pe. 3:6   *Whereby the world that then was, being overflowed with water, perished:*

Words from Genesis explain that the world of that day was destroyed by the flood. This includes the earth (as hearts) as well as heaven, which was charged with the task of lighting the path for a sinful world and which did not want to enter Noah's ark. Apostle Peter said this in the 6th verse: *Whereby the world that then was, being overflowed with water, perished.*

After the great flood, God once again created heaven and earth. It is written in the Book of the prophet Isaiah:

Is. 1:2   *Hear, O heavens, and give ear, O earth: for the LORD hath spoken, I have nourished and brought up children, and they have rebelled against me.*

Is. 1:3   *The ox knoweth his owner, and the ass his master's crib: but Israel doth not know, my people doth not consider.*

This means that the creation of the old covenant heaven and earth is at stake. The old covenant heaven lasted from the great flood until the crucifixion of Jesus. Prophet Jeremiah described the Jewish nation before they were led into captivity, through the symbols of heaven and earth:

Je. 4:22   *For my people is foolish, they have not known me; they are sottish children, and they have none understanding: they are wise to do evil, but to do good they have no knowledge.*

Je. 4:23        *I beheld* **the earth,** *and, lo, it* **was without form, and void; and the heavens,** *and they* **had no light.**

John's Revelation speaks the following words regarding the destruction of the old covenant heaven and earth:

Re. 6:12        *And I beheld when he had opened the sixth seal, and, lo, there was a great earthquake; and the sun became black as sackcloth of hair, and the moon became as blood;*

Re. 6:13        *And the stars of heaven fell unto the earth, even as a fig tree casteth her untimely figs, when she is shaken of a mighty wind.*

Re. 6:14        *And* **the heaven departed as a scroll when it is rolled together;** *and every mountain and island were moved out of their places.*

The Word of God says that the opening of the sixth seal caused heaven to depart as a "scroll when it is rolled together", the sun became black, and the moon became as blood.

The opening of the sixth seal on the Book was the crucifixion of Jesus. Through the spilling of His blood Jesus sealed the new covenant, i.e. empowered it.

He. 9:14        *How much more shall the blood of Christ, who through the eternal Spirit offered himself without spot to God, purge your conscience from dead works to serve the living God?*

He. 9:15        *And for this cause he is the mediator of the new testament, that by means of death, for the redemption of the transgressions that were under the first testament, they which are called might receive the promise of eternal inheritance.*

He. 9:16        *For where a testament is, there must also of necessity be the death of the testator.*

He. 9:17        *For a testament is of force after men are dead: otherwise it is of no strength at all while the testator liveth.*

With this deed the Old Testament, i.e. the old covenant heaven and earth, was abolished. Therefore, God terminated its importance and described this event through symbols. Heaven was rolled as a scroll. The "scroll" (Old Testament Book given by God) was not destroyed. If it were destroyed, it would no longer be a source of preaching. However, the rolling together of heaven caused the old covenant sun to darken. Because the sun (the priesthood in old covenant Israel) darkened (lacking spiritual life within themselves), it lost the ability to light the earth (the hearts of men believing in the Messiah's Law), and illuminate the darkness (people who live in unbelief and ignorance). When the sun blackened, the moon (old covenant church) could not receive light nor reflect it to illuminate the earth shrouded in darkness (ignoring the will of God) at night. The Word of God says that the moon was transformed into blood.

Why?

Because the soul is in the blood, which is life. The old covenant moon, a woman, i.e. the church delivering children to God, could not deliver living children. She did not receive light from the sun nor did the sun receive a blessing from God. Thus, the moon's blood must change into the blood "as of a dead man". These words are not directly written, because there are no words written "as of a dead man". These words are written indirectly, through the verses of Revelation 6:12-14. Here, everything is described in a negative sense. When words are written in a negative sense, we need to realize that an old covenant moon which fulfilled God's will did exist, as well as an old covenant moon which did not fulfill His will. The moon which fulfilled God's will was alive and delivering living children. Unfortunately, when the entire old covenant moon, through God's order, lost the right to continue its task, it was transformed into the blood "as of a dead man".

For the sake of clarity, let us recall what the meaning of Jesus' blood was. The blood of Jesus gives life to those who are in darkness. Most of Christianity as a new covenant moon in the new covenant heaven delivers living children. Also, the new covenant church feeds her children with Jesus' body (bread), and gives them drink – Jesus' blood (wine).

When the new covenant was empowered, a new covenant heaven was created. The new covenant heaven is third in line with the sun, moon and stars. This also applies to the new covenant earth (i.e. before Jesus' crucifixion the new covenant church, the priesthood and the nation believing in the new covenant were created, but received validity only after the crucifixion). This is the fourth spiritual day from the first chapter of Genesis.

Take note that the Word of God speaks of the destruction of heaven and earth as well as of their creation. The cause of this is sin. God did not execute the destruction of heaven and earth without ample warning to the generation concerned. This is why the seventh verse says that present-day Christianity and those believing in God and Jesus Christ will be kept unto the Day of Judgment. The remaining verses describe the judgment itself.

2 Pe.3:7     **But the heavens and the earth, which are now,** *by the same word are kept in store, reserved unto fire against the day of judgment and perdition of ungodly men.*

2 Pe.3:10    *But the day of the Lord will come as a thief in the night; in the which the heavens shall pass away with a great noise, and the elements shall melt with fervent heat, the earth also and the works that are therein shall be burned up.*

2 Pe.3:11    *Seeing then that all these things shall be dissolved, what manner of persons ought ye to be in all holy conversation and godliness,*

2 Pe.3:12    *Looking for and hasting unto the coming of the day of God, wherein the heavens being on fire shall be dissolved, and the elements shall melt with fervent heat?*

Today it is not preached that heaven and earth represent present-day Christianity. This is why we have trouble understanding the judgment and where it will take place.

When the coming of the last judgment is preached, it is stated that it will take place in heaven, and the universe as a material heaven and earth will be destroyed by fire.

The Bible speaks of catastrophic difficulties. It is not prophesied as a judgment, yet as a tribulation which will come upon all of humankind. This means that present-day Christianity understands the 10th and 12th verses as destruction of this Earth and as an entire universe. The other texts found in John's Revelation speak of the tribulation for present-day Christianity. These are therefore two separate events for Christianity.

If we read the Word of God carefully, we will understand that the universe cannot be destroyed because it is part of God. Scientists today already know that the galaxy dies and is reborn. This is an eternal process which is under God's supervision. This means that Peter's Epistle speaks of the judgment, or the last judgment, which will take place on this earth and which will be experienced by Christianity.

This last judgment which 2 Peter 3:7 speaks of encapsulates the realization that gentile Christianity will be rejected, and God's blessings, His mercy and His protection will be revoked. A testimony will be manifested through the realization of the removal of the Holy Spirit and through God's prohibition of the union of one fold and one shepherd (between Israel of Ephraim and Israel of Judah).

This is what apostle Peter says:

2 Pe.3:13      *Nevertheless we, according to his promise, look for new heavens and a new earth, wherein dwelleth righteousness.*

God will establish heaven and earth, fourth in line, named the new heaven and the new earth, after the executed judgment of Christians among the gentiles. God will establish this new heaven and new earth in Israel, for the sake of His new covenant nation and for the salvation of the Jewish people. There is a difference between the present heaven and earth and the new heaven and earth which God will soon create. The difference lies in the fact that righteousness will reign in the new heaven. In the present heaven, God called both bad and good, so that His house could be filled.

Mt.22:9       *Go ye therefore into the highways, and as many as ye shall find, bid to the marriage.*
Mt.22:10      *So those servants went out into the highways,* **and gathered together all as many as they found, both bad and good:** *and the wedding was furnished with guests.*

In such conditions, where good and evil coexist, where even spiritual Jerusalem was named Sodom by God, righteousness could not live, nor reign, in the present heaven.

Re. 11:8      *And their dead bodies shall lie in the street of the great city, which spiritually is called Sodom and Egypt, where also our Lord was crucified.*

This is why the last judgment must come. However, the description of the new heaven and the new earth does not mention the judgment. In that heaven righteousness will reign. There will also be no last judgment because death will not exist (Note: the new heaven and earth is not the kingdom of the millennium in a physical sense, as interpreted by present-day

Christianity). The new heaven, the new earth, and the New Jerusalem, in which the Lamb of Light reigns, will last forever.

Re. 21:4      *And God shall wipe away all tears from their eyes; and their shall be no more death, neither sorrow, nor crying, neither shall there be any more pain : for the former things are passed away.*

On the basis of everything which was quoted and explained, we see that the new heaven and earth represent Christianity in Israel, assembled from the ready virgins (Matthew 25:10), and the New Jerusalem is the spiritual building.

## The New Jerusalem

Evidence that New Jerusalem is a spiritual rather than physical building is found in the following words:

Re. 21:14     *And the wall of the city had twelve foundations, and in them the names of the twelve apostles of the Lamb*

The foundation of this town is the doctrine of Jesus Christ based on number 12 which establishes the new covenant priesthood — the twelve apostles of Jesus Christ. This is the reason why the foundation bears the names of the apostles:

Ef. 2:20      **And are built upon the foundation of the apostles and prophets,** *Jesus Christ himself being the chief corner stone;*

Ef. 2:21      *In whom all the building fitly framed together groweth unto an holy temple in the Lord:*

Ef. 2:22      *In whom ye also are builded together for an habitation of God through the Spirit.*

He. 6:1       *Therefore leaving the principles of the doctrine of Christ, let us go on unto perfection;* **not laying again the foundation** *of repentance from dead works, and of faith toward God,*

He. 6:2       *Of the doctrine of baptisms, and of laying on of hands, and of resurrection of the dead, and of eternal judgment.*

The principles of Christ's doctrine as repentance from dead works, faith toward God, baptism, laying of the hands, resurrection of the dead, eternal judgment etc. are the foundation on which the apostles and prophets based their teaching. It is what the Word of God speaks of in Revelation 21. This means that God's doctrine is the foundation of the New Jerusalem and all teaching which is based on this foundation bears the name of one of the twelve apostles of Christ. Only these twelve foundations support the wall of New Jerusalem. This wall symbolizes God's protection. In other words: only the hearts of men who are built on the foundation of the New Jerusalem – the doctrine of Christ – will have God's protection and possess the right to dwell in the New Jerusalem. Jesus Christ Himself is the cornerstone of the foundation.

Since the foundation of the New Jerusalem is spiritual it means that the whole town is spiritual, that it is already built and exists in heaven. The heavenly Jerusalem is filled with citizens who have surrendered their lives in purity up to this moment. The Word of God speaks of the construction of this spiritual heavenly Jerusalem which will come down from heaven onto this earth and whose tabernacle will dwell among men (live amongst people).

Re. 21:2　　*And I John saw the holy city, new Jerusalem, coming down from God out of heaven, prepared as a bride adorned for her husband.*

The New Jerusalem is a holy city and represents the Lamb's wife. It is described as a bride for the new earth because the Jewish people will repent and acknowledge Jesus Christ as her husband i.e. the Lord. On the other hand, Christians who are found worthy to go to Israel need to repent, because they are presently slumbering and sleeping (Matthew 25). This is a requirement for becoming citizens of the New Jerusalem, i.e. becoming the wife of the Lamb.

Re. 19:7　　*Let us be glad and rejoice, and give honour to him: for the marriage of the Lamb is come, and his wife hath made herself ready.*

Re. 19:8　　*And to her was granted that she should be arrayed in fine linen, clean and white: for the fine linen is the righteousness of saints.*

God testifies that nothing unclean will enter the New Jerusalem because it is established on twelve foundations, i.e. on the twelve apostles who watch the fulfillment of God's will. God will judge everything derived from the number twelve. There will be no tolerance for additions or subtractions to the Lord's doctrine.

What then does the apostle Paul, who is responsible for the gentiles as the 13th apostle, represent? Does he bring some other doctrine? Let us see what is written:

| | |
|---|---|
| Ac. 9:15 | *But the Lord said unto him, Go thy way: for he is a chosen vessel unto me,* **to bear my name before the Gentiles, and kings, and the children of Israel:** |
| Ac. 9:16 | *For I will shew him how great things he must suffer for my name's sake.* |

The Word of God says that he is responsible for all doctrine built on the twelve foundations to be brought before the gentiles. And not only before them, but before the children of Israel, so that God's name will be glorified. This means apostle Paul alone is included in the number twelve.

The number thirteen does not represent a separate doctrine. But it confuses the servants of Christ. The Word of God does not describe apostle Paul as the thirteenth apostle or Ephraim as the thirteenth tribe of Israel. On the contrary, the Word of God speaks of apostle Paul as being number one. He is a chosen vessel. He is not the thirteenth vessel, nor the thirteenth foundation. He is the one and very special foundation who contains all twelve foundations in himself.

The task of apostle Paul, who represents Christ's priesthood from the gentiles, is to bring God's doctrine to three groups of people: the gentiles, the kings of the earth, and the children of Israel. He must take the doctrine before all men. The kings of the earth are not a special group of people in the sense of rulers of this earth. The term refers to Christians who rule over sin. The gentile priesthood will present God's doctrine to the children of Israel when God creates the new heaven and the new earth.

In Revelation 21 it is written:

Re. 21:24     *And the nations of them which are saved shall walk in the*
              *light of it: and the kings of the earth do bring their glory and*
              *honour into it.*

These kings are the angels of the Son of man, repentant gentiles who will bring glory and honour of the nations into the New Jerusalem:

Re. 21:26     *And they shall bring the glory and honour of the nations into it.*

The time will then come for the Jewish nation to enter the New Jerusalem through our crucified Jesus Christ. This means, the walls of the New Jerusalem cannot have thirteen doors because twelve symbolizes God's nation. This is why Christians, the dear children of Israel from Ephraim, will enter New Jerusalem through walls containing twelve doors. This means that Ephraim, just as apostle Paul, alone contains the number twelve within himself.

What then does the door in the wall of the New Jerusalem symbolize?

It symbolizes the human heart — the image of Jesus Christ. Two Christians with identical hearts do not exist (i.e. the perfect fullness of Jesus Christ). It is, however, possible to classify hearts. The Word of God testifies that Jesus is the door from the New Jerusalem. This means that Jesus Christ is simultaneously the foundation, the door and the light of the New Jerusalem, which is established on the number twelve. There is no church in the New Jerusalem because the Lamb (Jesus crucified) is the Church. His citizens consist of sheep from the gentile and Jewish nations. There will be one shepherd and one fold. The New Jerusalem is the united body of Christ.

# 15

# THE BOOK OF THE PROPHET EZEKIEL, CHAPTER 37

The 37th chapter contains a memorable description of the past, present and future events through which we can see how God will create, step by step, one fold[17] with one shepherd. At the beginning of this prophecy God posed this question to the prophet Ezekiel: *"can these bones live"?* He was speaking of the bones which he saw in the spirit, thrown about in the valley:

| | |
|---|---|
| Eze.37:1 | *The hand of the LORD was upon me, and carried me out in the spirit of the LORD, and set me down in the midst of the valley which was full of bones,* |
| Eze.37:2 | *And caused me to pass by them round about: and, behold, there were very many in the open valley; and, lo, they were very dry.* |
| Eze.37:3 | *And he said unto me, Son of man, can these bones live? And I answered, O Lord GOD, thou knowest.* |

Since the prophet could not provide an answer, he said to the Lord: *Thou knowest.*

Verily, God knows the answer to this question. Further in the text God explains the steps through which the Jewish nation will be made alive. To become alive means to be one with the Lord and that is attainable only if Jesus Christ is recognized as our Saviour, for God and Jesus Christ are one. Because the Jewish nation still does not believe in the Son, they must first believe in Christ before the prophesied words "one fold" are fulfilled.

The whole text of chapter 37 speaks of how the Jewish nation will be brought to life spiritually, be grafted onto the olive tree and be merged into one fold led by one shepherd.

---

[17]  The unification of Christians and Jews in Israel.

The first eight verses speak of the Jewish people (captives of Zion) returning to their land but not of admitting their guilt. Having lived among the gentiles for nineteen hundred years did not help them in their understanding. Even those Jews who as *dry* through God's mercy were returned to their land did not comprehend their guilt although hundred years had passed since the beginning of their gathering. To be dry means to be without the Holy Spirit or to be spiritually dead, spiritually blind, living in unbelief and ignoring the will of God.

In order for the Jewish nation to be made spiritually alive, the Lord God will return the dry bones to their land. This has already been discussed. However, so that we may get a more complete picture, it is necessary to include several details.

Until now the Lord had twice delivered the Jewish people from slavery. The first instance of deliverance was from slavery in Egypt and the second from Babylonian slavery. We can now observe how God poured His mercy on His people a third time. This third instance is deliverance from the slavery of this world which will unfold in a different manner from the first two. This third exodus will have many components in common with the first two. One such is that these three instances take years to unfold and consist of several steps.

From these eight verses we will come to know by which steps the dry bones will be returned to their land:

- First through prophesying.
- Then there was a voice (referring to the Balfour Declaration of 1918).
- Next came the shaking (representing the murder of six million Jews between 1937 – 1945).
- The coming together of the bones.
- The bone came to his bone. The forming of the skeleton (the creation of Israel in 1948).
- The sinews and flesh came upon them (their gathering, which continued from 1948 to present day).
- The skin covers them above – the body is formed (representing the recognition of Israel's right to exist and the establishment of a border – a process which is presently unfolding).
- **But there was no breath in them** (there was no Spirit – Jesus Christ in the spirit as Holy Spirit)

The last step, or phase, in their return to their land is that their neighbours (enemies) must recognize that the dry bones have a right to exist as a country. When this happens, just as the prophet said, "in them (in the body) will be yet no spirit". They did not revive even though they were physically returned to their land.

However, it is not possible to revive without the Spirit:

Jn. 6:63  *It is the spirit that quickeneth; the flesh profiteth nothing: the words that I speak unto you, they are spirit, and they are life.*

In order for the dry bones to be revived, (the Jewish nation in Israel) the Lord must send the Holy Spirit. Here a big problem is created in the hearts of Christians because of their conception of the way God will accomplish this phase of the salvation of the Jewish nation. According to their belief, when we ascend into heaven God will revive the dry bones.

Nevertheless, it is better for us to carefully read God's Word in order to comprehend how God will order the occurrence of these events which will fulfill this phase.

God's plan to bring the Holy Spirit (who lives in repentant, baptized Christians) to the dry bones is described in the 9th and 10th verses.

Eze. 37:9  *Then said he unto me, Prophecy unto the wind, prophecy, son of man, and say to the wind, Thus saith the Lord GOD; Come from the four winds, O breath, and breathe upon these slain, that they may live.*
Eze. 37:10  *So I prophesied as he commanded me, and the breath came into them, and they lived, and stood up upon their feet, an exceeding great army.*

First God issues a command to the prophet to preach. This action takes place on earth for the Word can be prophesied or preached only to man. It is revealed in these verses that some people will receive the command, through the Spirit of the Word of God, to go and revive the slain.

The slain represent the dry bones, i.e. the Jewish nation which is spiritually, but not physically, slain. When we consider spiritual death, then their revival is spiritual as well. This is described in verses eleven through fourteen.

243

Eze. 37:11   *Then he said unto me, Son of man, these bones are the whole house of Israel: behold, they say, Our bones are dried, and our hope is lost: we are cut off for our parts.*

Eze. 37:12   *Therefore prophecy and say unto them, Thus saith the Lord GOD; Behold, O my people, I will open your graves, and cause you to come up out of your graves, and bring you into the land of Israel.*

Since the Jewish people are spiritually slain, their dead spirit is in a spiritual grave, in their heart (body). Their unbelief is like a door from the grave which is closed; it seals the dead spirit in its unlawfulness.

Thus God testifies that a veil of unbelief, which they have over their spiritual eyes, will be removed by His hand, i.e. He will open their grave so light may come in, illuminating the dead who lie in it.

Eze.37:13   *And ye shall know that I am the LORD, when I have opened your graves, O my people, and brought you up out of your graves,*

When their unbelief is removed, i.e. when they realize that they crucified their Messiah on Golgotha's cross, their grave (spiritual eyes of their heart) will be opened and they will see the light of the Word of God which our Lord Jesus brought from heaven. Only then will God be able to cause them to rise from their graves, namely from their lawlessness, where they spiritually lay helpless, firm in their untruth, for two thousand years. From the moment they are led out of their lawlessness into spiritual day, God will no longer call them the mountain of Israel, the dry bones, the house of Israel, or any other name. He will call them "my people". They will then have become His people, and will allow God to lead them, just as Moses led his people through the wilderness into the Promised Land. Only THEN will God, through the baptismal ordinance, bring them into their spiritual promised land, i.e. the kingdom of God.

Eze. 37:14   *And shall put my spirit in you, and ye shall live, and I shall place you in your own land: then shall ye know that I **the LORD have spoken it, and performed it**, saith the LORD.*

This is why the Word of God says that the Jewish nation will revive and shall be placed in their own (ours) spiritual land when they are sealed (baptized) with the Holy Ghost. This happens after baptism by water. They will then know that the Lord said it and performed it.

This means, God will raise (spiritually revive) the spiritually dead Jewish people so they will be:

- First returned to the Promised Land of Israel.
- Secondly, Christians will be brought unto them.
- Thirdly, trouble will come upon them that they might be taken out of their unbelief. Also, through Christians, i.e. baptism, they will be brought into their spiritual promised land, which is the kingdom of God.

From these fourteen verses it is clear that Christians will be brought into Israel for the purpose of breathing upon the dry bones. But the unification of Christians from the gentiles and from the Jewish nation is not yet evident, i.e. the unification of the seed of Abraham according to faith and the seed of Abraham according to the law. This is further shown in the text of the Book of the prophet Ezekiel 37.

| | |
|---|---|
| Eze.37:16 | *Moreover, thou son of man, take thee one stick, and write upon it, For Judah, and for the children of Israel his companions: then take another stick, and write upon it, For Joseph, the stick of Ephraim and for all the house of Israel his companions:* |
| Eze.37:17 | *And join them one to another into one stick; and they shall become one in thine hand.* |
| Eze.37:18 | *And when the children of thy people shall speak unto thee, saying, Wilt thou not shew us what thou meanest by these?* |
| Eze.37:19 | *Say unto them, Thus saith the Lord GOD; Behold, I will take the stick of Joseph, which is in the hand of Ephraim, and the tribes of Israel his fellows, and will put them with him, even with the stick of Judah, and make them one stick, and they shall be one in mine hand.* |

These four verses say that people, or rather, the Jews according to the law in Israel, will not understand God's will until they pose the following question to themselves: what does *Judah's stick for the children of Israel his companions* and also *the stick of Joseph which is in the hand of Ephraim and the tribes of Israel his fellows* represent? The Jewish nation cannot pose this question until they see it. For the Word of God says; *Wilt thou not shew us what thou meanest by these?* It means that God will first bring *the stick of Ephraim and the tribes of Israel his fellows* unto the Jewish people in Israel and then the deed of the prophet, which God commanded will appear.

This deed of the "prophet" – deed of the Word of God – is a testimony to the Jewish nation that it is the will of God to make these two sticks one, i.e. make one fold from the two. Let us recall the words of Moses:

Ro. 10:19     *But I say, Did not Israel know? First Moses saith,* **I will provoke you to jealousy by them that are no people, and by a foolish nation I will anger you.**

In this passage, the Word of God speaks the same words as are found in the Book of the prophet Ezekiel. The Jewish nation will be angered (into belief of Jesus Christ) by the gentiles when God brings the stick of Ephraim unto the Jewish people.

Why?

Because this will come from the blessing which rests upon Christians. Secondly, it will be a wonder to see them coming into Israel. The hearts of the Jewish nation will be filled with sadness (jealousy or anger) upon seeing God's blessing upon Christians. We will cite a few more verses which speak of the migration of Christians into Israel.

Ro. 10:13     *For whosoever shall call upon the name of the Lord shall be saved.*

Ro. 10:14     *How then shall they call on him in whom they have not believed? and how shall they believe in him of whom they have not heard? and how shall they hear without a preacher?*

Ro. 10:15     *And how shall they preach, except they be sent? as it is written,* **How beautiful are the feet of them that preach the Gospel of peace**, *and bring glad tidings of good things!*

In order for an individual to achieve salvation he must first believe. Faith comes only through the preaching of the Word of God. This is why "Ephraim" must be brought to "Judah" so that unfaithful Judah and his sons of Israel are angered into belief for the sake of their own salvation.

In Romans 10 we read the same thing, with only a slight difference. This chapter cites the task of the Deliverer, i.e. those in whom the Holy Spirit resides.

Ro. 11:25 *For I would not, brethren, that ye should be ignorant of this mystery, lest ye should be wise in your own conceits; that blindness in part is happened to Israel, until the fullness of the Gentiles be come in.*

Ro. 11:26 *And so all Israel shall be saved: as it is written,* **There shall come out of Sion the Deliverer, and shall turn away ungodliness from Jacob:**

The Jewish nation cannot attain faith on their own. God willed them to be spiritually blind until the number of gentiles in the new covenant bonds is fulfilled. When this happens, the Deliverer will come from Zion and will turn all ungodliness away from Jacob.

The coming of the Deliverer from Zion represents the migration of Christians to Israel, which will make possible the turning away of ungodliness from Jacob, i.e. from the Jewish nation already gathered in Israel.

These verses are identical to Ezekiel 37:19: *and make them one stick, and they shall be one in mine hand.* These cited words do not allow anything to be added or taken away. God testifies that He will make one nation from the Christians and the Jews. This means that the doctrine of the Lord's second coming being preached today in Christianity, that we will rapture into heaven, is not based on the foundation of the Word of God. Conversely, Christians must wait for the number of saved gentiles to be fulfilled before they can be led by the Spirit of God to Israel, to carry out His commanded task and fulfill His will concerning one shepherd and one fold.

# 16

# *JESUS' PARABLE*
# *OF THE TEN VIRGINS*

E very parable which our Lord Jesus Christ pronounced must be fulfilled in its entirety. Many parables which our Lord Jesus Christ spoke of have already been fulfilled. Others are being fulfilled now and some will be fulfilled in the near future. As a result, the question arises for many believers as to why the Word of God does not refer to the parables as prophecies? What is the difference between prophecies and parables if both describe events which will happen in the near future? The difference is explained in the following paragraphs:

**Prophecy** - The Lord through His servants, the prophets, sends a message to the Jewish nation that evil deeds (unfaithfulness, for example), will result in a particular punishment while good deeds, on the other hand, will reap blessings.

**Parable** - A parable is a prophecy presented as a story of an event which occurs in our everyday lives, so that we can more easily understand the manner in which spiritual events will occur. This is why events from our earthly lives are used: harvesting, planting a vineyard, sowing, a wedding, hiring reapers, fishing, the care of a shepherd for his flock etc. However, a parable in itself is composed of illogical events. This means, fulfilled actions which do not conform to our earthly laws and rules. For example:

Mt. 13:30    *Let both grow together until the harvest: and in the time of harvest I will say to the reapers,* **Gather ye together first the tares**, *and bind them in bundles to burn them: but gather the wheat into my barn.*

We all know that an earthly harvest is not carried out in this manner. First, we harvest the whole crop and then we separate the tares by winnowing the grain. At harvest-time, a farmer will never go through his field and pluck out the tares and bind them together in bundles because this action will destroy the crop. Spiritual events, however, which must happen on this earth, were ordered by God to occur in a different manner. To make it easier for us to understand these prophesies, the Lord ordered His Son, Jesus Christ, to relate the parables as stories, using events from our everyday lives. If we understand an earthly harvest, we will then be able to understand a spiritual harvest more easily. The Lord is speaking to us through parables for our benefit.

This means that a parable from Jesus Christ cannot be interpreted arbitrarily because it is a prophecy containing a specific meaning and a specific sequence of events. Therefore, every word must be interpreted:

Let us examine the words of a parable which has already been fulfilled:

| | |
|---|---|
| Mt. 21:33 | *Hear another parable: There was a certain householder, which planted a vineyard, and hedged it round about, and digged a winepress in it, and built a tower, and let it out to husbandmen, and went into a far country:* |
| Mt. 21:34 | *And when the time of the fruit drew near, he **sent** his servants to the husbandmen, that they might receive the fruits of it.* |
| Mt. 21:37 | *But **last of all he sent unto them his son, saying**, They will reverence my son.* |
| Mt. 21:38 | *But when the husbandmen saw the son, they said among themselves, This is the heir; come, let us kill him, and let us seize on his inheritance.* |
| Mt. 21:39 | *And they caught him, and cast him out of the vineyard, and slew him.* |
| Mt. 21:40 | *When the lord therefore of the vineyard cometh, what will he do unto those husbandmen?* |
| Mt. 21:41 | *They say unto him, He will miserably destroy those wicked men, and **will let out his vineyard unto other husbandmen**, which shall render him the fruits in their seasons.* |

This prophecy has been completely fulfilled. Every word is weighted with meaning. The Lord testified to the Jewish nation that they would kill Him, which was fulfilled. Also, through this parable, He prophesied to the Jewish nation that the wicked men would be miserably destroyed. We know that this has already happened through the destruction of Jerusalem in 70 A.D. In the same parable, the culmination of the punishment and tribulation of the Jewish nation are described in the following verse:

Mt. 21:43    *Therefore say I unto you,* **The kingdom of God shall be taken from you, and given to a NATION bringing forth the fruits thereof.**

The Lord testifies to the Jewish nation that the right to the salvation of their souls will be removed. A complete spiritual catastrophe, a spiritual darkness and a misinterpretation of His word is announced. The kingdom of God will instead be given to a nation bringing forth fruit. The nation which was given the right to enter into the kingdom of God and to bring the fruits thereof are the gentiles.

From these words we can conclude that the Jewish nation will never again find mercy before the God of Israel. If salvation is given to another nation, it is given for all time. But God reveals a mystery through His apostles:

Ro. 11:25    **For I would not, brethren, that ye should be ignorant of this mystery,** *lest ye should be wise in your own conceits;* **that blindness in part is happened to Israel, until the fulness of the Gentiles be come in.**
Ro. 11:26    *And so all Israel shall be saved: as it is written, There shall come out of Sion the Deliverer, and shall turn away ungodliness from Jacob:*

The Lord speaks of this mystery in the Gospel:

Mt. 23:38    *Behold, your house is left unto you desolate.*
Mt. 23:39    *For I say unto you,* **Ye shall not see me henceforth, till ye shall say,** *Blessed is he that cometh in the name of the Lord.*

The Lord testifies that God will grant salvation to the Jewish nation but they must first fulfill the condition which He requires, namely, to say to God's Zion: *Blessed is he that cometh in the name of the Lord.* Then the question arises as to why apostle Paul is informing us of a mystery which the Lord Jesus Christ had already revealed unto us? How can an announcement be a mystery?

251

If we return to the verse which states that the kingdom will be taken away from the Jewish nation and given to the gentiles, we will notice that the Word does not say that the gentiles will go astray from the faith, just as the Jewish nation had gone astray two thousand years ago. This will cause salvation to be **taken away** from the gentiles and once **again** returned to the Jewish nation.

The key to the salvation of the Jewish nation comes in the form of the number of saved gentiles. Consequently, this is a mystery. In that time, iniquity will be at its peak. This is described in Romans 11.

Apostle Paul draws our attention to this mystery, for he understood the parables of Jesus Christ. The question then arises: In which of Jesus Christ's parables is this recorded? It is recorded in many. Not only is the time of the removal of salvation recorded, but it is also described by our Lord how salvation will be transferred for the second time to the Jewish nation. This statement may appear somewhat strange. It seems strange only because we do not properly understand the parables of Jesus Christ. Apostle Paul draws our attention to this mystery with great concern because he knows that we will slumber spiritually and fall asleep. Also, this day will come suddenly and will bring spiritual destruction to many.

Lu. 21:29    *And he spake to them a parable; Behold the fig tree, and all the trees;*

Lu. 21:30    *When they now shoot forth, ye see and know of your own selves that summer is now nigh at hand.*

Lu. 21:31    *So likewise ye, when ye see these things come to pass, know ye that the kingdom of God is nigh at hand.*

Lu. 21:35    *For as a snare shall it come on **all** them that dwell on the face of the whole earth.*

From the above-cited verses we can see that Jesus gave the commandment to all his servants to look on the Jewish people (the fig tree). The question arises: Are we looking at the fig tree? Are we carefully following the events in the Middle East? Do we observe how the fig tree has renewed its branches? Do we see how it is turning green? Do we feel that summer is nigh? Do we know when summer will come, or which events will signal the beginning of summer? Why does the Word of God say that the kingdom of God was nigh, when we are already in the kingdom of God? Alternatively, how then can the kingdom of

God come unto us? Perhaps the Word of God speaks that the kingdom of God is nigh unto the Jewish nation, for they should receive grace?

Lu. 21:35    *For as a **snare shall it come on all them** that dwell on the face of the whole earth.*

Lu. 21:36    *Watch ye therefore, and pray always, that ye may be accounted **worthy** to escape all these things that shall come to pass, and to stand before the Son of man.*

Mt. 24:20    *But pray ye that your **flight** be not in the winter, neither on the sabbath day.*

Mt. 24:21    *For then shall be great tribulation, such as was not since the beginning of the world to this time, no, nor ever shall be.*

Let us not ignore the severity of the warning our Lord sent to us, His people. This is the reason why we should pay special attention to the parable of Jesus Christ, for it describes the time of our flight. The time when we will try to flee to safety from all the things which should happen on this earth. One such parable is that of the Ten Virgins, which we find in Matthew 25. However, prior to that, at the end of the 24th chapter of the same Gospel, in the verses that speak about God's servants who give food (Word of God) to the children of God, we find a description of the state of the Christians:

Mt. 24:45    *Who then is a faithful and wise servant, whom his lord hath made ruler over his household, to give them meat in due season?*

To give food in due season does not give the servant the option of giving meat occasionally, either when he is able to or when he wishes to do so. God does not allow His servant to put His children on a diet, or give His children only the meat he wants to give them. Instead, God clearly states that His servant must give all meat in due season. This means regularly and in fullness. Let us read Christ's Word so that we are not confused:

Mt. 28:19    *Go ye therefore, and teach all nations, baptizing them in the name of the Father, and of the Son, and of the Holy Ghost:*

Mt. 28:20    *Teaching them **to observe ALL things whatsoever I have commanded** you: and, lo, I am with you always, even unto the end o the world. Amen.*

The Lord testifies that the meat He left for His servants to give to His children is *"all things whatsoever I have commanded"*. This includes the complete Gospels, the Epistles, and John's Revelation. Jesus does not say in any letter in the New Testament: Do not preach this or that. Therefore, the duty of God's servants is to teach the complete Gospels. Let us, however, continue reading from Matthew 24:

Mt. 24:48    *But and if that evil servant shall say in his heart, My lord delayed his coming:*

Mt. 24:49    *And shall begin to smite his fellow-servants, and to eat and drink with the drunken:*

It is ordained that the complete word of the New Testament be preached. The Lord is calling those servants wise who fulfill His command. Conversely, the Lord testifies that evil servants will appear who will not fulfill this commandment. They will not give God's children meat in fullness and in due season. By not fulfilling God's commandment, these servants are also smiting their fellow servants.

What is the reason for this?

The Word of God is not revealed unto the evil in the same manner as it is revealed unto the wise. The meaning of these parables of Jesus Christ explained in a spiritual way through wise servants makes no sense to them. Because of this, they will forbid the explanations of God's parables to be spoken in fullness.

Jesus Christ does not allow such behaviour in His servants. This is why He announced a judgement upon them.

Mt. 24:50    *The lord of that servant shall come in a day when he looketh not for him, and in an hour that he is not aware of,*

Mt. 24:51    *And shall cut him asunder, and appoint him his portion with* **the hypocrites**: *there shall be weeping and gnashing of teeth.*

In the previous text from Matthew 24 the Lord gives a description of the spiritual state of the faith at the present time. Everyone who wishes to look the truth in the eye has to agree that the preaching about the departure of God's people to Israel is missing. Furthermore, the reunion of the Jewish nation with us, here on earth, is not preached. We do not feel like Israelis, and we do not feel that Israel is our land. Also, we do not feel that we are in "Egypt" until we fulfill a task in the gentiles. We do not feel that we are the thirteenth tribe of Israel, which is Ephraim, who received the largest first born blessing, although we acknowledge that our forefathers are Abraham, Isaac and Jacob. Finally, we do not accept the words of that blessing: *and will give this land to thy seed after thee for an everlasting possession,* nor do we consider that we are that seed though we originate from Abraham, Isaac and Jacob.

We do not feel that we are the sons of Ephraim who will be brought from "Egypt", and onto whom the Jewish people must be grafted.

Je. 31:9    *They shall come with weeping, and with supplications will I lead them: I will cause them to walk by the rivers of waters in a straight way, wherein they shall not stumble: for I am a father to Israel,* **and Ephraim is my firstborn.**

In the following verses, the Lord points to the extremely sad spiritual state which exists amongst us today: aside from our other shortcomings.

Mt. 25:1    *Then shall the kingdom of heaven be likened unto ten virgins, which took their lamps, and went forth to meet the Bridegroom.*
Mt. 25:2    *And five of them were wise, and five were foolish.*

In these verses, Jesus again testifies to the sad fact that there exists both wise and foolish servants in His flock. This is why the Lord describes them through the Ten Virgins, for not every one in His flock belongs to God. Not everyone possesses the kingdom of God, which is righteousness, peace and joy in the Holy Ghost (Romans 14:17). Every person will be granted this kingdom in his or her heart when they make peace with God through baptism.

This is why the parable of the Ten Virgins actually describes the judgment which God will proclaim against the evil servants, who smite the wise servants. In addition, the wise servants will receive a blessing which will become evident through many more details.

In order that we receive a more detailed description of the happenings in Christianity our Lord introduces the symbol of the Ten Virgins. What does this symbol represent? It represents the servants of God preparing the bride to be ready to meet her Bridegroom, to be prepared and properly adorned, to make a covenant of mercy with Him. Through this, a covenant of marriage is created. This means that not one of the virgins who prepare the bride can be the bride. What prepares the human soul to be ready to meet its saviour Lord Jesus Christ and to make a covenant of mercy? Only the Word of God, which resides in the servants of Christ, can prepare the human soul. We who are called from darkness into the light, into Christ's kingdom, have a duty to preach the Gospel regardless of what nationality we come from, the colour of our skin, our sex, our material wealth, etc. The Word of God gives every one of us a task in His vineyard. Jesus Christ is the head, like the high priest, and we are priests because we are a part of His body.

1 Pe. 2:9      *But ye are a chosen generation, a* **royal priesthood,** *an holy nation, a peculiar people; that ye* **should shew forth** *the praises of him who hath called you out of darkness into his marvellous light;*

Jesus Christ was born a Jew, and through this we are also Jewish because we are His body and have His Spirit:

Ro. 2:28      *For he is not a Jew, which is one outwardly; neither is that circumcision, which is outward in the flesh:*

Ro. 2:29      *But he is a Jew, which is one inwardly; and circumcision is that of the heart, in the spirit, and not in the letter; whose praise is not of men, but of God.*

The Word of God says that there is no difference between people. However, there are advantages to being a Jew.

Ro. 3:1      *What advantage then hath the Jew? or what profit is there of circumcision?*

Ro. 3:2      *Much every way:* **chiefly, because that unto them were committed the oracles of God.**

To those who are Jews inwardly are given the oracles of God. They are the servants of God who are sent to preach the eternal Gospel to sinful humankind.

Ro. 10:15      *And how shall they preach, except they be sent? as it is written, How beautiful are the feet of them that preach the Gospel of peace, and bring glad tidings of good things!*

Everyone who believes the words of the eternal Gospel, and preaches it, is preparing souls for repentance. All of God's servants who prepare people for repentance are indicated through the number ten. The number ten symbolizes an entity. Let us be reminded of the parable of the ten bags of silver. According to it, the Lord gave His servants the complete Word of God, which was given to Him by His father. Silver symbolizes the Word of God, and the ten bags symbolize the complete Word of God (Old and New Testament). The Ten Virgins also symbolize ALL of the servants of God. Of those, however, five were wise and five were foolish, that is, one wise group and one foolish group. There exists a difference between the bride and the virgin. Speaking carnally, the bride is the person who through her love made a promise of faithfulness to her Bridegroom. The Bridegroom is Jesus Christ, on a deeper level He is the Word of God. The Lord sends His virgins, the servants of God, to entreat sinful humankind to love the Word of God, or Jesus Christ. When a sinner turns to God, his soul is ready to give a promise of faithfulness to the Lord.

When a convert gives a promise to the Word of God, that is, to the Lord, we can compare this to an engagement. The convert becomes the bride, which the virgins – the servants of God – continue to prepare and to adorn, to enable him to make a covenant of mercy through the baptism of water and of the Holy Spirit. We should take note that every person who is waiting to make a covenant with God is a bride; this can also be applied to a whole nation.

Let us see what is written in the Old Testament concerning the engagement of the Jewish people:

Je. 2:2      *Go and cry in the ears of Jerusalem, saying, Thus saith the LORD; I remember thee, the kindness of thy youth, the love of* **thine espousals,** *when thou wentest after me in the wilderness, in a land that was not sown.*

When the Jewish people left Egypt and went with the Lord into the wilderness for forty years, this was their engagement period. We can compare this to our lives and to the time when we repented and left this world of sin; promised faithfulness to our Bridegroom until death, and became His bride.

The time we spend preparing ourselves to make a covenant of mercy is our engagement period.

Who represents Christ's wife? She is mentioned in John's Revelation.

Re. 19:7    *Let us be glad and rejoice, and give honour to him: for the marriage of the Lamb is come, and his **wife** hath made herself ready.*

The wife can only represent those who have made a covenant of mercy with our Lord Jesus Christ. This means that from the moment of baptism, the blessed soul has entered into the Body of Christ. From that moment on, Jesus is the husband of that soul. In Christianity, however, the belief is disseminated that those who pass through baptism are the brides of Jesus Christ, actually, of His church. Many of these people are expecting a wedding in heaven for they believe that is where the wedding will take place.

Jesus Christ, however, is our Lord, our husband. The body of Christ is His church. She is delivering His children to Him. If the congregation of the church is the bride, and the Lord is the Bridegroom, we will have to make another covenant in the future with Him. If this is the case, then it means that we will once again have to repent and pass through the ordinances of baptism, which is not possible.

Just as a ring in this world is a symbol of a marriage union, the sealing with the Holy Spirit is a sign to us that we belong to Him. The Lord testifies that He is the head and we are His body. This is why we are **one body** with our Lord.

In this parable the number ten envelopes all of God's servants in Christianity. That is why God divides them into two categories, the wise and the foolish, for wisdom hates sin while foolishness accepts sin. The wise teach sinful people to recognize their sin and to understand that they cannot be in sin however; the foolish do the contrary.

Pro. 8:13   *The fear of the Lord is to hate evil: pride, and arrogance, and the evil way, and the froward mouth, do I hate.*

The wise virgins, however, in addition to having the fear of God in them, hating evil and teaching in the same manner, have another important advantage in relation to the foolish virgins: they brought the **oil**. They have oil, which they did not use. To have the fear of God is to have God's wisdom, which is oil. To hate sin is also to have oil. To teach people in the same manner is knowledge, which is again oil. The wise virgins, however, took special oil with them which, when lit in that spiritual night, gave them the opportunity to see the Bridegroom. It is impossible to enter into the Supper of the Wedding Feast of the Jewish people with the Bridegroom without this oil. Every lamp without this oil will be extinguished.

Mt. 25:3    *They that were foolish took their lamps, and took **no** oil with them:*

Mt. 25:4    *But the wise took oil in their vessels with their lamps.*

The lamp is the Word of God, for King David speaks in the Psalms:

Ps. 119:105    *Thy word is a lamp unto my feet, and a light unto my path.*

Every virgin had the Word of God in her possession but only the wise had the knowledge of the Word of God. The knowledge of the Word of God is faith *for faith is the substance of things hoped for and the evidence of things not seen*, and is what God commanded and what we are patiently waiting for. We cannot believe in something that God did not command in His Word.

Only when we understand the meaning of the virgins, and what the oil and the lamp symbolize, what the kingdom of God is, and the difference between wisdom and foolishness – only then can we give an answer concerning other symbols from the first verse.

In the first verse of the parable of the Ten Virgins, the Lord testifies that those to whom the Word of God is given will, for some reason, go out and wait for the Bridegroom. On the other hand, the Word of God testifies that the Bridegroom is not coming to take His bride, but rather His virgins. This is why they are coming out to meet Him, but only those with oil and trimmed lamps will find Him and enter with Him into the Supper of the Wedding Feast of the Lamb.

According to our carnal thinking, the Bridegroom should come to take His bride. Similarly, the coming out of the virgins in front of the Bridegroom is not logical because the virgins should be concentrated on preparing the bride, not waiting for the Bridegroom. This is why the words from the first verse are completely illogical for many. Being human, we would first take care of our bride, and not the virgins preparing the bride.

Now, a problem arises because the virgins are already at the wedding and the salvation of the gentiles is not yet complete. Christ's servants are preparing the souls of the gentiles, but the parable does not concentrate on this. It says that the virgins went to meet the Bridegroom who will take them to someone's wedding.

There are those who believe that in the parable of the Ten Virgins, the coming of the Bridegroom is actually the second coming of our Lord Jesus Christ. This interpretation does not have any foundation in the Word of God. In order for us not to lose time trying to prove that this statement does not hold, let us pose a few questions. What does it mean to go out and meet the Bridegroom in the night? Does it mean that we should leave our houses with suitcases and wait to go into heaven? If this is the case, who do you think will slumber? To whom will sleepiness come? To whom will sleepiness come between 6:00 pm to midnight? Perhaps small children will fall asleep in their parents' arms. On the other hand, the Word testifies that none of us will know the hour or day in which this will happen. How then will believers in that night come to an understanding as to which night the Lord is speaking of? Through our own conclusions, we can see that God is speaking about a spiritual night and spiritual Bridegroom.

What are God's servants going out to meet the Bridegroom with? Obviously, servants can only go out before the Bridegroom through prayer and the preaching of His Word. At the beginning of the evening of the third spiritual day, the Lord allowed two important events to happen. Those events forced every virgin to go out and meet the Bridegroom. The prophecy of His Word started to be fulfilled. The horrible First World War began. The war was of a ferocity that humankind could not even imagine. What made the war even sadder was the fact that the main part of it took place in the heart of Christian Europe. Christianity received a testimony that they were not fulfilling God's will. God started to turn His face toward the Jewish nation. The Balfour Declaration allowed the Jewish nation to buy land in Palestine. This was a shock to the gentiles. It was a sign that the secret which apostle Paul spoke of was beginning to be fulfilled. The servants of God became disturbed. It became clear to everyone that the process of the abolishment of salvation from the gentiles had begun. On the other hand, the process of the building of the Jewish State had begun, which would have its peak when they entered into a covenant with God.

Through preaching, Christians were told that they should prepare themselves for big events. Therefore, the virgins went out to meet the Bridegroom as a result of preaching and prayers, to hear the Word of God, and the Spirit of God, say: the hour has come that we should go to the wedding feast of the Jewish people.

After thirty years of waiting, the state of Israel was created on May 14, 1948. This happened after the unimaginable bloodshed of the Second World War, where fifty million died and 200 million were injured. In addition, six million Jews were killed. The Second World War was five times worse than the First World War.

Instead of being better equipped with spiritual arms, just as the Word speaks in Ephesians 6, the virgins who went out to meet the Bridegroom slumbered,

Mt. 25:5        *While the Bridegroom **tarried,** they all slumbered and slept.*

Today the virgins are not waiting for their Bridegroom to take them to a new task. There is no preaching about going to the Supper of the Wedding Feast of the Lamb. Today we find that odd. We accept different spirits. We are waiting for the Lord to come and take us into heaven. We have forgotten our earthly brothers. Like Ephraim, son of Joseph, who received an inheritance in Israel, we have stopped thinking of granting mercy to our brethren from our father Israel. Suddenly, the Jewish nation is no longer our concern. We say, God, not we, will concern Himself with them. It is horrible to say something like this. Doesn't God do everything through His spirit, His servants?

Why did the Bridegroom tarry? There is obviously an important reason. We can pose this question: why did the virgins fall asleep? Really, couldn't events such as the First World War, the Balfour Declaration, the Second World War, the murder of six million Jews, the creation of the state of Israel, the gathering of the Jewish people, the five large wars between Israel and the Arab nations, and any other events, keep the virgins awake? They could not, because Satan began to sing an incredibly pleasant lullaby, which appealed to God's people: an explosion of materialism. We find it more important to live in a pleasant and leisurely manner, beyond our means, rather than to be on guard and suffer for Jesus Christ's name. We began to live according to our eyes. This is why many sealed in the faith suffer from materialism and as a result, the number of saved people did not grow quickly enough. Thus, the Bridegroom tarried. The words of Jesus Christ are fulfilled: *will I find faith when I return.*

| | |
|---|---|
| Mt. 25:6 | *And at midnight there was a cry made, Behold, the Bridegroom cometh; go ye out to meet him.* |

We are again confronted with illogical words. It is written in the first verse that the virgins went out to meet Him, and then, after a good sleep, when midnight began, a cry was made once again to go out and meet the Bridegroom. If someone goes out to meet the Bridegroom, then he is outside and waiting. How can someone go out to meet the Bridegroom when he has already gone out? To go out means to preach. When someone sleeps there is no preaching about the Bridegroom.

The Word of God says that someone made a cry to the virgins. Someone woke them up. The ministerial body, like a part of Christ's body, did not know that the spiritual midnight had begun while they were sleeping. Someone was warning them to go out and meet the Bridegroom. Without faith, it is not possible to satisfy the God of Israel. It is also not possible to enter the wedding feast without faith and knowledge. This means that God will make sure that there will be those who proclaim His Word.

However, it is necessary to note that a cry cannot begin if an earlier event has not occurred. This is announced through the words *everything is ready*. These same words can be found when the call for Dinner had gone out, which happened two thousand years ago. The call for the Supper of the Wedding Feast of the Lamb will also happen in the near future.

| | |
|---|---|
| Mt. 22:4 | *Again, he sent forth other servants, saying, Tell them which are bidden, Behold, I have prepared my **dinner**: my oxen and my fatlings are killed, and **all things are ready**: come unto the marriage.* |
| Lu. 14:17 | *And sent his servant at **supper** time to say to them that were bidden, Come; for **all things are now ready**.* |

The term *all things are now ready* summarizes the preparations which God was forced to make in order for the call (cry) for the Dinner of the Wedding Feast of the Lamb to go out.

In the past, when dinner began (everything was ready), apostle Peter and his eleven, raised his voice and then started to cry, to enter into a covenant through repentance and baptism.

Ac. 2:38      *Then Peter **said** unto them, Repent, and be baptized every one of you in the name of Jesus Christ for the remission of sins, and ye shall receive the gift of the Holy Ghost.*

These words are written as a call to the Wedding Dinner, and when we compare them to the words written for the call to the Wedding Supper, we can see the difference. At the Wedding Dinner, when the voice was raised (after the preaching of the apostles), the salvation of the gentiles began. Conversely, when the voice was raised at the Wedding Supper (*Behold the Bridegroom cometh; go ye out to meet him*), Christians were only then told that they needed to go to the Wedding Supper where the salvation of the Jewish nation will occur. In order for the call summoning Christ's virgins to the Wedding Supper to sound, the Lord has to prepare everything just as for the Wedding Dinner. The question then arises: what should the Lord do in order for the call – everything is ready – to go out?

1. Conditions will be created so that the Jewish nation may return to their land.
2. He will give them land; a country will be created.
3. He will gather them and strengthen them.
4. Skin will cover that "BODY" above.

All these steps are already described, in principle, in Ezekiel 37, which was analyzed in the light of the previous example describing the Christians' departure to the Supper of the Wedding Feast of the Lamb. The last step of this prophecy – a voice crying out *all is ready* – from the many stages of preparation described, is for the skin to cover the body above.

What does the skin covering the body above represent?

We can say that the skin is a border to our bodies just as a border is to a state. When neighbouring countries bordering Israel recognize its existence, the skin will cover the body. This action will mark the border. Let us see how this process has taken place up to this moment.

## Skin Covering the Created Body

The skin began covering the body in 1978. The signing of an agreement which caused Egypt to recognize the existence of Israel marked the beginning. Thus, a border was officially marked between Egypt and Israel. This became possible because Egypt lost every war against Israel. Chiefly in the last war, which occurred in 1973, Egypt lost all of Sinai. In order to return to peaceful means, they signed an agreement in which the United States acted as a mediator.

- **In 1994** the Palestinians in Gaza were given autonomy. Gaza was never given to the Jewish nation in their inheritance. The process of separation from the Palestinians had begun. In the same year, Jordan made an agreement with Israel concerning the border between them.

- **In the same year,** under pressure from Western countries, the Oslo agreement was signed. Through this agreement, the land of Israel and the city of Jerusalem should have been divided between the Palestinians and the Jews. As a result of this agreement, a Palestinian country should have been created within Israel. According to God's Word, this is not possible. Because the Israeli President, Isaac Rabin, signed the Oslo Accords, which was against God's will, he lost the blessing of God's protection and then he lost his life. This is a sign from God that this accord will not last. The promises of God which were given to Abraham, Isaac and Jacob cannot be sold.

- **In 2003** we watched the weakening of Israel's enemies: Muslim fundamentalism in Afghanistan, the war in Iraq, and pressure on every other Muslim-Arabic country because of terrorism. At the same time, we watched direct pressure being applied on Israel to divide itself into two countries: Israel and Palestine.

- **In 2006** Gaza received full independence from Israel which unilaterally withdrew its military and civilian population. At the same time, Israel took part in peace negotiations with Lebanon, Syria and Palestine.

Based on the agreement reached between Israel and Egypt, the skin was put on from the West. This means that it is not possible to cover Israel by skin without negotiations. This is why the Word of God says:

1 Th. 5:3    For **when they shall say, Peace** and *safety; then sudden destruction cometh upon them, as travail upon a woman with child; and they shall not escape.*

Through the peace process, Israel will receive a border and the neighbouring countries will recognize its existence. Only then will the word *all is ready* emerge (Luke 14:17). However, the Word of God in Matthew 25:6 says that this moment is described as midnight. Why is peace attained in the Middle East compared with a spiritual midnight? Wherein does the problem lie?

A problem arises because the dispute with neighbouring countries regarding Israel's borders wishes to be solved according to human intellect. The interference of the big powers is not what God ordered for the settlement of this issue. Israel will be forced to accept a solution to its border problem in a way that this world insists on. God and His Word will not be acknowledged, which is recorded in the Bible. This world and the Christian countries represent the culmination of ignorance, i.e. darkness. This is why the achievement of an agreement represents spiritual midnight.

When we see the **body** i.e. the country of Israel, recognized by her enemies – the neighbouring states, then everything will be ready for the call to come out to meet the Bridegroom. We should, however, heed the prophet who says that the *skin covered the body but there was* **no breath in them.** This means that there will be a short period between the time in which the skin completely covers the body and when the voice says, "GO and *say to the wind....*".

Eze. 37:9    *Then said he unto me, Prophecy unto the wind, prophecy, son of man, and* **say to the wind,** *Thus saith the Lord GOD;* **Come** *from the four winds,* **O breath,** *and breathe upon these slain, that they may live.*

This means that we are in the same situation which existed in times of old. In Matthew 22:4, the Lord made everything ready so that the **Dinner** of the Wedding Feast of His Son could begin. The Lord similarly testifies through Luke 14:17 that He will make everything ready for the Wedding **Supper** of His Son.

God's servants, whom He put on guard, will lift their voices and cry: virgins wake up, go and meet the Bridegroom. The Middle East serves as a testimony to us that the Jewish nation will soon enter into a new covenant bond. The servants of God are still crying today even though the virgins cannot hear the words of God, which are so clear. What do you think, will the sleepy virgins wake up when they see a recognized Israel and hear the cry from the guardsmen?

They will not. Why? The cry from the servants cannot wake them up unless God wakes them up. Particularly, the cry will not awaken the foolish virgins who do not have the fear of God in them. If it could be different, all the unbelievable events which have occurred to this day would not have allowed the virgins to sleep, and thus the cry from the guardsmen would not be necessary to try and awaken them. This means that another event must occur in the spiritual midnight. That "other event" will be so dramatic that it will wake both the wise and the foolish.

Mt. 24:21      *For then shall be great tribulation, such as was not since the beginning of the world to this time, no, nor ever shall be.*

In essence, the events which will cause the spiritual midnight to begin (events which will occur around Israel) will not awaken the virgins but rather additional events will eventually wake them up. Just as today the Word of God and the cry from the guardsmen is not waking up the virgins, the virgins will also not awaken in that time. Rather they will be awakened by fear. Imagine the foolish virgins who do not have the fear of God in them waking up. What tragic events must occur in order to wake the foolish? Great friction between nuclear powers will probably awaken the foolish.

In that time the guardsmen will cry: *go out and meet the Bridegroom.* This means, preach about the departure for Israel, for if you do not, God will ask blood from your hand for every destroyed soul. God will not allow you to enter into the Supper of the Wedding Feast.

In order to go out and meet the Bridegroom, the virgins must wake up, arise, and trim their lamps.

Mt. 25:7      *Then all those virgins arose, and trimmed their lamps.*

- **To wake up** means to come to the understanding that the salvation of the Jewish nation is at hand. The virgins will awaken and follow the events which are taking place. When they wake up, however, they will be surrounded by spiritual darkness[18].

- **To arise.** When man arises, his state of rest is finished and he is now in a state of action. This means that the virgins have repented. They are recognizing what they have done up to that moment. Even the foolish virgins, who do not have knowledge of sin, will repent out of fear.

- **To trim their lamps.** To light the oil means to fulfill God's will according to one's own abilities. The lamp must be trimmed and put in a high place. The foolish virgins, however, have two very big problems. Their light is dying, for they do not posses wisdom, nor do they have enough knowledge of sin within them. The second problem arises because they do not have any reserve OIL in their vessels (in their hearts). Trimming their lamps will allow them to SEE the Bridegroom when the hour to enter the Supper of the Wedding Feast comes. It is important to understand that the Bridegroom does not need the light. It is the virgins who need the light from the oil lamp in order to see the Bridegroom (the Word of God, which wants to save the Jewish nation). The Bridegroom is not coming to find the virgins, to compare the strength of their light, or to beseech them saying, "please go with me". The Word says in an additional text: *and the ready entered.* This means that some individuals are not more or less ready than others, but rather there are only those who are **ready,** who are able to hear, understand and fulfill the Word of God.

Mt. 25:8    *And the foolish said unto the wise, Give us of* **YOUR** *oil; for our lamps are gone out.*

The virgins cannot wait for the Bridegroom with their lamps not lit. The Bridegroom will not lead the virgins without lighted oil to the wedding of the Jewish nation. This is why the foolish virgins say: give us of YOUR oil.

---

[18]    Lack of God's knowledge.

Only that special oil (knowledge), when it is lit (fulfilled), can enable us to see the Bridegroom (will of the Word of God – the secret which the apostle Paul is speaking of) and enter unto the wedding. Be reminded of the words spoken in God's Word: *there shall come out of Sion the Deliverer and shall turn away ungodliness from Jacob.*

This time is approaching quickly, just as it was in the time of Noah and Lot. When this moment arrives, there will no longer be time to persuade, discuss, study, or analyze. We must do all of that now. In that night, in Lot's time, the angels said unto him: go and tell your sons-in-law to leave swiftly, for Sodom will be destroyed by fire and swiftly get out. Did Lot have time, for example, to say unto the angels: wait until tomorrow, or until I sell my property and fill my wagon with my possessions, gather my animals or other similar things? Read Lot's example. Let us also read Noah's example. We have time to read of their example now and be edified by them.

| | |
|---|---|
| Lu. 17:28 | *Likewise also as it was in the days of Lot; they did eat, they drank, they bought, they sold, they planted, they builded;* |
| Lu. 17:29 | *But the same day that Lot went out of Sodom it rained fire and brimstone from heaven, and destroyed them all.* |
| Lu. 17:30 | *Even thus shall it be in the day when the Son of man is revealed.* |
| Lu. 17:31 | *In that day, he which shall be upon the housetop, and his stuff in the house, let him not come down to take it away: and he that is in the field, let him likewise not return back.* |
| Lu. 17:32 | *Remember Lot's wife.* |
| Lu. 17:33 | *Whosoever shall seek to save his life shall lose it; and whosoever shall lose his life shall preserve it.* |
| Lu. 17:34 | *I tell you,* **in that night** *there shall be two men in one bed; the one shall be taken, and the other shall be left.* |
| Lu. 17:35 | *Two women shall be grinding together; the one shall be taken, and the other left.* |
| Lu. 17:36 | *Two men shall be in the field; the one shall be taken, and the other left.* |
| Lu. 17:37 | *And they answered and said unto him, Where, Lord? And he said unto them,* **Wheresoever the body is, thither will the eagles be gathered together.** |

What does the body or carcass mean? This word is describing the body, which does not have a spirit. In a spiritual sense, this symbolizes the recognition of Israel as a country separate from its neighbours. The body is present but without a spirit because they do not recognize Jesus as their King. The eagles (sons of God) will be gathered where the body is in that spiritual night.

We find the following words in the parable of the Ten Virgins:

Mt. 25:9    *But the wise answered, saying, Not so; lest there be not enough for us and you: but go ye rather **to them that sell,** and buy for yourselves.*

We are once again confronted with an illogical situation. Oil is the knowledge of God's will, actually the faith, which God gives to those who seek Him. If you tell someone that you believe this or that way, how is it possible to lose a part of your oil? How is it possible for the Word to say: *but the wise answered, saying, Not so; lest there be not enough for us and you: but go ye rather **to them that sell,** and buy for yourselves?*

It is meant the way it is written. This **oil**, which only the wise virgins will possess in their vessels[19], will not be for sale in that special moment.

Be reminded of the time when the Lord ordered the tenth plague against the Egyptians in Moses' time. This was the time when the Passover was supposed to be established. God sent a commandment that the lamb would be killed in that night and that every door would be marked with the lamb's blood. Whoever did not fulfill this, regardless of whether he was the firstborn of a Jew or an Egyptian, was killed. What do you think? Did every one know of this order in Egypt? They obviously did. Everyone was made aware of this. The wise and the foolish both knew, but in that night there was no time for the wise to sell their **oil,** to prove and argue with the Egyptians or the Jews, for the time had come to fulfill what was in their hearts, in the vessel.

In addition, there was no time for spiritual buying or selling.

The wise virgins are fulfilling their own faith by lighting up their oil. They are urgently preaching where they are ordered to preach. Everyone takes care of his own house. They are correcting their mistakes so that they may enter into the Supper with the Bridegroom. The hour for the departure to Israel has arrived, the place where they will serve their Lord at the Supper.

---

[19]    Human heart.

The wise virgins are advising the foolish virgins "go to them that sell". Who are those that sell? They are spiritual merchandisers, those who have the oil. They are the servants of God who have the required knowledge. This is why Lot and Noah did not say to the Lord: Lord, delay the catastrophes for some time so that we may speak, convince, explain, argue, and warn. That time will be difficult even for righteous people. When the decisive moment came, it was also not easy for Noah and his household. Therefore, the time will also not be easy for us. We will take care of our loved ones, according to the flesh and spirit, and of ourselves. Everyone will prepare his house in his domain.

Lu. 21:35     *For as **a snare** shall it come **on ALL** them that dwell on the face of the whole earth.*

However, every wise virgin will not be ready to go with the Bridegroom onto the wedding feast. Only those who are ready will be privileged to go.

Mt. 25:10     *And while they went to buy, the Bridegroom came; and they that were **ready** went in with him to the marriage: **and the door was shut.***

Mt. 25:11     *Afterward came also the **other** virgins, saying, Lord, Lord, open to us.*

Mt. 25:12     *But he answered and said, Verily I say unto you, **I know you not.***

Mt. 25:13     *Watch therefore, for ye know neither the day nor the hour wherein the Son of man cometh.*

The Lord does not suddenly divide the virgins into wise and foolish virgins. Rather, He refers to them as the other virgins and the ready virgins. Why does such a big difference suddenly appear? Because not every virgin will be ready to join the Bridegroom at the wedding, and only a small number of the wise virgins will join the Bridegroom.

Lu. 21:36     *Watch ye therefore, and pray always, **that ye may be accounted WORTHY to escape** all these things that shall come to pass, and to stand before the Son of man.*

This means that although the virgins are wise, have oil, get up, and light their lamps, **some** will not be considered worthy to enter unto the wedding. Why? Because wisdom, oil and everything else mentioned will not be enough; something is still missing.

Lu. 14:33    *So likewise, whosoever he be of you that forsaketh not all that he hath, he cannot be my disciple.*

These words apply to everyone, including preachers of God's word, God's people and those who are coming to God. The words have a significance for every one of these groups in their domain. This means that in addition to fulfilling the Lord's requirements, virgins must be ready to forsake all that they have in order to enter into the wedding with the Bridegroom. Unfortunately, everyone will not be able to do this. Only those who are ready to forsake all, will be **ready** to enter with the Bridegroom to the wedding of the Jewish nation.

The door will be shut when the ready virgins enter the wedding.

Mt.25:10    *And while they went to buy, the Bridegroom came; and they that were ready went in with him to the marriage: **and the door was shut**.*

Just as the Lord closed the door of Noah's ark, He will once again close a door, only this time it will be the door to the wedding, which will in the process disable those who are not worthy of entering.

We can see from the Word of God that the closing of the door is an extremely important event. Let us remember what the Word says: *But pray ye that your flight be not in the winter, neither on the Sabbath day.* Why? These words actually describe the closing of the door. The closing of the door describes three things, which are: fleeing, fleeing in the winter, and fleeing on the Sabbath. From this, we can see that there are three different periods.

## 1. Fleeing

When should we flee? When we see that trouble is coming. People take shelter in the face of trouble. Those who pay attention to the signs, and who see the storm approaching will make preparations and seek shelter, taking with them all things that are precious to them. We are looking realistically at man's reaction to approaching danger. This means that if the ready virgins do not see the Bridegroom they will not be able to go out to meet Him, and enter the wedding. This claim may sound strange to many hearts. Let us therefore consider an example. If someone turns to God and is not able to *see* his Saviour, he will never be able to make a covenant of mercy with Him. The condition which God sets is that man must first **see**. Every soul must first see with spiritual eyes in order to be able to do something:

Jn. 6:40      *And this is the will of him that sent me, that every one which SEETH the Son, and believeth on him, may have everlasting life: and I will raise him up at the last day.*

We all have to first see our Lord with spiritual eyes in some member of our family, through His people, in His congregation. We must believe that the Lord is within His congregation and then we must knock on the door and seek salvation for our souls. Without this, no one can pass through God's ordinances.

This is also the way for the departure unto the Marriage Supper of the Lamb. The foolish virgins do not have the necessary oil and are for that reason not able to see the Bridegroom. Even if they go out to meet the Bridegroom, knowing that salvation will be transferred to the Jewish people, they will not be able to understand how this will happen.

A different problem appears within the wise virgins. The wise virgins can see the Bridegroom but not every virgin is ready to enter with Him to the wedding. This means that some of the wise virgins are facing the problem of how to cope with the fear that enters their hearts, fear for our earthly bodies because of the turbulence and uncertainty in the Middle East at the time of departure. For this reason, many will not be willing to do what is asked of them at that time.

## 2. Fleeing in the Winter

When do we flee in the winter? The Word says: *pray ye that your flight be not in the winter*, actually, when the storm has already started. This storm is the nuclear war. The door will be left ajar. It will be difficult to travel as everything will be disrupted. Circumstances will be reversed in that time for it will become harder for our earthly bodies here, but easier in Israel.

The horror of nuclear war is unimaginable. Many will then strive to reach Israel, not because they are ready to sacrifice everything for the Lord but because they are fearful and are trying to satisfy their own interests. The Word of God describes this situation in this way:

Lu. 14:22    *And the servant said, Lord, it is done as thou hast commanded, and yet there is room.*

Lu. 14:23    *And the lord said unto the servant, Go out into the highways and hedges, and* **COMPEL them to come in,** *that my house may be filled.*

## 3. Fleeing on the Sabbath

When do we flee on the Sabbath? When there is no purpose in fleeing. When all spiritual work has ended among the gentiles. Rest for the virgins, or God's servants, begins on the spiritual Sabbath. The harvest will be finished in the gentiles and the **other** virgins, in their zealousness, will knock on the door of the wedding and say to the Lord: open the door unto us for we love Thee and would give anything to fulfill Thy will. Is this really the reason we know that even the spiritual winter, or nuclear war, will not be able to move them? No, the reason will be the panic that will consume people at the start of the Sabbath.

The virgins will suddenly be able to possess that special oil. Their spiritual eyes will open. They will be able to see the Bridegroom even if it is night. The Bridegroom has gone to the wedding some time earlier and the door is closed. Even in the darkness, they will know exactly where the door is and will thus knock. The foolishness of the virgins cannot suddenly turn into wisdom, which is ready to sacrifice everything for the Lord. Hopelessness will push them in the direction, which is the coming of the Antichrist. But the Lord says: *I know you not.*

# 17

# *WHEN THEY SHALL SAY PEACE AND SAFETY, 1 THESSALONIANS 5:3*

Each member of the world's vast population – at this point numbering some six billion people – places a different value on life and the direction of their hearts, being and energy. The goal of man is to live a life of material abundance rather than a life according to the Lord's will.

The main problem here is the will of mortal man. The will of man is ruled by the desires of the human heart and not by the laws of our Maker, the God of Israel.

Those who do not care for God and His proffered salvation, delivered by His mediator our Lord Jesus Christ, do not take note of what the Word of God speaks. The warnings uttered through the words of the prophets mean nothing to mortal man. These words, however, should mean a great deal to all the people who love the God of Israel and our Saviour Lord Jesus Christ. The desires of our soul should be directed **only** towards the fulfillment of His will, which made known the path assigned to us by His will. In order to be able to walk we must know that God had already prophesied all future events of the spiritual and material world. Therefore, by studying the Word of God we must determine which aspects of the prophecy have been fulfilled up to this point. We should also examine the events of today, so that we can direct our lives accordingly.

We must not be like those of whom the Word of God speaks:

2 Pe. 3:3    *Knowing this first, that there shall come in the last days* **scoffers,** *walking after* **their own lusts,**

Verily, these are very sad words. We can all recognize ourselves in these words. It is evident that by living in this materialistic system, we as well as our households are fulfilling our own desires. Surely, because our main concern is attempting to live a more comfortable and easygoing life, the day of the Lord shall come suddenly, as a thief in the night:

1 Th. 5:2    *For yourselves know perfectly that the day of the Lord so cometh as a thief in the night.*

1 Th. 5:3    *For when they shall say, Peace and safety; then sudden destruction cometh upon them, as travail upon a woman with child; and they shall not escape.*

It is difficult to determine when the day of the Lord will come and for whom it will come. The only certainty is that it will surely happen. However, consider if the Lord had not written the following words to Thessalonians: *When they shall say peace and safety; then sudden destruction cometh upon them, as travail upon a woman with child; and they shall not escape.* God's children should know the time period when these words will be spoken.

Let us phrase this differently: if the words had not been written in Thessalonians, which one of us would know, first, that this is the law of God and secondly, that the announcement of peace and safety is an opening for sudden destruction? Sadly, in addition to missing this knowledge, we have trouble understanding the meaning of these written and explained words.

God in His wisdom, knowing our limitations, announced His words to us, explaining ahead of time what will happen through words such as: day of the Lord, peace, safety, destruction, sudden coming, as a thief in the night, and so on.

However, if we take any word to meditate upon, we can see that there could be several possibilities. For example, consider the word "destruction". This could relate to:

- The Third World War
- Gog's battle
- Armageddon
- The destruction of Israel's enemy
- The destruction of the Christians' enemy
- Or several other possibilities

Conversely, the word "peace" could mean:

- World peace among all nations
- Peace between some big powers
- Peace between Israel and its enemies
- Nuclear disarmament
- Or other possibilities

When we are faced with so many possibilities the question arises: how should we begin explaining these few verses? The best way is to start with the words "day of the Lord". The reason is that the day of the Lord will cause the destruction of sinful souls. On the other hand, the "day of the Lord" has already been clearly explained in God's Word. It should also be noted that the words written in the Epistle to the Thessalonians are not provided so that we will be afraid of the destruction which is to come, but rather, they are given to us so that we may ponder the laws which rule in the "day of the Lord", and allow us to be spiritually prepared. Our salvation depends on these words.

Many believers will not agree with this statement because they think it is only important to be good and refrain from sin. Let us see what is written:

| | |
|---|---|
| 1 Th. 5:4 | *But ye, brethren, are not in darkness, that that **day** should overtake you as a thief.* |
| 1 Th. 5:5 | *Ye are all the children of light, and the children of the day: we are not of the night, nor of darkness.* |
| 1 Th. 5:6 | *Therefore let us not sleep, as do others; but let us watch and be sober.* |
| 1 Th. 5:7 | *For they that sleep sleep in the night; and they that be drunken are drunken in the night.* |
| 1 Th. 5:8 | *But let us, who are of the day, be sober, putting on the breastplate of faith and love; and for an helmet, the hope of salvation.* |
| 1 Th. 5:9 | *For God hath not appointed us to wrath, but to obtain salvation by our Lord Jesus Christ,* |

In 1 Thessalonians 5:2, we find the term **"the day of the Lord"**. In the fourth verse, however, the Word of God speaks only about **day**. This means that the term "day" is made equal with the term "day of the Lord". In other words, "day" and "day of the Lord" have the same meaning in our time period. The only question which remains is this: for whom? Obviously,

only for those who are in a covenant with God. The reason for this is in the meaning of the term "day of the Lord".

The general meaning of "day of the Lord" marks the time period when the sun of spiritual heaven will shine and break the spiritual darkness by lighting the path to salvation. This is when the Word of God is preached. This means it is given to humankind for the salvation of their souls. The day of the Lord is, however, both "great and notable" (Act. 2:20) and "great and very terrible" (Joel 3:11). To those who accepted the Lord Jesus Christ as their personal Saviour and King and live according to His will, the "day of the Lord" will be great and notable because they will be brought eternal life. However, to those who did not submit to His will, the "day of the Lord" will be a great and terrible day as they will be brought eternal damnation.

Since the gentiles accepted the Lord Jesus Christ as their king by faith, they are living in the light. The day of the Lord will not come to the gentiles because they are already in the **day**. They have the privilege of being able to turn to God through the Lord Jesus Christ and to save their souls. This privilege was received like a gift when the Jewish nation became unworthy of eternal life (Acts 13:46). This means that the gentiles are in the "day of the Lord". The gentiles themselves will define whether the "day of the Lord" will be glorious or terrible.

For the Jewish nation which lost the right of salvation after the destruction of Jerusalem, "the day of the Lord" has taken on the meaning of a great and terrible day. It is terrible because they have been unable to see spiritually for nineteen hundred years and to work for the salvation of their souls.

Ro. 11:8      *(According as it is written, God hath given them the spirit of slumber, eyes that they should not see, and ears that they should not hear;) unto this day.*

2 Co. 3:16    *Nevertheless **when it shall turn to the Lord**, the VAIL shall be taken away.*

The Lord clearly says that the veil is the spirit of slumber, which prevents the Jewish nation from believing the Lord Jesus Christ.

However, when God removes the veil and gives them the right to enter into the bonds of the new covenant through our Lord Jesus Christ, the day of the Lord will begin for them. The time period of light will begin for the

Jewish people. We should understand that only the Jewish people who are gathered in Israel will receive this grace.

The Word of God states that the Jewish nation will receive the right to enter into the bonds of the new covenant without any warning. It will happen in the same manner as when a thief comes at night to visit its prey. What does this mean? It means that the prey does not expect a visit from the thief.

Let us remember what happened in the past. God gave in to the desires of a small group of Jewish people to create the country of Israel and to work on its creation so that they could return from captivity to their homeland. God gave them His blessing in 1897, during the First Zionist Congress, when their hearts were united and they were able to bring about such a decision. The priesthood of the Jewish people, however, stood against such a decision. Let us note what God did following this action. He allowed an incomprehensible number of pogroms to take place in Europe, and the persecution and murder of the Jewish population had begun, in addition to inconceivable torment. The purpose of this was for the priesthood and the Jewish people to regain understanding. The Lord wanted them to understand that they would only feel security in a country where God reigned. The Jewish priesthood was not the driving force to teach their people, awaken them, and strengthen them in their resolve to strive and work on the creation of their own country. Events which occurred later show that the priesthood had not learned their lesson.

A parallel to these events is the time when Christian Europe received a message from God. God told them that the attitudes of Christianity toward their brothers from their father Jacob were not appropriate. God allowed Christian Europe to burst into flames during the First World War, so that brothers would kill one another and ten million people would perish. A plague then followed, in which ten to twenty million people perished. In addition, the Balfour Declaration was introduced which allowed the migration of the Jews into Palestine. This was a sign that God began to withdraw from the gentiles and to turn toward the Jewish people.

Just as the Christian world did not learn its lesson and did not repent, so did the Jewish people not turn towards their God.

By the terms of the Balfour Declaration of 1917, the Jewish people received the right to buy their own land and to emigrate to Palestine. They received mercy without admitting their sinfulness. They did not admit that they had killed Jesus Christ. When they received mercy through the Balfour Declaration they continued to work according to their own will and not according to God's will. A small number of Jewish people bought land, and emigrated to Palestine. Life in Palestine was very hard, which is why many did not want to leave their pleasant lives in Europe and elsewhere. God, however, sent the great depression at the beginning of 1930, giving the Jewish people a clear massage that they belonged in Palestine. Unfortunately, suffering in the captivity of the gentile world was a far more attractive option for these Jews. God provided a new warning through the Second World War and the killing of six million Jewish people by the Nazis in concentration camps.

What kind of a lesson did the Christian world receive at that time? They received an unusually crushing lesson. God warned the Christian world through the Great Depression that they should not live materialistically. The Christian world could not accept God's warning. Scientific development began full swing in industry and the world economy. World War II was God's answer to this. The war revealed the hearts of Christians towards God's commandments and towards their brothers, the Jewish people according to the flesh. Almost every Christian country, directly or indirectly, worked on the destruction of the Jewish people.

God brought down his judgment. In 1948 He gave the Jewish people a country named Israel. God acknowledged that He further turned towards the Jewish people. With a roar, the door of salvation began to close for the gentiles.

Christians did not learn their lesson from WWII. Similarly, the Jewish nation did not learn their lesson, for they did not comprehend God's prophecies. Let us take note of the two warnings we have already been given. God says; **I am reprimanding twice or thrice for the same thing.**

Following WWII, an unprecedented development of economic and capital goods and labour called materialism had begun. Christians, instead of repenting and becoming fearful of the events of WWII and the prophesied events, wholeheartedly embraced the materialistic lifestyle. Liberalism began to take the upper hand. In faith everything began to change and to adapt to the ways of the majority. If a Christian could not make changes in the congregation, he made changes in his home. A false spirit took hold of Christianity. The spiritual dark night had begun. Most believers pointed fingers at one another. Let us examine how we stand in the faith.

In order for the Jewish people to receive the right to enter into new covenant bonds, spiritual midnight must first come, not the Lord's coming with rapture of the righteous into heaven. Lawlessness in Christianity must be at the forefront and scoffers will follow their own lusts. Suddenly, in that spiritual night, the Jewish nation will receive the right to enter into the bonds of the new covenant. At this point, we can pose the question: who will be surprised by this? Obviously, everyone will be surprised.

Who worries about whether Christian countries are trying to block the fulfillment of God's will for Israel? Christian countries have the desire to create the Palestinian state on land which belongs to the tribe of Judah, divide Jerusalem, and make East Jerusalem the future capital city of the Palestinian state. What do the following words mean to you: *I will fulfill what I promised to Abraham, Isaac, and Jacob; Jerusalem is my city?* Do you know what kind of covenant God made with his servants Abraham, Jacob, Isaac, as well as with **us,** concerning this question? You might say that this is not important, since it is only important to be faithful.

However, God sends us the following warning:

| | |
|---|---|
| 1 Th. 5:4 | *But ye, brethren, are not in darkness, that that **day** should overtake you as a thief.* |
| 1 Th. 5:5 | *Ye are all the children of light, and the children of the day: we are not of the night, nor of darkness.* |
| 1 Th. 5:6 | ***Therefore let us not sleep, as do OTHERS;*** *but let us watch and be sober.* |

These unbelievable words of warning are pointed at Christians, His people. God knows that Christianity is in a deep sleep. Therefore, the Word says, *as do others:* But you, my chosen ones, do not be like others, that you do not know what the Word of God speaks of concerning the End Times: things which will happen in Christianity and with the Jewish nation. Let us be reminded of the words: *But of the time and seasons, brethren, ye have no need that I write to you, for yourselves know perfectly.* Verily, we should know perfectly when the Holy Spirit declares the truth beforehand. If that truth is not revealed to us, the Word of God says that we are sleeping. It is not possible for the Holy Spirit to conceal the truth if we pray in an appropriate manner. If we sleep, we will not be able to hear the words of the Spirit.

| | |
|---|---|
| 1 Th. 5:7 | *For they that sleep sleep in the night; and they that be drunken are drunken in the night.* |
| 1 Th. 5:8 | *But let us, who are of the day, be sober, putting on the breastplate of faith and love; and for an helmet, the hope of salvation.* |
| 1 Th. 5:9 | *For God hath not appointed us to wrath, but to obtain salvation by our Lord Jesus Christ,* |

We see the spiritual state of Christianity. It is the same among the Jewish people. Of those who survived WWII, more than half did not whish to settle in Israel after having been freed from captivity. According to statistics there are more Jewish people living outside of Israel than in Israel. In America alone, there are 4 500 000 Jewish people. And those who emigrated to Israel, had forgotten that the land promised by God to Abraham, Isaac and Jacob **cannot be sold**. Due to pressure from the most powerful countries of the world, negotiations had begun for the sale of the Promised Land to their neighbours, in exchange for peace. When this action began, God let trials and tribulations befall the Jewish people. Palestinians who lived in Israel rose in an armed struggle for their country. God is simply warning Israel's people. The Lord is saying to them: Because you are trying to sell the Promised Land, you will be afflicted by trouble and in danger of losing the whole land.

The Jewish people reaffirmed their stand in self-righteousness, from 1948, when they received their country from God. It never entered their mind to admit that they have been in captivity for nineteen hundred years and dispersed throughout the world through their own guilt. Verily, the day of the Lord must come as a thief in the night unto them. However, this day should not come as a surprise to us, God's people, those whom the Lord Jesus Christ redeemed. We are the sons of the day, and the knowledge of these future events must be in us. This is a commandment from God. God wants to help us, which is why the following words are written in the third verse:

| | |
|---|---|
| 1 Th. 5:3 | *For when they shall say, **Peace** and safety; then sudden destruction cometh upon them, as travail upon a woman with child; and they shall not escape.* |

Reading these words, the question arises: who will say "peace"? Obviously, someone who is described through the spiritual term "woman". When she says "peace" destruction will begin like a woman in travail about to deliver. This means, in order for us to understand these words it is necessary to understand what the woman symbolizes and what it means to be in travail.

In a carnal sense, the symbol "woman" describes the body, which carries the embryo. The man creates while the woman delivers. The man sows and the woman receives the seed. If the seed falls on good ground it will germinate well and in time bring forth good fruit.

In a **positive** spiritual sense the "woman" symbolizes the church, God's people of Israel, to whom God or our Lord Jesus Christ is a husband. In this union the seed represents the Word of God (spirit of His Word), pregnancy is the fulfillment of God's word (when a person possesses an idea, we say that he is conceived with a desire or an idea).

In a **negative** spiritual sense the "woman" represents this world, to which Satan is a husband. Seed is the word of this world (a worldly spirit, an idea); pregnancy is the fulfillment of some evil thought against God. (Note: there are several women in this world).

Through examples, we will now look at how God describes nations and people through the symbol "women":

## New Covenant Whore

A new covenant whore, whose name is Babylon[20], i.e. Christianity in this world gone astray, found where the Lamb's wife is hidden.

Re. 17:1    *And there came one of the seven angels which had the seven vials, and talked with me, saying unto me, Come hither; I will shew unto thee the judgment of **the great whore** that sitteth upon many WATERS:*

Re. 17:15    *And he saith unto me, The waters which thou sawest, where the whore sitteth, **are peoples, and multitudes, and nations, and tongues.***

---

[20]    Symbolizes disunity, Genesis 11:9.

A woman whore, from Revelation 17, represents Christianity that went astray. The term whore is used because rather than accepting the heavenly seed of her God (in the Spirit), which is the Word of God, she accepted the seed of Satan (materialism) into her heart. This is why we see materialism as an integral part of Christianity. She will deliver a son whose name will be Antichrist.

## New Covenant Church

Re. 12:1   *And there appeared a great wonder in heaven; a woman clothed with the sun, and the moon under her feet, and upon her head a crown of twelve stars:*

Re. 12:2   *And she being with **child cried**, travailing in birth, and pained to be delivered.*

Re. 12:5   ***And she brought forth a man child, who was to rule ALL nations with a rod of iron: and her child was caught up unto God, and to his throne.***

These words describe the new covenant church through the symbol *the woman* (people who believe in the Messiah), who is dressed in the sun. She conceived with the commandment that Jesus must be crucified. The realization of what Jesus must go through is torment for the woman, i.e. for those who follow Jesus. The peaks of this torment are travailing pains, which represent Jesus' crucifixion. The resurrection represents Jesus being revived for the spiritual world on this earth. By this Jesus becomes King, the Lord of life, child - Son, who will rule all nations with a rod of iron.

## Wife of Our God

The wife of our God is the Jewish nation, who received divorce papers from God. She represents the Jewish people who today are dispersed throughout the whole world. In the Old Testament, the Word of God describes the Jewish people as a nation, actually as a woman, married to God, who was adulterous with other spirits.

Je. 3:1   ***...but thou hast played the harlot with many lovers;*** *yet return again to me, saith the LORD.*

Je. 3:14       *Turn, O backsliding children, saith the LORD; **for I am marrried unto you:…***

Presently, the Jewish nation conceived of the idea of having its own state. Israel is the son-according to law. When he is delivered, i.e. separated by the events from the Diaspora (his mother) in the world, he will be a body, a son, who will direct his eyes toward God.

Conception took place at the proclamation of the state of Israel. When the embryo gains strength and comes to be delivered, it will not need water to guard him and help him in his growth. Water surrounding the embryo is that group of Jewish people around Israel who wholeheartedly help Israel develop and grow stronger. We know how the Jewish lobby, their organizations and the influential Jews all over the world work for Israel. Unfortunately, at a specific moment in time the Jews of the world will not be able to help the state of Israel. After peace is announced, certain events will occur which will spark anger against Jews throughout the world. Jews will be able to find salvation only if they enter Israel without delay. Through the battles of Gog and Magog, Israel will become independent and like a child will lift its eyes towards God, crying and being spiritually revived.

## Satan's Wife

Satan's wife represents a world which has fallen prey to the power of materialism. This world has conceived of the idea of destroying God's work in the Middle East. A son will be delivered, a body which will battle against the deeds of God.

1. Th. 5:3       *For when they shall say, Peace and safety; **then sudden destruction cometh upon them, as travail upon a woman with child; and THEY SHALL NOT ESCAPE.***

The process of delivering the "body" will occur when peace is announced. Travails of destruction will then come upon this world which will spare no one, just as a woman in travail is unable to escape her pain.

# Individuals Described as Women

As our fifth example we will look at words where the Lord describes every person through the symbol "women".

Mt. 24:19     *And woe unto them that are with child, and to them that give suck in those days!*

Ja. 1:14      *But every man is tempted, when he is drawn away of his own lust, and enticed.*

Ja. 1:15      *Then when lust hath conceived, it bringeth forth sin: and sin, when it is finished, bringeth forth death.*

Everything pertaining to a woman in the sense of nations or a church applies to every individual. When a sinful wish appears in someone's heart we say that it has been "conceived" and if a person does not battle against it but "nourishes" it, it brings forth the sin like a son.

## Lamb's Wife

Re. 19:7      *Let us be glad and rejoice, and give honour to him: for the marriage of the Lamb is come, and his wife hath made herself ready.*

Re. 18:4      *And I heard another voice from heaven, saying,* **COME OUT of her, my people,** *that ye be not partakers of her sins, and that ye receive not of her plagues*

The Lamb's wife is hidden in Babylon and conceived of the Word of God that God's servants should go to the Supper of the Wedding Feast. Once there, a son will be delivered whose name will be the new covenant Israel. Water (servants) guards and feeds this teaching until the embryo is strong enough to live on its own. This thought lives in present-day Christianity, i.e. Babylon, for the Lamb's wife is hidden in her. This means, that the idea was conceived by the Lamb's wife and not by Babylon. Because, the following words were written this idea is good and Babylon is evil: *COME OUT of her, my people.* The departure of God's people from Babylon is the departure of Christ's servants to Israel. This represents the beginning of the delivery process (appearance of the body) of the new covenant Israel.

From the material presented we can be certain that God sees mankind, or a nation, or an individual, as a body. This body can be of the male or female gender.

Likewise, we can understand that there exists a law which applies in these circumstances. Conception must first take place in order for an event to follow, either in a positive or a negative sense. After this, the "fetus" has to grow. Only when the "child" is ready to be delivered, does travail begin in phases.

We all know that our eyes are observing a war between the Spirit[21] of light and the spirit of darkness. In sermons preachers constantly emphasize that we are living in the End Times. Also, we all know that the mystery of the End Times will be explained in our lifetime. God will win. Satan has no hope of succeeding. God's wrath will be poured with full force upon those who oppose the Gospel of Jesus Christ. Knowing this, the question arises in the hearts of God's people: Am I fulfilling God's will? Will my house and I be spared from the tribulation which will come upon this world? How will God send me deliverance?

Presently, God is creating two sons. The first son is the state of Israel which today is already visible as a body and is shaped from the Jewish people according to the law. The second son is the new covenant Israel which will appear when Christians gather in Israel. The time will then come for these two folds to unite. One fold and one Shepherd, God's only son whose name will be the new covenant Israel – a new Adam.

Conversely, this world will be his enemy. The two sons will also unite, the first will be from this world and the second – the Antichrist[22]. There will only be two dominant spirits in the end; the Son of light and the son of darkness. These two sons will clash in the battle of Armageddon. God's Son will be victorious and will reign eternally.

Pose the following question to yourself: what is the purpose of the happenings occurring in the Middle East regarding Israel? The purpose is to destroy Israel. Verily, Satan is cunning. Satan knows that God's complete will must be fulfilled. He is a liar and when he decides to destroy God's creation,

---

[21]    Holy Spirit
[22]    The Antichrist will come from Christianity.

or man, he deceives our mother Eve. He succeeded in having Adam and Eve banished from paradise, who then became mortals. Satan knows that if he succeeds in deceiving a person and leading him or her to commit sin, God has no choice but to punish that person.

In the beginning, Satan did not need to destroy Israel. It was enough for him to deceive Israel or to transgress against the God of Israel. At that time God's only choice was to punish sin.

This world conceived of an idea. They developed a plan to force Israel to make peace with the Palestinians. They did not desire ordinary peace but rather peace which is against God's Word. Satan sowed this idea, as he believed that it would disable the fulfillment of God's plan to save the Jewish nation. The essence of the peace plan is to sell the land God pledged to Abraham, Isaac and Jacob, and their seed. Satan realizes that if Israel, God's land, is sold, the Jews are lost, for God will remove His blessing from them.

The question then arises: when did the world conceive this idea? Obviously, when the decision concerning the partition of Palestine was finalized by the UN on November 29, 1947. The Jewish delegation accepted this plan while the Palestinians rejected it. The Palestinians thought that the entire land of Palestine belonged to them and did not want to share it with the Jews. They expected to fulfill their intention through war, especially since their neighbours were from the Muslim states, and they had their support. The intention of the Palestinians was to regain the entire territory and pronounce it a Palestinian state.

Perhaps some will say that Israel had already sinned against God by accepting the UN plan concerning the partition of Palestine.

Israel, however, had not committed a sin. How is this possible? Because Israel did not exist at the time. Delegates of the Zionist movement and people from Palestine accepted the UN plan for partition. However, neither the Israeli nor the Palestinian state was recognized through the UN resolution. The plan for partition never materialized. There simply was no UN resolution. The Jewish people in Palestine pronounced a state on the territory which they kept under their control. Other countries, due to different circumstances, gradually accepted this newly pronounced state.

Verily, when the state of Israel was declared on May 18, 1948, the day of the British troops' withdrawal from Palestine, the Egyptian air force bombed Tel Aviv, and the old part of Jerusalem fell into Arab hands. War was declared from the moment of the pronouncement of the Israeli state. Up to this day, Israel has waged five wars against the Palestinians and its neighbouring Arab states. Israel has won every war and is constantly expanding its territory. Palestinian and Arab expectations did not materialize. When the Arabs realized that they did not have the power or the means to defeat Israel they changed their tactics and accepted the cooperation of the world. They actually accepted an idea from this world, which is under Satan's control, to divide Palestine (the Jewish Promised Land). They expected to fulfill their idea of the complete destruction of the Israeli state. With the acceptance of the plan for partition, they set the following additional conditions:

-    All refugees and their descendants must have the right to return to the land from which they fled
-    All property and land must be returned to its owners.

If Israel accepts these conditions the Jewish people will be a minority in their Promised Land. In reality, Israel will become a Muslim state.

Since the Arabs lost more territory through the five wars than their plan for partition defined, the idea to trade land for peace took on new meaning for the Palestinian and Arab states.

The initial agreement to trade land for peace was made with Egypt in 1978. By that treaty, Israel returned Sinai to Egypt. The border was marked and pointed toward the beginning of peace with Egypt.

Let us note: according to God's word, Sinai does not belong to Israel. This means that it was not a problem returning Sinai to Egypt. Israel did not commit a sin in God's eyes through this treaty. This treaty appeared to be fruitful for the world. Peace began to reign in that region and the Western countries reinforced their positions there.

The pregnancy lay ahead. The fruit in "the womb of the woman - this world", took shape. The idea to ruin the creation of Biblical Israel took root. In 2005 we heard in the news media the comments of those who made peace, that Israel had understood that it would not be able to achieve its idea concerning the creation of Biblical Israel. They have therefore stepped back from this idea. They are, however, only partially right. Due to pressure from this world only one part of the Israeli population was willing to submit to this.

However, the other part of the Israeli population is trying to oppose this. They are building settlements and settling their people on the territory which according to the partition plan belongs to the Palestinians. The world is not standing by idly; the world media calls these settlements illegal, putting pressure on Israel in an attempt to stop their efforts. There are a quarter of a million Jews settled in this territory today.

The Palestinian and Arab states have international support, both politically and financially. This has contributed to more tension, since the Arabs have lost every war with Israel. Their demands are as follows: withholding the single inch of land which the plan of partition of Palestine speaks of (and which they had initially rejected); removing every settlement from the territory; making East Jerusalem their capital city; taking possession of every Jewish holy place; returning every piece of land and buildings on it which belonged to Israel since 1947 (according to the plan of partition) to the Palestinians; returning all Palestinian refugees and their descendents to Israel – to the land which belonged to Israel according to the plan of partition. In essence, they are asking for the total capitulation of Israel.

Let us see what the Lord says:

Jl. 3:1    For, behold, **in those days, and in that time, when I shall bring again the captivity of Judah and Jerusalem,**

Jl. 3:2    *I will also gather ALL nations, and will bring them down into the valley of Jehoshaphat, and will plead with them there for my people and for my heritage Israel, whom they have scattered among the nations, and parted my land.*

Jl. 3:3    *And they have cast lots for my people; and have given a boy for an harlot, and sold a girl for wine, that they might drink.*

Jl. 3:4    *Yea, and what have ye to do with me, O Tyre, and Zidon, and ALL the coasts of Palestine? will ye render me a recompence? and if ye recompense me, swiftly and speedily will I return your recompence upon your own head;*

Jl. 3:5    *Because ye have taken my silver and my gold, and have carried into YOUR temples my goodly pleasant things:*

Jl. 3:6    *The children also of Judah and the children of Jerusalem have ye sold unto the Grecians, that ye might remove them far from their border.*

Jl. 3:7    *Behold, I will raise them out of the place whither ye have sold them, and will return your recompence upon your own head:*

Jl. 3:8          *And I will sell your sons and your daughters into the hand of*
                 *the children of Judah, and they shall sell them to the Sabeans,*
                 *to a people far off: for* **the LORD hath spoken it.**

The Word of God testifies that there will be no partition of the land because it is written: *and will return your recompense upon your own head.* These will be their wages: *"And I will sell your sons and your daughters into the hand of the children of Judah, and they shall sell them to the Sabeans, to a people far off: for the Lord hath spoken it"*.

However, through the prophet Joel we are provided with a description of what our eyes are seeing today in the Middle East. We see an attempt by Israel's enemies to reclaim what they had lost. The Word of God says; *what have ye to do with me, o Tyre, and Zidon, and ALL the coasts of Palestine?* Also the Word of God testifies that they will have the support of the world, because it is written: *I will also gather all nations....* They will come under judgment because they are making a concerted effort to battle against God and prevent the fulfillment of His will.

Jl. 3:12         *Let the heathen be wakened, and come up to the valley of*
                 *Jehoshaphat: for there will I sit to judge all the heathen*
                 **round about.**

Judgment in the valley of Jehoshaphat will occur before the day of the Lord comes to the Jewish people. Through this event the ideas of this world will materialize. The body will appear. The body will mature, which means that the desire to destroy Israel will not diminish but will grow and become stronger. In addition, when he becomes a powerful man, he will try to realize his evil thoughts with the cooperation of his mother; this will occur through Armageddon, the war between God and Satan. Satan cannot tolerate the existence of the son of God – Israel.

Some may pose a question in this manner: is judgment in the Jehoshaphat valley actually the spiritual midnight from the parable of the Ten Virgins (Matthew 25)? The answer is no. Spiritual midnight will arrive before the judgment in the Jehoshaphat valley. In order to know when this will occur, it is necessary to know what will happen during spiritual midnight.

The Jewish people had the idea and the desire to occupy their own country since 1897. In 1948 Israel was conceived as a body. The body began to grow. The pains of travail should begin in the spiritual midnight, through which Israel will be delivered and become spiritually alive in this world. Israel must then spiritually grow and come into full power to withstand an attack from Satan's son (this world).

In the spiritual midnight therefore, the body (Israel) will be ready to be separated (travail) from its mother – the Jewish Diaspora. Also, the body of this world will be ready. Peace will be announced and an agreement will be made. This world will overcome the Jewish lobby in the western countries and in the UN. Through this Israel will be forced to sign a treaty, or an agreement, which will not be in accordance with the Bible. Israel will be pressured to the point that will cause the agreement to fall apart. This will cause tribulation for the Jewish people, for Christianity and for the whole world, which is compared to pains in travail.

In order for peace to be achieved, in addition to Egypt and Jordan, other neighbours of Israel – Syria, Lebanon and Palestine – must recognize the existence of Israel. This means, *the skin* must be put on the body. In other words, borders must be established and drawn. This is the condition for the beginning of the delivery process.

Eze. 37:8     *And when I beheld, lo, the sinews and the flesh came up upon them, and **the skin** covered them above: but there was no breath in them.*

Israel must make concessions in order for these neighbours to recognize their existence. Also, in order for Israel to give in to the demands and make concessions the rest of the world must impose strong pressure. We can see today that Israel has already begun making many concessions. They accepted the creation of the Palestinian state on land which belongs to the tribe of Judah. As yet, they do not want to give in to the demands concerning Jerusalem. In essence, we are observing a Jewish nation on the brink of total catastrophe with the strong possibility of sinning against God. Perhaps you question why Israel had already made concessions? This is because Israel was threatened with UN sanctions. This would mean that the state would not be able to buy or sell anything outside of their country until they fulfilled the conditions which would be set by the rest of the world. In which case, according to the words of one politician, Israel would not be able to survive for more than three months. Israel will give in out of fear because they will not have enough faith in God to deliver them from the hands of their enemy.

From the time Israel was created, GOD DID NOT ALLOW Israel to sin so greatly that the plan for their salvation would come under question. Be reminded of events which have already occurred, such as when Isaac Rabin was the president of Israel. At that time, Israel was under great pressure from the whole world, because the Palestinians provoked unrest, which began in 1988 and which by that time had intensified. On September 13, 1993, as a result of pressure from the rest of the world, Isaac Rabin was forced to sign an agreement which would create the Palestinian state, in return for the cessation of unrest. This was the so-called Oslo Accords. What happened? President Rabin was assassinated on November 4, 1995. This was a sign from God that the God of Israel did not agree with this. Have you noticed that since the signing of the Oslo Accords, anytime there is the possibility of an agreement to bring about progress in negotiations to create the Palestinian state, terrorist action always interrupts negotiations? Today the Oslo agreement is dead. In this example we see a testimony of how God prevented Israel from sharing (sale for peace) the Promised Land with the Palestinians.

We will look at another example which took place in 2001, when two towers were toppled in New York. People see this event as simply a terrorist attack. This attack disrupted the unilateral intention to pronounce the Palestinian state with clear borders, with East Jerusalem as the capital city, without Israel's agreement. This announcement was postponed. At the same time the world economy experienced a shock. The global economy is the heart of this world. To this world, the existence of a Biblical Israel in the Middle East does not fit in with business. The business world and its global economy are opposed to the fulfillment of God's will. This is why the World Trade Center in New York, the heart of the business world, was destroyed. The will of God had to be fulfilled. This is an example of how God prevented this world from disrupting His plan of salvation for the Jewish people. This was the reason why God decided to destroy the World Trade Center. In addition, this means that God did not allow the Palestinian state to be proclaimed on land which He intended for us, the descendants of Abraham, Isaac and Jacob.

From these events we can deduce that when the time comes for peace to be proclaimed, the creation of the Palestinian state will not be pronounced, but rather only an agreement will be reached outlining the steps or stages to be brought to the proclamation of the Palestinian state. However, even this will suffice because soon after travail will come upon them as upon a woman with child. Events will occur which God will allow in order to make the proclamation of the Palestinian state impossible. The agreement then will be – for the neighbouring countries – the only recognition of Israel's right to exist. The plan to divide the Promised Land will fail.

Let us note what the Word of God says:

1 Th. 5:3    *For when they shall say,* **Peace and safety;** *then sudden destruction cometh upon them, as travail upon a woman with child; and they shall not escape.*

Something else will occur at the time of the proclamation of peace: "and safety" will be spoken. What does this mean? What is the world afraid of? The world is afraid of things that are prophesied through God's Word which will happen to this world. The key element of these things is the creation of Biblical Israel. This means that clauses will exist within the signed peace treaty which will make it impossible for the word of the Bible to be fulfilled. Also, the world will then be able to say: we should not be afraid. Israel accepted our conditions. Now we are certain that our plan to divide the Promised Land will be fulfilled. Actually, the Israelites sinned against God, and God's plan to save them will not be fulfilled.

Let us see what God says in the Gospel according to Luke:

Lu. 21:35    *For as a SNARE shall it* **come on all** *them that dwell on the face of the whole earth.*
Lu. 21:36    **Watch ye therefore,** *and pray* **always,** *that ye may be accounted worthy to escape all these things that shall come to pass, and to stand before the Son of man.*

In the spiritual sense a snare is the "word". Why? Because, the snare is a device by which you trap something. Be reminded of the parable about fishing. Fish are caught (trapped) by nets just as souls are caught and trapped by the Word of God and are seeking repentance. Also, the word, the announcement of peace, will be a snare for the beginning of travail as upon a woman with child.

The Word of God is warning His faithful children to be watchful. This means that we should examine the Word of God in order to understand future events and events which are unfolding before our eyes according to the Bible. If we are not watchful, do not pray, and start living according to the flesh as is written in the 34th verse:

Lu. 21:34  *And take heed to yourselves, least at any time your **hearts be overcharged with surfeiting, and drunkenness, and cares of this life**, and so that DAY come upon you unawares.*

The day of the signing of the treaty will come suddenly. That word "peace" will be a snare and events will begin to unfold. On this fateful day Christians will find themselves unprepared. In the parable of the Ten Virgins God describes this unreadiness in a dramatic way.

Mt. 25.5  *While the Bridegroom tarried, **they all slumbered and slept.***
Mt. 25.6  *And **at midnight there was a cry made**, ...*

The cry represents certain events (the beginning of travail), which will make the midnight, actually the signing of the treaty, possible. It is better to say: the events which will begin to occur will force the servants of God to cry out, for the situation will become urgent. These events will be so impressive that both the foolish and the wise or all those who do not watch, will arise.

In 2005 Israel started unilaterally handing over Gaza under the rule of the Palestinians. According to God's Word this is not a problem. Israel is not trespassing against God's will, because Gaza never belonged to Israel. However, the problem is the "package" ("Road Map"), which this world insists on attaching to the agreement. If this happens, and Syria and Lebanon are included, there will be a possibility to say peace, actually the start of spiritual midnight. Keep the following words in our hearts: a snare will appear suddenly, when we least expect it.

Up to this point we have been speaking of how and why the labour pains will begin and also that these pains will be felt by all those who do not find refuge, like Noah and his family, on "Noah's second ark". Noah's ark is Israel. This may seem illogical at first glance. However, remember that the region of spiritual darkness and of Antichrist will reign over the whole world. Only on Noah's ark will there be a light for God's servants who come to prepare the bride (Jewish nation) to make a covenant with the Bridegroom, Jesus Christ.

When all those who find mercy in God's sight are sheltered, God will pour His judgment upon those individuals from the gentiles who did not heed Christ's Gospel. The departure for Israel is recorded in many places in the Bible. This departure is described through the term "water" which will spill out during the delivery. In another sense, "water" is the spirit and the spirit is in God's people.

Four examples in which the loss of water appears will be explained. These four examples – from 1 Thessalonians 5, Ezekiel 37, Matthew 24, and 2 Thessalonians 2 – will be compared to the words from Jesus Christ's parable of the Ten Virgins (the fifth example). Jesus Christ's parable speaks of the loss of water in a similar yet different manner through the most descriptive steps. Lastly, John's Revelation will be used to show places where the Word of God speaks about the departure of God's people.

| | |
|---|---|
| Mt. 25:1 | *Then shall the kingdom of heaven be likened unto ten virgins, which took their lamps, and **went forth to meet** the Bridegroom.* |
| Mt. 25:2 | *And five of them were wise, and five were foolish.* |
| Mt. 25:3 | *They that were foolish took their lamps, and took no oil with them:* |
| Mt. 25:4 | *But the wise took oil in their vessels with their lamps.* |
| Mt. 25:5 | *While the Bridegroom tarried, they **all slumbered and slept.*** |
| Mt. 25:6 | *And **at midnight there was a cry made,** Behold, the Bridegroom cometh; go ye out to meet him.* |
| Mt. 25:7 | *Then all those virgins **arose,** and **trimmed their lamps.*** |
| Mt. 25:8 | *And the foolish said unto the wise, Give us of your oil; for our lamps are gone out.* |
| Mt. 25:9 | *But the wise answered, saying, Not so; lest there be not enough for us and you: but go ye rather to them that sell, and buy for yourselves.* |
| Mt. 25:10 | *And while they went to buy, the Bridegroom came; and they that were ready **went in** with him to the marriage: and **the door was shut.*** |
| Mt. 25:11 | *Afterward came also the other virgins, saying, Lord, Lord, open to us.* |

Mt. 25:12    *But he answered and said, Verily I say unto you, I know you not.*

The first twelve verses summarize the ten steps which will happen in our time, from the beginning of the creation of the Jewish state until their salvation. There are fewer steps in the remaining four examples. Only through comparison will we be able to see how everything is connected and that the Old Testament, the Letters, and John's Revelation speak of the same examples. For an easier orientation, the following steps of the prophecy of the Ten Virgins will give additional brief explanations.

The steps from the parable of the Ten Virgins:

1.  **They went forth to meet the Bridegroom** - Through the Balfour Declaration of 1917 the migration of Jewish people into Palestine was made possible. This started the formation of the state of Israel. According to the Zionist plan, Jews will return to their ancient homeland. Also, according to the prophecies, they will achieve salvation by believing in Jesus Christ, while the moved Christians will go out to await the Bridegroom (Jesus Christ who is coming in a spiritual sense through the voice of His word). The Bridegroom will come to take the virgins which He needs at the Supper of the Wedding Feast of the Lamb to make His bride (old covenant Israel people), ready for marriage, actually baptism. In this way, they will become part of the body of Christ.

2.  **Falling asleep** - The virgins fell asleep (they stopped preaching) because the Bridegroom was late. The Bridegroom's coming did not occur in time for the third spiritual night.

3.  **The coming of the spiritual midnight**- This represents peace between the state of Israel and the Palestinians and their supporters, Syria and Lebanon. Through this agreement the creation of a Palestinian state within Israel, with East Jerusalem as its capital, will be made possible.

4.  **There was a cry made**- The agreement for the creation of the state of Palestine on the soil of the "Promised Land", by dividing Jerusalem, making it Arab on the east side and Jewish on the west. This is not in accordance with the will of God. God will stand in

the way of the fulfillment of this agreement. He will allow events to occur which will annul the agreement- *at midnight there was a cry made*.

5. **Virgins arose from their slumber**- The virgins will be forced to arise due to events which will occur in the Middle East and in other parts of the world.

6. **They stood up**- The virgins who arose from their slumber will stand up and prepare themselves for the coming of the Bridegroom.

7. **Trimmed their lamps**- Because it is the spiritual night, it is necessary to have oil and trimmed lamps in order to be able to meet the dear guest.

8. **They that were ready WENT TOWARDS THE BRIDEGROOM**- The virgins went out to meet God's word (Bridegroom), Christ in the Spirit, who desires to save the Jewish people. The departure of Christ's servants (the Holy Spirit) from the gentiles is shown through the symbol "water" which is released from this world or Babylon.

9. **They entered the marriage feast**- This denotes the migration of Christ's servants into the state of Israel. They should help to graft the Jewish people onto the olive tree.

10. **Closing the door to the wedding feast**- This will mark the beginning of the spiritual awakening of the Jews in Israel. During this time Israel will be isolated from the rest of the world.

(**Note:** We will use these ten steps from the prophecy of the Ten Virgins to compare with other prophecies in order to establish similarities and differences.)

In the parable of the Ten Virgins, the Lord describes present Christianity by illustrating which types of servants — virgins who are awaiting the coming of the Bridegroom — Christianity consists of. He says that there are both foolish and wise servants; those who are not ready and will be late in entering, allowing the door to shut, and those who are wise and will be ready and prepared to enter the wedding feast with the Bridegroom. This means that every servant of God should, through the parable of the Ten Virgins, come to an understanding of whether or not he or she is prepared and ready to go to Israel. Those who are prepared to go are part of that "water" (faithful people) that will issue from the gentiles.

- COMPARISON with the prophecy of 1 Thessalonians 5.

| | |
|---|---|
| 1 Th. 5:2 | *For yourselves know perfectly that the day of the Lord so cometh as a thief in the night.* |
| 1 Th. 5:3 | *For when they shall say,* **Peace** *and safety; then sudden destruction cometh upon them,* **as travail upon a woman with child;** *and they* **shall not escape.** |
| 1 Th. 5:4 | *But ye, brethren, are not in darkness, that that day should overtake you as a thief.* |
| 1 Th. 5:8 | *But let us, who are of the day, be sober, putting on the breastplate of faith and love; and for an helmet, the hope of salvation.* |

The quoted words from 1 Thessalonians 5 contain only five steps:

1.  When they shall say peace
2.  Coming of sudden destruction like pain, which represents the beginning of travail upon a woman with child
3.  Coming out of the water (this step is not written directly but we will quote it as this prophecy was written for **us** so that we will be able to better understand the events which will cause us to depart for Israel)
4.  They shall not escape (gentiles from the destruction)
5.  Destruction

Now we will examine the steps of this Epistle together with the steps from the prophecy of the Ten Virgins for any similarities:

The First step of the First Epistle to Thessalonians is "when they shall say peace". This step is compared to the third step from the prophecy of the Ten Virgins which is the "coming of spiritual midnight".

We can understand that the coming of midnight and the moment of spoken peace are one and the same. Why? Because, the spiritual midnight is the culmination of not knowing God's will. The spiritual blindness which fell upon this world prevents many from understanding that God is returning His people to their homeland.

The Second step from 1Thessalonians is the "coming of sudden destruction like pain". This step is compared with the fourth step from the prophecy of the Ten Virgins which is: "there was a cry made".

We can conclude that the second and fourth steps have the same meaning. Why? After making peace, unforeseen events will happen to the Palestinian and Jewish people. The Jewish people will be forced to reject the signed peace treaty concerning the creation of a Palestinian state within Israel. The world meanwhile will be furious. To shelter Israel from the threat of this world, God will allow certain events to occur around the world, and will not allow the fulfillment of the signed treaty. These events are described in the parable of the Ten Virgins under the term "there was a cry made". Yet, in 1Thessalonians 5:3 the same events are referred to as the beginning of travail upon a woman with child, because they will unleash pain and suffering upon the world.

The Third step from 1Thessalonians is "coming out of the water". This step is compared to the eighth step from the prophecy of the Ten Virgins — "they that were ready went towards the Bridegroom".

Water symbolizes the Holy Ghost who lives in God's new covenant people. Therefore, the term "coming out of the water", describes the departure of Christ's faithful servants from the gentiles. It is only possible to depart with the Bridegroom, and that it is Christ who is in His word. The release of water is not directly written in 1Thessalonians 5. However, it is possible to understand that it is spoken of because it is written:

1Th. 5:4     *But ye, brethren, are not in the darkness, that that day **should overtake you** as a thief.*

The Word is saying that we should be watchful and understand the Word of God. We should know that the DAY, the time for their salvation, is approaching for the Jewish people. This DAY should not take us by surprise. It is important to know the time when we should go to Israel for the wedding, actually for their salvation. We cannot wait until the spoiled child of the woman (this world) is delivered. The deliverance of that child will come through the WORD. When this happens, it will be a sign for the world, Christians and Jews alike, who are outside of Israel, that they have entered the final period of destruction from which it will be impossible to escape. At the same time the DAY will begin for the Jews in Israel, the time when their salvation will occur, the day of the final battle between God and Satan.

The Fourth step from 1 Thessalonians is "they shall not escape" (the gentiles from the destruction). This step is compared to the 10ᵗʰ step from the prophecy of the Ten Virgins – "closing the door of the wedding feast". Why? The woman from this world will deliver her child, who has only one duty, which is to destroy Israel. This means that in that time no one will have a chance to enter into the state of Israel, for the "child" will not allow it. (The term "child" describes the newly created international body which is responsible for the enforcement of the treaty between the Palestinians and Israel).

The Fifth step from 1 Thessalonians is **"Destruction"**, or the pouring of God's wrath upon the gentiles. That is why apostle Paul sent a message to the faithful that they should be sober and put on the breastplate of faith and love; as well as a helmet, the hope of salvation, so that they would be able to escape the destruction which will fall upon the gentiles after the closing of the door to the Wedding Feast of the Lamb.

## • COMPARISON with Ezekiel 37:

| | |
|---|---|
| Eze. 37:7 | *So I prophesied as I was commended: and as I prophesied, **there was a noise**, and behold **a shaking**, and **the bones came together**, bone to his bone.* |
| Eze. 37:8 | *And when I beheld, lo, **the sinews and flash came upon them**, and **the skin covered them above**: but there was no breath in them.* |
| Eze. 37:9 | *Then said he unto me, prophecy unto the wind, prophecy, son of man, and **say to the wind**, thus saith the Lord god; **come from the four winds, o breath**, and **breathe upon these** slain, that they may live.* |

The words quoted from Ezekiel 37, contain the following eight steps:

1. There was a noise
2. A shaking
3. The bones came together
4. The sinews and flesh came upon them
5. The skin covered them above

6. Say to the wind
7. **Come from the four winds, o breath**
8. Breathe upon these slain

Of these eight steps five are the same as in the prophecy of the Ten Virgins in Matthew 25.

The First step from Ezekiel's prophecy is "there was a noise". This step is the same as the first step from the prophecy of the Ten Virgins – "they went forth to meet the Bridegroom".

Through the Balfour Declaration, the Jewish people were given the right to emigrate to Palestine and the right to buy land there. This is a sign for the virgins (for Christianity), actually a voice approaching the time when the Jewish people will receive the right to enter into the bonds of the new covenant. This is why the virgins will go out to meet the Bridegroom. They will go on faith to await the Bridegroom's call so that they will have a part in the preparations of the old covenant Jewish people to enter the covenant bonds through Christ. This means, that the old covenant Israel, or the Jewish people according to the flesh (in the state of Israel) are the bride of the future. They are those who will be grafted onto the natural olive tree (new covenant church) through baptism in the name of Jesus Christ.

The Fifth step from Ezekiel's prophecy is "the skin covered them above". This step is the same as the third step from the prophecy of the Ten Virgins – "the coming of spiritual midnight".

The skin did not cover the body – though it is already 2009 – yet this problem is still in the process of being solved. When Israel goes down on its knees and signs the agreement, spiritual midnight will begin. However, the Palestinian state will not be pronounced; steps will determine how this will be achieved.

The Sixth step from Ezekiel's prophecy is: "say to the wind". This step is the same as the fourth step from the prophecy of the Ten Virgins – "There was a cry made".

Due to extreme pressure from the world, Israel will sign an agreement that is not according to the will of God because God made a covenant with Abraham that He would give all the land of Canaan to him and his seed after him, for an everlasting possession. In addition, God is saying: Jerusalem is my town. This means that the essence of the disagreements in the Middle

East is the following: whose word (will) will be fulfilled – the word of this world or the Word of the Creator of heaven and earth, the God of Israel. God cannot allow the signed agreement between Israel, the Palestinians, and the Arabs to be fulfilled. Jerusalem will never be a divided city. Judea, the land where our Lord Jesus was born, cannot be under the rule of the Palestinian people or, rather, the people of this world. This is the reason why the CRY will start at midnight. Events which will occur in Israel, in its vicinity, and in the world at large, will prevent the fulfillment of a signed agreement. However, these events will be so monumental that they will strike fear into the hearts of people and cause every Christian, be he wise or foolish, to wake up spiritually. And those who possess oil will get ready for the departure to Israel.

On the other hand, these events in Ezekiel's prophecy are described in the sixth step through the words "say to the wind".

Why?

Because they are a testimony that the time for the virgins to depart for Israel has come. The servants of God to whom the truth has been revealed will receive the power to speak, or to preach about the departure for Israel.

The seventh step from Ezekiel's prophecy is "come from the four winds, o breath". This step is the same as the eighth step from the prophecy of the Ten Virgins – "they that were ready went towards the Bridegroom" and the ninth step from the prophecy of the Ten Virgins – "they entered the marriage feast".

It is evident that the seventh step from Ezekiel's prophecy: "come from the four winds, o breath" speaks about the departure of the ready virgins to the Marriage Supper of the Lamb, actually the salvation of the Jewish people.

The eighth step from Ezekiel's prophecy is "breathe upon these slain". This step is not directly quoted in the prophecy of the Ten Virgins. It is possible, however, to understand that the time of salvation of the Jewish people ("breathe upon these slain") may start only when the door to the wedding feast of the wedding is closed, actually the tenth step of the prophecy of the Ten Virgins.

Ezekiel's prophecy contains more steps than the prophecy of the Ten Virgins. The reason is that Ezekiel 37 describes events which are related to both the Jewish and the Christian nations. That which is related to us is generally described in the 8th and 9th verses and especially from the 16th to the 23rd verses and further. In addition, we realize that the Word of God in Ezekiel's prophecy describes the departure of the water like the departure of the wind.

- COMPARISON with Matthew 24:

We will not quote the whole prophecy consisting of 38 verses (Matthew 24:14-51); rather, we will quote only a few verses and steps.

| | |
|---|---|
| Mt. 24:15 | **When ye therefore shall see the abomination of desolation,** *spoken of by Daniel the prophet, stand in the holy place, (whoso readeth, let him understand:)* |
| Mt. 24:20 | *But prey ye that your* **FLIGHT be not in the winter, neither on the sabbath day***:* |
| Mt. 24:21 | **For then shall be great tribulation, such as was not** *since the beginning of the world to this time, no, nor ever shall be.* |
| Mt. 24:28 | *For wheresoever the carcass is, there will the eagles be gathered together.* |
| Mt. 24:29 | *Immediately after the tribulation of those days shall* **the sun be darkened***, and the moon shall not give her light, and the stars shall fall from heaven, and the powers of the heavens shall be shaken:* |

The sequence of events according to the Gospel of Matthew, which we quoted, are as follows:

1. When ye therefore shall see the abomination of desolation
2. Coming of tribulation
3. Flight in the winter, and on the Sabbath day:
4. Revealing of the place to which we will flee
5. The sun will be darkened

We will now compare these five steps from Matthew 24 to the prophecy of the Ten Virgins. We will see that these five steps are contained in the prophecy of the Ten Virgins. Also, we should note that every step from the prophecies compared to the prophecy of the Ten Virgins, has the same sequence of events.

Likewise, the first step from Matthew 24 "when ye therefore shall see the abomination of desolation" corresponds to the second step from the prophecy of the Ten Virgins – "falling asleep".

When Christianity falls asleep, the abomination of desolation will appear and stand in the holy place. Ponder these words for a moment because they are very important for every Christian. The Word of God says that a little leaven will leaven the whole lump. In the prophecy of the Ten Virgins the Word of God speaks about collective sleeping. It is written that they all slumbered and slept. Similarly, in Matthew 24, the Word of God speaks about the collective abomination of desolation, which stands in the holy place. The Word of God does not say that the abomination of desolation stands in some holy places or in many places, rather it speaks of the holy place. However, the word says, "when you shall see", which indicates that there will be those who will not be a part of the abomination of desolation. In the same manner the prophecy of the Ten Virgins states: *And at midnight there was a cry made, Behold, the Bridegroom cometh; go ye out to meet him.* This means that there were those who did not sleep because they were in a position to cry out and wake the sleeping virgins.

To sleep in faith is a sin. One who sleeps cannot live spiritually in the spiritual world. We can say this in a different way: the spiritual man who lives materialistically is asleep to the spiritual world.

Materialism is more important to many believers than the kingdom of God. These believers will adapt the Word of God to themselves, their children, their family or to this world so that their numbers will increase. The doctrine of God is no longer preached in its original strength. It has been watered down in an effort to adjust the Word according to this world. The abomination of desolation appeared to stand in the holy place. This means the doctrine of God is holy and stands in the holy place. However, the doctrine cannot be holy when it has been diluted and not preached in its fullness. This can vary from one denomination to another and from congregation to congregation, but it is still an abomination of desolation before God.

The second step from Matthew 24 is the "coming of tribulation". This step is compared to the fourth step from the prophecy of the Ten Virgins – "there was a cry made".

Signing an agreement of peace with the Arabs under unacceptable conditions for the Jews will cause tribulation. The Word of God says that great tribulation will begin, such as was **not** since the beginning of the world to this time, nor ever shall be. (Note: the words in this verse are related to the time even before they will say peace in 1 Thessalonians 5:3).

The third step from Matthew 24 is "flight in the winter and on the Sabbath day". This step is compared with the eighth step from the prophecy of the Ten Virgins – "they that were ready went towards the Bridegroom".

In Matthew 24:20 Jesus warns us that we should always pray to God so that our flight is not in winter, neither on the Sabbath day. This means that, even in this prophecy, God clearly describes the departure of the Holy Spirit for Israel.

The fourth step from Matthew 24 is "revealing of the place where we will flee". This step is compared with the ninth step of the prophecy of the Ten Virgins – "they enter onto the marriage feast".

The following words are found in the description of the place where we shall flee:

Mt. 24:28    *For whithersoever the carcass is, there will the eagles be gathered together.*

The word "carcass" denotes a dead body without a spirit. This means that the Jewish nation (like a body) is spiritually dead (dry bones Ezekiel 37:1,2) without the Holy Spirit. They should believe and make a covenant unto death with the Bridegroom, Jesus Christ. There will be a spiritual marriage in Israel. This is why the wise virgins will flee, actually enter the wedding feast with the Bridegroom.

The fifth step from Matthew 24 is "the sun will be darkened". This step is compared with the tenth step from the prophecy of the Ten Virgins – "closing the door to the wedding feast".

All of these events will occur in the third spiritual night, on the one hand through false doctrine and on the other hand through the departure of the wise virgins (Holy Spirit) to the wedding feast. The spiritual sun will darken for the gentiles and the stars – preachers, servants of Christ – will fall from the spiritual heaven. God will allow the door into Israel to be shut. The pleading of the foolish virgins will not be heeded.

306

The Word of God describes the departure of water from the woman through the words "flee away" in the quoted prophecy of the 24th chapter of Matthew.

- A COMPARISON with the second Epistle to the Thessalonians:

| | |
|---|---|
| 2 Th. 1:7 | *And to you who are troubled rest with us, when the lord Jesus shall be revealed from heaven with his mighty angels.* |
| 2 Th. 1:8 | *In flaming fire taking vengeance on them that know not God, and that they obey not the Gospel of our Lord Jesus Christ:* |
| 2 Th. 2:3 | *Let no man deceive you by any means: for that day shall not come, except there come **failing away** first, and that **man of sin be revealed**, the son of perdition;* |
| 2 Th. 2:7 | *For the mystery of iniquity doth already work: **only he who now letteth will let, until he be TAKEN OUT of the way.*** |
| 2 Th. 2:8 | *And than shall that Wicked be revealed, whom the **Lord shall consume with the spirit of his mouth,** and **shall destroy with the brightness of his coming:*** |
| 2 Th. 2:11 | *And **for this cause God will sand them strong delusion,** that they should believe in the lie:* |

In the steps quoted above we find:

1. Falling away from the faith (2 Thessalonians 2:3)
2. Removing Him who held back the coming of the Antichrist (2 Thessalonians 2:7)
3. Coming of the Antichrist (2 Thessalonians 2:8)
4. Sending a strong delusion (2 Thessalonians 2:11)
5. Lord Jesus Christ shall consume him with the spirit of his mouth (2 Thessalonians 2:8)
6. Enemies of the Gospel shall be destroyed with the brightness of His coming (2 Thessalonians 2:8; 1:7,8)
7. Those who are troubled will be delivered (2 Thessalonians 1:7)

By comparing these seven steps with the steps of the prophecy of the Ten Virgins, we notice that three of the steps are identical to one another. We will quote these three steps.

The First step from 2 Thessalonians — "falling away from the faith", is compared with the second step from the prophecy of the Ten Virgins — "falling asleep".

Falling away from the faith can happen only when a believer does not live according to God's teaching, when he is sleeping in the faith.

The second step from 2 Thessalonians — "removing Him who holds back the coming of the Antichrist" is connected with the eighth step of the prophecy of the Ten Virgins — "they that were ready went towards the Bridegroom".

Removing Him who holds back the coming of the Antichrist represents the departure of the wise virgins, God's people, to Israel, for the Wedding Feast of the Lamb. When the Holy Ghost, or God's people in whom the Holy Ghost resides — is removed, the way for the man of sin to be revealed will be opened.

The Third step from 2 Thessalonians — "coming of the Antichrist" is compared with the tenth step from the prophecy of the Ten Virgins — "closing the door to the wedding feast".

The remaining steps from 2 Thessalonians, will occur during a time which the prophecy of the Ten Virgins does not embrace. This means that the other steps will occur in the time of the seventh trumpet. These are the 4th, 5th, 6th, and 7th steps.

When we are comparing the words from the second Epistle to the Thessalonians with the words from the prophecy of the Ten Virgins, we must understand that only the Holy Ghost can hold back the coming of the Antichrist. The Holy Ghost resides within God's people. This is why His people must come from this world and enter Israel. When we leave this materialistic world the question then arises: what kind of life can we expect to have in Israel in that time? Shall we live in the same manner as we do today?

John's Revelation also speaks concerning the departure of God's people to Israel. In order to comprehend the description of the departure for Israel we must compare the words, which speak of the three big woes that will befall this world.

The first woe is described in the fifth trumpet, the second in the sixth trumpet, and the third in the seventh trumpet.

We will find a description of the horrible war in the second woe, actually the sixth trumpet. We read:

| | |
|---|---|
| Re. 9:12 | *One woe is past; and, behold, there come **TWO woes** more hereafter.* |
| Re. 9:13 | *And **the SIXTH angel sounded,** and I heard a voice from the four horns of the golden altar which is before God,* |
| Re. 9:14 | *Saying to the sixth angel which had the trumpet, **loose the four angels** which are bound in the great river Euphrates.* |
| Re. 9:15 | *And the four angels were loosed, which were prepared for an hour, and a day, and a month, and a year, for **to slay the third part of men.*** |

The Word of God clearly testifies that a big war will occur in the time of the sixth trumpet. Obviously, a nuclear war will occur during this time, when a third of mankind, approximately two billion people, will be slain. This means that peace will be announced before the war, for peace will come before destruction. Also, the Word of God clearly says that the war will be the second woe (Revelation 9:12) which will befall this world. We must read the next words to properly comprehend the weight of the events of the sixth trumpet. (Pay heed to the four angels. They are the same angels that are mentioned in the 9th chapter):

| | |
|---|---|
| Re. 7:1 | *And after these things I saw four angels standing on the four corners of the earth, holding the four winds of the earth, that the wind should not blow on the earth, nor on the sea, nor on any tree,* |
| Re. 7:2 | *And I saw another angel ascending from the east, having the seal of the living God: and he cried with loud voice to the four angels, to whom was given to hurt the earth and sea,* |
| Re. 7:3 | *Saying, hurt not the earth, neither the sea, nor the trees, till we have sealed the servants of our God on their foreheads.* |

These words explain that before the beginning of the sealing of the servants of our God on their foreheads (baptism in the name of Jesus Christ the crucified), the four angels who control the events on this earth received an order to protect three things. They received an order to hold the four winds (spirits) and thereby make the salvation (sealing with the Holy Ghost) of humankind possible. If we continue to read further in the seventh chapter, we will find that the Jews (up to the destruction of Jerusalem) and the people from the gentiles were sealed. A description of the salvation of the Jewish people will be found in Revelation 7:4 – 8 and of the gentiles in Revelation 7:9 – 17.

This means that for two thousand years the four angels did not allow the four earthly winds to harm the earth:

| | |
|---|---|
| The earth | - those who believe God and Jesus |
| The sea | - this world who does not know God and Jesus |
| The trees | - Servants of God (The tree grows on the earth. Those who believe and were baptized and grow like a tree. Also the tree brings forth fruit) |

However, when the voice of the sixth trumpet sounds, the angel will receive the order to unloose the four angels. This will be possible during the second woe. This means that the sounding of the sixth trumpet is a key moment. A new time period will start at that moment. The time of complete abolishment of salvation for the gentiles as well as the setting free of the four angels will begin.

In order to understand the voice of the sixth trumpet and the significance of the time in which we live, we will examine the events of the fifth trumpet:

The communist spirit appeared upon the sounding of the fifth trumpet. The sound of the fifth trumpet announced the reform movement in Christianity, a return to the foundation of the Word of God. In an attempt to stop the sound of the fifth trumpet, Satan launched the communist doctrine in which God did not exist, and people achieved happiness through the fair distribution of material goods. This spirit reigned in one part of the earth for five months (Revelation 9:5). The beginning of communism started when smoke (teaching) was released from the pit and heaven (Christianity) was darkened. Heaven was darkened only for those who raised their eyes unto heaven, for those who wished to repent. One month (Jewish) has thirty days. Five times thirty days is one hundred and fifty. This means that the communist regime would rule in one part of the earth for one hundred and fifty years. The Communist Manifesto was written in 1848, and if we add 150 years, we get the year 1998. Verily, just as the Word of God had predicted, in that year we witnessed the end of Communism. However, following the end of communism we should expect the sounding of the sixth trumpet, as the four angels will be set free in order for the second woe to come. The events of the fifth trumpet have passed; the first woe befell this world. The horrible evil occurred, because people did not have the opportunity to enter into a covenant with God through the mediator our Lord Jesus Christ. Let us be reminded that China, Kazakhstan, Russia, Belarus, Hungary, Czechoslovakia, Yugoslavia, Romania, Bulgaria, Estonia, Lithuania, Poland, Georgia, Vietnam, Laos, and countries from the African and American continents were all under the communist yoke. Truly, this was a major woe.

We have the testimony that in the time period of the fifth trumpet, actually up to 1998, it was not possible to announce peace. Similarly, we must understand that peace cannot be spoken in the fulfillment of the sixth trumpet because this is the time period when the four angels will be set free (the time of the delivery process). Also, this will be the time of the destruction of two billion people. This means that **PEACE can be spoken only in the time period from 1998 up to the time when the angel will sound the sixth trumpet.** Let us memorize this conclusion.

Now let us read the words which speak of the events which occurred after 1998:

Re. 9:12    *One woe is past; and, behold, there come TWO woes more hereafter.*

In this verse the Word of God speaks of events occurring after the fifth trumpet. The Word is warning us that the time period of communism is over and that two more woes are imminent.

We will quote three verses in which we find a description of events which will occur when the sixth angel sounds his trumpet.

Re. 9:13    *And the SIXTH angel sounded, and I heard a voice from the four horns of the golden altar which is before God,*

Re. 9:14    *Saying to the sixth angel which had the trumpet, loose the four angels which are bound in the great river Euphrates.*

Re. 9:15    *And the four angels were loosed, which were prepared for an hour, and a day, and a month, and a year, for to slay the third part of men.*

We can understand that four essential things are happening, the steps from Revelation chapter 9, which we will use when comparing the steps from the prophecy of the Ten Virgins.

311

1. Trumpeting of the SOUND of the sixth trumpet.
2. Coming of the voice to unloose the four angels
3. Unleashing of the four angels. Paralleled with the events that will gradually start the blowing of the four earthly winds, that will increase in intensity depending on the quickness of the unleashing of the four angels
4. Complete destruction = SECOND WOE

The above-quoted verses do not provide enough information to help us understand where the departure of God's people to Israel, actually the releasing of water from the woman, is described. In addition to the description of the second woe in the 9th chapter we can find a description of the second woe in the 11th chapter. This means that we have an additional explanation of the events that will cause the second woe to occur in the 11th chapter. Let us read on:

Re. 11:13     ***And the same hour was there a great earthquake, and the tenth part of the city fell, and in the earthquake were slain of men seven thousand:*** *and the remnant were affrighted, and gave glory to the God of heaven.*

Re. 11:14     *The SECOND woe is past; and, behold, the third woe cometh quickly.*

This means that the 13th verse describes the second woe. Yet a few verses before the 13th verse the time period that we are trying to better understand is described. We will quote these:

Re. 11:7     *And* **when they shall have FINISHED their testimony**, *the beast that ascendeth out of the bottomless pit* **shall make war against them**, *and shall overcome them,* **and kill them.**

Re. 11:8     *And their dead bodies* **shall lie in the street** *of the great city, which spiritually is called Sodom and Egypt, where also our Lord was crucified.*

Re. 11:9     *And they of the people and kindreds and tongues and nations* **shall see** *their dead bodies three days and an half, and* **shall not suffer their dead bodies to be put in graves.**

Re. 11:10    *And they that dwell upon the earth* **shall rejoice** *over them, and make merry, and* **shall send gifts** *one to another; because these two prophets tormented them that dwelt on the earth.*

Re. 11:11    *And after three days and an half* **the Spirit of life from God entered into them**, *and* **they stood** *upon their feet; and* **great fear fell upon them** *which saw them.*

Re. 11:12    *And they heard a great voice from heaven saying unto them,* **COME UP hither.** *And* **they ascended up to heaven in a cloud**; *and their enemies beheld them.*

In the verses quoted above, we can find a description of the events that MUST occur before the coming of the second woe, when a third of mankind will perish.

The steps from the 11th chapter of Revelation:

1. Two prophets will finish their testimony
2. The beast will initiate a war against two prophets
3. The beast killed the prophets
4. He leaves them to lie in the streets
5. He shall not suffer their dead bodies to be put into graves
6. They shall rejoice
7. They will send gifts to each other
8. AFTER three and a half days they will come back to life.
9. They stood upon their feet
10. A VOICE came up hither
11. They ascended up to heaven in a cloud
12. Their enemy is in fear
13. There was a great earthquake
14. Seven thousand men were slain = the SECOND WOE
15. Others become afraid

Repeat the steps from Revelation chapter 9 once again:

1. **Trumpeting of the SOUND of the sixth trumpet** (a good sound for the servants of God)
2. There came a voice that four angels will be unloosed (a bad voice for those who do not obey the Word of God)

3. Unleashing of the four angels. Paralleled with the events that will gradually start the blowing of the four earthly winds, which will increase in intensity depending on the quickness of the unleashing of the four angels

4. Complete destruction = **second woe**

The text speaks of the coming of the second woe. Therefore, if we compare the steps from the 9th chapter with the steps of the 11th chapter, we can see that the two steps from the 9th chapter, the first (trumpeting of the sound of the sixth trumpet) and fourth steps (complete destruction - second woe), are identical to the tenth (a voice came up hither) and fourteenth steps (seven thousand men were slain - the second woe) from the 11th chapter.

By comparing the 9th and 11th chapters of John's Revelation you can easily understand that the voice, which "come up hither", is actually "the sound of the sixth trumpet". In previous comparisons of the prophecies with the prophecy of the Ten Virgins, we have seen that the voice is actually God's call to His people to come to the Supper of the Wedding Feast of the Lamb. It is interesting to note the discrepancy that appears in the Word. In Revelation 9 the Word of God states that a third of mankind will be killed and that after this catastrophe, people will not repent from their murders, fornication etc. However, Revelation 11 describes the same event through an earthquake and says that seven thousand men of the city were slain and after this catastrophe the remnant was affrighted, and gave glory to God. Why is it written in this manner?

This means that Revelation 9 speaks concerning events which will happen to this world, to people who do not repent or accept Christ's Gospel. The Word testifies that these people will remain ungodly. However, the 11th chapter describes what will happen to those Christians who choose not to go to Israel, or the foolish virgins. It proceeds to say that seven thousand men will be killed in the city where the beast killed two prophets and left them to lie in the street as the citizens rejoiced. The number seven thousand should be represented as seven times one thousand. Seven represents a complete entity (perfection), while one thousand represents a countless amount (eternity on earth). Because we have a case in which God's wrath is exercised, the number means that an infinite number of Christians will die because they will be cast from God's kingdom.

We will provide a short explanation to help make the steps from the 11$^{th}$ chapter clearer.

1. **Two prophets finished their testimony** - the two prophets represent the word of the Old and the New Testaments – the Bible. When God turned His face towards the Jewish people, the plan of their return to their land began being fulfilled. Also, the testimony of the two prophets among the gentiles was reaching its completion. We can say that this corresponds to the time after the First World War.

2. **The beast lifted a war against two prophets** - The beast symbolizes materialism. This means that materialism waged war against the two prophets. We can say this in a different way: liberalism had taken root in Christianity.

3. **They were killed** – After a certain time the beast had a chance to kill the two prophets. In other words, the Word of God had no influence on a certain number of the liberal Christians.

4. **They were left in the street of that town** – This happened when liberalism (liberal Christians) had achieved its end. The two prophets (the Word of God) were left in the street of the town. This town is sinful, and the street symbolizes the heart. The street is actually the road the two prophets walked.

5. **They will not allow their bodies to be put into graves** – In denominations and congregations the system of democracy started to predominate. This means that the majority rules. Since the majority has a liberal understanding of the Word of God, it does not allow the pure Word of God to be preached. Simply put, it does not allow the Word to be preached in a manner required by God. What does it mean to "bury"? Recall the parable of the sower. The word was sown. The word fell on good ground which was the heart. The word must die, be buried in the heart. If it is not, fowls will come and take it away.

6. **They shall rejoice** – The liberal members are joyful when they dominate a denomination or a congregation. How is this joy manifested? Look around you and you will understand.

7. **They will send gifts to each other** - Verily, God beautifully describes the present Christian era. This seventh step describes

the activities of the liberal denominations or congregations. They begin scrutinizing the Word of God, discussing and analyzing it, and making all kinds of stories according to the eyes and to human reasoning. The real meaning and clarity of the Word of God is not being presented to the members and to those seeking salvation.

8. **AFTER three and a half days they will be revived** - This description is very hard to understand simply because it is necessary to know the law of 42 months or 1260 days or 3.5 years, or a week and a half, or a time and a half time (which makes 3.5) etc. We notice that their joy lasted only three and a half days and the turning point suddenly came when the prophets were revived. Why do you think they were revived? Because liberal Christians had come to an understanding through their searching of the Word of God. It is necessary to understand that those who are departing from the truth are doing so because they are losing their fear of God. In the present time many Christians have become scoffers only because they are losing their fear of God. The manner in which one lives depends on how much fear of the Lord has been lost. This applies to myself and my household as it does to you and your household. The fear of God is an invisible power which moves the human heart. When I fall in fear, God's word and its fullness revives me. This means, the prophets revived some hearts only because the spiritual midnight and voices had come. The pains of the delivery process will begin. The prophets will only revive the hearts of the wise virgins.

9. **They stood upon their feet** – We have already explained this step in the prophecy of the Ten Virgins. Here the Word says that the virgins arose, while in Revelation the Word says that the prophets stood upon their feet. This means that those hearts in which the two prophets received strength were ready to fulfill the **whole** will of God.

10. **A VOICE came up hither** - The sixth trumpet sounded. The call for the Marriage Supper of the Lamb went out.

11. **They ascended up to heaven in a cloud** – The departure of Christians for Israel. The clouds symbolize Christians who live spiritually. This means the Word of God, which wants to save the

316

Jewish people, revived the hearts of God's servants. Also, the clouds ascended up to heaven through them (spiritual sphere).

12. **Their enemy is in fear** - When the departure for Israel begins, those who do not have the spirit in them will be in fear. Surely, they will be frightened; they fought the preaching of the departure for Israel and now it is happening.

13. **There was a great earthquake** – This is the beginning of several very big events.

14  **Seven thousand men were slain** – the SECOND WOE

15. **Others became afraid** - Christians who survive and are not in Israel will give glory to God but will not be allowed to enter into Israel.

The prophecy of our Lord Jesus Christ in the 9th and 11th chapters of John's Revelation provides a detailed description of past, present and future happenings. Every reader can be persuaded that the descriptions of events from John's Revelation are written in chronological order according to the sequence of their occurrence. This principle, which God uses in His prophecies, enables every reader to be convinced of the authenticity of His word. This is why the words in the Bible are living words, and every one who believes the God of Israel and his son Jesus Christ can follow the fulfillment of His prophesied happenings and thereby reinforce one's own faith.

In addition, through prophecies quoted in this book, one can realize that many happenings which should be fulfilled are before Christians, rather than the rapture of His church. This is why it is necessary for Christians to synchronize their beliefs and their lives with these impending events. Only through this will it be possible to become worthy and to be spared from the events which will befall this earth.

The illustrated examples should confirm the departure for Israel of the Holy Spirit residing in God's faithful people. In addition, the entire Word of God should permeate with the same ideas and speak of identical beliefs in different ways. Furthermore, an endless source of unimagined depth of wisdom and instruction is presented for man which is impossible to withdraw.

It is known to all that after the third World War a new world order will emerge which will have one specific attribute and that is to completely dishonour the law of God and Jesus Christ. We know that every servant of God who fails to hide himself/herself in Noah's second ark, i.e. Israel, will perish when the great spiritual flood (as in Noah's time) arrives. Thus, it is worth making every effort to receive God's guidance, so that we will be able to come to a proper understanding of God's will revealed (ascertained) for the End Times.

I do believe that with God's help and through the selected examples and explanations in this book, you will be able to find truth. God will bless you with His mercy so that you may be His choice at the Great Supper of the Lamb.

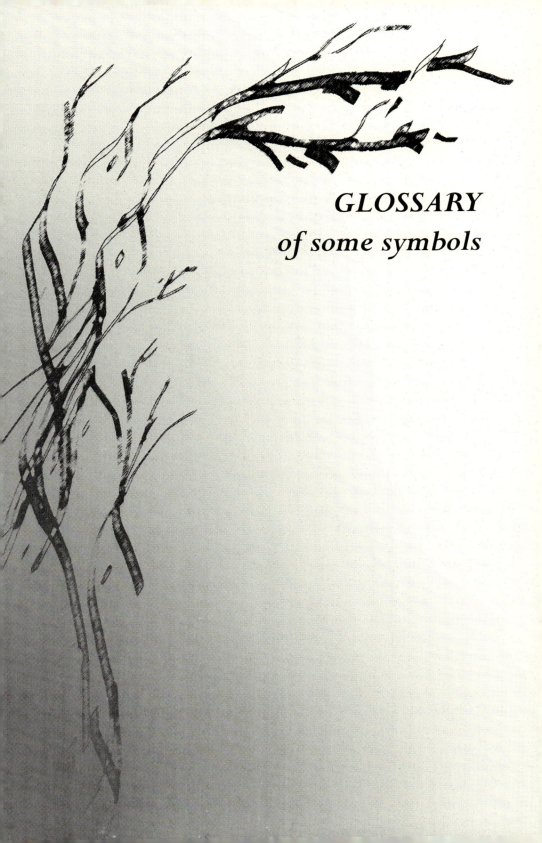

# GLOSSARY
## *of some symbols*

The necessity to interpret the Word of God by using spiritual symbols instead of literal interpretations was emphasized in the chapter Symbolism in the Bible. It was demonstrated that what appears to be a simple text contains a hidden message. Through the history of the Jewish people God's plan for the salvation of mankind was revealed. This plan was revealed only to those who understand the language used in the Bible, while for others only a moral lesson was given. By doing this God did not do injustice to those who do not possess this understanding, because the spiritual growth of man goes gradually, depending on the conditions in which he is approaching God. Therefore, man must first become moral in every aspect of his life and only in that condition, if he directs his life towards love for God and for his neighbour, can he achieve knowledge. Spiritual growth has four levels and begins with understanding the law and acquiring moral qualities, and culminates with the understanding of spiritual law and with acquiring spiritual qualities. This is why it is so important to understand the Holy Scripture not only literally but also in a spiritual sense. These conditions and understanding of the Word of God depend exclusively on the individual and are not a matter of inheritance or predestination. Depending on how much one consecrates himself that much will he be enlightened. By reading this book the reader will not automatically acquire the necessary state of mind to understand the entire Bible, but it will put him on the right path.

For a better understanding of the quotations used a Glossary of the most important symbols adapted to the actual text of the book will follow. It is important to know that symbols have other meanings as well as the one given here.

# GLOSSARY

# OF SOME SYMBOLS

## Numbers as symbols

**1**

**one day with the Lord** – Spiritual day in which one fold can find salvation, 2 Peter 3:8

**one flesh** – Christ and the church, Ephesians 5:31

**one flesh** – Husband and wife, Ephesians 5:31

**one fold** – Christians from gentiles united with Christians from the Jewish nation (will occur in Israel), John 10:16

**one shepherd** – Lord Jesus Christ, John 10:16

**one stick** – Judah and the children of Israel his companion, or the Jewish nation according to the law (old covenant), Ezekiel 37:16

**one woe** – The Communist system, Revelation 9:12

**one of the days**

    – Second and third new covenant day, Luke 17:22

    – Day of the Lord, Isaiah 9:14

**2**

**two men in one bed** – One group of righteous Christians and another group of unrighteous Christians, Luke 17:34

**two women shall be grinding** – Two groups of Christian denominations which prepare the doctrine (food), Matthew 24:41, Luke 17:35

**two men shall be in the field** – Two groups (kinds) of priesthoods in Christianity. The one which is according to the will of God and the other which is not, Luke 17:36, Matthew 24:40

**two pence** – The Old and the New Testament, Luke 10:35

**two sons**

    – Two covenants, Galatians 4:22

    – Isaac and Ishmael, Galatians 4:22

**two wings** – God's two commandments, Matthew 23:37, Revelation 12:14

**two woes** – Third world war and the Antichrist system, Revelation 9:12

**3**

— Trinity, John 21:11

**4**

— Number which describes the material world, Revelation 7:1
**four angels** — Angels of this world, Revelation 7:1
**four winds of the earth** — Spirits of this world which bring trouble. They are in the human heart. Revelation 7:1
**from the four winds** — From the spirit (as a whole). From Christianity, with no restrictions on the denomination, Ezekiel 37:9

**5**

— The sum of the numbers two and three. Unity of the corporal (spirit and flesh) and the heavenly (Trinity). The number five has an individual character while number six has a general meaning, Matthew 25:2
**five yoke of oxen** — Priesthood which an individual chose for himself to spiritually lead him, Luke 14:19

**6**

**sixth angel sounded** - Call for Christians to come to Israel, Revelation 9:13

**7**

— Unity of material (presented through number 4) and spiritual (presented through number 3) worlds. This is perfection, completeness, Revelation 11:13,
**seven angels**
    — The new covenant priesthood, Revelation 1:20, Revelation 17:1
    — United Christian priesthood in Israel, Revelation 15:1
**seven churches** — New covenant church, Revelation 1:20
**seven pillars** — Servants of God in whom the perfect will of God is manifested, Proverbs 9:1
**seven thousands** — Complete number, refers to Christians who are in the spiritual eternal kingdom ( on earth), Revelation 11:13
**seven trumpets** — Perfect messages which will be announced to God's people unto the end of salvation of humankind, Revelation.8:6
**seven vials** — Seven events as punishment, Revelation 17:1

**10**

— Everything, all, complete (wise — foolish, old — new, physical — spiritual), Luke 19:12
**ten cities** — Spiritual and physical congregations, Luke 19:17
**ten pounds** — The complete Word of God, as well as the Old and the New Testament, Luke 19:13
**ten servants** — All servants, Luke 19:13
**ten virgins** — Christians, denominations, congregations as a whole. Matthew 25:1
**tenth part** — All who lost the mercy of God, Revelation 11:13

— Tribe, nation

**twelve thousand** — People who have a part in the eternal kingdom of Jesus Christ on this earth (from Jewish tribe), Revelation 7:4

**twelve tribes of Israel** — The lost sheep of Israel, Matthew 19:28

**twelve thrones** — Power of the new covenant church, Matthew 19:28

**50** — Pentecost, Holy Spirit, John 21:11

**100** — Little flock, John 21:11

**153** — The new covenant church, John 21:11

**666** — Unity of three unclean spirits, Revelation 13:18

**1000**

— Eternity on earth, Christians who are in the kingdom of God, Revelation 11:13

**thousand years** — Eternal kingdom in the spirit on earth, 2 Peter 3:8

**144 000**

— Christians who are of Jewish origin up to the time that four angels shall be loosed, Revelation 7:4

— Christians from the gentiles who are ready to fulfill God's will in the time of the sixth trumpet, Revelation 14:1

# A

**Abraham**

— Father of many nations in the spiritual sense, Genesis 17:5

— Father of circumcision to those who are from circumcision and to those who walk in the faith of Abraham, Romans 4:12

**Agar**

— Mount Sinai represents those who are in sin, Galatians 4:25

— Present Jerusalem, delivers from bondage, Galatians 4:25

**abomination**

**abomination of desolation** — Doctrine of God which is not presented in its fullness (twisted), Matthew 24:15

**adultery** — Spiritual adultery, materialism, 2 Peter 2:14

**alive**

**alive again** — To be spiritually alive again, Luke 15:22

**all**

**all nations** — All Christians in Israel, Matthew 25:32

**all the tribes of the children of Israel** — All generations up to the time when the four angels will be loosed, Revelation 7:4, Revelation 7:3

**all things are now ready** — All preparations for the Marriage Supper are completed, Luke 14:17

**all these things shall be dissolved** — Abolishment of salvation of the gentiles, 2 Peter 3:11

**all the holy angels** — All Christians who will come into Israel, Matthew 25:31

**on all** — All who believe God, Luke 21:35

**Ancient** – God, Daniel 7:22

**angel**

> – Jesus Christ, Revelation 19:17

> – Jesus, Revelation 20:1

> **with his angels** – Servants of Christ, Matthew 16:27

**another, other**

> **another angel** – The resurrected Jesus Christ, Revelation 7:2

> **another sign** – United Christianity in Israel, Revelation 15:1

> **another stick** – Joseph, the stick of Ephraim and all the house of Israel and his companions, Ezekiel 37:16

> **other husbandmen** – Priesthood from the gentiles, Matthew 21:41

> **other servants** – Servants who are sealed with the Holy Spirit, Matthew 22:4

> **other sheep** – Lost sheep of Israel from the gentiles, John 10:16

> **other virgins** – Everyone who did not enter into Israel, Matthew 25:11

**archer**

> **archers** – Joseph's brothers, Genesis 49:23

**army**

> **his armies** – Army of the Roman Empire, Matthew 22:7

**arise, arose (to wake up)**

> – To come to the knowledge that the will of God was not exercised in their lives, Matthew 25:6

> – To be ready to fulfill the will of God, Matthew 25:7

> **sheaf arose** – The sheaf is ready for action; the Messiah came, Genesis 37:7

**array** – To perform deeds of repentance, Revelation 19:8

**ascend**

> **ascendeth out of the bottomless pit** – Liberalism, materialism, Revelation 11:7

**ash**

> - Shame which torments the soul

> **wallow thyself in ashes** – Revealed fact that God rejected them, Jeremiah 6:26

**as**

> **as it were a sea of glass mingled with fire** – The Jewish nation mingled with Christians, Revelation 15:2

**ass**

> – Jewish nation or a Jewish man, Luke 14:5

> – Jewish nation who accepted Jesus' doctrine (was released from Mosaic Law), Matthew 21:7

> **ass's colt** – The new covenant priesthood, Genesis 49:11

# B

**baptize**
 **baptized into Christ** – To be dressed into Christ (put on Christ), Galatians 3:27
 **(baptized) with fire** – Go through trials, Matthew 3:11
**barn** – Israel, Matthew 13:30
**beast**
 – Spiritual beast which destroys the children of God. Jewish priesthood which stood against Jesus Christ, Daniel 7:11
 – The old covenant priesthood, Revelation 20:4
 **her beasts** – Servants of God, Proverbs 9:2
 **the beast that ascendeth out of the bottomless pit** – Christianity which is in spiritual death. The sinfulness is presented as light (righteousness of God) and reigns in a place where it should not, Revelation 11:7
 **ravenous beast** – Unclean people, Isaiah 35:9
**bed**
 – Covenant
 – Covenant with God through Jesus Christ, Luke 17:34
**Bethel** – The gate of heaven, Genesis 28:17
**bid**
 **bid to the marriage** – Preaching to the gentiles, Matthew 22:9
 **those which were bidden** – Jewish nation who fulfilled (ate) the Mosaic Law, Luke 14:7
 **bade many** - To reveal the meaning of the Wedding Supper to many, Luke 14:16
**bind, bound**
 – Resurrection of Jesus, Revelation 20:2
 – To bind with the Holy Spirit, Genesis 49:11
 **bind (the tares)** – To believe twisted explanations of the Word of God; false spirits, Matthew 13:30
 **bind the strong man** – Through the resurrection of Jesus; Satan was bound, Matthew 12:29
 **binding sheaves** – Binding people with the Word of God, Genesis 37:7
 **bound up his wounds** – The new covenant law gives protection, Luke 10:34
**blessing**
 **blessings of the breasts** – In a spiritual sense this is the Word of God, Exodus 49:25
 **blessings of the deep** – Material world (forgiveness to trespassers of God's will), Exodus 49:25
 **blessings of heaven above** – The spiritual world (prophets, contact with angels, …) Exodus 49:25
 **blessings of the womb** – A spiritual birth of the children of God, Genesis 49:25
**blind**
 – Christian or Jews who does not see (believe) spiritually. He needs someone to spiritually lead him, Luke 14:13, Luke 14:21

**blindness**

— Not believing Jesus Christ, Romans 11:25

**blood**

— In a negative sense, this represents the Mosaic Law which lost power, Acts 2:19

**blood of the dead man** — Changed law of God that there is no life in it, Revelation 16:3

**lamb's blood** — Jesus' life, Exodus 12:13

**bondage**

**in bondage** — To be a slave of sin, John 8:33

**body**

— Church, God's people, Ephesians 5:23

— A spiritually dead body. Or the Jewish nation in Israel, Luke 17:37

**body is of Christ** — Part of God's people, Colossians 2:17

**their dead bodies** — The Word of God not exercised or believed, Revelation 11:8

**bone**

**bones** — Servants of God, Psalm 22:14

**bones are out of joint** — My servants left me, and they became afraid, Psalm 22:14

**bones come together** — Work on the creation of the state of Israel, Ezekiel 37:8

**these bones live** — To receive the Holy Spirit, Ezekiel 37:3

**those bones** — The whole house of Israel, Ezekiel 37:11

**book**

**book of life** — The Book in which the spiritually born are entered, Revelation 20:15

**born**

**born again** — Spiritually born through baptismal ordinances, John 3:3

**born of God** — Spiritually born through baptismal ordinances. Those who do not sin, 1 John 5:18

**was born** — Jerusalem was born when Jacob won the battle in Peniel, Ezekiel 16:4

**bough** — Generation, Genesis 49:22, Luke 21:32

**bow** — Joseph's firstborn blessing which Rachel bought from Leah, Genesis 49:24

**branch**

— Generation which kept the Mosaic Law, Isaiah 9:14

— People who believe Jesus, John 15:2

— Generation, Ezekiel 36:8

— Jesus, Isaiah 11:1

**branch is yet tender** — When generations multiply, Matthew 24:32

**branch run over the wall** — Went astray in the faith (place where God does not protect), Genesis 49:22

**some branches broken off** — Through the Jewish nation's unfaithfulness some generations lost the right to salvation, Romans 11:17

**bread**

**bread of life** — Jesus Christ, Word of the new covenant, John 6:35

**unleavened bread** — To be sinless, pure life, Exodus 12:8

**breastplate** – Faith and love, 1 Thessalonians 5:8

**breath**

– Spirit of God, Ezekiel 37:10

**breath of his lips** – Spirit of Jesus, Holy Spirit who condemns sinfulness, Isaiah 11:4

**breathe** – To preach the Word of God for repentance, Ezekiel 37:9

**breast**

**breast are fashioned** – Knowledge of God increased, Ezekiel 16:7

**Bridegroom** – The Word of God which speaks about salvation. This verse is directed toward Jewish nation, Matthew 25:1

**bring**

– Bring into new covenant bonds, John 10:16

**bring them from the north country** – Come to Israel from a country where they do not like you, Jeremiah 31:8,9

**bring into the land of Israel** – Bring them into the spiritual land of Israel (God's kingdom), Ezekiel 37:12

**brother**

**thy brethren** – Those who are baptized, Luke 14:12

**bull**

**bulls of Bashan** – God's priests, Psalm 22:12

**building**

– Church of God, Ephesians 2:21

**bundle** – Congregation, Matthew 13:30

**burn**

**burn them** – Trouble brought upon Christians so their faith is tried. This will be the Antichrist system, Matthew 13:30

**burned up their city** – Destruction of Jerusalem in 70 A.D., Matthew 22:7

**buy**

– To believe God's Word, Isaiah 55:1

– To find an explanation of God's Word and to accept it, Matthew 25:9

– To accept someone or something, then he or it becomes his possession, Luke 14:18

**I have bought a peace of ground** – To accept the teaching of some denomination which now feeds him, Luke 14:18

# C

**call**

**called unto the marriage supper** – The call is pointed out to every person who heard that Christians should go to Israel, Revelation 19:9

**shall call upon him** – To be baptized in the name of Jesus Christ and to live a life which pleases God, Romans 10:13

**Cana** – Cane, John 2:1

**candlestick** – Church, Revelation 1:20

**carcass** – Spiritually dead body. Jewish nation in Israel, Matthew 24:28

**cast**

— Jesus gave the Spirit to His disciples and through this became the king of eternal life, Revelation 20:3

**cast him out of vineyard** —To condemn Jesus to death, Matthew 21:9

**cast it out** — To be rejected as a servant, Luke 14:35

**cast the net** —To preach, John 21:6

**cast them to the earth** — To teach God's people contrary from God's commandments, in such way that they are not able to honour God and live spiritually, Revelation12:4

**cast out in the open field** — The Jewish nation was taken away into Egypt, Ezekiel16:5

**casteth her untimely figs** —To be rejected from God (God's nation), Revelation 6:13

**certain**

**certain noble man** – Resurrected Jesus, Luke 19:12

**chain**

**great chain** – Jesus received the right from his Father to be crucified and resurrected, Revelation 20:1

**chicken**

**chickens** – God's people, Matthew 23:37

**child**

— Born after the Spirit, Galatians 4:29

— Christians, Galatians 4:28, Romans 9:8

**being with child** –To learn that Jesus will be crucified, Revelation 12:2

**brought forth a man child** –Resurrected Jesus, Revelation 12:5

**travail upon woman with child** – This world which become ripe with the idea to force Israel to divide the Promised Land among its enemies, 1 Thessalonians 5:3

**with child** –To develop sinful thoughts in the heart, Matthew 24:19

**children**

**children (have you any meat)** – Jesus' disciples.Those who are not fully matured spiritually.Those who are not sealed with the Holy Spirit, John 21:5

**children of Ammon** – Jordanians, Isaiah 11:14

**children of God** – Children of promise (are received for the seed), Romans 9:8

**children of Israel from among the hidden** – Israel from Judah and Israel from ten tribes, Ezekiel 37:21

**children of promise** – Spiritual children, Galatians 2:29, 4:28, Romans 9:8

**children of the day** – A new generation created in the Lord's day, 1 Thessalonians 5:5

**children of the flesh** – Children of this world, Romans 9:8

**children of the light** –The new generation in Jesus, 1 Thessalonians 5:5

**church**

**church of the firstborn** – Those who are spiritually born again through Jesus Christ, Hebrews 12:23

**circumcision**

– Circumcision of the heart, Spiritual circumcision, Romans 3:1

**sign of circumcision** – Sign of righteousness, Romans 4:11

**uncircumcision** – To be without the seal of righteousness in the flesh, Romans 4:11

**city**

– Spiritual Jerusalem, Luke 14:21

– Jewish nation, Matthew 21:18

**city of the living God** – Heavenly Jerusalem and spiritual Jerusalem, Hebrews 12:22

**five cities** – Christian congregations, Luke 19:19

**great city** – Christianity gone astray, Revelation 11:8

**citizen**

**citizens** – Citizens of spiritual Jerusalem, Luke 19:14

**cleanse**

**cleanse them** – To give forgiveness to the Jewish nation, Ezekiel 37:23

**clothe**

**clothed with white robes** – Clothed in righteousness and truth, Revelation 7:9

**clothes**

**their (disciples) clothes** – The fulfillment of Jesus' will, Matthew 21:7

**cloud**

– God, Acts 1:9

**bright cloud** – God, Matthew 17:5

**clouds**

– Christians, Jude 12

– In a negative sense, these are servants of God who live according to the spirit of this world,

2 Peter 2:17

– Righteous Christians, Matthew 26.64, Revelation 11:12, Revelation 1:7

– Christians who will go to Israel, Matthew 24:30

**clouds that are without water** – Christians without the Holy Spirit, Jude 12

**clothes**

**their (disciples) clothes** – Fulfilment of Jesus' will, Matthew 21:7

**come**

**come and gather** – Gathering in Israel, Revelation 19:17

**come down** – To return to living according to the eyes, Luke 17:31

**come down** – To be born in the flesh (Jesus), Revelation 20:1

**come up** – Living Word of God can live only in the clouds (servants of God) who are in heaven (who are living spiritually). By this act, salvation of the gentiles is abolished, Revelation 11:12

**come up out of your graves** – Repentance of the Jewish nation, Ezekiel 37:12

**the Son of man shall come in glory** – Jesus Christ who came through the Word of God (Comforter), Matthew 16:27

**they would not come (to the wedding)** – Not to believe Jesus that He is the Messiah, Matthew 22:3

**thou art come to excellent ornaments** – To gain knowledge about God, Ezekiel 16:7

**your Lord doth come** – Jesus Christ in Spirit coming through the Word of God (third night), Matthew 24:42

**when the Son of man shall come in his glory** – When Jesus Christ in the Spirit as the Word of God shall come to Israel (third night), Mat. 25:31

**coming in the clouds of heaven** – Seeing Jesus Christ in Christians who live spiritually, Matthew 26:64

**see the Son of man coming in a cloud with power and great glory** – Jewish nation in Israel will see Jesus Christ in righteousness (third night), Luke 21:27

**see the Son of man coming in his kingdom** – To see Jesus Christ in the spirit in His spiritual kingdom which our eyes see and our hearts feel, Matthew 16:28

**shall also the coming of the Son of man be** – Jesus Christ in Spirit which comes through the Word of God to Christians calling them to migrate to Israel, Matthew 24:37

**compass**

**Jerusalem compassed with armies** – Army of the Roman Empire surrounded Jerusalem in 70 A.D., Luke 21:21

**compel** – Great trouble, WWIII, Luke 14:23

**conceive** – To put certain thoughts in the heart, James 1:15

**couch**

**he couched** – To be fortified (in sin), Genesis 49:9

**caught**

**caught nothing** – Nobody accepted the crucified Jesus as Messiah, John 21:3

**country**

**far country** – Heaven where God's throne is, Luke 19:12

**cover**

**cover them above** – Proclamation of the treaty, Ezekiel 37:8

**crib**

**master's crib** – Lord's table, Isaiah 1:3

**cross** – Burdens of life, Matthew 10:38

**crown** – Eternal life, Ezekiel 16:12

**crucify**

**crucify among you** – Not obeying the truth, Galatians 3:1

**cry**

– Events in the world from which Christians will awake, Matthew 25:6

**crying** – Spiritual crying, Revelation 21:4

**crieth** – To preach, Proverbs 9:3

**cut**

**cut him asunder** – The removing of the Holy Spirit from a Christian, Matthew 24:51

**cut off** – To lose God's mercy, Isaiah 9:14

**cut off** – To be rejected by God, Romans 11:22

# D

**darkness**

– Lack of God's knowledge, John 1.5, 1 Thessalonians 5:5, Genesis 1:5

**mist of darkness is reserved forever** – Confusion, misunderstanding, eternal death, 2Peter 2:17

**power of darkness** – Beginning of the second spiritual night in the new covenant period, Luke 22:53

**day**

– Day of salvation of the Jewish nation in Israel, Luke 21:34, 1 Thessalonians 5:4

**certain day** - Certain day equals "today", Hebrews 4:7

**day of God** – When the Jewish people will once again believe in, 2 Peter 3:12

**day of the Lord will come as a thief in the night** – The day of the Lord is announced in a negative sense. This is why this verse represents the abolishment of salvation given to the gentiles, 2 Peter 3:10, 2 Thessalonians 5:2

**day of the Lord is near in the valley of decision** – Spiritual deliverance will come to the Jewish people (valley), while destruction will come to the enemy of the Jewish people, Joel 3:14

**first day** – The time period from Adam up to the time when Noah's sons departed from God, Genesis 1:5

**great and dreadful day of the Lord** – The announcement, through the coming of the Comforter that one portion of the Jewish nation will not recognize Jesus Christ as their Messiah, Malachi 4:5

**great day of His wrath** – Coming of the Comforter and the beginning of salvation of mankind, Revelation 6:17

**great and notable day of the Lord** – An announcement that one part of the Jewish nation will recognize Jesus Christ as their Messiah through the coming of the Comforter, Acts 2:20

**last day** – Describes the time given to mankind as a last chance for salvation, John 6:40

**last day** – Lord's day, John 11:24, and John 12:48

**last days** – From the year 1897 up to the words in Revelation "it is done", Genesis 49:1

**sabbath day** – The time when Jews should live in righteousness, Luke 14:5

**sabbath day** – Antichrist system, Matthew 24:20

**seventh day** – The spiritual day in which God rests from all His works, Hebrews 4:4

**terrible day of the Lord** – An announcement that everyone who will not accept Jesus Christ in the day of the Lord will not inherit eternal life, Joel 2:31

**today** – The time when a person hears the Word of God and believes it, Hebrews 4:7

**today** – Second day light time and the third spiritual day in the new covenant period, Hebrews 4:7

**in the days of Noah** – The sinful man in the time of Noah, Matthew 24:37, Luke 17:26

**in the days of the Son of man** – The time from Pentecost up to the migration of believers to Israel, Luke 21:24

**in the days of the Son of man** – The second spiritual day (time of the light) and the third spiritual night in the new covenant time, Luke 17:26

**David**

**my servant David** – Jesus Christ, Ezekiel 37:25

**daughter**

**daughter of Zion** – The Jewish nation (new generation) who turned their hearts toward God, Jeremiah 6:2

**dead**

– People (Christians) who are not spiritually alive, Revelation 20:12

– Spiritually dead, Luke 15:22

– Dead to sin, Colossians 3:3

**dead works** – Sinful works, Hebrews 9:14

**half dead** – Bodily alive and spiritually dead, Luke 10:30

**dead – small** – Christians who did not teach people properly as God requires, Revelation 20:12

**dead – great** – Christians who did teach people properly as God requires, Revelation 20:12

**rest of the dead** – Gentiles, Revelation 20:5

**death** – Spiritual death, Revelation 21:4

**deep**

**into the deep** – Among sinners, Luke 5:4

**face of the deep** – Eternal death, Genesis 1:2

**defile** – Accept a teaching which is not based on the foundation of the Word of God and to live by it, Revelation 14:2

**Deliverer** – Holy Spirit, Romans 11:26

**depart**

**heaven departed** – Importance of the old covenant heaven come to an end, Revelation 6:14

**sceptre shall not depart … until** – To lose the firstborn right, Genesis 49:10

**desolate** – Jerusalem which now is in bondage with her children, Galatians 4:27

**desolation**

– To take a nation into captivity, Luke 21:21

**died**

**died in the sea** – All those not reborn through baptism, i.e. the spiritually dead, Revelation 16.3

**dig**

**digged a winepress** – A heart which keeps God's knowledge, Matthew 21:33

**dinner**

>**my dinner** – Salvation of the Jewish nation up to the destruction of Jerusalem and the salvation of the gentiles, Matthew 22:4

**divide** – The great flood in Noah's time. Darkness was divided from light, Genesis 1:4

**dog**

>**dogs** – Someone who is a friend to this world; gentiles; Roman soldiers, Psalms 22:16

**door**

>– Jesus, John 10:9

>– Righteousness and truth, John 10:1

>**at the doors** – At their heart (Jewish nation), Matthew 24:33

**dragon** – The devil and Satan, Revelation 20:2

**draught** – onverting human souls, Luke 5:4

**draw, drew**

>**and his tail drew** – To preach different doctrines, Revelation 12:4

**drunkenness** – A negative spirit through which carnal desires such as pride, lack of love, disfavour are fulfilled Luke 21:34

**dry, dried**

>– To be without the Holy Spirit, Ezekiel 37:2, Ezekiel 37:11

>**our bones are dried** – They came to an understanding that they are in sin, Ezekiel 37:11

**drink**

>**drink of the wine** – To live in Christ's spirit, Proverbs 9:5

>**drink with drunken** – To be the same as the Christians described in 2 Timothy 3:1-5, Matthew 24:49

**dropsy** – In a spiritual sense, this is a sickness of the spirit, Luke 14:2

**dunghill** – Christians who do not possess the Holy Spirit, Luke 14:35

**dwelling place** – Deeds in the body, Ezekiel 37:23

# E

**eagle**

>**eagles** – Sons of God, Luke 17:37, Matthew 24:28

**earring**

>– Sign that certain individuals are "slaves" to God, i.e. they fulfill the law which they hear, Ezekiel 16:12

**earth**

>– In a general sense, a human heart which believes God

>– The Jewish nation in the old covenant time period, Isaiah 1:2

>– Hearts of the Jewish nation in present Israel, Hosea 6:3

>– Hearts that believe God, Revelation 7:1, Genesis 1:1

>– Hearts of gentiles in the time of the Antichrist, 2 Peter 3:1

>– Hearts of Jewish people in the time of the prophet Jeremiah, Jeremiah 4:23

>– Human hearts from Adam and Eve up to the great flood, 2 Peter 3:5

>**earth was without form** – An unreasonable nation, Genesis 1:2

**called the dry land Earth** – Hearts of the Jewish nation in the old covenant time period. They are dry because they did not contain the Holy Spirit, Genesis 1:10

**new earth** – Hearts of those who believe Jesus Christ in Israel (in the future), 2 Peter 3:13

**the earth which is now** – Unrepentant gentiles who believe in Jesus Christ, 2 Peter 3:7

**earthquake**

**great earthquake** – Hearts of the sinful Christian world shaken by a great event, the Third World War (nuclear war), Revelation 11:13

**great earthquake** – Hearts (earth) of the Jewish nation shaken by some event. This was Jesus' crucifixion, Revelation 6:12

**eat**

**eat of my bread** – To perform deeds according to the will of God, Proverbs 9:5

**eat bread in the kingdom of God** – To live according to Christ's commandments, Luke 14:15

**eat bread on the Sabbath day (in the Pharisees house)** – To live according to the Mosaic Law, Luke 14:1

**eat the flesh (of the lamb)** – To fulfill the will of Jesus Christ, Exodus 12:8

**eat and drink with drunken** – To perform deeds in the name of God, in a manner contradicting His commandments, Matthew 24:49

**eat fine flour** – To fulfill the Word of God, Ezekiel 16:13

**eat fine honey** – Deeds done through the mercy of God, Ezekiel 16:13

**eat oil** – Deeds done in the Holy Spirit, Ezekiel 16:13

**Egypt**

– The land of slavery; people who are slaves to sin, Exodus 12:12

– Not knowing God, Revelation. 11:8

**Elijah** – John the Baptist, Malachi 4:5

**enemy**

– The spirit of the devil materialized in Christians, Matthew 13:27

**enter**

**enter in** – Enter into the spiritual world through baptism, John 10:9

**Ephraim**

– Christians from gentiles, Jeremiah 31:9, Genesis 48:19,20

**espousal**

– The time the Jewish nation spent in the wilderness. In a spiritual sense, this represents the repentance process, Jeremiah 2:2

**evening** – The first guard from the fifth night, or the first guard from the second new covenant night, Exodus 12:6

**eye**

– Spirit, Genesis 49:12

**eyes full of adultery** – Human spirit, 2 Peter 2:14

**eyes shall be red** – The spirit is overwhelmed (drunk) with fulfillment, Genesis 49:12

# F

**face**

    **my face** – My law, Hosea 5:15

    **face of the serpent** – Laws of the unclean spirit, Revelation 12:14

**fall**

    – Transgress God's will, Luke 14:5

    **fallen into a pit** – When a person falls into a sin from which he cannot remove himself without the help of others, Luke 14:5

    **fell among thieves** – Accept false gods, Luke 10:30

    **the stars of heaven fell unto the earth** – Lost spirituality, to became carnal, and to lose the mercy of God, Revelation 6:13

    **the tenth part of the city fell** – To depart from God, Revelation 11:13

**farm**

    – The Jewish nation, Matthew 22:5

**father**

    **father was an Amorite** – Satan, Ezekiel 16:3

**fatling**

    **fatlings** – Prophets (and Jesus), Matthew 22:4

**feast**

    **feast with you** – Work together in God's vineyard with the righteous one, 2 Peter 2:13

**feet**

    **beautiful feet of them** – Christians filled with the Holy Spirit, Romans 10:15

**field**

    – The world where the Word of God is preached, Luke 17:36

    **his field** – This world, i.e. Christianity, Matthew 13:24

**fight** - Jesus was allowed to be judged and crucified, Revelation 20:2

**figs**

    **untimely figs** – Jews in the time of Jesus' crucifixion, Revelation 6:13

**fire**

    – In a negative sense the tongue which speaks evil words, Acts 2:19

    – Holy Spirit, Christians, Revelation 15:2

    **fire of the Lord** – To hate evil, Proverbs 8:13

    **fire that burneth all the day** – The Holy Spirit condemning God's servants trespassing the will of God, Isaiah 65:5

    **it is set on fire of hell** – Fire (as an evil spirit) which is initiated and multiplied by Christians who are in sin, James 3:6

**firstborn**

    – The chosen son who will stay in the house of his Father and to whom the possessions of his Father will belong. Christians are firstborn through Christ, Jeremiah 31:9

**fish**

    – The human soul, John 21:3, Luke 5:4

**great fishes** – People who feel that they are great sinners, John 21:11

**multitude of fishes** – People who believe that Jesus was resurrected, John 21:6

**fishing** – Converting people to God, John 21:3

**flame**

**burning flame** – Constant troubles, Daniel 7:11

**fly**

**fly** –To live spiritually, Revelation 19:17

– Wage war, Isaiah 11:14

**flesh**

–The Word of God, John 1:14

**born after the flesh** – Born as a sinner, Galatians 4:23

– Jewish people, Ezekiel 37:8

**flight** – Christians departing to Israel, Matthew 24:20

**fold**

– A part of the Jewish nation which is spiritually awake and awaiting their Messiah, Luke 2:8

– May represent Jews, gentiles or Christians, John 10:16

**sheepfold** – The Jewish nation, or the old covenant church, John 10:1

**foolish** – Sinful, Proverbs 9:6

**former**

**former things** – Corruptible things, Revelation 21:4

**foundation**

– Part of God's doctrine, Revelation 21:14

**foundation of the apostles and prophets** – The Word of God coming through the apostles and prophets, Ephesians 2:20

**found** –To repent, Luke 15:24

**fowl**

**fowls that fly in the midst of heaven** – Servants of God who live spiritually, Revelation 19:17

**friend**

**thy friend** –A person who knows the will of God and wants to come closer to Him, Luke 14:12

**fruit**

**fruit withereth** – Not having deeds in God, Jude 12

**fruit** (from vineyard) – Fulfilment of God's will, Matthew 21:34

fruit (from tares) – Deeds of darkness, Matthew 13:26

**furnace**

**furnace of fire** –The Antichrist system, Matthew 13:42

# G

**garment**

– Wisdom, Genesis 49:11

**his garment** – Jesus' righteousness, Geneses 49:11

**gather**

    – Through divisions and liberalism, the hearts of Christians are gathered, Matthew 13:30

    **gather all nations into the valley of Jehoshaphat**– Bring nations together against the Jewish people gathered in Israel (they will rely on God rather than weapons), Joel 3:2

    **gather them up** – Excommunicate, Matthew 13:28

**generation**

    – Seventy to eighty, Matthew 24:34

    **chosen generation** – Christians, 1 Peter 2:9

**gird, girt**

    – Truth, Ephesians 6:14

    **girt about** – To put in mind, to accept, Ephesians 6.14, Jeremiah 6:26

    **gird thee with sackcloth** – To recognize the fact (sin) which is tormenting the soul, Jeremiah 6:26

    **loins girded** – To put the Word of God in mind, Exodus 12:11

**give**

    **judgment was given unto them** – To go through the ordinance of baptism, Revelation 20:4

    **judgment was given to the saints** – Judgment which happened in the spirit before the destruction of Jerusalem 70 A.D., and was applied to the Jewish nation and Christians of that time. This is described in the parable of 10 silver pounds (Luke 19:12-27), Daniel 7:22

**gnashing**

    **gnashing of teeth** – Trouble which will come upon souls because they lost God's protection, Matthew 24:51

**goat**

    **goats** – Servants of God who did not fulfill the will of God, Matthew 25:32

**god**

    **gods of Egypt** – Gods of the gentiles. Idols and materialism, Exodus12:12

**Gog** – Materialism, Revelation 20:8

**gold**

    **my gold** – Servants of God, Joel 3.5

    **decked with gold** – To perform deeds which please God, Ezekiel 16:13

**go, went**

    – Fulfill, Luke 14:18

    **will go** – To go to Golgotha, Hosea 5:15

    **went** – To return to the old covenant doctrine, Matthew 22:5

    **went in** –Christians departing to Israel, Matthew 25:10

**go out**

    – To the light of the spiritual day, John 10:9

    – To preach, Luke 14:23

    **went down** – To depart from God's law (Mosaic Law), Luke 10:30

    **went forth** – To preach, Matthew 25:1

—To preach the departure for Israel, Matthew 25:1

**good**

    **good seed** – Sons of the kingdom, Matthew 13:24

    **good wine** – The new covenant doctrine, John 2:10

**goods**

    – Human souls, Matthew 12:29

    **spoil his goods** – To redeem souls from the captivity of sin, Matthew 12:29

**grow** – To live in faith, Matthew 13:30

**graft**

    **grafted in** – To be baptized and become a part of God's new covenant nation, Romans 11:17

**grapes**

    **(washed) clothes in the blood of grapes** – Jesus' deeds, Genesis 49:11

**grave**

    – The spiritual grave where dead spirits lie in unbelief, disregard godliness, Ezekiel 37:12

    **graves** – Unbelief, sinfulness, where dead spirits lie, Revelation 11:9

**girdle**

    **girdle of his loins** – Righteousness, Isaiah 11:5

    **girdle of his reins** – Truth, Isaiah 11:5

**grind**

    – To preach, Luke 17:35

**ground**

    **good ground** – A heart which believes in God and accepts His Word, Matthew 13:8

    **piece of ground** – A place of sowing; human hearts, congregations, denominations, Luke 14:18

# H

**hair** – As a general term, it represents a man who keeps some service to God, Ezekiel 16:7

**harvest**

    – End Times, Matthew 13.30

    **in the time of harvest (gather the wheat)** – The migration of Christians to Israel, Matthew 13:30

    **in the time of harvest (gather the tares)** – The beginning of the harvest which began after the first Zionist congress. This is also when industrialization started, Matthew 13:30

**have, had**

    **hath the son** – To believe in Jesus Christ, 1. John 5:12

    **had the trumpet** – To have the message, Revelation 9:14

**he**

    **he who now letteth will let** – The Holy Spirit, God's people, 2 Thessalonians 2:7

**head**

    – The ancient and honourable, Isaiah 9:15

    – The husband is the head of the wife, Ephesians 5:23

    **the head of the church** – Christ, Ephesians 5:23

**heal**

    **heal us** – Renew His mercy, Hosea 6:1

**hear**

    **hear my voice** – To put one's faith in the crucified and resurrected Jesus, John 10:16

**Heaven**

    **Firmament of heaven** – Spiritual people, Genesis 1:8

    **in the firmament of heaven** – Christianity, Genesis 1:14

**heaven**

    – In general sense it represents the spiritual nation on this earth

    – The old covenant heaven (moon, stars, sun), Revelation 6:13

    – A spiritual nation up to the time of Christ, Genesis 1:8, Revelation 6:14

    – A spiritual nation up to the great flood, Genesis 1:1

    – A spiritual nation out of this earth, Revelation 20:1

    – A spiritual world in the new covenant, Revelation 12:1

    – Christianity, 2 Peter 3:12

    – Israel (old covenant), Isaiah 1:2

    – Old covenant Israel in the time of the prophet Jeremiah, Jeremiah 4:23

    **first heaven** – Christianity, Revelation 21:1

    **in heaven** – A new heaven in Israel, Matthew 24:30

    **in the midst of heaven** – Christianity, Revelation 19:17

    **new heaven** – The spiritual nation in Israel, Christianity in Israel, Revelation 21:1, 2 Peter 3:13

    **under heaven** – A spiritual nation which needs repentance, Luke 17:24

**heavens**

    **heavens were of old** – A spiritual nation up to the great flood, 2 Peter 3:5

    **heavens which are now** – A spiritual nation from the gentile nations; Christianity, 2 Peter 3:7,10

    **powers of the heavens** – The laws of God which reign in the spiritual world, Matthew 24:29

**hedge**

    – God's law which protects them, Matthew 21:33

    **hedges** – Man made commandments, Luke 14:23

**heirs** – Christians of the seed of Abraham, Galatians 3:29

**hell** – Christians who sin, James 3:6

**helmet** – Salvation of the soul, Thessalonians 5:8

**hen** – Church, God, Matthew 23.37

**herb**

    **bitter herbs** – Bring fruits of repentance, Exodus 12.8

**hewn** – Trouble which moulds the heart of a servant, Proverbs 9:1

**highway**

— Jesus Christ's doctrine, Isaiah 35:8

**highways** — Interpretations which are not based completely on God's Word. Those who add or take away from God's Word, Luke 14:23

**hill**

**hills** — A group of Jewish people who believe certain promises from the Word of God, bat not in its fullness (watered down), Ezekiel 36:6

**everlasting hills** — Promises of God which are spiritually exalted forever, Genesis 49:26

**his**

**his day** — The Lord's day, Luke 17:24

**his farm** — The Jewish nation who accepted the Mosaic Law, Matthew 22:5

**his merchandise** — Preaching of the old covenant doctrine, Matthew 22:5

**hold** — Not allowing certain words (spirit) to go out, Revelation 7:1

**hope**

**hope lost** — To lose hope in finding mercy before God, Ezekiel 37:11

**horn** — Someone who has power. The Jewish priesthood who keep obeying the Mosaic Law, Daniel 7:21

**host** — The new covenant priesthood, Luke 10:35

**house**

— A body where the spirit of God lives

— The human heart, Proverbs 9:1

— A body (where the spirit of man lives), Exodus 12:13

— The human body, Luke 17:31

**householder** — God of Israel, Matthew 21:33

**house of Israel** — The Jewish nation which has a veil over the eyes, Ezekiel 36:22

**house of one of the chief Pharisees** — The old covenant church, Luke 14:1

**my house may be filled** — Church of God in Israel, Luke 14:23

**desolate house** — Spiritually desolate, i.e. to be a nation without the Holy Spirit, Matthew 23:38

**spoil his house** — To deliver sinners from eternal death, Matthew 12:29

**strong man's house** — Satan's house; the materialistic world, Matthew 12:29

**housetop**

**to be upon the housetop** — To be above carnal desires, Luke 17:31

**hunger** — To have the desire to fulfill God's will, Matthew 21:18

**hurt**

**hurt not** — To not bring different spirits against the doctrine of God, Revelation 7:2

**husbandmen** — The priesthood of the Jewish nation, Matthew 21:33

# I

**image** — The Mosaic Law which lost priority over the law of grace, Revelation 20:4

**inheritance** — To be in possession, Ezekiel 36:2

**inn** — The old covenant church, Luke 2:7

**island** – All the gentiles who believe in the Mosaic Law, Revelation 6:14

**Isaac** – Children of promise, Galatians 4:28

**Israel**

    –The Jewish nation according to the law, Romans 10:19

    –The Jewish nation having a veil over the eyes to this day, Romans 11:25

    **my people of Israel** – The new covenant Israel, Ezekiel 36:8

# J

**Jacob**

    –The Jewish nation which does not live according to the laws of Moses or Christ's Law, Romans 11:26

**Jehoshaphat**

    –The king of Israel who relied on God and not on his weapons, Joel 3:2

**Jericho** –The town upon which God's curse stands; paganism, Luke 10:30

**Jerusalem**

    –The town of peace in the Old Testament; people who are at peace with God, Luke 10:35

    **Jerusalem which is above** – Mother to new covenant children, Galatians 4:26

    **from Jerusalem** – From the spiritual Jerusalem, Isaiah 2:3

    **heavenly Jerusalem** – Christianity which fulfills God's will, Hebrews12:22

**jewel**

    **jewel on thy forehead** – Truth, Ezekiel 16:12

**Jordan**

    **beyond Jordan** – The left side of Jordan symbolizes the hearts of men (land), who are in sin, Matthew 4:14

**Joseph** –The Jewish nation awaiting the Messiah, Genesis 49:22

**Judah** –The Jewish nation according to the Mosaic Law, Deuteronomy 33:7

**judging** – Baptizing, Matthew 19:28

# K

**key**

    **key of the bottomless pit** – The new covenant Word of God, Revelation 20:1

**kill, slain**

    – To sacrifice, Exodus 12:6, Proverbs 9:2, Matthew 22:4

    **kill (the lamb)** – Reject Jesus as the Messiah, Exodus 12:6

    **kill them (the Word of God)** –To make it impossible to preach, Revelation 11:7

    **the beast was slain** – The soul of the beast was taken away (destroyed), and this was the temple in Jerusalem, Daniel 7:11

    **my oxen and fatlings are killed** – Servants are sacrificed, Matthew 22:4

    **killed her beasts** – Servants are sacrificed, Proverbs 9:2

**king**

    **one king** – Jesus Christ in the spirit, Ezekiel, 37:22

    **kings** – Christians, Acts 9:15

    **kings of the earth** – Christians from the gentile nations, Revelation 21:24

**kingdom**

 – Spiritual kingdom of Jesus Christ, Luke 22:29

 **kingdom of God is nigh** – Kingdom of God is nigh for the Jewish people in Israel, Luke 21:31

 **kingdom of heaven** – Peace with God, Matthew 22:2

 **his kingdom shall not be destroyed** – Spiritual kingdom, Daniel 7:14

 **to receive for himself a kingdom** – To sit at the right hand side of the Father's throne, Luke 19:12

**kinsmen** – Members of other Christian denominations, Luke 14.12

# L

**lake**

 **lake of fire** – Antichrist system, Revelation 20:15

**lamb**

 – Jesus in the flesh who desires to be sacrificed for humankind

 – The man who possessed the nature of the lamb and was born again (spiritually), Isaiah 11:6

**Lamb**

 – Jesus Christ in the spirit. The Word of God who wishes to be sacrificed for the Jewish nation (gathered in Israel), Revelation 14:1

 – Jesus, Exodus 12:3

 **before the Lamb** – Jesus Christ in the spirit, Revelation 7:9

**lame** – Christian in the process of repentance not completely fulfilling his commandments or the ordinances of baptism (he/she was born with a certain spiritual problem). This is why he/she is not able to completely fulfill God's will. Is spiritually lame, Luke 14:13, Luke 14:21

**lamp**

 – Word of God, Psalm 119:105, Matthew 25:1, Mathew 25:3

 **took their lamps** – To believe the Word of God, Matthew 25:1

 **trimmed their lamps** – Multiply deeds in Christ, Matthew 25:7

**land**

 **land of Canaan**

 – Promised Land, Genesis 17.8

 – Land where mercy and the Word of God flows, Genesis 48:3

 **land of Egypt** – Land of unbelief, Genesis 48:5

 **(the land) Galilee of the gentiles** – People who are rejected from the Jewish nation. Jews and gentiles who are in sin, Matthew 4:15

 **land of Israel** – Kingdom of God, Ezekiel 37:12

 **land of Nephthalim** – People (son from Rachel's bondmaid) who are in sin and believe in Jesus, Mat. 4:15

 **land of Zabulon** – Group of people or a tribe who does not obey the law of Moses. Matthew 4:14

 **dry land** – Hearts who believe God but do not contain the Spirit of God, Genesis 1:10

**my land** – Land which is given to the tribes of Israel as an inheritance, Ezekiel 36:5

**lawgiver** – God, Genesis. 49:10

**leaf, leaves**

> **leaves (green)** – People who call upon God only by mouth, Mat. 21:19
>
> **putteth forth leaves** – To begin believing God, Luke 21:32, Matthew 24:32

**leave, left**

> – To be left among the gentiles, Luke 17:34
>
> – To be left under the Antichrist's reign, Matthew 24:41

**lift**

> **lifted up mine hand** – God stood against the enemy of Israel, Ezekiel 36:7

**light**

> – Appearing of the Word of God in which eternal life is found, Genesis 1:3
>
> – Day, Genesis 1:5
>
> – Eternal life, John 1:4
>
> **light is sprung up** – Offer of eternal life, Matthew 4:16
>
> **light of the world** – Jesus, John 8:12
>
> **had no light** – Israel did not live according to the Word of God given through Moses, Jeremiah 4:23

**lightning** – Eternal life, Jesus Christ in the Spirit, Luke 17:24

**like**

> **like the Son of man** – Jesus Christ in the spirit as a King who comes to punish His servants, Daniel 7:13

**lion**

> – Man possessing a lion's nature, Isaiah 35:9
>
> **roaring lion** – Satan, Psalms 22:13
>
> **Judah is a lion whelp** – The Jewish nation according to the Mosaic Law who trusted God. Time when Judah took the firstborn blessing from Reuben, Simeon and Levi (departure of the ten tribes of Israel), Genesis 49:9
>
> **couched as a lion** – Jewish nation killed Jesus and did not want to accept Him as their Messiah, Genesis 49:9

**Lord**

> – Spirit, 2 Corinthians 3:16,17
>
> **where our Lord was crucified** – Place where they sinned, i.e. killed the Messiah, Revelation 11:8

**lose, lost**

> – To be in sin, Luke 15:24
>
> – To come to a realization that they will not find mercy before God, Ezekiel 37:11

**loose**

> – Make possible, Revelation 9:14
>
> **to loose four angels** – Words (spirit, wind) of intolerance concerning nationalism, religion, racism, higher interest – Materialism, will start to appear causing a new world system to come, Revelation 9:14
>
> **he must be loosed a little season** – The first loosening of Satan. This occurred before the destruction of Jerusalem 70 AD., Revelation 20:3

**Leah** – Jerusalem that delivers according to the law, Genesis 30:14

**lust** – Seed of sin, James 1:14

# M

**manger** – Lord's table, Luke 2:7

**Magog** – Idolatry, Revelation 20:8

**maimed (cripple)** – Was born healthy but sinned in the faith. Repented and was healed however a spiritual consequences remains, Luke 14:21

**man**

> **certain man** – Lost sheep of Israel (Jewish nation), Luke 10:30, Luke 14:2
>
> **man of sin** – Antichrist, 2.Thesslonians 2:3

**Manasseh** – Christians from the Jewish nation. Manasseh was born (spiritually) before Ephraim (Christians from Gentiles), Genesis 48:20

**mandrake** – Gains fertility and riches, reveals the future, Genesis 30:14

**mark**

> – Visible or invisible sign of something
>
> **mark upon their foreheads** – To be a member of the old covenant church. To accept the Mosaic Law fully with heart and mind, Revelation 20:4
>
> **received his mark** – Perform deeds in the Mosaic Law, Revelation 20:4

**marriage**

> – Salvation of the lost sheep of Israel, i.e. salvation of humankind. The place where a covenant with God is made, John 2:1
>
> **marriage for His son** – Salvation of humankind, Matthew 22:4
>
> **marriage supper of the Lamb** – Salvation of the Jewish nation in Israel, Revelation 19:9

**master**

> **master of the house** – God of Israel, Luke 14:21

**meat**

> **meat in due season** – Explanation of the Word of God, Matthew 24:45
>
> – To fulfill God's will, John 21:5

**melt**

> **elements shall melt** – Faith in the hearts shall collapse, 2 Peter 3:12

**merry** – Fulfilling God's will, Luke 15:22

**messenger** – John the Baptist, Matthew 11:10

**midnight**

> – A complete lack of understanding of God's will.
>
> – Announced peace in the Middle East between Israel and its neighbours, Matthew 25:6

**milk**

> – Doctrine of repentance, baptism, etc., Isaiah 55:1
>
> – Word of God, Genesis 49:12

**mingle** – To show, Proverbs 9:2

**mist**

    **mist of darkness** – Servants of God who are insincere, 2 Peter 2:17

**moon**

    – In a general sense it represents the body which receives light from the sun. It is always of the female gender

    – Rachel, Genesis 37:9

    – The old covenant church, Acts 2:20, Joel 2:31

    **(shall turn) the moon into blood** – From the beginning of Jesus' preaching, the Mosaic Law began losing priority. It turns into the law (blood) which cannot give life, Joel 2:31, Acts 2:20

    **the moon under her feet** – Abolished the old covenant church, Revelation 12:1

    **the moon becomes as blood** – The old covenant church (moon) does not contain life in itself, Revelation 6:12

    **the moon shall not give her light** – Rejected Christianity in front of God, Matthew 24:29

**morning**

    – The morning of the first spiritual day in the new covenant time period, Matthew 21:18

    – Last vigil of the second spiritual night, John 21:4

**mother**

    **mother of Jesus** – Jews who believe Jesus, John 2:1

    **thy mother an Hittite** – Idolatry, Ezekiel 16:2

**morrow** – Second spiritual day in the new covenant period, Luke 10.35

**mountain**

    – Belief

    – Belief of the Jewish people, Ezekiel 37:22

    – Group of Jewish people who believe God's promises, Revelation 6:14

    **mountain of the Lord** – Belief of God's people, Isaiah 2:3

    **mountain of the Lord's house** – House of Jacob's God, God's nation, Isaiah 2:3

    **holy mountain** – Zion of God, Isaiah 11:9

    **on the mountain Sion** – Belief of God's people (our present time), Revelation 14:1

    **mountains** – Group of Jewish people who believe certain promises of God which are exalted above every other belief, Ezekiel 36:6

    **mountains of Israel** – Jewish nation according to the law which believes in God's promises which is exalted above every other belief, Ezekiel 36:1

**mourn**

    – Jewish nation in Israel shall recognize their sin and repent, Matthew 24:30

**move, moved**

    **every mountain and island where moved out** – To doubt in faith, Revelation 6:14

**multitude**

    – Nations without the Spirit of God, Joel 3:14

    **great multitude** – Christians from the gentile nations, Revelation 7:9

**mystery**

– transfer of salvation to the Jewish nation when the fullness of the gentiles be come in, Romans 11:25

**mystery of iniquity** – Antichrist system, 2 Thessalonians 2:7

**mysteries of the kingdom of heaven** – Happenings which will occur in the spiritual world, Matthew 13:11

# N

**naked, bare** – To live in sin, Ezekiel 16:7

**nation**

**foolish nation** – Christians from the gentiles, Romans 10:19

**one nation** – Unification of old covenant Israel, Ezekiel 37:22

**navel**

**navel was not cut off** – To have contact with idolatry, Ezekiel 16:4

**neighbour**

**rich neighbours** – Those who believe and know everything, Luke 14:12

**net**

– The Word of God, John 21:6, Luke 5:4

**net brake** – Weakness in the preaching of repentance and eternal life prior to Jesus' suffering on the cross. First spiritual night in the new covenant period, Luke 5:6

**let down the net** – To preach, Luke 5:5

**launch out the net** – To preach, Luke 5:4

**night**

– First spiritual night in the new covenant time period, Luke 5;5

– Second spiritual night in the Old Testament time period, Exodus 12:8

– Spiritual night; not knowing the will of God, 1 Thessalonians 5:5, John 9:4

**all the night** – First spiritual night in the new covenant period, Luke 5:5

**that night** – Second spiritual night in the new covenant time period, John 21:3

**noise**

– Announcement of the Balfour declaration which gave the Jewish nation the right to buy land and emigrate into Palestine, Ezekiel 37:7

# O

**obeisance**

**made obeisance** – To admit, recognize, Genesis 37:9

**made obeisance to my (Joseph) sheaf** – Recognize Jesus Christ as their king, Genesis 37:7

**oil**

– Holy Spirit, spirit of love, Luke 10:34

– Knowledge (faith) of the will of God, Matthew 25:3

**occupy** – Preach, Luke 19:13

**olive**

**fatness of the olive tree** – Holy Spirit, Romans 11:17

**root of the olive tree** – Jesus Christ, Romans 11:17

**wild olive tree** – gentile nations, Romans 11:17

**open**

– To do some deed, Revelation 6:12

**had opened sixth seal** – Crucifixion of Jesus, Revelation 6:12

**ornaments** – Spiritual ceremonies and feasts, Ezekiel 16:11

**others** – Other Christians, 1 Thessalonians 5:6

**ox**

– Jewish priesthood, Luke 14:5

– Priest, Isaiah 1:3

# P

**palm**

**palms in their hands** – They possess the deeds of peace and victory over sin, Revelation7:9

**pain** – Spiritual sickness, Revelation 21:4

**pasture**

**find pasture** – Work spiritually in the kingdom of God, John 10:9

**peace**

– Peace treaty between Israel, Palestine and their neighbours to create a Palestinian state in the Promised Land which God gave by covenant to Abraham, Isaac, Jacob and their seed, 1 Thessalonians 5:3

**Philistines** – Palestinians, Isaiah 11:14

**pillar**

**pillars** – Servants of God, Proverbs 9:1

**place**

**ancient high places** – Promises of God which have eternal value, Ezekiel 36:2

**holy place** – God's altar, Matthew 24:15

**highest places** – Promises from God given to spiritual Jerusalem, Proverbs 9:3

**I shall place you** – Place them in the kingdom of God, Ezekiel 37:14

**plant**

**planted vineyard** –To bring the Jewish nation into the Promised Land, Matthew 21:33

**poor**

–Those who feel a lack of spiritual knowledge, Luke 14:13,21, Isaiah 11:4

**porter** – God, John 10:3

**pour**

**poured out** – To bring a new law, Revelation 16:3

**prepare** –To finish all preparation for the salvation of mankind, Matthew 22:4

**prey**

**from the prey, my son, thou art gone up** – Return from committed sin. He killed Jesus, Genesis 49:9

**priest**

**certain priest** – Old covenant priesthood, Luke 10:31

**priesthood**

    **royal priesthood** – Christ's priesthood, 1 Peter 2.9

**profane** – To put to shame, Ezekiel 36:22

**prophecy**

    – To preach the Word of God, Ezekiel 37:9

    **prophecy unto the wind** – Preach to Christians, Ezekiel 37:9

**pull**

    **pull out** – To be directed on the path of righteousness and truth, Luke 14:5

**put**

    – Accept

    **put their clothes on them** – Accept Jesus' disciples for the priesthood, Matthew 21:7

# R

**Rachel** – Jerusalem from above which delivers children through love, Genesis 30:14

**raiment** – Righteousness, Luke 10:30

**rain**

    – Preaching of the Word of God, Hosea 6;3

    **as the latter and former rain** – Preaching of the Word of God to the Jewish people, Hosea 6:3

**ready**

    – Everything necessary is done so the salvation of mankind can start, Matthew 22:4

    **my wife hath made herself ready** – She repents, Revelation 19:7

**reaper**

    **reapers** – Angels, Christian priesthood, Matthew 13:30

**repay** – The repayment are cities from the parable of the Ten Pounds (Luke 19.17), Luke 10:35

**resurrection**

    **resurrection of the just** – The moment when a Christians receives a testimony that they satisfied God, Luke 14:14

    **first resurrection** – Baptism, Revelation 20:5

**redeem**

    **redeemed** – God's new covenant people, Isaiah 35:9

**regeneration** – Spiritual regeneration through baptism, Matthew 19:28

**reign**

    – Jesus Christ in the spirit, Luke 19.27

    **shall reign with him a thousand years** – Christ's spiritual kingdom (second) given to the gentiles, Revelation 20.6

**rest**

    **my rest** – Make peace with God, Hebrews 4.5

    – Spiritual rest, not to sin, Hebrews 4.10

**return**

    **in the morning as he returned** – In the first spiritual day when Jesus came to the Jewish nation, Matthew 21:18

**return to my place** – Ascend into heaven, Hosea 5:15

**when he was returned** – Through the Comforter, Luke 19:15, and Luke 10:35

**Reuben** – Firstborn according to the law. Beginning of the Jewish nation, Genesis 30:14

**ride**

**(they set him thereon)** – Jewish nation (ass) submitted to Jesus, Matthew 21:7

**rise**

**rise again** – To resurrect, John 11:23

**river**

– Jews who preach the Old Testament doctrine, Ezekiel 36:6

– Spirit, 9:14

–The Word of God, Jeremiah 31:9

**great river Euphrates** – Christianity, Revelation.9:14

**roast**

**roast with fire** – Jesus suffering on the cross, Exodus 12:8

**rod**

**rod of iron** – Word of God which reproaches; crumble our carnal mind, Revelation 12:5, 2;27

**rod of his mouth** – The new covenant word. Jesus' preaching, Isaiah 11:4

**rod of his mouth** – Word of God as law, Isaiah 11:5

**room**

**chief rooms** – To be a priest, Luke 14:7

**root**

**roots** – Jesus Christ, Jude 12; Romans 11:17

**plucked up by the roots** – Lawlessness which removes the soul from the body of Christ, Jude 12

**rouse**

**who shall rouse him up** – Who will deliver him from his sin, Genesis 49:9

# S

**sackcloth** – Knowledge which torments, Jeremiah 6:26

**saint**

**saints** – Those who possess the Holy Spirit, Christians, Daniel 7:21

**salt**

– Christians who do God's will, Luke 14:34

– Deeds in God, Ezekiel 16:4

**Samaritan**

**good Samaritan** – Jesus, Luke 10:30

**sanctuary** – Resurrected Jesus, Ezekiel 37:26

**save** – To give power to the Jewish nation so they repent, Ezekiel 37:23

**sceptre** – Mosaic Law, Genesis 49:10

**scoffer** – Christian who lives according to his desires, 2 Peter 3:3

**schoolmaster** – The law, Mosaic Law, Galatians 3:24

**sea**

– Unrepentant hearts of man, sinful world, Revelation 7:1

—The world, Revelation 16:3

**sea (Galilee)** – Mosaic Law, Matthew 4:18

**seal**

**seal of the living God** – Ordinance of baptism, Revelation 7:2

**seal upon him** – Through the arrival of the Comforter, the door of the bottomless pit is sealed so that Satan cannot change anything, Revelation 20:3

**which were sealed** – Baptized with new covenant baptism, Revelation 7:4

**second**

**second death** – Eternal death, Revelation 20:6

**see**

—To see Jesus with spiritual eyes in Christians who gather in Israel, Matthew 24:30

– To rejoice, Luke 14:18

– To see with spiritual eyes, Matthew 26:64

**cannot see** – Those who do not have righteousness, peace, and joy in the Holy Ghost, John 3:3

**which seeth the Son** – To see Jesus in Christians, John 6:40

**seed**

—The Word of God or spirit of His word

**Abraham's seed** –Christians, Galatians 3:29

**good seed** –The Son of man, the Word of God, Jesus Christ in the Spirit, Matthew 3:25

**his seed** – Christians, Galatians 3:16

**thy seed** – People who have faith of Abraham, Genesis 48:4

**sell**

– Preach

**go ye rather to them that sell** – Those who are knowledgeable about the Word of God and preach, Matthew 25:9

**serpent** – Evil spirit, Revelation 20:2

**servant**

– Jesus Christ in the spirit as the Word of God, Luke 14:17.

**sent his servant** – Word of God which comes from Christians who speak God's will, Luke 14:17

**servants**

– Apostles and Christians before the destruction of Jerusalem, Matthew 22:6

– Children of the kingdom, Matthew 13:27

**again, he sent forth other servants** – When the Comforter descended from heaven the apostles became other servants, Matthew 22:4

**he sent other servants** – Prophets, priests, faithful Jews (from Babylonian captivity up to the time of Jesus' birth), Matthew 21:36

**sent his servants** – Prophets, priests, faithful Jews (up to Babylonian captivity), Matthew 21:34

**sent forth his servants** – Jesus and His disciples first sent a call to the Jewish nation, Matthew 22:3

352

**then saith he to his servants ...** – Christians from the Jewish nation sent unto gentiles after the destruction of Jerusalem Matthew 22:8,9

**set**

**set him thereon** – The new covenant priesthood (disciples) accept Jesus as their King, Matthew 21:7

**shadow**

**shadow of things to come** – Old Testament, Colossians 2:17

**shake**

**shaking** – Killing Jews in the Second World War from which the hearts of the Jewish nation were shaken, Ezekiel 37:7

**shall be**

**shall be one** – Unification of the Jewish people with Christians in Israel, Ezekiel 37:19

**shall be one fold** – Grafting of the Jewish people gathered in Israel on the body of Christ, John 10:16

**shall be their inheritance** – They will be brothers in Christ, Ezekiel 36:12

**shall be tilled** – Will be forced to repent, Ezekiel 36:9

**smite his fellow servants** – To do wrong to his brother for reasons of discord in the understanding of God's Word, Matthew 24:49

**sheaf**

– Person (Jesus), nation, tribe

**sheaf (Joseph's)** – Part of the Jewish nation who awaited the Messiah, Genesis 37:7

**sheaf (of Joseph's brothers)** – Jewish nation who upheld Mosaic Law, Genesis 37:7

**stood upright (Joseph's sheaf)** – Jesus became the King. Members of Joseph's sheaf became Christians, Genesis 37:7

**sheep**

– Jewish nation, John 10:3

– Christians in Israel, Matthew 25:32

**my sheep** – Jesus' followers, John 10:27

**shepherd**

– Jesus, John 10:16

– Priest, priesthood, Genesis 49:24

**shepherd of the sheep** – Messiah, John 10:2

**shepherds abiding in the field** – Watchful priesthood from the old covenant church, Luke 2:8

**shine**

– To believe, 2 Corinthians 4:4

– Offer of eternal life through preaching, Luke 17:24

**ship**

– Teaching, belief, John 21:3

– Belief, John 21:6

**shoes** – The Gospel of peace, Exodus 12:11, Ephesians 6:15

**shoot** – To deliver children, Ezekiel 36:8

**shut**

> **door was shut** – Departure to Israel was completed, Mat. 25:10
>
> **shut him up** – Jesus ascended to heaven and through this the faith of Satan was sealed, Revelation 20:3

**side**

> **right side** – According to the will of God, John 21:6

**silk**

> – Righteousness, Ezekiel 16:13
>
> **fine linen** – Righteousness of the saints, Revelation 19:8

**silver** – Word of God, Joel 3:5, Ezekiel 16:13

**simple** – Person who did not submit himself to wisdom, Proverbs 9:4

**sign**

> **the sign of the Son of man** – United Christian priesthood, the new covenant Israel, Matthew 24:30,

**Sion**

> – The new covenant nation, Romans 11:26
>
> **mount Sion** – Belief of God's people, Hebrews 12:22

**sit, sat**

> – To be firm in something or preoccupied with something
>
> **sit in the throne** – To be fortified in power, Matthew 19:28, Revelation 20:4
>
> **sit on thrones** – To be established in the doctrine of Christ. In the spirit which Christ reigns over sin, Luka 22:30
>
> **sit upon the throne of his glory** – (The Word of God) To be fortified in the power on the altar, Matthew 25:31
>
> **people which sat in darkness** – People who are immersed in sin. Lack of knowledge of God's will, Matthew 4:16
>
> **sat at meat** – To be firmly established in the Mosaic Law, Luke 14:15
>
> **sat in the region and shadow of death** – Part of the Jewish nation who knows the will of God and has sinned against God, Matthew 4:16
>
> **whore that sitteth** – Part of Christianity who reigns, Revelation 17:1

**skeleton** – Proclamation of Israel as a state

**skin**

> **skin covered them above** – Border of the Israeli state, Ezekiel 37:8

**slay, slain**

> – Destruction of Jerusalem (Jewish nation) 70. A.D., Luke 19:27
>
> – Spiritually slain because God put a veil over their eyes, Ezekiel 37:9
>
> **slay them before me** – Spiritual slaying: to put a veil upon the eyes so a person's soul cannot be saved, Luke 19:27

**sleep**

> – Changed faith. The Word of God does not influence the life of a Christian, Matthew 25:5
>
> – Lack of fulfillment of God's commandments, 1 Thessalonians 5:6
>
> **while men sleep** – Start to transgress against God, Matthew 13:25

**slumber** – To know God's will and to not live accordingly, Matthew 25:5

**smoke**

>**these are a smoke in my nose** – Servants of God as spirits who are not pleasing God, Isaiah 65:5

>**vapour of smoke** – Evil spirits who produced evil tongues through words, Acts 2:19

**snare** – The word, for the soul is caught with the word, Luke 21:35

**sober** – To be preserved from twisted interpretations of the Bible, 1 Thessalonians 5:8

**Sodom** – Those who are twisting the law of God, Revelation 11:8

**son**

>– Generation which is repenting and returning from sin, Luka 15:21

>– Covenant, Galatians 4:22

>– Jesus, Matthew 21:37

>**his son** – Jesus, Matthew 22:2

>**son of perdition** – Antichrist, 2 Thessalonians 2:3

>**(two sons),…other by a freewoman** – One who is righteous, Galatians 4:26

>**(two sons), the one by a bondmaid** – One who lives by the flesh, i.e. sins, Galatians 4:23

**Son of man**

>– Jesus Christ in the Spirit, Matthew 16:27, Matthew 26:64, Luke 17:24

>– Jesus in the flesh, Matthew 20:18

>– The Word of God, Matthew 25:13

>– Resurrected Jesus, Matthew 19:28

>– The Word of God in Israel, Luke 21:36

**soul**

>**souls of them that were beheaded** – Those who were excommunicated from the old covenant church in the time of Jesus' preaching, Revelation 20:4

**sound**

>**sounded** – To preach, Revelation 9:13

>**and the sixth angel sounded** – Call for the departure to Israel, Revelation 9:13

**sow**

>**sowed good seed** – Properly preached the Word of God, Matthew 13:24

>**sowed tares** – To allow unrepentant people to enter into the covenant, or liberal teachings which influence the hearts of Christians, Matthew 13:25

>**sown** – Jesus Christ's doctrine will be preached, Ezekiel 36:9

**Spirit**

>**Spirit of life** – The Word of God, Revelation 11:11

>**spirit** – Words of Jesus are spirit and life. Only spirit quickeneth, John 6:63,

**spoil** – Body of Christ, human souls, Isaiah 53:12

**spring**

>**sprung up** – Belief of a Christian manifested through deeds, Matthew 13:26

**staff** – Word of God, Exodus 12:11

**stand, stood**

>– To be ready for action, Luke 21:36

**stand in the holy place** — To be strengthened in the holy place, Matthew 24:15

**angel standing in the sun** — Jesus Christ in the spirit as one with God ready for action, Revelation 19:17

**stood** — To be ready for action, Revelation 7:9

**stood on the shore** — To be spiritually exalted and ready for action, John 21:4

**stood upon their feet** — To be ready for action, Ezekiel 37:10, Revelation 11:11

**Lamb stood on mount Sion** — Jesus in the spirit (as Word of God) ready to be sacrificed and ready for action in the hearts of His servants Revelation 14:1

**star**

— In a general sense represents the spiritual children who were delivered through a union between the sun and the moon

— Angel, Revelation 1:20

**morning star** — Spirit of Jesus Christ which announced the coming of a new day, Revelation 2:28

**the stars of heaven** — The old covenant people in the time of Jesus' preaching, Revelation 12:4, Revelation 6:13

**the stars of heaven fell unto the earth** — Downfall from a higher sphere unto the lower sphere represents the loss of salvation for the stars (Jewish nation). This happened when the Holy Spirit came and the Jewish nation refused to recognize Christ as their king, Revelation 6:13

**the stars shall fall from heaven** — The stars (Christians from the gentiles) who do not go to Israel will lose the mercy of God. They will believe in God but with no hope for eternal life, Matthew 24:29

**eleven stars** — Joseph's brothers, eleven tribes of Israel, Genesis 37:9

**stem**

**stem of Jesse** — Descendants of Jesse, Isaiah 11:1

**stone**

**corner stone** — Jesus Christ, Ephesians 2:20

**stoop**

**stooped down** — To decide not to admit sin, Genesis 49:9

**street**

— The heart, Revelation 11:8

**streets of the city** — Hearts of Christians (city). Spirit of love, spirit of suffering ..., Luke 14:22

**strip**

**stripped him of his remnant** — To lose righteousness, Luke 10:30

**stumble** — Transgress God's law, Jeremiah 31:9

**suck** — Fulfilled sinful thoughts. Sin is born and this sin becomes part of the life of the spiritual person. He feeds the sin, Matthew 24:19

**sun**

— In a general sense it represents the body which preaches eternal life after the death of the flesh. It is always described in the male gender.

— God, Revelation 19:17

— Israel (Jacob), Genesis 37:9

356

— Old covenant Israel, old covenant priesthood who did not accept Jesus Christ as their Messiah, Acts 2:20

— Priesthood in Christianity (the new covenant Israel), Matthew 24:29

**sun became black** — The old covenant priesthood (Israel) who did not accept the resurrected Jesus as their Messiah, Revelation 6:12, Joel 2:31, Acts 2:20

**shine forth as the sun** — Fulfill God's will, Matthew 13:42

**strong**

**strong man** — Satan, Matthew 12:29

**summer**

— The time when preaching and the spiritual harvest starts, Matthew 24:32

**summer is nigh** — Harvest is at hand, Luke 21:30

**summer is nigh** — Salvation of the Jewish nation is at hand (occurring in the future), Matthew 24:32

**supper**

**great supper** — Salvation of the Jewish nation in the future, Luke 14:16

**taste my supper** — To be a partaker of the salvation of the Jewish nation, Luke 14:24

**surfeit** — In a negative sense represents the fulfillment of carnal desires as deeds, Luke 21:34

**swaddling clothes** — Mosaic Law, Luke 2:7

**sword** — Word of God, Matthew 10:34

# T

**tabernacle** — Spiritual body of Christ, Ezekiel 37:27

**table**

— Congregation, Proverbs 9:2, Matthew 22:10

**furnished table** — Word of God (Holy Spirit) in the congregations, Proverbs 9:2

**tail**

— False prophesying of the Jewish priesthood in Jesus' time, Revelation.12:4

— The prophet who taught lies in the name of God, Isaiah 9:14

**take**

**take away their sins** — To force them to repent, Romans 11:27

**taken** — To lead them into Israel, Luke 17:34, and Matthew 24:41

**tares** — Children of the wicked one. Those who offend and do iniquity, Matthew 13:25

**teeth** — Strength, power, son, servant, Genesis 49:12

**tell**

**tell them which are bidden** — Preach to them, Matthew 22:4

**tempest**

**carried with a tempest** — Servants of God who are influenced by the spirit of this world, 2 Peter 2:17

**temple**

**your temples** — Temples which are not of the God of Israel, Joel 3:5

**that**

    **that night** – Third spiritual night, Luke 17:34

    **that night** – Second spiritual night, John 21:3

**them**

    **say to them** – Christians, Luke 14;17

    **tell them** – Jewish nation in the time when the Comforter was sent, Matthew 22:4

**thief**

    – False Messiah, John 10:1

    **thieves** – Evil spirits, Luke 10:30

**thing**

    **my goodly pleasant things** – Promises of God to the Jewish nation, Joel 3:5

**third**

    – Third day in the old testament time period, John 2:1

    **third day** – Day given to the Jewish nation for their salvation, Hosea 6:2

**thirst** – To have a desire for righteousness, Isaiah 55:1

**throne**

    – Governing power

    **sit in the throne of his glory** – To start exercising heavenly power, Matthew 19:28

    **sit upon twelve thrones** – Exercise power of the new covenant church, Matthew 19:28 and 14:12

**thy** – Those who know God's will, Luke 14:12

**till**

    **till the thousand years should be fulfilled** – Kingdom of Christ on earth (first) which was given to the Jewish people and lasted until Jerusalem was destroyed in 70A.D., Revelation 20:3

    **till we have sealed** – Until the salvation of the gentiles is abolished, Revelation 7:3

**time**

    **the time of love** – The time came to make a covenant (time of the marriage), Ezekiel 16:8

**token**

    **token upon the houses** – Token upon them, Exodus 12:13

**tongue** – Fire, a world of iniquity, James 3:6

**torn** – To lose the right for salvation, Hosea 6:1

**tower** – Congregation, Matthew 21:33

**travail**

    – Distress; friction between nuclear powers, economic misery …, 1 Thessalonians 5:3

**tree**

    – Righteous man, Revelation 7:1

    **all the trees** – Christianity, Luke 21:29

    **fig tree** – Jewish nation, seed of Abraham according to the law, Matthew 24:32, Luke 21:29

**table**

>**my table in my kingdom** – Righteousness and truth, Luke 22:30

**trumpet** – Voice of God; the Word of God, Revelation 8:6

**turn**

>**I will turn unto you** – I (God) will bless you with faith, Ezekiel 36:9

**twice**

>**twice dead** – The first time men died to their sinful lives by repentance. The second time they died with their sinfulness to eternal life, Jude 12

# U

**until**

>**until Shiloh comes** – Jesus, Genesis 49:10

# V

**veil**

>– The spirit of slumber, 2 Corinthians 3:16, Romans 11:8, 2.

>**veil of the temple** – Body of Jesus, Matthew 27:51

**valley**

>– Human sinfulness

>–This sinful world (valley), Ezekiel 37:1

>**valley of decision** – It is the valley of decision because the Jewish nation in Israel will make a decision to turn (rely) toward God (accept Christ), Joel 3:14

**vessel**

>**chosen vessel** – Apostle Paul, Acts 9:15

>**vessels of a potter** – Carnal nature of man, Revelation 2:27

>**vessels** – Hearts, Matthew 25:4

**vine**

>**chosen vine** – God's people, Genesis 49:11

**vine**

>– Jesus, Genesis 49:11, John 15:5

>**choice vine** – Christians, Genesis 49:11

**vineyard** – Jerusalem as a spiritual town of peace; Jewish nation, Mat. 21:33

**virgin (maiden)**

>– In a general sense those who call sinners to repentance, Proverbs 9:3

>**wise virgins** – Christians who have a fear of God and knowledge about the Word of God, Matthew 25:2

>**foolish virgins** – Christians who do not have knowledge of the Word of God and do not hate sin, Matthew 25:3

>**ready virgins** – Christians from the wise virgins who went to Israel, Matthew 25:10

>**virgins who follow the Lamb** – Christians from the gentiles who will go to Israel, Revelation 14:4

**voice**

>**my voice** – The Word of God, John 10:16

# W

**wall**

– God, Genesis 49:22

**wall of the city** – Doctrine of God, Revelation 21:14

**wash**

– To show, to perform, Genesis 49:11

**washed his garment in wine** – Jesus showed and performed His deeds of righteousness, Genesis 49:11

**wash in water** – Repent through the Word of God, Ezekiel 16:4

**washed I thee with water** – To clean human conscience through deeds done through the Word of God, Ezekiel 16:9

**watch**

– To study the Word of God and follow events/occurrences in the world, Luke 21:36

**water**

– Doctrine of God, Isaiah 55:1

– World up to the great flood, 2 Peter 3:5

**waters** – People, multitudes, nations, and tongues, Revelation 17:15

**wast thou washed in water** – Jewish nation was not passing through repentance, Ezekiel 16:4

**way**

**way of Balaam** – The way which brings wages for unrighteousness, 2 Peter 2:15

**way of holiness** – Jesus Christ's doctrine, Isaiah 35:8

**his ways** – Jesus Christ's doctrine, Isaiah 2:3

**prepare the way** – Preach repentance to the Jewish nation, Matthew 11:10

**right way** – God's way of righteousness and truth, 2 Peter 2:15

**straight way** – Righteousness and truth, Jeremiah 31:9

**weep**

**weeping** – Weeping for the lost salvation, Matthew 24:51

**well**

– Fountain of God's doctrine

– New covenant doctrine, Exodus 49:22

**wells without water** – Heart of man which is not a well of the Spirit, 2 Peter 2:17

**wheat** – Righteous Christians, Matthew 13:30

**when**

**when the Son of man is revealed** – Jesus Christ in the Spirit through the Word of God is revealed to those who pay heed to the voice of the Spirit. That is, pay attention to the announcement for the departure to Israel, Luke 17:30

**when thousand years are expired** – The end of the kingdom of a thousand years for the gentiles. End of salvation for the gentiles, Revelation 20:7

**whore**

**great whore** – In a spiritual sense represents Christianity having contacts with strange spirits, i.e. materialism, Revelation 17:1

**wife**

– The new covenant church, Revelation 19:7

**married a wife** – To enter into a new covenant, i.e. in new belief, Luke 14:20

**wives** –The church, Ephesians 5:22

**wind**

– Christians in whom the Spirit of God resides, Ezekiel 37:9

– Man, nation, spirit

– Spirit, Revelation 7:1

– Doctrine of Jesus Christ, Revelation 6:13

**(wind) come from four winds** – Christians come to Israel, Ezekiel 37:9

**winds** – Ungodly spirits, Jude 12

**wine**

– Blood of Jesus, Genesis 49:11

– Love of God towards sinners, Genesis 49:12

– New covenant doctrine, Luke 10:34

– Spirit of Christ, Isaiah 55:1

– Spirit of the new covenant doctrine, Proverbs 9:2

**no wine** – Mosaic Law which lost power in the hearts of the Jewish nation, John 2:3

**winter**

– The battle in the valley of Jehoshaphat which will lead the world into the Third world war, Matthew 24:20

**wisdom** – God, Proverbs 9:1

**withered** –To lose the right to be green; to believe in Jesus Christ, Matthew 21:19

**woe**

**second woe** –Third world war, Revelation 11:14

**third woe** – Antichrist system, Revelation 11:14

**wolf** – Man who has the nature of a wolf. Because he dwells with the lamb, they say to us that he is spiritually reborn, Isaiah 11:6

**woman**

– In a general sense the church or this world

**woman clothed with the sun** –The new covenant church, Revelation 12:1

**were not defiled with women** –Teaching of different denominations, Revelation 14:2

**word** – God, John 1:1

**words that I speak** – Spirit which quickeneth, Jovan 6:63

**world**

**the world that then was** – Sinful people up to the great flood, 2 Peter 3:6

**worship** – To accept, Revelation 20:4

**worthy**

    **were not worthy** – Jewish nation lost the right to enter into new covenant bonds, Matthew 22:8

**wound**

    **wounded** – Somebody who is sinning or sinned against God, Luke 10:30

**wrap**

    **wrapped him** – Teach him, Luke 2:7

# Y

**yoke** – God's doctrine, Matthew 11:29

**youth**

    **thy youth** – Time spent in Egyptian bondage, Jeremiah 2:2